ADVANCE
THE COLORS!

☆

VOLUME I

ADVANCE THE COLORS!

★

PENNSYLVANIA CIVIL WAR BATTLE FLAGS

Richard A. Sauers ★ Capitol Preservation Committee

ISBN: 0-8182-0090-1

This book has been typeset in 11 point ITC Garamond Light.

Typography:	Batsch Spectracomp, Mechanicsburg, PA
Design/Art:	John P. Wattai, Wattai Design Associates, Lebanon and Palmyra, PA
Color separations:	Colortech, Inc., Lebanon, PA
Printing:	Sowers Printing Co., Lebanon, PA
Binding:	The CHM Edition, Ltd., Andalusia, PA

Overleaf: The Rescue of the Colors *by William T. Trego, 1899, portraying Sergeant Hiram Purcell's rescue of the Colors of the 104th Pennsylvania during the Battle of Fair Oaks, May 31, 1862. The original painting is in the Mercer Museum, Bucks County Historical Society.*

Photograph by AL FRENI © 1984 TIME-LIFE Books, Inc. from *The Civil War* Series.

Dedication

*"Wherefore Governments rather depend upon Men,
than Men upon Governments. Let Men be good, and the
Governments cannot be bad; if it be ill, they will cure it.
But if Men be bad, let the Government be never so good,
they will endeavor to warp and spoil it to their Turn."*

— William Penn

This Documentary History of Pennsylvania Civil War Flags is dedicated to two outstanding Commonwealth officials whose inspiration and leadership in the cause of preserving and passing onward the Pennsylvania heritage made this work possible.

These distinguished officials are the Honorable K. Leroy Irvis of Allegheny County, Speaker 1977-78, 1983-84, 1985-86, 1986-87, and the Honorable Matthew J. Ryan of Delaware County, Speaker 1981-82, of the Pennsylvania House of Representatives.

In their respective service as Members of the House, Floor Leaders, and Speakers of the House, they have provided bipartisan leadership and support for a variety of endeavors dedicated to the preservation of Pennsylvania heritage, the heightening of citizen awareness of their birthright, and the transmission of that inheritance to future generations.

In concert with the joint observance of the 300th Anniversary of the Commonwealth and the 75th Anniversary of the State Capitol Building, Representatives Irvis and Ryan provided leadership in statutorily creating the Pennsylvania Capitol Preservation Committee. This Committee, in turn, is sponsoring numerous conservation, preservation, and restoration programs to ensure that the Pennsylvania State Capitol and its public treasures will be passed onward intact to Pennsylvanians of future generations.

Among these programs is that of providing conservation care to the Civil War Flag collection with funds raised from the Commonwealth's citizens, and publishing a documented history of these Flags, and the military units which they symbolized in the war to preserve the Republic.

The role of many others, in private and public life, who have joined in this program to preserve the Flags carried by Pennsylvanians in the Civil War, and to publish the story of the Flags and the men and units they represented, is recognized and honored by the Capitol Preservation Committee, the publishers of this work.

In view of the unique contributions made by the Honorable K. Leroy Irvis and the Honorable Matthew J. Ryan, it is fitting that they be extended special Commonwealth recognition for their indispensable service.

—Rep. Joseph R. Pitts, Chairman,
Capitol Preservation Committee

HONORABLE K. LEROY IRVIS
Speaker of the House
1977-78, 1983-84, 1985-86, 1986-87

HONORABLE MATTHEW J. RYAN
Speaker of the House
1981-82

Capitol Preservation Committee Members 1985-1986

Front row
Mrs. Renee Jones, Chief Justice Appointment; Robert Glenn, Secretary-State Art Commission; Senator John J. Shumaker; Representative Joseph R. Pitts, Chairman; Representative Peter C. Wambach, Secretary; Senator William J. Moore.

Back row
Walter Baran, Secretary-Department of General Services; Representative Thomas R. Caltagirone; Honorable Richard A.

Snyder, Governor's Appointment; Representative James L. Wright, Jr.; Senator Edward P. Zemprelli; John M. Dickey, Architect-Governor's Appointment

Absent from picture
Senator James R. Kelley, Vice Chairman; Dr. Larry E. Tise, Executive Director-Historical & Museum Commission; Denise Scott Brown, Architect-Governor's Appointment

The Capitol Preservation Committee is an independent Commonwealth Committee established by the General Assembly in 1982 for the purpose of coordinating and overseeing programs to conserve, restore, preserve, and maintain the Pennsylvania State Capitol and its historic contents for all future time.

The Capitol Preservation Committee consists of fifteen members who are appointed by officials of the Legislative, Executive, and Judicial branches of Commonwealth government, or who hold membership

by virtue of office. This Committee meets regularly in Harrisburg to make decisions concerning the ongoing restoration and preservation programs.

In creating the Committee, the Legislature provided for establishment of a "Capitol Restoration Trust Fund" which may receive both public funds and contributions from the private sector. This fund is independent of the Commonwealth General Fund and used for various conservation projects.

Capitol Preservation Committee Staff

Front row
Arlene Brown, Secretary-Capitol Preservation Committee Office; Ruthann Hubbert, Administrative Assistant; Mary Ashton, Chief Textile Conservator

Back row
Karen LaFaver, Project Assistant; Marta Rothwarf, Textile Conservator; Sue Ann Ellison, Secretary to Chairman; Richard A. Sauers, Military Historian

Advance the Colors!

Table of Contents

Appendixes

Introduction

The date was May 6, 1864. The Federal Army of the Potomac, under the tactical supervision of Major-General George G. Meade, was locked in a titanic struggle with General Robert E. Lee's Army of Northern Virginia. One of the regiments fighting in the smoky, tangled underbrush in the Wilderness was the 45th Pennsylvania. After maneuvering around for some time, the regiment was ordered forward to attack the Rebel breastworks. The 45th reached the enemy line and planted its colors on the works, but other troops were repulsed and the regiment was forced to withdraw and reform.

Captain Rees G. Richards was attempting to rally his company when he came upon Colonel John I. Curtin standing alone in the drifting gunsmoke, apparently greatly disheartened. Richards approached his colonel and asked where the regimental colors were. "I do not know," replied the distraught Curtin. But soon, the color-bearer emerged through the smoke, still holding the precious banner. Captain Richards rushed over, seized the flag, "and with an energy born of the calamity and inspired by a realization of its meaning, sang out:

> Rally round the flag, boys!
> Rally once again!
> Shouting the battle cry of freedom."

Other soldiers heard the captain's voice and joined in the song. Although the air was filled with smoke from burning underbrush and echoed with whistling bullets, "there rose in clear and blood-stirring strains:

> The Union forever, hurrah, boys, hurrah!
> Down with the traitors and up with the stars."

As the song spread down the line, the regiment rallied and held its position.

This incident illustrates the effect a regiment's flag had on the men. The national flag's role in the Civil War has not yet received the attention it should command. The flag meant everything to a regiment of soldiers. In an era when most people in the country did not travel great distances from their homes, the flag was a tangible symbol of the national government. It was to be protected at all costs. Even though the flag might be reduced to scraps of silk clinging tenuously to the fringe, it was still a proud symbol of the United States and the men were no less willing to carry their old tattered banners than a brand new color. Indeed, many regiments were loath to turn in their treasured, battle-torn flags for a new stand of colors. On more than one occasion after a hard-fought battle, a colonel apologized to his superiors when his flag did not receive an appropriate amount of damage to prove his regiment's bravery.

The wartime reverence for the colors epitomized the growing national popularization of the stars and stripes. Most of the best-known songs of the Civil War era, such as "The Battle Cry of Freedom" and "The Vacant Chair," contained stirring references to the national flag. Newspapers of the period, especially during the military fervor stirred in 1861, printed all sorts of poems about the flag. Many papers incorporated the image of the flag in their mastheads. The newspapers also contained numerous stories of local flag-raisings as people freely exhibited their patriotism. The stationery used by the soldiers prominently featured the flag and its associated poetry. The Civil War and its image of the flag led to a growing "cult of the national flag" in the decades following the war. Indeed, it was a veterans group, the Grand Army of the Republic, that led the move to enshrine the American flag with rituals such as the salute to the flag.

Because the flag was so important in the Civil War, and because over 300,000 Pennsylvanians helped to defend the Federal Union, the Capitol Preservation Committee is proud to help maintain the memory of the thousands of Keystoners who gave their lives to preserve the United States as a free and united nation.

Arrangement of this Book

Owing to the lack of detailed Civil War flag studies, the research for this book has brought together a wide range of material. Primary sources have furnished the bulk of material for the work. The oft-used *Official Records* is the starting point for any serious Civil War research. Samuel P. Bates's five-volume *History of Pennsylvania Volunteers*, although error-filled in both the regimental narratives and muster rolls, is still an invaluable reference tool. The regimental letter and order books in the National Archives contain a wealth of information on the flags carried by many Pennsylvania commands, as does the collection of regimental papers and muster rolls in the State Archives. Contemporary newspapers contain many items of interest, primarily soldier letters and reports of local flag presentations. Letters and diaries of the combatants also house useful material, but it takes an inordinate amount of time to weed through the mass of existing manuscript material scattered in hundreds of repositories. Regimental histories also are useful, but must be used with caution because of the tendency to overglorify a regiment's role in the war. Last, but certainly not least, contemporary photographs and illustrations provide key information about the wartime appearance of the flags.

The book is organized into three introductory chapters that describe the history of pre-Civil War Pennsylvania military flags, the wartime flags themselves, and the postwar history of the banners. Thereafter, the book contains sketches of each regiment's flags in numerical order. Each sketch is designed to be read independently of the others. Since Pennsylvania was the only Northern state to issue colors and standards to each regiment, this is the common denominator chosen to describe the regiment's movements. In general, the history of the flag is the history of the regiment. Each state-issued flag is followed by a general description of the regiment's movements while carrying that banner. Although it is dangerous to assume too much in the absence of concrete information, the author has assumed that each regiment carried its state flag in every battle or campaign in which it participated until either it was disanded or received a replacement flag. This was not always true, and those instances where a state flag was kept out of a battle are documented when known. Battles for which there is verifiable evidence of the flag being carried are more fully described than those for which there is no information available about the flag.

Presented Flags: Flags received from non-state sources are described under appropriate headings. In many cases, no information is known other than the physical description and presentation dates of such flags. Many of these local flags are not in the state collection; if not, their present location (if known) is indicated.

Color-Bearers: This section includes the names of bearers for whom an exact flag cannot be determined. If a regiment carried more than one flag simultaneously and the nature of the source does not identify which flag each bearer was carrying, then the names are listed in this section.

Notes: All references are restricted to specific mention of the regiment's flags and their bearers. The general background information for each regiment has been compiled from reading Bates, the regimental history if existing, and the battle reports printed in the *Official Records*. Notes referring to lists of flags located in Record Groups Nineteen and Twenty-five in the State Archives are not included. Instead, each list is described below.

Bibliography: This section lists all known bibliographic material for each regiment, and is included as an aid for those readers seeking further information about a selected regiment.

A note on names of generals: In order to avoid repetition of the names of the most prominent Civil War generals mentioned in this book, the author has used last names in some cases. The full name and rank of less well-known officers are printed in full. Those abbreviated include: Lieutenant-General Ulysses S. Grant (Grant); Major-General Joseph Hooker, commander of the Army of the Potomac, January-June 1863 (Hooker); Major-General George B. McClellan, commander of the Army of the Potomac until November 1862 (McClellan); Major-General George G. Meade, commanding the Army of the Potomac, June 1863-1865 (Meade); Major-General John Pope, commander of the Army of Virginia, June-August 1862 (Pope); Major-General William T. Sherman, commander of the Military Division of the Mississippi, 1864-1865 (Sherman); and on the Confederate side, General Robert E. Lee, commanding the Army of Northern Virginia, June 1862-April 1865 (Lee); Lieutenant-General James Longstreet, First Corps, Army of Northern Virginia (Longstreet); and Major-General Thomas J. "Stonewall" Jackson, Lee's Second Corps commander until his death in May 1863 (Jackson).

Missing Regiments: Although Pennsylvania regiments were numbered consecutively from 1 to 215, several regiments were never formed because the men authorized to raise a certain unit could not get enough recruits to fill the ranks and the regiment was broken up and the men distributed to other units. Units which did not survive were the 66th (in existence from July 1861 to March 1862), 86th, 94th (10th Cavalry), 120th, 144th, 146th, 156th, 164th, 170th, and 189th (4th Artillery, in existence from April through August 1864). Flags were made for all these regiments except the 164th. Most were altered for use by other regiments.

Pennsylvania Civil War Flag Lists Mentioned in the Text

1) "Battleflags of Penna. Regiments Turned Over By Adjt-Genl. Russell to QMr Genl. PA. Febry 25/65, and those received subsequently." In RG 25.
This list includes those flags already in state care and transferred to the quartermaster-general in February 1865. Additional entries end on October 21, 1865. In many cases, the condition of the flag was noted, as well as those without staffs. Officers who turned in the flags were noted also.

2) Letter from Colonel Frank Jordan to Adjutant-General A. L. Russell, February 10, 1866. In RG 25. In this letter, Colonel Jordan listed the flags located at the State Agency building in Washington. These banners had been deposited at the agency when units left for home or had not been picked up at all.

3) Letter from Major William B. Lane to Adjutant-General A. L. Russell, April 20, 1866. In RG 19. Lane, the Chief Mustering Officer in Philadelphia, compiled a list of those flags left in his office when regiments mustered out of service. The list includes flags for Pennsylvania's black infantry regiments.

4) "Catalogue of Colors and Standards of the various Pennsylvania Regiments and Batteries deposited in the Capitol buildings in Harrisburg, with the names of Colonels commanding, from organization to muster-out."

This list is dated May 25, 1887. Local photographers F. E. Musser and Wilson C. Fox each received permission from Adjutant-General Daniel Hastings to photograph the flags and sell the pictures to veterans. This list contains the number of flags to be found on each photograph. The list may not be comprehensive and may only include those flags actually photographed, not the entire collection as it existed in 1887.

5) Untitled list dating from circa 1895, with pencilled 1914 corrections. In RG 25.

This important list, apparently dating from the old Flag Room in the Executive Library and Museum Building, is an itemized list of flags, listed by regiment and type, as well as by case number and section. This document lists camp colors, company markers, artillery flags, cavalry flags, and infantry colors. There is a pencilled 1914 inventory check against the list, with additions and corrections noting any differences.

6) List of flags in the 1896 adjutant-general's report. This list is prefaced by: "As no list of flags deposited in the flag room has been published since 1866, and some additions having been made thereto since that time, a revised list will no doubt be of interest, and is given herewith:"

Abbreviations

Bates	Bates, Samuel P. *History of Pennsylvania Volunteers 1861-5*. 5 volumes. Harrisburg: B. Singerly, 1869-1871.
Beyer-Keydel	Beyer, Walter F., and Keydel, Oscar F. *Deeds of Valor: How America's Heroes Won the Medal of Honor*. 2 volumes. Detroit: Perrien-Keydel Company, 1901. All references are to volume one.
Captured Flags Document	United States Congress. 50th Congress, 1st Session. Executive Document No. 163. "Captured Battle Flags. Letter from the Secretary of War, with inclosures, in response to a resolution of the House calling for information relative to captured standards, flags and colors." Washington, 1888.
CW Misc Collection	Civil War Miscellaneous Collection.
CWTI Collection	Civil War Times Illustrated Collection.
EH	Evans & Hassall (used in photograph identifications).
HB	Horstmann Brothers & Company (used in photograph identifications).
HbCWRT Collection	Harrisburg Civil War Round Table Collection.
MASS-MOLLUS	Massachusetts-Commandery, Military Order of the Loyal Legion of the United States. Photograph collection located at USAMHI.
MOLLUS	Military Order of the Loyal Legion of the United States.
Mulholland	Mulholland, St. Clair A. *Military Order, Congress Medal of Honor Legion of the United States*. Philadelphia: Town Print, 1905.
O.R.	United States. War Department. *The War of the Rebellion: A Compilation of the Official Records of the Union and Confederate Armies*. 70 volumes in 128 parts. Washington: Government Printing Office, 1880-1901. All citations refer to Series I unless noted. Succeeding numbers refer to volume and part. For example, *O.R.* 27.1 means volume 27, part 1.
PHMC	Pennsylvania Historical and Museum Commission (Used in photograph credits).
Pennsylvania at Antietam	Pennsylvania, Antietam Battlefield Memorial Commission. *Pennsylvania at Antietam: Report of the Antietam Battlefield Memorial Commission and Ceremonies at the Dedication of the Monuments Erected by the Commonwealth of Pennsylvania to Mark the Positions of Thirteen of the Pennsylvania Commands Engaged in the Battle*. Harrisburg: Harrisburg Publishing Company, 1906.
Pennsylvania at Chickamauga	Pennsylvania. Chickamauga-Chattanooga Battlefields Com-

mission. *Pennsylvania at Chickamauga and Chattanooga. Ceremonies at the Dedication of the Monuments Erected by the Commonwealth of Pennsylvania to Mark the Positions of the Pennsylvania Commands Engaged in the Battles.* Harrisburg: W.S. Ray, State Printer, 1897.

Pennsylvania at Gettysburg

Pennsylvania. Gettysburg Battlefield Commission. *Pennsylvania at Gettysburg: Ceremonies at the Dedication of the Monuments Erected by the Commonwealth of Pennsylvania to Mark the Positions of the Pennsylvania Commands Engaged in the Battle.* 2 volumes. Harrisburg: E. K. Meyers, State Printer, 1893.

RG 19

Pennsylvania State Archives. Record Group 19. Records of the Department of Military Affairs. Unless noted, all references are to the General Correspondence File of the Office of the Adjutant-General.

RG 25

Pennsylvania State Archives. Record Group 25. Records of Special Commissions. All refer-ences are to the Records of the Flag Transfer Commission.

RG 94

National Archives. Record Group 94. Records of the Office of the Adjutant-General.

Scharf - Westcott

Scharf, John T., and Westcott, Thompson. *History of Philadelphia, 1689-1884.* 3 volumes. Philadelphia: L. H. Everts & Company, 1884. All references are to volume one.

Soldiers & Sailors

Soldiers and Sailors Memorial Hall, Pittsburgh.

Taylor, *Philadelphia*

Taylor, Frank H. *Philadelphia in the Civil War 1861-1865.* Philadelphia: Dunlap Printing Company, 1913.

USAMHI

United States Army Military History Institute, Carlisle Barracks, Pennsylvania.

Wallace, *Schuylkill County*

Wallace, F. B. *Memorial of the Patriotism of Schuylkill County, in the American Slaveholder's Rebellion, Embracing a Complete List of Names of All Volunteers from the County During the War, Patriotic Contributions by the Citizens,* . . . . Pottsville: Benjamin Bannan, 1865.

Glossary

I: Flag Terms

Arms The term "arms" is used to refer to two distinctly different types of emblems. a) The arms of the Commonwealth of Pennsylvania consists of a shield displaying a ship, a plough, and three sheaves of wheat; an eagle for the crest; two horses as supporters; and the motto "Virtue, Liberty, and Independence" below the other devices on a scroll. An olive branch and cornstalk are crossed below the shield, while stalks of corn occasionally were added behind the horses. b) The arms of the United States consists of a bald eagle, holding an olive branch in his right talon and a bundle of arrows in his left, while a scroll with the motto "E Pluribus Unum" is in his beak. A shield emblazoned with red and white stripes is usually found on the eagle's breast, but sometimes is located beneath the eagle, who crouches above the shield.

Battle Honors The names of the battles or engagements in which the unit fought. Often painted or sewn onto the unit's flag or displayed on attached streamers and replacement banners.

Camp Colors Small bunting flags used to mark a unit's camp, the color line, and some regimental maneuvers.

Canton A quadrant of a flag. Common usage with Civil War flags refers to the top hoist quadrant which usually displays a blue field with stars representing the states in the union. Pennsylvania state-issue colors also display the state arms as well as the stars in the blue field.

Color In general, the flag of a military unit. Historically, the term was specifically applied to the flags carried by infantry and artillery regiments. Thus, the term is a very broad description which includes national colors, state colors, and regimental colors. In this book, the term "color" represents a single flag, but Civil War-period literature often used the term "colors" to indicate either one or more flags. The term "stand of colors" was also used interchangeably to mean one or more flags.

Cord A length of two to four plied silk cord connecting two decorative tassels. The midpoint of the cord is usually tied around the finial base of the staff.

Ferrule The metallic tip at the lower end of the staff, used to plant the flag in the ground and rest the flag in the sling worn around the neck.

Field The principal area of a flag, prior to any additions or embellishments. This is usually made up of a single fabric or several joined fabrics.

Finial The decorative ornament found on the top end of the staff. Federal Civil War colors usually contained a spearpoint or eagle as a finial device. The finial was normally made of a metallic. It could be a single piece construction or more commonly appears to be composed of a finial base attached to the staff and the decorative device attached by a screw mount to the base.

Flank Markers Small flags carried at each end of an infantry regiment's line of battle to mark the flanks. If carried on long staffs, these flags are properly termed "flank markers." If carried on smaller staffs fitted into the rifle barrels of the guide sergeants, they are called "general guide markers."

Fly The length of the flag measured from the outer pole sleeve to the free edge. Also understood as the outer half of the flag.

Fringe A woven band with decorative ends extending from one side. The ends can be plied cut ends, plied knotted cut ends, or self plied loops. The band is usually attached to the free edges of the flag though it often does extend over the top and bottom ends of the pole sleeve. This serves as decoration and helps to accentuate the body and drape of the unfurled flag by weighting the light edges of the silk.

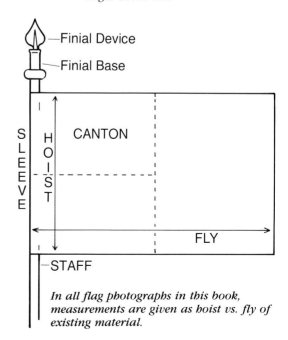

In all flag photographs in this book, measurements are given as hoist vs. fly of existing material.

General Guide Markers	See Flank Markers.
Guidon	The term applied to the type of flag carried by an artillery or cavalry company. Guidons were usually swallowtail in appearance, according to army regulations. Some infantry regiments carried guidons as flank markers (q.v.).
Hoist	The width of the flag measured along the staff edge, excluding the fringe. Also understood as the half of the flag nearest the staff.
National	The term applied to any flag (color, regimental, or standard) displaying the national arms or a stars and stripes color which does not have any state emblems added.
Obverse	View of the flag as seen when the staff edge is to the viewer's left.
Regimental	The term applied to a flag consisting of a monocolor field with either national or state symbols added for identification.
Reverse	View of the flag as seen when the staff edge is to the viewer's right.
Sleeve	The part of the flag usually reinforced and doubled over, through which the staff is slipped prior to attachment. The reinforcement is referred to as the 'inner sleeve' while the doubled flag fabric is referred to as the 'outer sleeve'.
Staff	The wooden pole on which any type of military flag is attached. In specific Civil War military usage, the infantry staffs were termed 'pikes' while cavalry regiments carried flags mounted on 'lances'. "Staff" is used in the text to represent both terms to minimize confusion.
Standard	The type of flag carried by a cavalry regiment. It is smaller than the infantry and artillery colors.
State Flag	Any flag containing the Pennsylvania coat-of-arms. The arms can be found on state colors, state standards, and state regimental colors.
Streamer	A band or ribbon, usually made of silk, displaying the battle honors (q.v.) of a particular regiment. One or more of these were attached to the finial end of the staff after the war.
Tassels	Two pendant ornaments connected by the cord (q.v.). These are often made up of a tassel head and several layers of self-loop plied free ends. The tassel head is usually made of one or more adjacent wooden core shapes covered with knotted, plaited, or wrapped silk. Army Regulations specified the colors used for infantry and artillery colors but local presentation flags incorporate various colors of silk or metallic threads and boullion.

II: Military Terms

Army	A military formation composed of at least two corps (q.v.) and other attached units. Northern armies were usally named after rivers (Army of the Potomac, Army of the Cumberland, etc.) while Confederate armies were named for geographic areas (Army of Northern Virginia, Army of Tennessee, etc.).
Battery	The usual name for a company of artillery, consisting of approximately one hundred soldiers and four or six cannon, commanded by a captain. Batteries were subdivided into two-gun sections.
Battalion	A unit of troops consisting of between two and nine companies. For purposes of field command, infantry regiments were referred to as battalions when officers issued commands.
Brigade	A formation consisting of two or more regiments (q.v.). The "average" Civil War brigade consisted of four to eight regiments. A brigade was led by a brigadier-general, or often by the senior regimental colonel.
Company	A unit of soldiers consisting of approximately one hundred officers and men, commanded by a captain.
Corps	A formation consisting of two or more divisions (q.v.). Federal corps averaged three divisions plus attached artillery and cavalry units. A major-general was the usual officer commanding a corps, although Southern corps were usually led by lieutenant-generals.
Division	A formation of troops consisting of two or more brigades. Federal divisions usually contained three brigades, while Confederate divisions numbered up to six brigades. Major-generals or brigadier-generals commanded divisions.
Muster in/out	The formal procedure of swearing recruits into or out of government service. State volunteers first took an oath to defend their state, then were sworn into national service. In this book, the muster out dates for regiments reflect their discharge from federal service.
Regiment	A unit formed of an exact number of companies. Ten companies comprised an infantry regiment, while cavalry and artillery regiments consisted of twelve companies. A colonel was the field commander of a regiment.

PART I

Chapter I
Pre-Civil War Pennsylvania Military Flags

With a strong Quaker influence in the provincial legislature and the comparative solitude of its borders, Pennsylvania was the only one of the thirteen original British colonies not to organize a militia for home defense. However, the threat of a French attack in 1747 influenced Benjamin Franklin to anonymously propose that citizens form voluntary "military associations" to protect themselves against French and Indian depredations. No enemy raids occurred, and despite the formation of several "Associator" units, Franklin's idea and his proposed voluntary militia system were allowed to lapse into obscurity.[1]

The French victory over General Edward Braddock's British regulars near Fort Duquesne in 1755 again led some concerned Pennsylvanians to clamor for military defense against the now-serious French threat. Governor Robert Morris called upon the people to again form voluntary military associations, but the response was very modest, with a total of only 2,265 Associators on the muster rolls. The province did recruit a regiment of three (later reduced to two) battalions to serve with the British forces in North America during the resulting French and Indian War (1756-1763). It is not known if either this provincial regiment or the local Associator battalions carried any military colors, for none seem to have survived.[2]

On the eve of the American Revolution, several local unauthorized militia units came into existence throughout Pennsylvania. On June 4, 1774, concerned citizens meeting in Lancaster County's Hanover Township voted to form a military unit to oppose British tyranny. The actual existence of this force has been questioned, but the company was authorized to procure a flag. If this company ever did acquire a flag, the actual color has not survived, although a color print was published in *Pennsylvania Archives*, 2nd Series, Volume XIII. The crimson flag depicts a rifleman, clad in a green hunting shirt and buckskin leggings, standing on guard and accompanied by the motto "Liberty or Death" on a yellow scroll.[3]

On November 17, 1774, a group of men meeting in Philadelphia formed the Philadelphia Troop of Light Horse, which later was renamed the First Troop,

Revolutionary War Standard of the First City Troop

Philadelphia City Cavalry, or more simply the First City Troop. This unit is still in existence, and is the oldest continuous military unit in America. Captain Abraham Markoe, the troop's first elected commander, had a flag prepared especially for his command.[4]

This 33″x40″ flag is made of yellow silk edged with a silver fringe, and originally contained the British union as the canton. Sometime afterwards, thirteen alternating blue and silver stripes were painted over the union. The central motif of the flag depicts a blue shield with a golden knot, from which radiate thirteen golden scrolls. The head of a bay horse with a white star on its forehead appears as a crest. The two supporters represent the figures of America and Fame. The left figure, that of America, is an Indian holding a golden staff topped by a Liberty cap. Fame, the right-hand figure, is represented as an angel with a staff in one hand and a trumpet in the other. Beneath the motif is a scroll with the motto "For These We Strive," a reference to the supporters.[5]

Shortly after Associator units such as these began forming, the Pennsylvania legislature officially recognized them. As a result, scores of Associator battalions were formed across the province. One battalion of two companies, commanded by Colonel John Proctor, was recruited in Westmoreland County. The flag adopted by this infantry unit appears to be the only infantry Associator color to have survived to the present day. Like many other early American flag designs, the banner carried by Proctor's command was based on the English flag with the addition of an anti-English motif. In this case, the coiled rattlesnake design is accompanied by a scroll with the now-familiar motto "Don't Tread on Me." The letters above the snake, "J. P. I. B. W. C. P.," stand for "John Proctor's Independent Battalion Westmoreland County Provincials (or possibly Pennsylvania).[6]

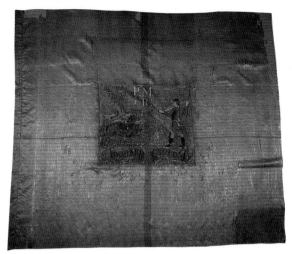
Revolutionary War Standard, 1st Pennsylvania

Revolutionary War Standard of Proctor's Battalion

Most of the Associator battalions were swept out of existence when Pennsylvania enacted its first genuine militia law in March 1777. This law provided for a more organized system of militia units. Although this militia force was designed to be used primarily for home defense, Pennsylvania battalions frequently augmented Washington's main army at various times.[7]

In addition to the militia units, some of the Continental regiments were also raised in Pennsylvania. Of these, only two flags carried by the 1st and 7th Pennsylvania regiments have survived. The flag of the 1st Pennsylvania was first described in a letter dated March 8, 1776, and thus may be assumed to have actually been furnished shortly thereafter. This 53″x60″ color has a deep green field with a red square in its midst. Within this central square is a picture of a hunter about to strike a lion entangled in a net. The Latin motto "Domari Nolo" (I Refuse to be Subjugated) appears on a scroll beneath the two figures. The flag of the 7th Pennsylvania Regiment of 1776 is

described by Richardson as a division color, and is now owned by Independence National Historical Park. This 54″x52″ color is composed of a faded red field and a canton of stars and stripes. The canton of this smaller flag is white, and the eight-pointed stars are red. A few remants of a red fringe are still extant. According to tradition, this flag was carried in the Battle of Brandywine on September 11, 1777. Little else is known about the history of this flag.[8]

When the Revolutionary War ended, Congress disbanded the Continental Army on June 2, 1784. A meager standing force of a few hundred soldiers was authorized by the new Confederation government, but each state was forced to rely on its own militia force to counter any Indian threat and to maintain internal order. Although the 1792 Militia Act passed by the national government advocated a "well regulated" militia system in each state, most states allowed their militia to become completely disorganized. The Pennsylvania legislature did pass several militia-related laws, but enforcement was spotty at best and most able-bodied men qualified for membership in the state militia were indifferent about both enrolling and turning out for the few annual drill days.[9]

After a number of less-than-comprehensive militia laws were enacted, Pennsylvania finally overhauled the entire system in 1799. One of the sections of this new law provided that each militia regiment should receive two colors to carry, described as follows:[10]

There shall be two colors or standards provided at the expense of the State for every regiment, so that each battalion may have one, and they shall be uniform throughout the State, and of the following dimensions and devices, to-wit: The length or height of the staff of each of the said colors shall be nine feet, with a brass spear on the top thereof, the fly of each of the said colors shall be six feet, two inches in length, and four feet, six inches in height on the staff. On the fly of one of the said colors, to be made of a dark blue-colored silk, there shall be painted an American eagle, with

Advance the Colors!

expanded wings, supporting the arms of the state, or some striking part thereof. In the upper corner, next to the staff, there shall be inserted, in white letters and figures, the number of the regiment, and the word "Pennsylvania," encircled or ornamented with thirteen white stars. The fly of the other color shall be composed of thirteen red and white alternate stripes, with the upper corner next to the staff colored and appropriated as above directed, and each color shall be ornamented by two silk tassles; and the two colors or standards now deposited in the office of the Secretary of this Commonwealth shall be preserved as models for the colors of the State, agreeably to which all the regimental colors of this Commonwealth shall be made.

The law describing the regimental colors was amended on March 30, 1824, to read: "In the future, every stand of colors for a militia regiment, shall be marked 'Pennsylvania Militia,' and not with the number of the regiment."[11] One of these militia regimental flags has survived and is now owned by Soldiers and Sailors Memorial Hall in Pittsburgh. This flag contains twenty-four six-pointed stars, which dates the flag sometime during the period 1822-1836. The central scrollwork surrounds the word "Regt." in white letters, and "Pennsylvania" in gold letters on a red scroll. Thus, it is not quite regulation. The number of the regiment does not appear on the flag, although a slight tear and evidence of defacing suggests that it may have been painted on at one time.

Pennsylvania Militia National Color, 1822-1836

The use of two flags by each regiment referred to the tactical organization of the militia at that time. Each regiment of ten companies was divided into two battalions of four companies each, the remaining two companies being assigned as flank companies or skirmishers, and thus not in the regular line of battle.[12] However, in spite of the large number of regiments carried on the militia rolls, there is little evidence to suggest that any militia regiments ever were assembled on any occasion.

By the outbreak of the War of 1812, the Pennsylvania militia system had already begun to degenerate

into two classes—the "uniformed militia" and the "general militia." The first class was, as a rule, more uniformly equipped and theoretically better prepared than was the general militia, whose ranks were to be found more on paper than in reality. Still, chronic shortages and lack of any standardized equipment plagued the entire militia system.[13]

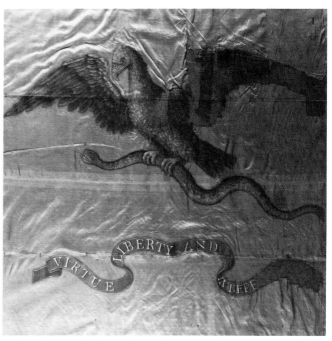

War of 1812 Color of the York Volunteers

Pennsylvania supplied more militiamen than any other state during the War of 1812. Of the many companies called upon for active service, only the flag carried by the York Volunteers still exists. This volunteer company, together with two companies of general militia from York, went to Baltimore and served as part of a Maryland regiment during the Battle of North Point. The battle resulted in the defeat of the British land force sent to storm the city's defenses while the Royal Navy bombarded Fort McHenry. An unweighted silk flag was presented to the company by the "Ladies of York," and was given to the Commonwealth through the Flag Room sometime prior to 1914. The central feature of this color, an eagle grasping a serpent in its claws, is quite rare after the Revolution. The motto "Virtue Liberty and Independence" on the scroll beneath the eagle, is, of course, that of the Commonwealth.[14]

Upon the outbreak of the Mexican War in 1846, the federal government, in order to augment the small Regular Army, asked each state to provide a quota of regiments to be known as "state volunteers." This system of recruitment would later be used in the Civil War to raise the necessary men to defend the Union. Pennsylvania's quota was two regiments, designated the 1st and 2nd Pennsylvania Volunteers. Both units were attached to Major-General Winfield Scott's army, which landed at Vera Cruz and marched overland to capture Mexico City on September 14, 1847. The 2nd Pennsylvania was directly involved in the battles around the Mexican capital, while the 1st Pennsylvania guarded the army's forward supply depot at Puebla. The regiment was besieged here by a large enemy force until relieved in mid-October 1847. Both regiments were then sent home and were mustered out of service in August 1848.[15]

Both regiments carried battleflags during the war. Shortly after the capture of Mexico City, General Scott personally presented a United States infantry regimental color to each regiment in appreciation for their gallantry during the campaign. Both colors were the standard federal design, with the appropriate regimental designation embroidered on the red scroll beneath the national eagle. These flags were presented to the Historical Society of Pennsylvania by the survivors of the "Scott Legion," a Mexican War veterans' association, on April 18, 1893, and can still be found among the Society's museum collections.[16]

Mexican War Regimental Color of the 1st Pennsylvania

The 1st Pennsylvania also carried other colors during its term of enlistment. The Historical and Museum Commission has custody of a 29-star United States flag which measures 78″x93″. It was formerly owned by Captain Francis L. Bowman, commanding Company I, the Wyoming Artillerists. This color was donated to the Commonwealth through the Flag Room sometime prior to 1914, when it was transferred to the Historical Commission.[17]

Since the 1st Pennsylvania left for the war without receiving any flags, Captain William F. Small of Company C gathered what materials he could and

Mexican War National Color, 1st Pennsylvania

fashioned a crude replica of the state flag while the regiment sailed en route from New Orleans to Vera Cruz. This small flag is reputed to have been carried during the Mexican Campaign. Its present disposition is unknown.[18]

Company B of the 1st Regiment, the Washington Artillery of Pottsville, carried a locally-presented flag when it marched off to war. In order to show their appreciation of the patriotism of the hometown boys, the ladies of Pottsville presented a homemade American flag to the company. Miss Lydia Gilbert collected the money needed for the materials. The flag itself was sewn by Mrs. Harrison Hartz, while Mrs. Jane Elliott and Miss Jane Loeser embroidered the stars, circular wreath design, and the legend "Presented by the Ladies of Pottsville." The flag was presented to the company on May 5, 1846, just before the men boarded a train for Philadelphia. After the Mexican War was over, the flag came into the possession of the family of Captain Daniel Nagle, commander of the

Mexican War Flag of the Washington Artillery
Size: 54″ × 72″

6

company. It remained in the Nagle family until December 14, 1913, when it was transferred to the custody of the Historical Society of Schuylkill County . It remained in the Society's care until March 1984, when the Society donated it, as part of its Civil War flags collection, to the Commonwealth for inclusion in the conservation program.[19]

During the years between the Mexican War and the outbreak of the Civil War in 1861, the distinction between the uniformed militia companies and the general militia increased rapidly. Indeed, by 1861, the general militia consisted more of lists of names on paper (essentially, a draft registration), than actual bodies of troops. Each county still represented a brigade of militia, and the statewide structure of twenty divisions was maintained. But in reality, the local volunteer companies became the only active units. As a result, regulations were relaxed so that companies could be formed with only thirty men. A mere three companies could constitute a battalion, and a regiment might consist of only five companies instead of the required ten.[20]

The men in the volunteer companies usually had to obtain their own uniforms and equipment under standards set by the state adjutant-general. Many of these companies existed more for the social gatherings than for any actual love of the military by most of the members. Many companies were very ephemeral, forming and disbanding on the whims of their members, and thus the militia system became very confused indeed. Similar conditions developed in other states, and the degeneration of the state militia was not confined to Pennsylvania alone.[21]

The flags carried by these companies were unique colors made especially for each company, and thus no two are exactly alike. One of the earliest of these company flags is that of the Columbia Volunteer Battalion, also known as the Columbia Battalion of Volunteers, part of the Columbia Guards, a Montour

County unit formed in 1837. Owing to confusion of its re-enlistment during the Mexican War, the battalion ceased to exist by 1848, so its colors can be dated only to the period 1837-1848. One of its colors, measuring 55″x61″, is made of dark blue silk with a gold fringe. The name of the battalion is painted in gold letters on a red scroll, beneath which is a dramatic rendition of the state coat-of-arms.[22]

A second color of this battalion measures 57″x57″ square, of the same dark blue silk, but the coat-of-arms is vastly different on this flag. The differences between two flags of the same unit illustrates only two of the many artists' renditions of the state coat-of-arms. The Commonwealth had adopted an official coat-of-arms, designed by Caleb Lownes in 1778. This version of the state arms was cut into printer's metal to be used on all official state documents. According to the State Librarian's 1893 report, the original version of the early plates was still in use as late as 1865, when the Telegraph printing office burned, destroying the last known original.[23]

In spite of an official state design, independent artists soon were creating their own versions of the state design. The earliest surviving representation of the state arms on a flag dates from the War of 1812. One of the militia companies from the conflict, the State Fencibles, dissolved itself after the war. A new com-

Reverse, Columbia Volunteer Battalion

War of 1812 Color of the State Fencibles

pany with the same name was formed shortly thereafter. On November 29, 1819, the old State Fencibles presented their standard to the new company in a brief ceremony in Philadelphia. This second State Fencibles company is still in existence and retained the banner until 1985, when it was transferred to the State Museum.[24]

Writing in 1893, State Librarian William H. Egle chronicled the major changes that resulted:

> As referred to, the first innovation made upon the Arms proper, was in 1805, or thereabouts. A rude engraving of the arms was used, omitting the stocks of maize in the rear of the supporters and also the harnessing of the horses. The olive branch is also omitted. Various changes were made from that period down to the year 1874. In all instances the engraver left off the harness, while in some cases two white horses were in proper position; again we find one black and one white horse; at another time both horses were in a semi-recumbent position; and, more frequently, each in different posture. It appeared to be impossible for any two engravers to give the same design for the Arms, from the fact that so many innovations had been made coming down for almost three quarters of a century, that scarcely any one knew what was really the authorized Arms of the Commonwealth.

The many discrepancies with the coat-of-arms were finally resolved in 1874, when the legislature approved a new law authorizing the adoption of Caleb Lownes's version as the official arms of the Commonwealth.[25]

Other flags contain different motifs on each side of the color. An example is the color of the First State Troop, Philadelphia County Cavalry, now owned by the Atwater Kent Museum. This standard, 30″x38″, contains on the obverse side the state coat-of-arms with the name of the troop on a scroll beneath. The reverse depicts a uniformed horseman in the act of urging his horse forward in the charge. The color is signed "Woodside," and thus is thought to be the work of noted Philadelphia flag artist John A. Woodside.[26]

Several other militia company flags exist throughout the Commonwealth. Among these are the flag of the Woodward Guards, owned by the Lycoming County Historical Society, the flag of the Lancaster Fencibles, complete with its metallic fringe, in the Lancaster County Historical Society, and the cavalry standard of the Juniata Cavalry, in the Historical and Museum Commission's holdings. All are unique pieces, for the Pennsylvania militia system had declined to the local company level, and when war was declared in April 1861 the existing system was found to be totally useless. It was scrapped after the war and the present national guard emerged from the ashes.

When Lincoln issued his call for 75,000 three-months militia to supress the Southern rebellion, he asked Pennsylvania for two regiments. The decline of the state militia was no more clearly seen than when only five companies were able to respond promptly to the President's call. These five companies, the Washington Artillery and National Light Infantry from Pottsville, the Logan Guards of Lewistown, the Ringgold Light Artillery of Reading, and the Allen Guards of Allentown, are collectively known as the "First Defenders," as these Pennsylvanians, estimated at between 475 and 530 men, were the first troops to reach Washington in response to Lincoln's call.[27]

These five companies reached Washington on April 18, one day before the much-heralded arrival of the 6th Massachusetts. The companies went by train from Harrisburg to Baltimore, where they had to detrain and march through the city to another rail station with a direct link to the capital. As the men, mostly unarmed, accompanied by Lieutenant John C. Pemberton and a detachment of Battery H, 4th United States Artillery, marched through the streets of the city, a pro-Southern mob began to form. The crowd bullied and threatened the Pennsylvanians as they went from station to station. Nicholas Biddle, the colored servant of the Washington Artillery's Captain James Wren, was hit in the head by a flying brick and seriously cut, the first man to shed his blood in defense of the Union. Although the military importance of the First Defenders was minimal at best, their arrival in Washington was of great morale value to the beleaguered capital. Lincoln, overjoyed to see the men, personally shook each man's hand after the companies were quartered in the Capitol itself.

In addition to the Washington Artillery's Mexican War flag described above and not carried in 1861, there are flags for two of the other First Defenders companies.[28] There are two flags of the Ringgold Light Artillery of Reading, a company formed in 1850 and named after Major Samuel Ringgold, an American officer killed during the Battle of Palo Alto in 1846. One, currently owned by the Historical and Museum Commission, contains two different motifs. The obverse side depicts the state coat-of-arms, while the reverse

Reverse, Ringgold Light Artillery

Advance the Colors!

has an illustration of a cannon with the legend "Stand By the Flag and Don't Give Up the Guns" on a scroll beneath the gun. There is no evidence to suggest that this flag was carried by the company in 1861. It was donated to the Flag Room sometime prior to 1914, as it is listed among the miscellaneous colors transferred to the Historical Commission when the Civil War colors were placed in the Rotunda that same year.[29]

A second color attributed to the Ringgolds was placed in Flag Case #1, bearing a placard with the inscription "This Flag was carried by the Ringgold Light Artillery of Reading, Pa., which reported for duty at

Close up of reverse, Logan Guards

Ringgold Light Artillery, National Color
Size: 68³/₄″ × 118¹/₄″
1985.007

Harrisburg April 16, 1861. The first United States flag to enter the city of Washington, D.C." Other than this single bit of writing, the author has found no contemporary accounts that substantiate this claim. However, since this flag is in the Civil War collection and was placed in the case, its history was probably verified at one time, but this evidence has not been located.

A single flag exists for the Logan Guards of Lewistown, Mifflin County, a company organized in July 1858. The new company received a flag presented to it by the women of Lewistown during a militia encampment in September 1859. This flag was furnished to the women by Horstmann Brothers & Company, a Philadelphia-based military supplier. The

Logan Guards color has a different image painted on each side. The obverse shows an American eagle with the details of the presentation of the flag inscribed in a circle around the bird. The reverse honors the Logan's namesake, the famous Indian Chief Logan, with his picture, accompanied by the legend "Heroic Actions Win Immortality."[30]

This flag was carried by Private William G. Mitchell when the company went to Washington in 1861. Mitchell later became the chief aide-de-camp of Major-General Winfield Scott Hancock. After the three-months term of enlistment expired, many of the Logans re-enlisted and became Company A, 46th Pennsylvania. Since the federal government discouraged the use of company flags, and judging from the state of preservation of the Logan flag, it seems highly unlikely that it was carried during the war. The flag came into the possession of Captain John B. Shelheimer's family, where it remained until sometime between 1909 and 1914. During this period, the flag became the property of Colonel Edward E. Ziegler of Lewistown, who had it placed between two panes of glass to preserve it from deteriorating. Colonel Ziegler then donated the flag to the state. Two surviving members of the Logans, Franklin H. Wentz and William Weber, went to Harrisburg and placed the banner in the Flag Room. It remained there until 1914, when it was transferred to the Historical Commission, in whose custody it remains.[31]

Notes

[1]Colonel John B. B. Trussell, "The Pennsylvania Militia," in Bruce S. Bazelon, *Defending the Commonwealth: Catalogue of the Militia Exhibit at the William Penn Museum, Harrisburg, Pennsylvania* (Providence: Mobray Company Publishers, 1980), pp.1-2.

[2]*Ibid.*, p. 2.

[3]Frank E. Schermerhorn, *American and French Flags of the Revolution, 1775-1783* (Philadelphia: Pennsylvania Society of Sons of the Revolution, 1948), p. 98.

[4]*Ibid.*, p. 38.

[5]*Ibid.*; Major William P. Clarke, *Official History of the Militia and the National Guard of the State of Pennsylvania from the Earliest Period of Record to the Present Time.* 2 volumes. (n.p.: Published by Captain Charles J. Hendler, 1909), 1: Frontispiece caption; Edward W. Richardson, *Standards and Colors of the American Revolution* (Philadelphia: University of Pennsylvania Press, 1982), pp. 113-115.

[6]Trussell, p. 2; Schermerhorn, p. 99; *Defending the Commonwealth*, p. 14.

[7]Trussell, pp. 3-4.

[8]*Defending the Commonwealth*, p. 14; Schermerhorn, pp. 51-52; Richardson, pp. 116-117, 120.

[9]Trussell, p. 4

[10]*Laws of Pennsylvania*, volume 5, pp. 214-215. The original is heavily punctuated with commas and is a long sentence. To make it easier to read and comprehend, I have eliminated some of the unnecessary commas and made it into sentences.

[11]Clarke 1: 35.

[12]*Ibid.*, p. 26.

[13]Trussell, p. 6

[14]*Ibid.*, p. 7; *Defending the Commonwealth*, p. 18; "Old Flags, from State Flag Room," document, bearing the "copied" date, October 10, 1930, in RG 19.

[15]Trussell, pp. 10-11. For a concise account of Pennsylvania's commitment in the Mexican War, see Randy Hackenburg, "Pennsylvania Volunteers in the War with Mexico," *Pennsylvania Heritage* 4, #2 (March 1978): 27-30.

[16]"Mexican War Battle-Flags Presented to the Historical Society of Pennsylvania," *Pennsylvania Magazine of History and Biography* 17 (1893): 185, 187

[17]*Defending the Commonwealth*, p. 17; "Old Flags" document, RG 19.

[18]"Mexican War Battle-Flags," p. 185.

[19]"Proceedings and Speeches Made at the Transfer of Battle Flags to the Historical Society of Schuylkill County, December 14, 1913," *Publications of the Historical Society of Schuylkill County* 5, #2 (1932): 12-15.

[20]Trussell, p. 11; Clarke 1: 39.

[21]For an excellent history of the American militia, see John K. Mahon, *History of the Militia and the National Guard* (New York: Free Press, 1983).

[22]*Defending the Commonwealth*, p. 25.

[23]William H. Egle, "The Arms of Pennsylvania and the Great Seal of the Commonwealth," in *Annual Report of the State Librarian for 1893*, pp. 3-4.

[24]Details of the flag transfer can be found in Minute Book 1, State Fencibles Papers, State Archives.

[25]Egle, "Arms of Pennsylvania," pp. 3-4.

[26]*Defending the Commonwealth*, p. 23.

[27]This material on the First Defenders is taken from Heber S. Thompson, *The First Defenders* (n.p., n.d.), the most complete work on all five companies yet written.

[28]None of the references to the Washington Artillery mention any colors being carried. Captain Wren's account (see bibliography) is very detailed, and since he fails to include any mention of a flag, I am inclined to think that the company did not carry one in 1861.

[29]*Defending the Commonwealth*, p. 26; "Old Flags" document, RG 19.

[30]Copeland, *Logan Guards*, pp. 11-12, 62.

[31]*Ibid.*, pp. 16, 62-63; Clarke 2: 133.

Bibliography—The First Defenders

Copeland, Willis R. *The Logan Guards of Lewistown, Pa. Our First Defenders*. Lewistown: Mifflin County Historical Society, 1962.

Downey, Edgar. "History of the First Defenders." *Schuylkill County Historical Society Publications* 6 (1952): 29-34.

Fernald, Granville. *The Story of the First Defenders*. Washington, 1892.

Gay, James D. "Ringgold Light Artillery at the Outbreak. A Pennsylvanian in Washington Early in 1861." *National Tribune*, September 29, 1887.

Heister, William M. *The Place of the Ringgold Light Artillery of Reading, Among the First Five Companies from Pennsylvania Which Marched to the Defense of Washington, April, 1861, A Paper Read Before the Historical Society of Berks County, June 14, 1870*. Reading, 1870.

Mackay, W. F. "The First Defenders." *Philadelphia Weekly Press*, April 28, 1886.

Schaadt, James L. "The Allen Infantry in 1861." *Pennsylvania German Magazine* 12 (1911): 149-162.

Strohecker, John E. "The First Defenders." *Berks County Historical Review* 26 (1960/61): 40-48.

Thompson, Heber S. *The First Defenders*. N.p., n.d.

Wren, James. "The First Defenders. The Washington Artillery of Pottsville." *Philadelphia Weekly Press*, July 21, 1886.

Chapter II
Pennsylvania Civil War Flags

After the First Defender companies reported to Washington, Pennsylvania was called upon to furnish fourteen complete regiments as the state's quota for the volunteer militia. However, the popular response was so great that the Commonwealth eventually fielded twenty-five infantry regiments to serve for three months. No cavalry or artillery units were accepted because the federal government believed that the war would be very short; hence the enlistment period of a mere three months. Owing to the rush to get these troops into the field as soon as possible, scant provision was made to completely supply each regiment. Since the state's military stores were woefully inadequate to meet the needs of twenty-five completely-equipped regiments aggregating nearly 21,000 men, state authorities depended, in most cases, on the federal government to supply the new regiments with necessary equipment. Whenever possible, the state government attempted to purchase whatever equipment could be had on the open market.[1]

Because these twenty-five regiments were organized and sent to the front within a hectic ten-day period, the state did not issue any flags to the three-months volunteers. Any flags carried by these units were locally-presented banners. Many, if not all, of the first twenty-five regiments seem to have received such colors, which generally were regulation 34-star American flags with local inscriptions added. Some of the regiments that later re-enlisted as three-years units kept their presented colors and continued to carry them throughout the war. For example, most of the soldiers of the 4th Pennsylvania re-enlisted in the 51st Pennsylvania. During the Battle of New Bern, North Carolina, on March 14, 1862, the 51st advanced and helped drive the Confederates out of their earthworks defending the city. Captain William J. Bolton of Company A, who would later become the regiment's colonel, wrote that the flag presented to the 4th Pennsylvania on April 20, 1861, was the first to be planted on the enemy works on that part of the battlefield.[2]

Following is a brief descriptive list of flags presented to the three-months regiments. On the whole, these units were not heavily engaged in combat. Only

three regiments, the 4th, 11th, and 15th, suffered any battle casualties, which totalled forty for these three units. Of these losses, the 15th Regiment suffered thirty-six of them when most of Company I was captured by Rebel cavalry on July 2, 1861, as Federal troops crossed the Potomac and advanced into Virginia. No Pennsylvania units were engaged in the Battle of Manassas on July 21, the war's first major battle. Most of the flags presented to these regiments have been lost. A few were retained and carried by three-years regiments; these are identified as such and are more fully described in the appropriate regimental sketches.

1st Regiment

There is no evidence that this regiment received a flag, but each of the five companies recruited in Northampton County received a flag from local citizens. Company A, the Washington Grays, was the recipient of a "beautiful silk flag" from the ladies of Bethlehem just prior to their departure for Harrisburg on April 19. On April 20, Company B, the Citizens Artillery, obtained two silk flags from the ladies of Easton. Companies C (Easton Invincibles) and D (Scott Guards) each received a flag on April 18. Company H, the National Guards, received a "silk bunting" flag on April 19. Company K, the Jackson Rifles of Lancaster County, received a 34-star national color from the ladies of Gap, Bellevue, and vicinity while the regiment lay in camp near Chambersburg.[3]

2nd Regiment

On an unspecified date, Company I, the State Capital Guards, was presented with a "splendid flag" by Mrs. Marion Verbeke while the regiment lay at Camp Scott.[4]

4th Regiment

On April 20, Judge Daniel G. Smyser presented two flags to the regiment, the ceremony taking place in front of the Montgomery County Court House in Norristown. When most of the regiment re-enlisted for three years as the 51st Pennsylvania, these flags were carried during that unit's term of service. They are more fully described in the sketch of the 51st Regiment.[5]

5th Regiment

Sometime in July, Mrs. Dr. Hiester of Reading presented a stand of colors to the regiment with the provision that it be returned to her by Company H (the Union Light Infantry) when the regiment disbanded.[6]

7th Regiment

On May 15 while the regiment lay encamped at Camp Slifer, the ladies of Chambersburg presented a national color to the regiment. Company E, the Allegheny Light Guards, received a "beautiful flag" from the ladies of Allegheny City sometime in April.[7]

8th Regiment

This regiment also received a flag from the ladies of Chambersburg while at Camp Slifer. It was presented on May 11 by Mr. J. K. Shyrode on behalf of the donors. Captain William W. Wise of the Brookville Rifles accepted the flag for the regiment. A member of the 8th, W. W. Valentine, wrote that the ladies also presented a flag on May 8, but the second color received on the eleventh "far surpassed the other in size and beauty."[8]

9th Regiment

When the Easton Jaegers (Company G) left Bethlehem for Harrisburg on April 22, the ladies of Bethlehem gave them a flag just prior to their departure.[9]

11th Regiment

The loyal ladies of Martinsburg, Virginia, gave flags to the 11th Pennsylvania and 1st Wisconsin on July 12 to honor them for their part in the small victory at Falling Waters on July 2. This color was carried after the 11th became a three-years regiment, and is fully documented in that sketch. Company H, the Danville Rifles, received a "beautiful silk flag" from the ladies of their hometown on April 22.[10]

12th Regiment

On April 24, the ladies of Allegheny presented a flag to the 12th Regiment, which was received on behalf of the officers and men by Captain R. Biddle Roberts of the U.S. Zouave Cadets. Company E, the Washington Invincibles, received a flag from the ladies of that borough on April 20. Mr. Robert H. Koontz presented the flag to the company in front of the Washington County Court House.[11]

13th Regiment

Two companies of this regiment received flags in April 1861. The Duquesne Greys (Company K) received a flag from the Honorable A. W. Loomis on April 24. The Fort Pitt Guards (Company E) were given a flag by the ladies of the 7th and 8th Wards on April 24.[12]

14th Regiment

Bates wrote that the regiment was presented a flag by the ladies of Martinsburg, Virginia, but no further information has been located about this presentation.[14]

16th Regiment

At the request of a delegation of York ladies, Horstmann Brothers & Company manufactured a flag that the women presented to the regiment on June 8, in a ceremony in front of the York County Court House. This flag, now owned by the Historical Society of York County, is a 52½″ × 69″ 34-star national flag, with "16th Regt. Penna. Vols." painted on the center red stripe. The Latin motto "Semper Paratus" (Always Prepared) is painted in the midst of the blue canton. "Suspended from the heavily gilt spear and battle axe, on the staff, was a pair of magnificent gold tassels and cord." Horstmann also supplied the leather covering and carrying belt.[14]

18th Regiment

Women friends of the regiment presented two flags— a national and a state—to the unit on May 9. Colonel William D. Lewis, Jr. accepted the colors for his command.[15]

19th Regiment

According to Taylor, several young ladies of the High School presented a silk flag to this Philadelphia regiment on May 14. The *Philadelphia Inquirer* reported that the women of the Girls' High and Normal School presented a flag on April 29. This color was made of the finest silk, stitched by the pupils themselves. The flag included the names of the donors within the canton. Colonel Peter Lyle marched his troops to the school, located on Sergeant Street, to receive the flag. The *Public Ledger* reported that the regiment received another flag on April 29. After finishing their daily drilling at Franklin Square, City Solicitor Charles E. Lee presented a silk flag to Colonel Lyle on behalf of the ladies of the Sixth Ward.[16]

22nd Regiment

This regiment received two flags during its term of enlistment. The first color was presented sometime prior to May 13 by Miss Freeman of Philadelphia. A second, the gift of the loyal women of East Baltimore, was received on June 8. A soldier writing home described it as a "beautiful silk regimental flag."[17]

23rd Regiment

This unit received a flag from a delegation of Philadelphia women sometime during its term of service. The flag was most likely carried after the regiment re-enlisted for three years, and is described within the 23rd's sketch.[18]

25th Regiment

On May 27, the soldiers of the 25th Regiment were the recipients of a flag obtained for them by Joseph W. Cake of Pottsville. It was presented to Major James H. Campbell by Colonel John W. Forney on behalf of the absent donor. The presentation took place in the square east of the capitol in Washington, D.C. This flag was later carried by the 96th Pennsylvania.[19]

On April 30 the Pennsylvania legislature convened in a special session called by Governor Curtin. The rush to place troops in the field had revealed the inadequacy of the existing military laws, so the governor wished the legislature to upgrade them. As the legislature debated the question of new laws, the idea of providing state-issued colors to Pennsylvania regiments surfaced. The existing militia law concerning flags had first been passed in 1799 and amended in 1824, providing two colors for each militia regiment, as described in Chapter 1. However, these flags were

Governor Andrew Gregg Curtin

at variance with United States Army Regulations and were designed for the militia, not state volunteers.

State militia officer Henry J. Biddle noted the discrepancies between the state and national regulations, and wrote a letter to State Senator Heister Clymer of Reading, explaining his own recommendations on the question of state-issued colors. Biddle called the senator's attention to the regulation differences and suggested that the state and national colors could be combined into one flag for use by the volunteer units:[20]

> 1st Our U.S. colors are readily distinguishable from the colors of the Insurrectionist confederacy, and any state colors, whereas state colors not being well known, officers might mistake and fire on the colors of loyal sister states.
>
> 2d The colors of Pennsylvania regiments should when in U.S. service proclaim their allegiance to the constitutional government by subordinating her nationality on the flag for the time being.
>
> 3rd It is very desirable in a mixed force of volunteer and regular troops that the enemy should not be able to distinguish which were regulars or volunteers, and the appearance of all being regulars would in itself have a strong effect in damaging the courage of the opponents.

In the case of regimental flags with the national eagle on them, Biddle suggested that the scroll beneath the eagle denote that the regiment was from the Keystone State. Again, he suggested that the state coat-of-arms not be placed on these blue flags, for the reasons given above.

As a result of the debate over state-issued colors, the legislature passed Joint Resolution #6, which was signed into law by Governor Curtin on May 16. This law read as follows:[21]

> Joint Resolutions
>
> Relative to the procuring of Standards for the several Regiments of Pennsylvania called or to be called into Service of the United States.
>
> Section 1. Resolved by the Senate and House of Representatives of the Commonwealth of Pennsylvania in General Assembly met, That the governor of the Commonwealth be requested to ascertain how the several regiments raised in Pennsylvania during the war of the revolution, and the war of 1812, and the war with Mexico, were numbered, among what divisions of the service they were distributed, and where the said regiments distinguished themselves in action. That having ascertained the particulars aforesaid, he shall procure regimental standards, to be inscribed with the numbers of those regiments respectively, on which shall be painted the arms of this Commonwealth, and the names of the actions in which the said regiments distinguished themselves. That the standards so inscribed shall be delivered to the regiments now in the field or forming, bearing the regimental numbers corresponding to the regiments of Pennsylvania in former wars.
>
> Section 2. That the governor do procure regimental standards formed or to be formed in Pennsylvania, beyond the numbers in former wars, upon which shall be inscribed the number of the regiment, and painted the arms of this

Commonwealth; and that all these standards, after the present unhappy rebellion is ended, shall be returned to the adjutant general of the state, to be further inscribed, as the valor and good conduct of each particular regiment may have deserved; and that they then be carefully preserved by the state, to be delivered to such future regiments as the military necessities of the country may require Pennsylvania to raise.

The intent of the legislature in regard to honoring Pennsylvania commands of earlier wars was good, but this resolution shows the lack of information that the Civil War legislature had about the earlier Pennsylvania commands. As described in Chapter 1, Pennsylvania did contribute several regiments numbered 1st through 13th to the Continental Army. The units engaged in the War of 1812 were militia commands that ceased to exist after the war except at the company level. Mexican War commands included only the 1st and 2nd Pennsylvania Regiments. The legislature's attempt to honor these former units by inscribing their battle honors on flags for active regiments with the same numbers as earlier units was laudable, but all of the earlier regiments had been disbanded. And even though there were three-months volunteer regiments with the same number, by the time the legislature passed this resolution, and the state awarded contracts for the supply of these colors, the regiments with corresponding numbers of earlier regiments had been mustered out of service.

In addition to the resolution on state colors, the legislature also enacted a resolution authorizing Governor Curtin to use the $500 given to the state by the Pennsylvania Chapter of the Society of the Cincinnati to purchase regimental flags for some of the regiments. This Society, a patriotic order embracing descendants of Revolutionary War officers, had donated the money to be used to help equip Pennsylvania soldiers.[22]

By the time the legislature adjourned, Pennsylvania had supplied more than enough troops to meet its quota, and all further federal recruiting was suspended. But the fielding of twenty-five regiments had seriously depleted the state militia units, and many Pennsylvania leaders feared that a Rebel invasion was possible, especially since the Commonwealth was bordered by Maryland, a state of dubious allegiance to the Lincoln government. Thus, one of the legislative acts authorized the governor to raise and equip a reserve corps of fifteen three-years regiments (thirteen infantry, one cavalry, and one artillery) to defend the state borders. This law provided that the corps would be federalized if the national government needed the troops.[23]

In accordance with the legislative authority to both raise a reserve corps and issue flags to these regiments, state Adjutant-General Edward M. Biddle, on

June 18, published the state's bid proposals for contracts to supply the state with flags for the reserve corps regiments. Biddle advertised for both national and regimental colors for the single artillery regiment, the rifle regiment, and the ten infantry regiments then forming. He also sought a standard and ten company guidons for the cavalry regiment. All flags were to be made in accordance with United States Army Regulations, except that the state coat-of-arms was to be embroidered on the national colors, within the blue canton, with the thirty-four stars to be arranged symmetrically about the arms. The arms were also to be embroidered on the regimental colors, in the upper corner next to the staff. The state arms would also be placed on the cavalry standard and on each of the company guidons. Bidders were required to place their proposals no later than June 26, with the speedy delivery of the flags to be considered together with the prices.[24]

Three Philadelphia firms placed bids for the flag contract. The most important and largest of the three

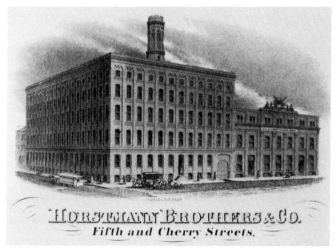

Horstmann Factory in Philadelphia

was that of Horstmann Brothers & Company. This company had been established by William H. Horstmann (1785-1850), a native of Cassel, Germany, who emigrated to Philadelphia in 1816. Horstmann, a passementier by trade, went into partnership with a coach-lace maker in the city. He eventually married the boss's daughter and went into business for himself, gradually expanding into the areas associated with all sorts of garment manufacturing. Horstmann bought out a local swordmaker in 1828 and thereafter entered the military goods field as well. The company built a large brick factory at the corner of 5th and Cherry Streets in 1852, and by 1861 the firm was perhaps the largest military goods manufacturer in America. The Horstmann business consisted of two related firms: 1) William H. Horstmann & Son, specializing in ornamentation and garments, and 2) Horstmann Brothers & Company, the military goods department. Although the company suffered huge losses when the Southern states seceded from the Union, the January 1863 business rating commented that the $400,000 loss did not cripple the firm at all. Indeed, the 1864 report noted that the Horstmann business was doing very well as a result of the war, and was "the largest business in the line in the United States," with an estimated worth of over one million dollars.[25]

The second firm was that of George O. Evans and William S. Hassall, two men who had worked in the Horstmann firm before starting their own business in 1859. The new company was rated in 1859 as building up a profitable business, but the majority of the company's garment trade was with the Southern states. Hence, the outbreak of the war hurt Evans & Hassall, but government contracts bailed the firm out of immediate danger. By June 1864, the firm's estimated worth was about $400,000. However, the war seemed to have had an adverse effect on the two part-

ners, for they withdrew from the company in 1866 after admitting others into the firm.[26] A third man named Samuel Brewer also applied for the contract, but, except for his proposal, nothing is known about his business, in which he claimed to have had twenty-five years experience.[27]

When the bids were opened and examined, they were found to be as follows:

	Horstmann	Evans & Hassall	Brewer
national/regimental pair	$160	$135	$110
cavalry standard	35	35	30
cavalry guidon	12	22.50	15

After deliberation over the bids, state Inspector-General Henry Coppee decided to award the contract to Horstmann Brothers & Company, whom Coppee considered as the "most responsible partner," even though their bid was not the lowest of the three. However, before accepting the Horstmann bid for the contract, Coppee recommended reducing the price of their bid as follows: pair of colors from $160 to $150, the cavalry standard reduced from $35 to $33, and the guidons from $12 to $11.[28]

Coppee's letter to one of Governor Curtin's aides about his decision was dated July 22, 1861. On the previous day, the Federal army commanded by Brigadier-General Irvin McDowell had been defeated at the First Battle of Manassas. The panic-stricken army retreated to Washington, where the terms of service of most of the three-months regiments expired within a few days after the battle. The Lincoln government suddenly was faced with a crisis as few troops remained to defend the capital. On the very day that Coppee announced the bid decision, Lincoln issued a call for troops to serve for three years. The government also asked that Pennsylvania tender its Reserve Corps for immediate mustering into federal service, which was granted by Governor Curtin.

Faced by this sudden emergency call for Pennsylvania troops, Adjutant-General Biddle realized that more flags would be needed. As a result, he contracted with both Horstmann Brothers and Evans & Hassall for flags on August 9. The Horstmann contract specified the colors to be supplied as follows:[29]

> . . . That the said Horstmann Brothers & Co., their heirs, executors, and administrators shall make and cause to be delivered at the office of the Adjutant General in the City of Harrisburg, one National Color for United States Artillery and twelve National Colors for United Stated Infantry, all to be in every respect as described in the U.S. Army Regulations, Paragraphs No. 1369, 1370, except that the Arms of

Evans & Hassall Advertisement

Pennsylvania are to be painted on the National Colors in the centre of the union, their size not to exceed one-fourth of its area and the thirty-four stars to be arranged symmetrically around them; all to be entirely complete with pike, spear, ferrule, cords, tassels, fringe, ready for use and marked with no. and name of Regiment according to regulations above mentioned.

Also, one National Color for Rifle Regiment; as above described for Infantry Colors except the no. and name of Regiment are to be painted in gold instead of silver to be complete ready for use and marked as above mentioned.

Also, one Standard and ten Guidons for Cavalry Regiment as described in Paragraphs 1372 & 1373 of U.S. Army Regulations. the Arms of Pennsylvania of suitable dimensions to be painted on each; to be complete ready for use and marked as above mentioned.

The workmanship and materials in every Color and Guidon to be equal to U.S. standard patterns; the material of the paint not to be injurious to the silk; and the whole to be subject to inspection by an officer appointed for that purpose whose decision shall be final and conclusive.

And the said Horstmann Brothers & Co. are to deliver the said Colors and Guidons at the rate of two Colors or four Guidons per day—the first delivery to be made not later than twelve days from the date of this contract.

The cost was placed at $65 for each national color, $33 for the cavalry standard, and $11 for each guidon. However, owing to the confusion over what the exact design of the guidons was to be, Horstmann Brothers asked for, and received, the price of $20 per guidon, which included the state coat-of-arms painted on each. Extra lettering was priced at 12¢ for each gilt letter, or 8¢ for painted lettering. These colors were assigned to the Pennsylvania Reserve Corps, and were delivered in time for Governor Curtin to present them to the regiments on September 10.

Evans & Hassall received a contract similar to Horstmann Brothers. This firm was contracted to supply twelve infantry colors, also at a per-flag price of $65. These colors were assigned to the infantry regiments numbered 45th through 56th, and were completed by September 14. Neither contract specified that leather covers for the flags were to be supplied. It is quite possible that both companies did furnish them, as several contemporary accounts include references to such covers. Also, a May 31, 1866, list of flags "on hand" in the adjutant-general's office includes 135 flag covers and 10 standard covers.[30]

These two firms supplied all state-issued flags during the course of the war. As more and more regiments were recruited, each company was asked to provide flags for specific regiments. Horstmann Brothers & Company furnished 134 state colors, 1 artillery national color, 29 cavalry standards, and 112 cavalry company guidons. Evans & Hassall furnished 88 state colors, 2 artillery standards, and 4 cavalry standards. Neither company furnished any regimental flags as proposed by the original bids. All colors, stan-

dards, and guidons contained the state coat-of-arms. Any regimental flags were obtained by federal requisition or by local presentation. Owing to the increased cost of labor and supplies, both firms raised their prices as the war progressed. Horstmann's prices for colors went from $65 to $80, and standards increased to $40. The price charged by Evans & Hassall for infantry colors went from $65 to $85, with their price for cavalry and artillery standards increasing at first to $55, and finally to $60. A complete list of all flags purchased by the Commonwealth follows.[31]

HORSTMANN BROTHERS & COMPANY
Flags Furnished to Pennsylvania

Abbreviations: st=standard   g=guidon

date	number	regiments	price
9/6/61	14	30-43(PaRes)	910.
	1 st	44(1stCav)	33.
	10	44(1stCav)	210.
		additional lettering	90.
10/24/61	2 g	44(1stCav),L,M	40.
11/1/61	14	flag belts	21.
11/4/61	10	66-69, 71-76	650.
	2 st	59,60(2d,3dCav)	66.
	20 g	59,60(2d,3dCav)	220.
	34	flag belts	51.
11/18/61	1	84	65.
	1 st	92(9thCav)	33.
	10 g	92(9thCav)	110.
11/19/61	43	flag belts	64.50
11/22/61	4	86,101,103,111	260.
	2 st	70,80(6th,7thCav)	66.
	20 g	70,80(6th,7thCav)	220.
12/6/61	2	90,91	130.
	3	flag belts	4.50
12/7/61	1 st	Anderson Troop	33.
	5 st	64,65,89,94,108(4th,5th,8th, 10th,11thCav)	165.
	50 g	64,65,89,94,108(4th,5th,8th, 10th,11thCav)	550.
12/9/61	10	23,81,82,83,87,88,98,99,100,102	650.
12/13/61	6	95,105,106,107,109,110	390.
3/11/62	1	112(2dArty)	65.
	3	114,115,116	195.
5/5/62	1 st	113(12thCav)	33.
9/24/62	10	138-142,145,148,149,150,155	650.
10/17/62	1	153	65.
11/8/62	2	143,151	130.
11/22/62	2	147,158	130.
1/12/63	3 st	161,162,163(16th,17th,18thCav)	99.
	5	165-169	325.
	3 st	117,159,160(13th,14th,15thCav)	99.
3/9/63	1	61(altered from 144)	65.
5/14/63	1	48(altered from 146)	65.
5/16/63	3	54(altered from 154),83(altered from 157),158	195.
5/12/63	1	77(altered from 156)	65.
6/22/63	1	152(3dArty)	65.
11/14/63	1 st	64(4thCav)	33.
11/17/63	1	silk flag	75.
12/1/63	4	98,101,106,115	260.
12/9/63	7	35-41(PaRes)	455.
2/15/64	6	29,53,61,91,57,111	390.
5/20/64	1 st	80(7thCav)	33.
	1	79	65.

Advance the Colors!

date	number	regiments	price
6/6/64	2	200(altered from 71),188	130.
	1 st	92(9thCav)	33.
3/12/64	4	45,46,(altered from 48),93,147	260.
6/20/64	1	75	65.
7/2/64	2	85,184	130.
7/14/64	2	51,97	160.
7/27/64	1	188	80.
8/12/64	3	193,194,195	240.
9/21/64	2	201,202	160.
10/3/64	6	49,55,203,209,210,211	480.
11/23/64	1	183	80.
12/12/64	2	45,76	160.
	1 st	44(1stCav)	40.
1/3/65	1	102	80.
1/28/65	1	143	80.
2/6/65	2	47,139	160.
2/28/65	1 st	59(2dCav)	40.
4/10/65	1 st	70(6thCav)	40.
4/26/65	3 st	64,113,162,(4th,12th,17thCav)	120.
	4	52,83,157,192	320.
5/8/65	1 st	112(2dArty)	40.
5/16/65	2	116,145	160.
7/1/65	1	76	80.
7/11/65	1	81	80.
7/15/65	1	53	80.

EVANS & HASSALL
Flags Furnished to Pennsylvania

date	number	regiments	price
9/14/61	12	45-56	780.
		additional lettering	
		(240 gold letters, 20 on each, @12¹/₂¢)	30.
9/18/61	1	bunting flag (14 foot)	14.
10/30/61	12	26,27,28,29,57,58,61,62,63,77,78,79	780.
11/4/61	5	11,93,96,97,104	325.
11/9/61	1	85	65.
9/24/62	20	118-137	1300.
1/5/63	9	170-178	585.
		lettering on 29	6.
3/19/63	1	179	65.
12/3/63	4	63,69,78,85	262.
12/12/63	4	30,32,33,34(PaRes)	262.
4/5/64	6	50,51,77,102,110,116	390.
5/2/64	1	56, with additional lettering	95.
	1 st	89(8thCav)	40.
9/28/64	6	100,187,207,208,213,214	535.
		205(altered from 120),206(altered from 170)	
10/5/64	2 st	204,212(5th,6thArty)	110.
10/25/64	1	58	85.
11/15/64	1 st	60(3dCav)	55.
1/10/65	3	81,190,191	255.
	2 st	159,189(14thCav,4thArty)	120.
2/6/65	3	28,73,104	255.

The flags made by these two military manufacturing establishments generally followed the guidelines established in the bid proposal of June 1861, but there were some minor adjustments. Evans & Hassall alerted General Biddle that it would be impossible to embroider any of the flags because there was only one high quality embroideress in the entire city of Philadelphia, and thus it would be impossible to meet the delivery dates. Thus, all state symbols were painted rather than embroidered. Horstmann suggested that gold paint be used for all lettering on the flags, as the firm had inquired about paint colors with the War Department and learned that the use of silver paint had been discontinued because of its propensity to blacken after exposure to weather. Thus, both firms used gold paint for all regimental designations.[32]

Nearly all regiments recruited in Pennsylvania received at least one state-issued color. Units that did not receive any were the 154th (which only recruited to a battalion level and thus was not authorized any flags according to army regulations), 186th, 196th, 197th, 198th, 199th, and 215th infantry regiments. The 19th, 20th, 21st, and 22nd cavalry regiments also did not receive any state standards.

Many regiments later were given replacement colors for flags lost by accident or capture, or for those which had been literally shot to pieces in battle. The state legislature took the lead in authorizing replacement colors with Joint Resolution #6, which was signed into law by Governor Curtin on February 14, 1863. This act authorized the governor to procure a replacement state color for the 54th Pennsylvania, which had lost its state flag by accident. Joint Resolution #11, approved April 11, 1863, authorized replacement flags for the 78th, 80th (7th Cavalry), 83rd, and 111th regiments.[33] After these two resolutions became public, many colonels or other commanding officers of Pennsylvania regiments wrote the governor to request new flags, primarily to replace those that had been torn to pieces by hard service. No requests seem to have been turned down, and thus many regiments received at least two flags if they served more than two years in the field.

Once the state flags were completed by the Philadelphia manufacturers, they were ready to be given to the regiments. This was accomplished is a variety of ways. First, and especially during the first year of the war, Governor Curtin took great delight in presenting the flags in person to regiments at Camp Curtin or elsewhere in the Commonwealth, before the units took the field. It appears that he presented 55 flags himself. One of his aides, Colonel Samuel B. Thomas, presented another 29 in the name of the governor. A total of 34 colors were sent directly to regimental headquarters, while at least 5 were sent to Adjutant-General Russell's office in Harrisburg at the end of the war. These flags were those finished for delivery after the end of hostilities, and were never used in combat.[34]

The most common practice was to forward the state flags directly to the Pennsylvania State Agency, established in Washington during the first year of the war, "to provide for the comfort and efficiency of our volunteers, the care of the sick and wounded, the sending of dead bodies of those who might die in the

Lieutenant-Colonel J. H. Puleston

Pennsylvania Regiments and Their Flags I: Infantry

In addition to the state-issued colors, many Pennsylvania infantry regiments carried flags issued by the federal government. United States Army Regulations provided that each infantry regiment should carry two silk flags. One was the national flag, with the name and number of the regiment embroidered in gold letters on the center red stripe. The flag measured six feet hoist by six and one-half feet fly, mounted on a staff nine feet, ten inches in length, which included the brass spearpoint finial, and the brass ferrule at its base. The attached cords and tassels were of blue and white silk intermixed, the standard infantry colors.[36]

The second flag prescribed by Regulations was termed the regimental color. This banner was made of dark blue silk, with the arms of the United States embroidered in the center. The name and number of the regiment was embroidered on a red scroll beneath the national eagle. The staff, flag size, and cords and tassels corresponded to the national flag. Although the infantry regiments of the Regular Army carried both of these flags, it seems from the surviving evidence that these two types of flags were not automatically issued to volunteer regiments. The regulation flags were a sort of "generic" flag, manufactured for the government by a number of independent contracted firms. These flags were supplied to the government without the name and number of the intended regiment inscribed on the flag. It was the individual preference of a regimental commander whether or not to requisition one or both types of flags from the government. If he did so, he was re-

service, and for such other purposes as might be necessary for the benefit of Pennsylvania soldiers." The directors of this important, but overlooked, agency were:

Colonel J. H. Puleston, through December 1862
Colonel Matthew S. Quay, January-April 1863
Colonel R. Biddle Roberts, April-December 1863
Colonel Frank Jordan, January 1864 through 1866

A similar agency was established at Nashville, Tennessee, in May 1864, which was supervised by Colonel James Chamberlin until it ceased operation on April 1, 1866. The Washington agency received 118 colors to forward to regiments, while Colonel Chamberlin was sent 5 state flags for regiments in the "Southwestern Department." The directors obtained the flags either from Philadelphia or Harrisburg and kept them until someone from the regiment showed up to claim the flag, presented the colors themselves, or forwarded the flags by Adams Express to regiments already in the field.[35]

Unmarked Infantry Regimental Color
Size: 71-3/8" × 75-7/8"
1985.173

18

sponsible for having the name and number of his regiment painted on the flag. He could either have one of his men do it, or send it out to a professional to have the flag completed with the proper designation. In the case of Pennsylvania regiments, many seem not to have carried government flags in addition to the state-issued flag.

Many regiments also received flags presented by local citizens. The design of these flags varies greatly. Several carried by Pennsylvania commands are United States national flags of many differing designs. Until 1912, there were no specific regulations about the appearance of the American national flag, except that it was to contain thirteen alternating red and white stripes, and a blue field with the appropriate number of stars matching the number of states in the Union. However, there was no specific regulation about the placement of the stars, so the Civil War period flags depict numerous star patterns. President Taft's 1912 Executive Order also regulated the proportions of different sections of the flag, and thus the nineteenth century national colors exhibit a wide range of size variations for the canton, as well as the widths of the stripes. The majority of the locally-presented colors are the national flag with appropriate local inscriptions. Others are more elaborate, such as the flag presented to the 138th Pennsylvania by the loyal ladies of Norristown and Bridgeport. This flag contains the state arms surrounded by a red circle, centered on a regulation-size blue silk flag.

When any type of flag was issued to a regiment, it was placed under the care of a color-guard. The tactical manuals in use in 1861 specified the composition and selection of the members of the guard:[37]

43. In each battalion* the color-guard will be composed of eight corporals, and posted on the left of the right centre company, of which company, for the time being, the guard will make a part.

44. The front rank will be composed of a sergeant, to be selected by the colonel, who will be called, for the time being color-bearer, with the two ranking corporals, respectively, on his right and left; the rear rank will be composed of the three corporals next in rank; and the three remaining corporals will be posted in their rear, and on the line of file closers. The left guide of the color-company, when these three last named corporals are in the rank of file closers, will be immediately on their left.

45. In battalions with less than five companies present, there will be no color-guard, and no display of colors, except it may be at reviews.

46. The corporals for the color-guard will be selected from those most distinguished for regularity and precision, as well in their positions under arms as in their marching. The latter advantage, and a just carriage of the person, are to be more particularly sought for in the selection of the color-bearer.

*For the purposes of field command, regiments were called battalions.

But these regulations were very rarely followed. Regulations specified the use of two colors, but the paragraphs quoted above refer to the appointment of only one color-bearer! It is hard to reconcile this discrepancy, except to state that regulations were followed very loosely by volunteer regiments. If more than one flag was carried simultaneously, the usual practice was to keep both flags together in the color-guard, which was placed in the center of the regimental battleline, following the regulations quoted above. According to Casey's *Infantry Tactics*, the standard tactical manual used by Federal troops, Company C was assigned as the color company. The ten companies of an infantry regiment were assigned an exact place in line depending on the seniority of each captain. From right to left, the original order of battle was as follows: A, F, D, I, C, H, E, K, G, B. This order could be changed when officer casualties revamped the seniority order of the company commanders. Thus, any company could be rotated as the color company.[38]

The large size of the infantry colors made them very important to the regiment. The usual battle formation alluded to in the passage on the position of the color-guard was in two ranks, the men marching shoulder-to-shoulder, the rear rank thirteen inches behind the front rank. A third rank of file closers marched behind the two battle ranks, the file closers aiding in keeping the lines straight and echoing the verbal orders given to the regiment. A full-strength regiment of approximately 1,000 officers and men, when deployed, occupied a lengthy battleline. When advancing, a usual command was to "Guide on the colors," which meant that the soldiers were to keep their eyes on the flags in reference to keeping the lines straight to prevent confusion. Thus, the large size of the flags was extremely important in minimizing the confusion so prevalent on a battlefield. The large size also was important because of the black powder muskets of the Civil War era. Each volley of .58 and .69 caliber muskets produced clouds of hazy, white smoke that obscured vision and made regimental maneuvers difficult. The large colors aided in keeping the regiment aligned during such fighting. Where the flag went, so went the regiment.

Even more importantly, the flags represented an intangible part of the regiment's personality. They represented the honor of the regiment, to be protected and guarded with the lives of the soldiers at all times. It was regarded as a point of honor not to let the flag touch the ground or allow the enemy to gain possession of it, or else the regiment would be disgraced. Thus, to be a member of the color-guard or actually carry the flag itself was a great honor. But at the same time the mortality rate of the color company was very great, as the flags drew a great amount of enemy fire. It is no coincidence that of the 1,200 Congressional Medals of Honor awarded during the war to Federal army soldiers, many were given to men who picked up the flag after the guard had been shot down, or rescued their colors from capture. Hundreds of other men received Medals for capturing Confederate flags during a battle.

The loss of the flag in battle represented the ultimate insult to a regiment. Many regimental commanders were embarrassed by the capture of their colors, and in many instances refused to acknowledge such a loss when writing their official battle reports. In some cases, reporting the loss of a flag meant censure by general officers, and thus many colonels hesitated before making such a report.

By the summer of 1864, when Grant's campaign against Lee's army required more and more new recruits to replace the thousands of casualties suffered by the Army of the Potomac, several generals began to notice the decline in both effectiveness and patriotism of their troops. After the disastrous Battle of Reams' Station in August 1864, Brigadier-General John Gibbon, commanding the Second Division, Second Corps, made an inquiry into the loss of so many flags to the enemy during this engagement. As a result of his inquiry, Gibbon stripped the right to carry colors from the 36th Wisconsin, 8th New York Heavy Artillery, and 164th New York, commenting that:[39]

> The officers and men of the command should understand that their colors should be the last thing surrendered, and that in all well-regulated military organizations, it is considered a disgrace for a majority of the command to return from the field of battle without them.

After a short delay, General Meade approved Gibbon's order to his division and had it extended to apply to the entire army. This action disturbed Gibbon very much, for he had intended that the order should apply to his command alone, and when his superior pointed out these three regiments before the entire army, Gibbon considered it bad politics to have his men disgraced publicly when other regiments in the army had also lost their colors under somewhat dubious circumstances. After the three regiments fought well at Hatcher's Run on October 27, 1864, army headquarters permitted these units to receive new flags and carry them in future engagements.[40]

But there were still problems with the large numbers of recruits and draftees and their unwillingness to defend their colors. Many regiments lost flags to the Confederates in the summer and autumn operations around Petersburg, and because of Gibbon's orders, regimental commanders reported with great detail the loss of their colors so that the regiment would be absolved of any blame for losing their flags so easily. Some regiments, such as the 7th Michigan, resorted to other means to prevent their colors from falling into enemy hands. In one of the Petersburg battles, the regiment's flag was in danger of capture, so the color-guard tore the flag from the staff and ripped it into bits. This action was not without precedent, but such a deed was seen at headquarters as quite unorthodox. Second Corps headquarters viewed the Michiganders' action as having the proper motive but devoid of good precedent. It would have been "much more glorious . . . had this regiment escaped from its perilous position with its colors at its head, or lost them to the enemy after a gallant and desperate resistance."[41]

In addition to the large regimental flags, each regiment was authorized to carry two types of smaller flags. One of these types was the "camp color," described by Paragraph 1371 of the Army Regulations:

> The camp colors are of bunting, eighteen inches square; white for infantry, and red for artillery, with the number of the regiment on them. The pole eight feet long.

In January 1862, the War Department changed the design for camp colors and ordered that they be made "like the United States flag, with stars and stripes." Such flags continued to be made of wool bunting rather than silk.

Camp colors, as their name suggests, were used to mark the limits of a regimental camp. In addition, Major William Gilham's *Manual of Instruction for the Volunteers and Militia of the United States* specified that camp colors should also be used to "mark the color line, points of wheeling, etc.; they are also carried by the markers in the evolutions." Gilham's manual was used by many Federal units, including some of Pennsylvania's black regiments. Some states obtained camp colors from contractors to give to their regiments. The number of colors distributed to infantry regiments varied considerably. For example, New Jersey usually issued two to each regiment, but sometimes allotted four per regiment. New York obtained large numbers of ten per regiment. There is no surviving evidence to suggest that Pennsylvania obtained colors from federal depots and issued them to her units. Rather, it seems that they were received by local presentation. Most have not survived, thus prohibiting identification of types and sources.

Another type of small color used by infantry regiments was known as either a general guide marker or flank marker, depending on the type of staff used for such flags. The two sergeants posted at each end of the line of file closers were called "general guide sergeants." They were responsible primarily for maintaining the integrity of the battleline by making sure the men stayed closed up in the ranks and by echoing the verbal orders given to the regiment. Many times, each sergeant carried a small marker fastened on a

Skirmish at Lee's Mills, Virginia, *1862, showing left general guide marker*

staff tapered to fit into the rifle barrel. When the rifle was carried at "shoulder arms," the guide marker could be seen fluttering above the heads of the men in the ranks and thus the flanks of the regiment could be identified. These flags are more properly termed "flank markers" if the staff was the usual eight feet long and carried by a soldier detailed as a "marker" rather than borne by the guide sergeants.

However these small markers were carried, they were not covered by Army Regulations. The Regular Army did not formally adopt such flags until 1885. The Civil War volunteer regiments carried a wide variety of styles of these flags, which were usually obtained by local presentation. Usage of such flags stemmed from European armies, notably the French and British. Since the flags were non-regulation, swallowtail, rectangular, square, and triangular styles were used. Most were silk, but bunting flags also have survived. On occasion, it seems that unmarked cavalry company guidons were requisitioned to use as flank markers. Again, most of these flags have not survived, a fact which hinders research.[42]

II: Cavalry

Most Pennsylvania cavalry regiments received the state-issued standard, which conformed to Army Reg-

ulations with the exception of the state arms being painted on the flag rather than the national arms. Regulations specified the following size and appearance of the cavalry standard and company guidons:[43]

1372. Each regiment will have a silken standard, and each company a silken guidon. The standard to bear the arms of the United States, embroidered in silk, on a blue ground, with the number and name of the regiment, in scroll underneath the eagle. The flag of the standard to be two feet five inches wide, and two feet three inches on the lance, and to be edged with yellow silk fringe.

1373. The flag of the guidon is swallow-tailed, three feet five inches from the lance to the end of the swallow-tail; fifteen inches to the fork of the swallow-tail, and two feet three inches on the lance. To be half red and half white, dividing at the fork, the red above. On the red the letters U.S. in white; and on the white, the letter of the company in red. The lance of the standards and guidons to be nine feet long, including spear and ferrule.

The cavalry standards manufactured for the national government were similar to the infantry regimental flags, both types issued without the name and number of the regiment. Again, the colonel was responsible for requisitioning national standards and having his regiment's state and number painted on it. Thus,

*Unmarked Federal Cavalry Standard
Size: 27" × 30¼"*

On January 18, 1862, the War Department issued General Orders #4, which stated in part:[45]

1. Under instructions from the Secretary of War, dated January 7, 1862, guidons and camp colors for the Army will be made like the United States flag, with stars and stripes.

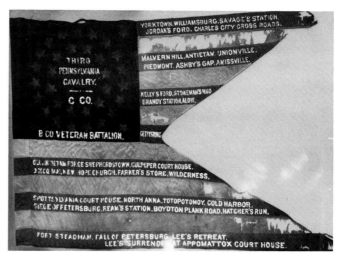

Federal Guidon of the 3rd Pennsylvania Cavalry

some Pennsylvania cavalry regiments carried such standards, while many did not, preferring instead the state standard.

Horstmann Brothers & Company furnished company guidons for the first eleven Pennsylvania cavalry regiments, which were equipped in 1861. The Horstmann guidons were similar in design and size to the Federal guidons as described in Paragraph 1373 of the Army Regulations, but contained the state coat-of-arms on the red field rather than the white letters "U.S." Horstmann supplied ten guidons for the 1st

Horstmann-made Company Guidon of Company G, 1st Cavalry

Pennsylvania Cavalry as per his 1861 contract, then added two more, for Companies L and M, later. However, the company furnished only ten guidons per regiment for the 2nd through the 11th Pennsylvania Cavalry. In 1861, cavalry regiments were authorized four, five, or six squadrons, each squadron comprising two companies. In practice, most regiments orginally fielded ten companies. By September 1862, the War Department set twelve companies as the authorized complement for each volunteer regiment.[44]

Under this order, the old-style company guidon, half red and half white, was replaced by a swallowtail United States flag, which remained in effect until the army reverted to the pre-war style in 1885. Surviving examples of the 1862-65 guidons show that the flags contained the company letter within the star pattern of the flag. Pennsylvania did not modify this design or issue any such guidons to its cavalry regiments, and thus it appears that cavalry officers had to requisition the guidons from the federal government.

Owing to the different fighting styles and deployment of the cavalry and infantry, the cavalry standards seem not to have been as important as the infantry colors were. Cavalry regimental histories contain few references to the flags when compared to published infantry accounts. In general, cavalry regiments rarely operated as complete units during the first years of the war. Individual companies were detached as guards for headquarters, railways, supply depots, and many other such duties, leaving the regiment much depleted in strength. And owing to the wooded and hilly nature of much of the theater of war, cavalry regiments rarely had the opportunity to conduct massed charges against the enemy, as Napoleon's cavalry had once done but which cavalry tactics still taught. More often than not, cavalry regiments were used as scouts, sent on raiding expeditions, and used as skirmishers to cover the deployment of the infantry. The cavalry standards, although used in combat, were not as important for keeping the horsemen in straight lines. The regimental historian of the 3rd Pennsylvania Cavalry wrote

Advance the Colors!

that it was not usual "for the cavalry of the Army of the Potomac, at least after the battle of Brandy Station, to carry its flags and its guidons flying on the battlefield, as was the case with the infantry."[46]

III: Artillery

Artillery regiments, organized into batteries, were allocated two regimental colors by Army Regulations:[47]

> 1369. Each regiment of Artillery shall have two silken colors. The first, or national color, of stars and stripes, as described for the garrison flag. The number and name of the regiment to be embroidered with gold on the centre stripe. The second, or regimental color, to be yellow, of the same dimensions as the first, bearing in the centre two cannon crossing, with the letters U.S. above, and the number of the regiment below; fringe, yellow. Each color to be six feet six inches fly, and six feet deep on the pike. The pike, including spear and ferrule, to be nine feet ten inches in length. Cords and tassels, red and yellow silk intermixed.

Unmarked Artillery Regimental Color
Size: 71" × 75"

These regimental colors were used primarily as headquarters flags because the ten or twelve batteries comprising an artillery regiment rarely fought as a complete unit. The individual batteries were attached to division or corps artillery brigades, which usually averaged no more than five batteries, and thus the regimental headquarters became superfluous. The War Department issued General Orders #86 on April 2, 1863, reducing each active artillery regiment to six batteries, and abolished the grade of colonel, two of the three majors, and the assistant surgeon. This order recognized the fact that artillery regiments operated as detached batteries and therefore regimental officers were reduced to a minimum.

Artillery regiments were classified as either "light" or "heavy." The light artillery regiments were composed of the field artillery batteries that were actively engaged in the operations of the army and provided the artillery support in all battles. The heavy artillery regiments were organized along similar lines as the light regiments, except the heavy artillery batteries were specially trained to use the heavy artillery pieces not usually found in field operations. Cannon such as mortars, Columbiads, and other large guns were restricted to offensive siege operations against enemy fortifications and used as defensive cannon in similar fortifications. Thus, many heavy artillery regiments were used as garrison troops in the defenses of Washington, Nashville, Fort Monroe, and other important fortified cities and military installations. As a result, many heavy artillery regiments contained the maximum number of soldiers, since an enlistment in a heavy artillery unit usually meant a safe tour of duty with only an occasional brush with the enemy.

However, faced with a need for more troops in the spring of 1864, General Grant ordered many of the heavy artillery regiments garrisoning the Washington area to join the Army of the Potomac for offensive operations. The units that joined the main army were armed with rifles and expected to fight as infantry rather than serve as artillerists. When organized as infantry, a heavy artillery unit was divided into three battalions of four companies each, for ease in maneuvering the oversized regiment, which might contain as many as 1,800 officers and men. The many heavy regiments that fought in Grant's operations against Lee's army used their flags as the regular infantry regiments did, and thus some of the artillery regimental flags did see some active combat service.

Pennsylvania furnished one regiment of light artillery—the 43rd—five of heavy artillery, numbered 112th, 152nd, 189th, 204th, and 212th, and nine independent batteries of light artillery. Of the five heavy artillery regiments, the 189th, or 4th Heavy Artillery, was formed from the surplus of men of the 2nd Heavy Artillery in April 1864 to be used as infantry. The new regiment suffered heavy losses and the survivors were returned to the 2nd Heavy Artillery in August 1864. Pennsylvania issued state artillery flags to the 43rd, 112th, and 152nd. The remaining three regiments—189th, 204th, and 212th—received a state artillery standard, which appears to be a cavalry-sized, blue standard with the state coat-of-arms painted on both sides.

Artillery batteries carried a battery guidon, but except for one brief mention of the guidon in the artillery tactical manual written by the War Department, the official sources are silent on the design specifications of this flag.[48] The usual design seems to have been a swallowtail design of the stars and stripes configuration, although some examples illustrate the

*Reverse, Guidon of Independent Battery F
(Hampton's) Size: 23" × 30"*

early-war red/white design, while other swallowtail guidons are made entirely of red silk. Other surviving guidons are rectangular American flags, illustrating the wide variety of guidons carried by volunteer artillery batteries. Since Pennsylvania did not issue any guidons to her artillery batteries, it is assumed that battery commanders acquired flags for their commands either by requisition from the federal government or by local presentation.

IV: Battle Honors

The practice of painting on the regimental colors the names of battles in which a regiment was engaged became widespread during the Civil War. Some units in the Regular Army had begun this prior to 1861, but as a rule, no regulations had been developed to standardize this procedure. Owing to the bravery of the Federal troops during the engagement at Wilson's Creek, Missouri, on August 10, 1861, Congress granted the authority for all units that fought in this battle to inscribe "Springfield" on their national colors.[49] This was implemented by a War Department order that was routinely issued to all commanders, and this order may have prompted other units to seek similar recognition for their own colors. As a result of the growing demand for battle honors, the War Department issued General Orders #19 on February 22, 1862:[50]

It is ordered that there shall be inscribed upon the colors or guidons of all regiments and batteries in the service of the United States the names of the battles in which they have borne a meritorious part. These names will also be placed on the Army Register at the head of the list of the officers of each regiment.

It is expected that he troops so distinguished will regard their colors as representing the honor of their corps—to be lost only with their lives; and that those not yet entitled to such a distinction will not rest satisfied until they have won it by their discipline and courage.

The General Commanding the Army will, under the instructions of this Department, take the necessary steps to carry out this order.

Even though this order was promulgated, there were no follow-up orders as to how the battle honors were to be inscribed. What was meant by "meritorious part?" With such a vague order, and no succeeding specifications, the inscriptions of the battles on colors followed no set pattern. Many generals issued their own orders regarding this subject. For example, on February 19, 1863, Major-General William S. Rosecrans, commanding the Department of the Cumberland, ordered all regiments and batteries engaged in the recent Battle of Stones' River to inscribe that battle on their colors. After the capture of Atlanta in September 1864, Major-General John M. Schofield, commanding the Department of the Ohio, ordered that the Knoxville and Atlanta Campaigns should be inscribed on the flags of the regiments in the Twenty-third Corps that participated in these two campaigns. Major-General Philip H. Sheridan, commanding the Middle Military Division, issued orders on November 22, 1864, listing the battles that could be inscribed on the colors of each regiment under his command.[51]

To further confuse matters, many state governors issued their own orders to state regiments about battle honors. Governor Curtin was no exception. He instructed Adjutant-General Russell to authorize battle honors for Pennsylvania units engaged in certain battles. General orders on this subject are extant through General Orders #19, dated May 31, 1862, which authorized battle honors for thirteen regiments engaged in five different campaigns.[52] It is not known if Pennsylvania issued any more such orders after June 1862.

A major impetus toward standardization of battle honor inscriptions was Major-General Gouverneur K. Warren, commander of the Fifth Corps of the Army of the Potomac. On September 19, 1864, Warren wrote to General Meade about the morale problems in his corps. To excite the "energy and soldierly pride" of his men, Warren suggested that army headquarters publish a list of the battles that each regiment could inscribe on its colors. The general also recommended that a board of general officers be appointed in each corps to ascertain the list of battles for the regiments in each corps.[53]

On the next day, Warren again inquired about his idea, stating that General Sherman had ordered "Atlanta" to be inscribed on the flags of his army. The Fifth Corps commander also commented that many regiments were already painting names of battles on their flags without proper authorization. Warren noted further that Governor Curtin had ordered

Pennsylvania regiments to inscribe lists of battles on their colors. All in all, Warren hoped for a standard system of battle honors.[54]

General Meade doubted that he had the authority to publish such a list of battles, but upon determining that the commanding general of the army had not published any orders other than General Orders #19, Meade authorized each of his corps commanders to appoint a board of three officers to examine the service record of each regiment.[55] The final result of this research was the Army of the Potomac's General Orders #10 of March 7, 1865. This order listed every volunteer regiment and battery then in the army, together with a list of battles that each unit could inscribe on its colors. Pennsylvania was represented by sixty-two infantry, cavalry, and artillery regiments. However, the units represented were those remaining with the army in March 1865; all regiments that had

served previously and mustered out prior to 1865 were ignored.[56]

As a final conclusion to the subject of battle honors, there is no such thing as any standardized system. The Army of the Potomac seems to have been the only large body of troops that attempted to regulate battle honors, and this army's list is by no means complete. And, as General Warren commented, many regiments had been in the habit of inscribing their flags without waiting for the proper authority to do so. Many regiments added unauthorized engagements in which the regiment may have been present on the field but did not fire a shot. Other units painted on their colors the names of minor skirmishes to embellish the authorized list. And many colors of the veteran regiments were so reduced to scraps of silk by battle and weather that any painting upon them was out of the question.

NOTES

[1]For a general survey of Pennsylvania's military in 1861, see Edward G. Everett, Pennsylvania's Mobilization for War, 1860-1861," Ph.D. dissertation, University of Pittsburgh, 1954; excerpts as "Pennsylvania Raises an Army," *Western Pennsylvania Historical Magazine* 39 (1956): 83-108.

[2]William J. Bolton, "War Journal," p. 55, unpublished manuscript in War Library and Museum, Military Order of the Loyal Legion of the United States, Philadelphia.

[3]*Easton Argus*, April 25, 1861; "Departure of the Volunteers," *Northampton County Journal*, April 24, 1861; "Bethlehem Volunteers," *Ibid.*; "The War in Easton," *Easton Argus*, April 25, 1861; "Flag Presentation to the Jackson Rifles," *Lancaster Intelligencer*, July 2, 1861.

[4]"Camp Scott Correspondence," *Pennsylvania Daily Telegraph*, May 1, 1861.

[5]Bolton, "War Journal," p. 32.

[6]*Lebanon Courier*, July 18, 1861.

[7]*Philadelphia Inquirer*, May 22, 1861; Bates 1: 68; *Daily Pittsburgh Gazette*, April 22, 1861.

[8]*Philadelphia Inquirer*, May 13, 1861; *Wilkes-Barre Record of the Times*, May 22, 1861.

[9]"Departure of the Volunteers," *Northampton County Journal*, April 24, 1861.

[10]"Departure of Our Soldiers," *Danville Intelligencer*, April 26, 1861; Bates 1: 108-109.

[11]*The Rebellion Record of Allegheny County, from April, 1861, to October, 1862* (Pittsburgh: W. A. Lare and W. M. Hargzell, 1862), pp.6-7; "Departure of the Washington Invincibles," *Washington Reporter and Tribune*, April 25, 1861.

[12]"The Duquesne Greys," *Pittsburgh Gazette*, April 29, 1861, "Presentations," *Pittsburgh Gazette*, April 25, 1861.

[13]Bates 1: 135.

[14]"Flag Presentation," *York Gazette*, June 11, 1861.

[15]Scharf-Westcott, p. 765.

[16]Taylor, *Philadelphia*, p. 346; "Presentation of a Flag to the National Guards," *Philadelphia Inquirer*, April 30, 1861; *Philadelphia Public Ledger*, April 30, 1861.

[17]"Flag Presentation," *Philadelphia Inquirer*, May 13, 1861; "Letter from Camp Cadwalader," *Philadelphia Inquirer*, June 7, 1861.

[18]Wray, *23rd Pennsylvania*, p. 31.

[19]Wallace, *Schuylkill County*, p. 49; Bates 1: 227; "Flag Presentation," *Pottsville Miners' Journal*, June 1, 1861.

[20] H. J. Biddle to Hiester Clymer, May 13, 1861, RG 25.

[21]*Laws of Pennsylvania, 1861*, p. 776.

[22]*Ibid.*, pp. 777-778.

[23]*Ibid*; *The Union Army*, 1: 327-328; Josiah R. Sypher, *History of the*

Pennsylvania Reserve Corps (Lancaster: Elias Barr & Company, 1865), pp. 57-60.

[24]"Proposals. National and Regimental Colors," copy in RG 25. This notice appeared in many Pennsylvania newspapers, such as the *Philadelphia Public Ledger* in its June 21 edition.

[25]For information on the Horstmann Company, see *One Hundred Years 1816-1916, The Chronicles of an Old Business House in the City of Philadelphia* (Philadelphia: J. B. Lippincott Company for the W. H. Horstmann Company, 1916), pp. 7-29; and the Dunn & Bradstreet ratings, Harvard University, Baker Library, volume 132, p. 402.

[26]Dunn & Bradstreet ratings, Harvard University, Baker Library, Volume 137, p. 612.

[27]Samuel Brewer to Adjutant-General E. M. Biddle, June 26, 1861, RG 25.

[28]For the bids, see the following, all in RG 25: Horstmann Brothers & Company to E. M. Biddle, June 25, 1861; Evans & Hassall to Biddle, June 25, 1861; Brewer to Biddle, June 26, 1861. Evans & Hassall wrote to Governor Curtin on July 23, listing the bids and complained that Horstmann had received the primary contract even though that company was not the lowest bidder. For the bid award, see Henry Coppee to Horstmann Brothers & Company, July 22, 1861, also in RG 25.

[29]For the contracts, both dated August 9, see RG 19, Office of the Quartermaster General, Contract Book, 1861-1862.

[30]RG 19, Adjutant-General's Office, Civil War Records, Miscellaneous Accounts, Box 1.

[31]Both lists can be found in RG 25, Box 1, General Correspondence & Accounts, Folder 1.

[32]Evans & Hassall bid, June 25, 1861; Horstmann Brothers & Company to J. B. Parker August 15, 1861, August 22, 1861, all in RG 25.

[33]*Laws of Pennsylvania, 1862*, pp. 607, 610.

[34]An incomplete listing of flags and how they were delivered to each regiment can be found in RG 25, in a document titled "Flag Memorandum."

[35]For the actions of the Pennsylvania State Agency, see *Annual Report of the Adjutant-General of Pennsylvania, 1866*, pp. 22-24. Brief annual reports of the Washington agency exist for the years 1862-1866, and for the Nashville branch for 1864-1866. None of these reports includes any mention of flags.

[36]*United States Army Regulations of 1861*, paragraph 1370.

[37] Silas Casey, *Infantry Tactics for the Instruction, Exercise and Manoeuvres of the Soldier, A Company, Line of Skirmishers, Battalion, Brigade, or Corps D'Armee*, 3 volumes (New York: D. Van Nostrand, 1862), 1: 15-16.

[38]*Ibid*, unnumbered frontispiece page.

[39]*O.R.* 42.2, pp. 559, 595.

[40]*Ibid.*, pp. 981, 1071-1072; *O.R.* 42.3, pp. 13-14, 40, 493-500.

[41]*O.R.* 42.3, pp. 479-480, 524-525, 544.

[42]The material on camp colors, guide flags, and flank markers, has been supplied by Howard Madaus, who is preparing a lengthy study of these flags.

[43]*General Orders of the War Department, Embracing the Years 1861, 1862, & 1863*, 2 volumes (New York: Derby & Miller, 1864), 1: 33, 85, 386.

[44]*United States Army Regulations of 1861*, paragraphs 1372-1373.

[45]*O.R.*, Series 3, volume 1, p. 803.

[46]*History of the Third Pennsylvania Cavalry, Sixtieth Regiment Pennsylvania Volunteers in the American Civil War, 1861-1865* (Philadelphia: Franklin Printing Company, 1905), p. 511. The standard cavalry manual in effect during the war, *Cavalry Tactics*, 3 volumes (Philadelphia: J. B. Lippincott, 1861), rarely mentions the standard, only referring to the composition of the escort for the standard (pp. 19-20). Plate 1, depicting the order of battle of a cavalry regiment, places the standard in the middle of the 3rd Squadron, but nowhere is the color-guard mentioned.

[47]*United States Army Regulations of 1861*, paragraph 1369.

[48]United States Department, *Instruction for Field Artillery* (Philadelphia: J.B.Lippincott & Company, 1861), p. 68,

[49]Todd, *American Military Equipage,*, volume 2, p. 300.

[50]*O.R.*, Series 3, volume 1, p. 898.

[51]General Orders #24, Department of the Cumberland, February 19, 1863, in *O.R.* 23.2, p. 77; Special Field Orders #104, Army of the Ohio, September 8, 1864, in *O.R.* 38.2, p. 521; Special Orders #91, Middle Military Division, November 22, 1864, in *O.R.* 43.2, p. 659, with an amendment, Special Orders #108, December 10, 1864, *Ibid.*, p. 772.

[52]See the following orders, all in RG 19: General Orders #19, March 21, 1862; General Orders #20, April 4, 1862; General Orders #21, April 30, 1862; General Orders #27, May 31, 1862.

[53]G. K. Warren to George G. Meade, September 19, 1864, *O.R.* 42.2, p. 922.

[54]Warren to Meade, September 20, 1864, *Ibid.*, p. 942.

[55]Adjutant-General Seth Williams to Warren, September 20, 1864, *Ibid.*, pp. 942-943; Special Orders #255, Army of the Potomac, September 21, 1864, *Ibid.*, p. 954.

[56]General Orders #10, in *O.R.* 46.2, pp. 865-878.

Chapter III
Postwar History of the Flags

Joint Resolution #6 of May 1861 provided that all flags issued by the state were to be returned to state care after the Rebellion was crushed. However, prior to the end of the fighting, no specific provisions had been made to comply with this law. As regiments mustered out of service prior to 1865, it seems that many officers and color-bearers took their flags along home, since no apparatus had been devised to care for the colors. Many flags were collected at the chief mustering out camps in Harrisburg (Camp Curtin), Philadelphia (Camp Cadwalader), and Pittsburgh. But, on the whole, no system was formed to ensure compliance with the 1861 law.

To confuse matters further, the federal government took steps to regulate the discharge of volunteer regiments by issuing General Orders #94, dated May 15, 1865. Under this regulation, once a volunteer regiment returned to its home state for muster out, it was to report to and be taken control of by the Chief Mustering Officer of the state or one of his assistants. This officer was responsible for all public property of the regiment, including the regimental and company records, as well as the colors, and he was to take possession of them pending further orders from the Adjutant-General's Office.[1]

However, by the time this order was issued, many regiments had already been mustered out of service and many of the specific instructions contained in the order could not be applied with any regularity. Thus, on June 13, 1865, the War Department, after receiving instructions from Secretary of War Edwin Stanton, ordered the chief mustering officers to turn over all colors in their possession to the governors of the individual states.[2]

By the time this order was written, Pennsylvania flags were scattered throughout the state. Many of the regiments that had already been discharged prior to 1865 had taken their flags home. Other units had deposited their flags at Harrisburg, Philadelphia, or Pittsburgh, with the Chief Mustering Officer at those points. Some regiments had left their flags with Colonel Frank Jordan at the Pennsylvania State Agency in Washington. A few colonels, alarmed at the seeming lack of care for the flags, kept them, pending some future order which would provide better care for their treasured banners. Thus, when Colonel John Glenn of the 23rd Pennsylvania went to Harrisburg to return his state color, he found that those already returned had been tucked away in the corner of a staircase and were covered with dust. Colonel William Wilson of the 81st Pennsylvania wrote that his men stood around for three days in an open shed at Camp Cadwalader, and when no one seemed disposed to take their flags, he took them home, where they were properly respected. Colonel Thomas F. B. Tapper, 4th Pennsylvania Reserves, remarked that he had been told not to be in any hurry to return his flags because no provision had been made to take proper care of them. With problems such as these, many flags remained in private hands at the end of the war.[3]

The flags that had been returned to the state prior to the end of the war were occasionally used for public displays. In May 1863, Governor Curtin granted permission for returning regiments to take their flags home to use in public receptions before sending them to Harrisburg for safekeeping. The United States Sanitary Commission held a public fair in Philadelphia in June 1864 to raise money to help the soldiers then in service. Many relics from the war as well as from America's earlier military involvements were displayed at this fair. Among the trophies on exhibition were approximately forty Pennsylvania colors and standards. These were primarily those flags returned for replacements, but included some local presentation flags as well. The battle-scarred relics excited the public imagination and proved a valuable addition to the fair's museum exhibition. A similiar fair in Pittsburgh featured a display of flags of Pennsylvania regiments from the western part of the state.[4]

By the end of 1865 it seems that some discussion had already taken place regarding the final disposition of Pennsylvania's battleflags. It was decided that all Pennsylvania flags were to be formally returned to state care at a ceremony to take place on July 4, 1866, at Independence Hall, Philadelphia. The state legislature passed a resolution on April 16, 1866, allotting the sum of $5,000 to defray the expenses incurred by this ceremony.[5]

Even before the exact date for the ceremony had been decided upon, Adjutant-General A. L. Russell began to compile lists of absent flags, writing letters to colonels of regiments whose flags were not yet under state control. As a result of Russell's work, all flags were temporarily placed under the control of Quartermaster-General James L. Reynolds, who was ordered to assemble the flags prior to the Independence Day ceremony. Owing to the work of these two agencies of the state military department, nearly all of the missing state flags were accounted for prior to July 4.[6]

While the military department worked to gather the battleflags, a committee was appointed to make arrangements for the ceremony. This committee first met on May 12, and convened four additional sessions thereafter. Under the leadership of Harry White, with assistance from Philadelphia Mayor William McMichael and Governor Curtin, the committee of war veterans planned a magnificent spectacle for the return of the battleflags. Among the major points of business conducted by this committee was the appointment of Major-General Winfield S. Hancock to command the parade, the decision to allow free railroad passes to all color-bearers and guards, and to transport to Philadelphia the children of the Commonwealth who were attending special schools established for war orphans. All in all, with the complete cooperation of the City of Philadelphia, which voted $10,000 to cover the costs of the ceremony, the Commonwealth of Pennsylvania, and the eager participation of the veterans, July 4, 1866, promised to be a memorable day in Pennsylvania history.[7]

Independence Day 1866

The day dawned bright and sunny—so sunny that members of the press referred to the sun as worthy of the tropics—and by mid-morning, several spectators had fainted from a combination of the intense heat and the immense throng of people who lined the streets along the parade route. The troops forming the seven divisions of the parade formed in alternate streets entering Broad Street south of Penn Square. By seven o'clock the flags already in possession of the state and housed temporarily in the City Armory were being released to color-sergeants of each regiment present to participate in the procession. By eight, the regiments were seen forming in the streets assigned to them, as more and more people began lining the nearby streets. At precisely nine a.m. a gun was fired in Penn Square, the signal for the regiments to form in line and be prepared to move off. General Hancock's aides spread the commands, and at ten o'clock sharp, General Hancock, followed by his headquarters flag and staff, proceeded to the head of the column and

ordered it forward.[8] The divisions of the parade marched as follows:[9]

Mounted Police Officers
Liberty Cornet Band
Henry Guard, Captain Henry Spear,
Major-General Hancock & Staff, escorted
by a detachment of the First City Troop

First Division
Major-General James S. Negley & Staff,
Logan Guards, National Light Infantry,
Washington Artillery, Allen Light Infantry

Second Division
Major-General Robert Patterson & Staff
Infantry regiments and detachments in numerical order

Third Division
Brigadier-General Charles T. Campbell & Staff,
Artillery regiments and detachments

Fourth Division
Major-General David M. Gregg & Staff,
Cavalry regiments and detachments,
Major-General George G. Meade & Staff,
followed by invalid officers riding in carriages

Fifth Division
Major-General John W. Geary & Staff,
Color-bearers and guards who did not parade
as regiments or detachments, followed by
United States Marines

Sixth Division
Major-General Samuel W. Crawford & Staff,
Governor Andrew G. Curtin, followed by the soldiers' orphans,
who were escorted by members of volunteer fire departments

Seventh Division
Major-General John R. Brooke & Staff,
Colonel Charles Prevost's Grey Reserves,
a Pennsylvania militia regiment, fully armed and uniformed.

In spite of all the meticulous planning, some minor scrapes occurred during the forming of the parade. The First Division was to consist of the five "First Defenders" companies, those militia companies that were the first troops to answer President Lincoln's call for 75,000 three-months militia in April 1861. These five companies were to parade in the exact order in which they had marched into Washington. However, a fight broke out between Reading's Ringgold Artillery and the National Light Infantry of Pottsville, both of which claimed the honor of marching first in the parade. And even though General Hancock issued a march order in an attempt to clear up the bad feelings between these two groups, the Reading company felt it had been slighted and refused to take part in the proceedings. Further back in the column, Gregg's division faced a minor problem when the 2nd Pennsylvania Cavalry refused to march as a brigade with the 3rd and 6th cavalry regiments, the veterans complaining that the old 2nd Regiment should be first in the brigade line.[10]

But these minor affronts of honor did not mar the glorious Independence Day procession. The police at the head of the column had much difficulty in keeping the streets clear of appreciative Pennsylvanians, and the troops, marching eight abreast, could barely squeeze through the overcrowded thoroughfares.[11] General Hancock, riding near the head of the parade, was constantly cheered as he rode along the crowded avenues. General Meade was cheered lustily as the "Hero of Gettysburg," and it seemed that the crowd's loudest applause was for Meade, Pennsylvania's best-known officer. Governor Curtin also received sustained public appreciation.[12] The several score (1,128) of orphan children, the boys walking and the girls riding in wagons, were the object of much sympathy from the adoring populace.[13]

The greatest attention was focused on the scores of battle-scarred banners that fluttered over the heads of thousands of war veterans, now parading with their colors for the last time.[14]

> They were present in such great abundance as to distract the eyes of those who loved them most. . . . Many of the veteran regiments carried the bare staff. . . . From the tops of many of these bare staffs floated gay ribbons, of red, white and blue, with the names of the battles in which these staffs had lost their burden of bunting. Others again had the blue field or Union shot at, and the stripes all faded and torn, but through the dingy ribbons gleamed in letters of gold the name of victorious fields, never to fade while human annals endure. A few of the staffs not having a shred of flag left, had the number of the regiment engraved on a silver plate and secured to the staff.

The parade began on Broad Street, turned east down Arch Street to 12th Street, then proceeded south on 12th to the intersection with Chestnut Street. Here the parade route went east on Chestnut to 2nd Street, turned south along 2nd to Walnut, thence westward along Walnut to the gateway at Independence Square.[15]

At the Walnut Street entrance to Independence Square, the parade turned up the gravel walkway toward the old state house, now heavily decorated for the occasion. Large flags draped the tower of Independence Hall, hanging from the tower clock, some 120 feet above the ground. At a height of sixty feet, the coats-of-arms of the City of Philadelphia, the state, and the nation, framed a large portrait of the late President Lincoln. In front of the hall was a semicircular wooden amphitheater, said to be large enough to hold over 6,000 spectators, who were given red, white, or blue tickets, according to seating preference. The two wings of this monstrous construction, extending toward Walnut Street, were reserved for invited guests and the orphaned children of the fallen defenders of the Union. More distinguished guests were seated in the center of the curve, directly be-

hind the speakers' platform, which was ten feet high, elevated enough so that all could see the proceedings about to unfold. Directly in front of the state house, but behind the oval-shaped amphitheater, was a platform reserved for the Handel and Hayden Musical Society, whose members were to provide the music for the occasion. The trees lining the entire length of the gravel walkway were decorated with strips of red, white and blue bunting, ending at the Walnut Street entrance in a canopy shaped like an American eagle with outstretched wings, which served as the keystone for the flags over the entrance.[16]

The head of the procession reached the Walnut Street entrance fifty minutes after starting from Penn Square. General Hancock and staff rode into the area at eleven o'clock, and the cheers for that general were only eclipsed by the deafening cheers for General Meade, who entered half an hour after Hancock. The tumultuous reception given the generals continued as flag after flag entered Independence Square, the bearers lining both sides of the walkway leading to the wooden stands. Governor Curtin finally reached the crowded stands at noon, and the ceremonies began.[17]

After an instrumental rendition of Mendelssohn's "Triumphal March" by Professor Bergfeld's band, General Harry White, on behalf of the organizing committee, briefly addressed the seemingly endless sea of upturned faces. The crowd was everywhere. Many even had climbed into the branches of the trees lining the central walkway to obtain a better view. Then the Reverend Thomas Brainerd delivered an eloquent prayer, followed by an inspiring vocal and instrumental rendition of the "National Anthem."[17]

General Meade stood up and walked to the edge of the speakers' platform. He reached down to the assembled color-bearers below and took the state flag of the 82nd Regiment in his hands. The general then turned to Governor Curtin and spoke the following words:[19]

> At the request of the brave and noble men, who on the field of battle represented our beloved State of Pennsylvania, I am here upon this occasion to present to you, sir, honored Chief Magistrate of our Commonwealth, these battle-stained banners, which for four years were carried by these noble men amidst the bullets and cannon roar, and in the face of the enemy.
>
> Sir, of all the honors that have been showered upon me for the humble services which it has been in my power to render to my country, none have been so grateful to me, and of none am I so proud, as being on this occasion the representative of these hardy and noble men who stand before you.
>
> Sir, in the dark days of 1861, when treason and rebellion lifted their impious heads, and the people of eleven States of this blessed Union, forgetful of the memories and associations which had bound us together for three-quarters of a century, and made us a great and happy people, but

blinded by passion, raised their impious arm and threatened the life of this Government; at that time when you, sir, then as now Chief Magistrate of this Commonwealth, it is a matter of historic record that Pennsylvania was the first State to fly to the rescue of our country, and send her sons to the endangered capital of the nation.

Sir, in that noble procession which today has marched through our streets, at the head of the column were the representatives of the men, who, at the first alarm, rushed to the rescue of the capital, and from that time to the conclusion of the war, Pennsylvania was ever prompt to send her men into the field. More than 360,000 soldiers carried the banners of their country on the battlefield. When it was found what the proportions of this war would reach, you, sir, with a sagacity highly creditable and honorable to you, in conjunction with the action of the Legislature, devised a banner which should be presented to the Pennsylvania regiments in the army of the Union. It was no unworthy or improper State right which you, on this occasion, claimed. It was a legitimate pride in the prowess and deeds of valor in the noble sons of the State which you were satisfied they would honor and appreciate. These flags were presented by you on many occasions in the presence of these regiments. I have often heard your fervent and eloquent appeals to the soldiers, to their patriotism and strict attention to their duty. I say that on this occasion, which is due to you and your personal services in inspiring the soldiers of Pennsylvania on the field of battle—the soldiers of Pennsylvania for four years have carried these banners with honor to themselves and to their native State. I will not attempt here to recount the deeds of the soldiers of Pennsylvania. To do so would be to repeat the history of this war, for with few exceptions there is not a battlefield from Gettysburg to Mobile that the ground has not been stained by the blood of the soldiers of Pennsylvania; and, sir, there is not a State, either loyal or insurrectionary which was the seat of the war, which does not at this moment hold within it the honored and sacred remains of the heroes of Pennsylvania. Whilst we as soldiers of Pennsylvania claim no pre-eminence over the soldiers of our sister States, we at the same time cannot acknowledge any; and I claim, sir, in the name and on behalf of the soldiers of Pennsylvania that, in the illustrious roll of honor, whether it be among the immortal dead or among the distinguished living, that the names of the sons of Pennsylvania officers and soldiers will stand as high as the representatives of any other State.

This war is over; peace has returned to bless our happy land. By the concurrent action of the Legislature it has been determined that you should receive on this day, sacred to the memory of liberty, these battle-stained banners, that have passed through their fiery ordeals. In the name of the soldiers of Pennsylvania, I present to you these banners, which were received from the State, and which were borne through the war with honor and credit, and of which we, as soldiers, are justly proud. Receive them, sir, as mementoes of the prowess and deeds of valor of the noble sons of Pennsylvania. Cherish them for all time to come, and place them in the State Capitol, where our posterity for all generations may see them, to know what their forefathers have done in the hour of trial, and where they may stand a warning to all future traitors to shun the fate of those who dare to attempt the life of the nation.

I will conclude by praying the Great Giver of all Good that He will bless this great country, upon which He has been pleased to send peace once again, that never again may it be necessary for the sons of Pennsylvania to take up arms against those who should be their brothers, to put down insurrection and Civil War and treason, but that God will ever bless us, that we may be a united and happy people, so that we shall look back to this day and these colors for the proud associations they carry with them.

Governor Curtin then rendered an eloquent acceptance speech, praising the valor of Pennsylvania's soldiers and admonishing the crowd not to forget about the cherished relics that he was accepting back into state care. Perhaps the following paragraph best expresses the tenor of the Governor's address:[20]

To the men who carried the steel, the musket and the sabre—to the private soldier, to the unknown dead—the demi-gods of the war, we this day seek in vain to express all our gratitude. If there be men more distinguished than others, more entitled to our highest veneration, it is the private soldier of the Republic. If we follow him through all the sufferings and privations of the service, his long, weary marches, his perils on the outposts, his wounds and sickness, even in this article of death, we trace him back to that sentiment of devotion to his country that led him to separate from home and its ties, and to offer even his life a sacrifice to the Government his fathers gave him and his children. As the official representative of the Commonwealth, I cannot take back the remnants of the colors she committed to your keeping without attempting to gather into my arms the full measure of her overflowing gratitude and lay it at your feet. I therefore present you with the thanks of your cherished mother, this ancient and goodly Commonwealth of Pennsylvania, for the great glory you have given history. She fully realizes, and while public virtue remains she will never cease to realize, that she could better afford to lose the sources of her natural wealth, her rich fertile valleys, her great cities, her exhaustless minerals, than to lose from her archives a single one of these torn, faded precious, consecrated flags of battle and its history, and of the brave men who suffered and fought around them. A Commonwealth may exist without cherishing her material wealth, but no Commonwealth can worthily, or should exist, which does not cherish, as the joy of life, the heroic valor of its children.

At the conclusion of Governor Curtin's speech, the band played Handel's "Hallelujah", after which Army Chaplain William R. Gries spoke the prayer "Thanks to Almighty God for Victory and Return to Peace." Then the Handel and Hayden Society performed the standard hymn "Old Hundred." This was followed by the musical rendition of Meyerbeer's "Coronation March", signalling the end of the formal presentation ceremony. Bishop Simpson then pronounced the Benediction.

However, before the crowd dispersed, General Hancock made a few brief remarks in response to the continued loud calls for such an appearance. Generals Geary and Negley also spoke briefly to the adoring crowd, after which the immense number of people began to leave the area. The gigantic fireworks display planned for that evening was washed out by some heavy thunderstorms that began shortly after five

Advance the Colors!

o'clock in the afternoon. Even so, the day's activities had gone according to plan.[21]

Once the ceremony was over, General Joshua T. Owen, representing the committee that had planned the festivities, formally turned the flags over to the care of the state, represented by Adjutant-General Russell. Then, under the supervision of Chief of Police Harrison G. Clark, the Henry Guards removed the colors to Sansom Street Hall, where they were guarded throughout the night. The sacred banners were shipped to Harrisburg on the morning of July 5.[22]

The Flags, 1866-1914

The flags shipped from Philadelphia to Harrisburg numbered 270 pieces. Most of these were the state-issued flags, although some regiments which did not have their state colors immediately at hand for the

G.A.R. Parade in Albany, New York, June 1879, Showing Pennsylvania Flags Passing By

ceremony used instead either government-requisitioned flags or those presented by friends at home. The Adjutant-General's Office had retained most of these two types of flags as unnecessary for the parade, which featured the state-issued flags. However, only a fraction of the locally-presented flags had been turned over to state care by the regiments. Many were returned to those citizens who had taken their time and money to make the flags for the units. Some of these were eventually given to county historical societies and other museums, some to local veterans posts such as the Grand Army of the Republic, while others were taken home by veterans to keep as mementos. Of the hundreds of flags dispersed across the state in 1865, very few have survived to the present era.

Once the flags arrived in Harrisburg, they were stored in cases provided for them in the State Armory in Capitol Park. They were there in 1871, when the Adjutant-General reported that the flags were never removed from the cases "unless to gratify a soldier or

the heirs or representatives of a soldier desirous of seeing the flag under which he fought or fell. To such they are always cheerfully exhibited." It seems that General Russell influenced members of the Legislature to take steps to provide necessary funds to outfit a room in the Capitol so that the flags could be displayed to the public. But, after the final adjournment of the Legislature, the line item for such money had disappeared from the general appropriations bill, and no action was taken.[23]

However, the 1872 appropriations bill included Section 57, which authorized the Adjutant-General to spend $1,000 to refurbish a room on the east side of the South Executive Building for the reception and proper display of the battleflags collection. A year later, Joint Resolution #10 authorized an additional $1,500 to complete the necessary work.[24]

This new "Battle Flag Room" was located on the

Pennsylvania State Capitol in the 1880s

second floor of the South Executive Building, directly opposite the Adjutant-General's Office. The 29x84 room had been used during the war for the offices of both the Quartermaster-General and the Surgeon-General. The floor was laid with elegant Brussels carpet and the walls were newly papered. The entire room was furnished with ornately-carved Gothic-style wood work. In the center of the room, two large pedestals were installed, each large enough to hold twenty-seven flags. Brackets of differing sizes were mounted along the walls and over the room's four windows, the brackets holding from seven to twenty-eight colors each. The flags were installed on the brackets in an upright position, unfurled, each regiment's colors grouped together. Each flag was also marked with a small metal plate bearing the name of the regiment to prevent misidentification, as many colors were so battle-scarred as to be almost unrecognizable.[25]

The flags remained in the South Executive Building until 1893, when they were temporarily moved into the State Arsenal while repairs were made. During the two decades (1873-1893) the banners were in the Flag Room it became more and more crowded as several additional flags were deposited with the collection. The largest gift was in 1887, when the 51st Pennsylvania Regimental Association donated to the state eight flags carried by the regiment during the war, and an Illinois officer returned a state color of the 56th Pennsylvania he had found in Raleigh in 1865. Many veterans who visited the flag room also deposited relics in the room, such as minie balls, uniform buttons and artillery shell pieces, and the room began to look overcrowded. At some time prior to 1887, the flags were removed from the brackets and placed in glass cases.[26]

Owing to this condition, the flags were again moved in 1895. Two years earlier, the Executive Library and Museum Building had been constructed south of the Capitol. A new flag room was established in this building, directly at the head of the main stairs. The tattered banners were placed in four long, glass cases, but were still displayed unfurled. Peter F. Rothermel's large painting of the repulse of Pickett's Charge at Gettysburg dominated the east wall of this room, with his smaller paintings of the battle hung elsewhere on the walls. Even though the Adjutant-General considered this new room much better than the old one, he remarked that there was still not enough space to display all the relics and the flags with the proper viewing conditions that the size of the collection warranted. The Adjutant-General also

Executive Library and Museum Building in 1894

thought that the collection should be housed in a fireproof building. The need for better protection was accented when the Capitol Building burned to the ground on February 2, 1897.[27]

A major addition to the collection was made in 1905, when the War Department returned all captured battleflags to the states of origin. Although the majority of the War Department's collection consisted of Confederate colors captured during the war, over two hundred pieces were Federal flags captured by Rebel forces and surrendered to the government in 1865. Congress approved a joint resolution on February 28, 1905, to return the flags to the states, a similar measure having failed in 1888, a time when passions caused by the war still ran too high to allow the

Flag Room in Executive Library and Museum Building, CA. 1895

Advance the Colors!

former Rebel states to retrieve their captured colors. On March 31, 1905, Acting Secretary of War Robert Shaw Oliver informed the several governors of the states that he was sending all identifiable flags to each state. Pennsylvania received eleven flags representing the 11th, 27th, 40th, 46th, 65th, 77th, 100th, 105th, and 149th regiments. These flags were added to the collection shortly after their receipt by the Adjutant-General's Office, which first verified each flag by corresponding with the survivors' associations of the regiments.[28]

Four years later, Adjutant-General Thomas J. Stewart recommended that the flags be taken out of the cramped quarters in the Library and Museum Building and placed in the new Capitol Building. By this time, the Executive Department had moved into the new Capitol, leaving the smaller office building to the library and museum, both of which needed more space. On the main floor of the Rotunda, niches had been designed to contain decorative statuary. Instead of statues, Stewart recommended that those niches be modified to house the battleflags of both the Civil War and the Spanish-American War. When Stewart first announced his plans, at least one G.A.R. post took exception to it. On November 23, 1911, John B. Clark Post 162 entered a protest against the removal of the flags from the Flag Room to the Capitol, sending a formal letter of protest to Stewart.[29]

Stewart's idea was finally adopted in the form of Joint Resolution #291, signed into law by Governor John K. Tener on June 5, 1913. This resolution authorized the establishment of a commission to arrange for the transfer of the flags from the Library and Museum Building to the Capitol Rotunda, on a date to be selected by the Committee. The sum of $6,000 was appropriated to defray all expenses. The major disbursement was made to purchase railroad passes, which would be given gratis to all veterans who would come to Harrisburg to carry the flags from the Flag Room to the Capitol. Twenty new flag staffs were purchased from Horstmann, primarily to be used for the captured flags that had been returned in 1905. The Confederates had taken the flags off the staffs, and the banners were still without poles when returned. Since they were not placed on staffs until 1914, it is possible that they were never displayed in the old Flag Room. The Committee planned a suitable parade and ceremony for Monday afternoon, June 15, 1914.[30]

Flag Day 1914

Long before one o'clock that afternoon, the aged war veterans had begun to assemble at the entrance to the Library and Museum Building. When the doors were opened at 1 p.m., the veterans marched up the broad

Head of the Parade Forming Near the Capitol

View of the Parade, Showing 29th Regiment Flags and Bearers on Right

Flag Bearers on State Street, Moving Toward the Capitol

staircase to the Flag Room, where Deputy Adjutant-General Frank D. Beary and Major L. V. Rausch handed each man his regimental flag. Many of the veterans wept openly as they received the tattered banners, and there was a slight delay of the start of the parade, as many of the elderly men were loath to go out in public with their faces still wet with tears.[31]

However, the parade got off nearly on schedule from its starting point on Fourth Street in the rear of the Capitol Complex. The marchers were divided into four divisions, as follows:[32]

First Division
Major E. M. Vale
Six companies of the 8th Regiment, Pennsylvania National Guard, and the Governor's Troop of cavalry.

Second Division
Commonwealth Band, followed by members of the Grand Army of the Republic from the Eastern and Western Pennsylvania Districts

Third Division
C. R. Lantz, Marshal
Steelton Band, members of G.A.R. posts in the Central Pennsylvania District, Spanish-American War Veterans, Spanish-American Foreign Service Veterans, Regimental Associations.

Fourth Division
Lieutenant C. F. Gramlich, Marshal
Soldiers' Orphans Industrial School Band, followed by the battleflags, each carried by representatives of the respective regiments.

The aged color-bearers with their prized possessions attracted the most attention. Before the flags were removed from the Library and Museum Building, each had been encased in a silk chiffon sleeve, as by this date many of the colors had begun to crumble with age. One reporter who witnessed the parade compared the men carrying their silk-encased flags with a forest of masts. In addition to the numerous photographers who captured the parade with their cameras, the *Harrisburg Telegraph* filmed the entire proceedings, showing them later in the week at a local theatre. Pennsylvania officials then made arrangements with the Telegraph Press to have copies of the film sent to the Pennsylvania building at the San Francisco Panama Exposition of 1915, where the film would be shown daily.[33]

Many of the men who bore the Civil War colors were the very same boys who had carried the flags in 1866. The very same Harry White who helped organize the 1866 ceremony marched in the 1914 parade. White was now a young 84. Color-bearer Zacharias Rost, 73rd Pennsylvania, carried his unit's flag with one hand, while with the other he led blind comrade Benjamin F. O'Donnell, who had saved one of the 73rd's flags from capture at the Battle of Missionary Ridge in November 1863. O'Donnell had been captured when the 73rd was driven back by the Rebels, but he managed to conceal a guide flag in his uniform and was taken to Andersonville Prison, where he gave the flag to Rost when he thought he might die. Francis H. Hoy carried the same flag of the 201st Pennsylvania that he carried during the war. His son, Francis Jr., carried the banner of the 3rd Pennsylvania, Spanish-American War. This was the only father-son combination in the entire parade.[34]

The marchers paraded down Fourth Street to Market, thence to Front Street, turning from Front onto State Street, toward the Capitol. The sun was warm, but a lively breeze kept the temperature bearable for the majority of the aged veterans. Thus only three men were not able to complete the half-mile route of the parade. As the parade turned up State Street, the National Guard members turned aside and lined each side of the street, forming an honor guard as the flag-bearers proceeded up the hill toward the grandstand and seats that had been erected near the Hartranft Statue. The parade reached the grandstand area at 2:40 p.m. and the ceremony began by 3:15 p.m.[35]

After the vocal and instrumental playing of "Pennsylvania," the Reverend J. R. Boyle, Chaplain of the Military Order of the Loyal Legion of the United States, gave the Invocation. That was followed by another musical number, "Battle Hymn of the Republic." Governor Tener then made a short welcoming speech to both the assembled veterans and the immense crowd of people who witnessed the parade. When Tener finished speaking, Senator Franklin Martin, chairman of the Flag Transfer Commission, expressed his thanks to the Committee for its cooperation in the arrangements. Martin briefly recounted the history of the flag collection, ending his speech by stating:[36]

These torn and tattered battle-rent emblems of national pride need no eulogy. Their history is written in the blood of Pennsylvania's loyal sons who fought and died for the preservation of the nation. Therefore, let them be preserved, as a tribute to our fallen heroes, and as an ever-living inspiration of loyalty and patriotism to the generations that follow.

After Senator Martin's speech, a poem, "Pennsylvania's Battle Flags," especially written for the occasion, was sung by the chorus of Harrisburg school children who provided the musical background for the other numbers performed. Then Major Moses Veale, a veteran of the 109th Pennsylvania, delivered the oration for the ceremony. Veale spoke about the extreme youth of the masses of soldiers who served during the war and what the war did for that generation. He praised the victory of the Union, and how it resulted in the present strength of the nation. Veale also surveyed the contributions of Pennsylvania troops during the war. As he told the audience how a Pennsylvania flag was first to reach the summit of Lookout Mountain, one of the bearers jumped up and shouted "There she is, Major!" holding up the flag of the 29th Pennsylvania. Once Veale finished, the song "America" was sung by both the chorus and the audience. Finally, the Reverend M. L. Ganoe, Chaplain of the Pennsylvania Department of the Grand Army of the Republic, pronounced the benediction.[37]

Then, as the band played a medley of Civil War songs, the veterans filed out of their chairs and went

Advance the Colors!

into the Capitol Rotunda single file, each giving up his banner to attendants to be placed in the specially-designed display cases. Civil War flags were installed in five of the cases, the sixth containing the state's Spanish-American War colors. The cases were designed to be air-tight in the hope of preserving the remnants of the 352 flags installed that afternoon.[38] All the relics and several miscellaneous flags that had been in the old Flag Room were transferred at first to the Department of Public Grounds and Buildings for storage, and later to the Pennsylvania Historical Commission. This material is now stored and displayed in the William Penn Museum.[39] After the installation of the flag collection, other colors were received as late as 1922, when the guidon of Battery F, 112th Pennsylvania (2nd Heavy Artillery) was received and placed in Case #3.[40]

The Flags, 1914-1985

After the 1914 ceremony, the battleflags collection was largely forgotten by the majority of Pennsylvanians. However, the active participation of the Commonwealth in World War I did stir some members of the Legislature to inquire about the condition of the collection. In 1929, the flags of Pennsylvania's World War regiments were stored in the State Arsenal ready to be displayed once a proper location was provided. This activity led to the investigation of the Civil War flags and resulted in a legislative appropriation of $30,000 for the Department of Property and Supplies to use in the "preservation and reconditioning of Pennsylvania regimental flags, standards and guidons of the regiments that served in the Civil War, Spanish-American War and the World War." After some deliberation, Governor John S. Fisher vetoed the bill, remarking that:[41]

I am reliably informed that there has been no deterioration in their condition since they have been permanently placed in these cases. Their tattered condition at the present time is due, no doubt, to the fact that prior to the year 1914 they were not properly cared for.

With the failure of the 1929 bill, it seems that the rapidly developing affairs of the twentieth century deflected attention from the preservation of this part of Pennsylvania's Civil War heritage. In 1939, someone did take the time to notify Roger V. Rowland, the Secretary of Property and Supplies, that the flags seemed to be disintegrating. The Secretary launched an investigation, which showed that the cases were not as air-tight as was planned and that the flags did seem to be disintegrating with age. However, nothing further was done in this matter.[42]

Even the Civil War Centennial of the 1960s failed to revive interest in the battleflags collection. The

Flag Case #1, Capitol Rotunda

Centennial did result in a revitalized interest in battle re-enactments. This in turn led to the formation of many re-enactment groups, each based on a particular Civil War regiment. One such unit, Company A of the 87th Pennsylvania, expressed an interest in raising money to have the flag of the original 87th taken out of Case #2 and conserved. Keith Keller, the 87th's commander, approached Capitol Curator Ruthann Hubbert with this idea in 1981. This year was also the 75th anniversary of the Pennsylvania Capitol Building, and, with the approval of the Tercentenary Committee, Mr. Keller was given the signal to raise the necessary funds for the conservation of this flag.

Accordingly, Case #2 was opened on August 26, 1981, and the 87th's flag was removed. Five other flags were also removed, pending further study for the possible conservation of these colors as a prelude to a major effort to conserve the entire collection. The 87th's flag was delivered to Mr. Les Jensen, a contract historian at Williamsburg, Virginia. He removed the silk chiffon sleeve from the flag and discovered that most of the original state flag had been literally shot to pieces in battle and but little remained. The regiment's veterans had attached a small banner to the staff in place of the flag. This banner contained the names of the principal engagements in which the regiment had fought. Mr. Jensen conserved the banner in time for it to appear in the Capitol rededication ceremony on October 19, 1981.[43]

The publicity attending the conservation of this banner resulted in many queries throughout Pennsylvania about the further conservation efforts with other flags. As a result, the Capitol Preservation Committee—an independent Commonwealth agency formed in 1982 to coordinate and oversee programs to conserve, restore, preserve, and maintain the Capitol and its historic treasures—decided to launch a "Save-the-Flags" campaign to raise money to perform badly-needed documentation and conservation work on the entire Civil War flags collection. Under the chairmanship of Representative Joseph R. Pitts (R-Chester), the Committee received unanimous support from both political parties in the House and Senate. Foremost in their enthusiastic support of this program were Speaker of the House Matthew J. Ryan (R-Delaware) and Democratic Leader K. Leroy Irvis (D-Allegheny).

In 1983 the Committee began a public campaign to raise funds to advance the conservation program. Several professional consultants had been hired to aid in establishing the program until the Committee

Members of the 87th Pennsylvania Receiving Their Citation During the 75th Anniversary Celebration of the Dedication of the State Capitol Building (1906-1981). Left to Right: *Hon. Matthew J. Ryan,* Speaker of the House; *Timothy Pritchard; Donald Howard; Jeffery Halterman; Hon. Henry Hager,* President Pro-Tempore; *Keith Keller,* Governor *Dick Thornburgh*

could interview and hire its own personnel. Based on information provided by Mr. Jensen, the Committee decided to initiate a sponsorship program for individual flags at the cost of $1,000 per flag. Pennsylvanians began to support the program, as corporations, groups, and individuals contributed money for specific flags. A complete list of contributors will be included in Volume Two.

The flag collection received a new group of additions in March 1984. As a result of negotiations between the Capitol Preservation Committee and Mr. Russell L. Hershberger, President of the Historical Society of Schuylkill County, the Society donated its collection of about twenty Civil War flags to the Commonwealth for inclusion in the conservation program. These banners were locally-presented flags of Schuylkill County units, and had been in the care of the Historical Society since the veterans donated them in December 1913.[44]

As the Committee matured plans to start conservation work on the flags collection, it began to develop a cooperative effort with the Pennsylvania Historical and Museum Commission. The Commission had planned to construct a Commonwealth Conservation Center for its own use, and with much planning and cooperation, the Commission received funding to begin development of its center ahead of schedule. The Textiles Division of this new center was constructed with Committee funds, with the division to be used for the flags program, after which the space would be turned over to the PHMC. General Services Secretary Walter Baran generously donated space for the new facility on the third floor of the Commonwealth Publications Building at Tenth and Market Streets in Harrisburg.

Construction of the new facility began in mid-1984 and was primarily completed one year later. Two professional conservators—Mary Ashton and Marta Rothwarf—were hired to work on the flags. Karen LaFaver was hired as Project Assistant. With construction of the textile laboratory almost finished, plans were made to open Case #1 in the Rotunda and remove the flags. This case was opened on June 17, 1984, and the eighty-four flags were moved to the conservation laboratory. Because of the condition of the flags and the time it would take to do even a cursory conservation treatment, the conservators decided that each flag would be unrolled and photographed in preparation for flat storage in a new flag room. Once the initial program of unrolling and photographing was completed, those flags which had $1,000 sponsors would be accorded a more comprehensive conservation treatment. A summary and analysis of the initial conservation program will be included in Volume Two.

Advance the Colors!

Notes

[1]*O.R.*, Series 3, volume 5, pp. 20-22.

[2]*Ibid.*, p. 54.

[3]John Glenn to James L. Reynolds, April 21, 1866; Thomas F. B. Tapper to J.L. Reynolds, April 16, 1866; William Wilson to Reynolds, May 23, 1866; William B. Lane to A. L. Russell, April 20, 1866; John Elliott to A. L. Russell, May 4, 1866, all in RG 19. See also Frank Jordan to A. L. Russell, February 10, 1866, in RG 25.

[4]"The State Regimental Flags," *Pittsburgh Evening Chronicle*, May 23, 1863; Department of Arms and Trophies, Great Central Fair, *Catalogue of the Museum of Flags, Trophies, and Relics, . . .* (Philadelphia: Crissy & Markley, Printers, 1864); "The Display of Flags at the Old Curiosity Shop," *Pittsburgh Gazette*, June 13, 1864.

[5]*Laws of Pennsylvania, 1866*, p. 1126.

[6]See above, Note 3, for examples of correspondence concerning the locations of the missing flags. RG 19, Boxes 27 and 28, and RG 25, Box 2, contain the correspondence relating to this subject.

[7]For a complete account of the work of the committee, see "Ninety Years. Pennsylvania, Indiana, Michigan and Kansas To-day Receive Back from their Soldiers the Battle-torn State Standards." *Philadelphia Press*, July 4, 1866.

[8]"Yesterday. A Day of Flags, Festivals, Speeches, Fun and Processions—A Nights of Fireworks and Illuminations," *Philadelphia Press*, July 5, 1866; "Our Battle Flags. Return of our War-worn and Victorious Standards to the State. The Old Keystone's Honors to Her Veteran Defenders," *Philadelphia Inquirer*, July 5, 1866.

[9]*Philadelphia Press*, July 4, 1866. The regiments did not march in numerical order and thus the reporters present did not manage to obtain a complete list of all units that returned their flags on July 4. The *Inquirer* and *Press*, in the July 5 editions, each has a different list, both papers commenting that it was impossible to print an accurate and complete list.

[10]*Ibid.*

[11]*Ibid.*

[12]*Philadelphia Inquirer*, July 5, 1866.

[13]Specific details of the arrival, care, and descriptions of the orphan children are found in "The Celebration. Preparations for the Flag Presentation," *Philadelphia Inquirer*, July 4, 1866. Nominal lists of the attending children, descriptions of their costumes, et cetera, are in the *Philadelphia Press*, July 4 and 5, 1866.

[14]*Philadelphia Inquirer*, July 5, 1866.

[15]*Philadelphia Press*, July 4, 1866.

[16]*Ibid.*; *Philadelphia Inquirer*, July 5, 1866.

[17]*Philadelphia Inquirer*, July 5, 1866.

[18]The entire program is printed in the *Philadelphia Inquirer*, July 4, 1866; White's and Brainerd's parts are in the *Philadelphia Press*, July 5, 1866.

[19]This version is taken from the *Philadelphia Press*, July 5, 1866. A slightly different version appears in the *Philadelphia Inquirer*, July 5, 1866.

[20]*Ibid.*

[21]*Philadelphia Press*, July 5, 1866.

[22]*Ibid.*; *Philadelphia Inquirer*, July 5, 1866.

[23]*Annual Report of the Adjutant-General, 1871*, p. 7.

[24]*Laws of Pennsylvania, 1872*, p. 15; *Laws of Pennsylvania, 1873*, p. 896.

[25]"An Hour Among the Battle-Flags," *Harrisburg Daily State Journal*, September 22, 1873; George H. Preble, *Origins and History of the American Flag*, 2 volumes (Philadelphia: Nicholas L. Brown, 1917), 2: 574.

[26]*Annual Report of the Adjutant-General, 1887*, p. 11; "Veterans Carry War Flags Through Streets to Last Resting Place in Capitol," *Harrisburg Star-Independent*, June 15, 1914.

[27]*Annual Report of the Adjutant-General, 1894*, p.ix; *1895*, p. 15.

[28]See *Annual Report of the Adjutant-General, 1905*, pp. 12-13, for list of flags returned. For the 1888 document, see 50th Congress, 1st Session, Executive Document 163, Captured Battle Flags, twenty pages in length. A complete list of all captured flags and their disposition since the war is found in the National Archives, RG 94, Records of the Office of the Adjutant-General, Entry 178, Register of Captured Flags.

[29]"Stewart Arranged the Plans for the Noble Ceremony," *Harrisburg Telegraph*, June 16, 1914; *Personal War Sketches of the Members of Colonel John B. Clark Post No. 162, of Allegheny* (Philadelphia: Louis M. Everts, 1890), p. 440.

[30]*Laws of Pennsylvania, 1913* p. 438; Circular, "Information Regarding Transfer of Flags," dated March 25, 1914, Adjutant-General's Office, copy in RG 25.

[31]*Harrisburg Star-Independent*, June 15, 1914; "Veterans Weep as Old Flags Again Handed to Them," *Harrisburg Patriot*, June 16, 1914.

[32]*Harrisburg Star-Independent*, June 15, 1914.

[33]"Hearts Throb as Battle Scarred Flags Pass By," *Harrisburg Patriot*, June 16, 1914; "Impressive Scenes as Veterans Carry Colors for the Last Time," *Harrisburg Telegraph*, June 16, 1914.

[34]"Military Lives of Sire and Son Closely Parallel," *Harrisburg Patriot*, June 16, 1914; *Harrisburg Star-Independent*, June 15, 1914; "Blind Veteran at Last Proves He Bore Colors," *Harrisburg Star-Independent*, June 16, 1914.

[35]"Veterans Weep," *Harrisburg Patriot*, June 1, 1914; *Harrisburg Star Independent*, June 15, 1914.

[36]The program is listed on the program card, RG 25. Martin's speech is printed in the *Star-Independent*, June 15, 1914. For more details, see also "Veterans Weep," *Harrisburg Patriot*, June 16, 1914.

[37]Major Veale's speech is printed in the *Star-Independent*, June 15, 1914. For the 29th Pennsylvania flag incident, see "Veterans Weep," *Harrisburg Patriot*, June 16, 1914.

[38]"Veterans Weep," *Harrisburg Patriot*, June 16, 1914; "Photographs of Flags are in Great Demand," *Harrisburg Star-Independent*, June 11, 1914.

[39]"List of Old Flags, from State Flag Room," dated May 12, 1915, RG 19, Adjutant-General, General Correspondence File. The collection included 22 camp colors and 32 company markers at one time. Their exact postwar history is not well-documented. A printed list of flags in RG 25 includes a pencilled note that these smaller flags had been transferred to the State Arsenal in 1880. However, an undated list of flags in the Flag Room after 1895 includes all these flags, so they must have been added to the displayed collection between 1880 and 1895. When the flags were placed in the Rotunda, these 54 small markers were given to G.A.R. Post 58 in Harrisburg. In 1929, the Post gave these flags to the Historical Commission. It appears that the flags were placed in storage, and by the time the William Penn Museum opened in 1965, these flags had disintegrated and the remnants were discarded. According to the 1895 list, these flags belonged to the following regiments, with the number for each unit in parentheses: camp colors—52nd(2), 100th(2), 104th(1), 148th(2), 201st(2), 205th(2), 208th(1), 209th(1), 214th(2), 215th(2), unknown(5); company markers—49th(2), 50th(1), 55th(2), 56th(2), 76th(2), 78th(3), 83rd(2), 97th(1), 116th(2), 141st(1), 180th(1), 182nd(1), 205th(2), 207th(1), 210th(4), Battery F(1), Battery I(1), 3rd Provisional Cavalry(1), unknown(2).

[40]Receipt dated May 25, 1922, "Received from Brigadier-General Frank D. Beary, Adjutant-General by S. B. Rambo, Deputy Superintendent, Department of Public Grounds and Buildings," Headquarters Flag, 2nd Division, Fifth Corps, Company C, 100th Pennsylvania, and Battery F, 112th Pennsylvania.

[41]*Vetoes by Governor, 1929*, pp. 237-238.

[42]L. L. Dunkle to Roger V. Rowland, June 30, 1939, RG 20, Records of the Department of General Services, State Archives.

[43]"Conservation Report, Flag of 87th Pennsylvania Volunteers, Civil War," by Les Jensen, October 10, 1981, in Capitol Preservation Office files. There are several other pieces of correspondence in this file that pertain to this topic.

[44]For the 1913 ceremony, see "Proceedings and Speeches Made at the Transfer of Battle Flags to the Historical Society of Schuylkill County, December 14, 1913," *Publications of the Historical Society of Schuylkill County* 5 (1932): 1-43.

Chapter III Appendix
Flag Bearers in the 1914 Parade

The following list of those veterans who participated in the 1914 parade is based on a memorandum book found in RG 25. Any problems with the handwritten names were checked against the regimental rosters compiled by Samuel P. Bates. Still, some errors may result. Asterisked (*) names are those veterans who also carried flags in the 1866 parade, for which no similar list is extant.

1st	Frank H. Wentz	51st	Nathan Ramsey		Francis Miller
Defenders	F. M. Yeager		Montgomery S. Smith	76th	Albert Sanders*
11th	John H. McKalip		Louis Fisher		Michael Post
	Henry B. Temple		Isaac Treat		D. O. Kiser
	John Zimmerman		R. A. M. Harner	77th	John Obreiter
23rd	Philip Stengle		Albert List		Henry P. Krebs
26th	Richard H. O'Donnel		Allen J. Clifton		D. W. Cox
27th	H. A. Hoopes		David Reichley	78th	William T. Powell
	T. J. Bretz	52nd	Irwin E. Finch		A. B. Richey
28th	John O. Foering		Smith B. Mott		John W. Thompson
	P. F. Routke	53rd	David B. Rothrock		J. H. Stoer
	Thomas Munroe		William H. Rodgers	79th	Peter Sensenderfer
	George W. Rhoads		Farnham E. Lyon		E. M. Boring
29th	George W. Brown	54th	W. A. Slick	80th	Daniel W. Rank*
	John Graham	55th	Augustus Flanagan		H. P. Loveland
30th	George W. Palmer		Edward Looker		S. W. Dimock
	Wesley McBride		Joseph J. Leonard	81st	Frank McCoy
31st	Thomas J. Goldey	56th	Isaac G. Ridabaugh		Jacob Hentz, Sr.
	John McGinnis		Allen McCall	82nd	John G. Morris
32nd	William Clark		Warren L. Smith		Thomas H. Marston
	Henderson Synnamon	57th	Thomas Stewart	83rd	Isaac Lunger
33rd	Joseph M. Fries		Robert I. Campbell		Jacob E. Swap
	Alexander F. Nicholas		Henry H. Forrest		Orlando Kinnear
34th	William H. Grier	58th	William H. Blair	84th	Joseph Griffiths
	George Eicholtz		William H. Freeman		A. J. Hertzler
35th	O. Fred Benson	59th	D. E. Spear		J. J. Wirsing
	C. S. Fornwald	60th	John Clark	85th	Alexander Ross
36th	Edwin M. Hoffman		William E. Miller		Walter C. Craven
37th	R. A. Sayers	61st	John C. Matthews	87th	Daniel Reigle
	James Towell		John P. Batt	88th	Robert Herron
38th	Robert Taggart		William B. Stahl		Michale Conover
	Jesse M. Corbus	62nd	B. J. Coll		E. L. Gilligan
39th	Samuel Hamilton	63rd	Robert Orr	89th	William T. Broadhead
	John C. Gaither		John Newhouse	90th	Charles Breyer
40th	John T. Kelly	64th	John H. Ulrich	91st	Charles Beaver
41st	Emory Strock		Samuel Lowry		William H. Geary
	Joseph N. Clark		Henry Raiger	92nd	Amos R. Stoner
42nd	Jonathan V. Morgan	65th	William B. Morgey		George G. Myer
	William H. Rauch		George W. Uber	93rd	George Imboden
43rd	Luther Seiders	67th	T. P. Stephens		William Boeshore
44th	John P. Taylor		Charles Yetter	95th	John P. Griffith
	David Gardner		Joseph L. Leonard		David S. Ayres
45th	John B. Emery	68th	Charles Naylor		William Jamison
	William H. Musser		John S. Harvey	96th	George W. Foltz
46th	Joseph Matchette		Robert Fogg		Frank Knittle
	H. A. Weidensaul	69th	Michael Brady	97th	John Wainwright
	Lewis H. Ruble		David Kiniry		William S. Underwood
47th	James Stuben	70th	J. R. Green	98th	Philip H. Fratz
	Edward H. Keiper	71st	Benjamin Butterworth		Michael Henninger
48th	Samuel A. Beddall	72nd	Thomas H. Eaton	99th	Amos S. Casey
	Daniel F. Bausum	73rd	Benjamn F. O'Donnell	100th	John W. Morrison
49th	Henry B. Minichan		Frank Sauerlander		N. M. Maxwell
	Frank H. Eckelman		Adam Loos	101st	John A. Reed
50th	Aaron Osman		Adam C. Dieffencach	102nd	W. L. Jones
	Levi Eckert	74th	John J. Shive		William A. Dawson
	John B. Mishler	75th	Charles Dreusch		Henry M. Serena

Advance the Colors!

103rd	Samuel M. Evans
104th	George W. Michener
	Isaiah Vanhorn
105th	S. A. Craig
	James G. Mitchell
	James Penfield
106th	Rufus G. Brown
107th	Byron Carpenter
	E. W. Pierce
108th	James E. McFarlan
109th	Fergus Elliott
	Luther Van Orden
110th	Michael Feathers*
	James Kreps
	W. W. Speer
111th	C. G. Malin
	A. W. Merrick
	Ashibal Orton
112th	George M. Green
	Charles H. Dorr
	W. H. Bratton
113th	T. J. Shepard
114th	William J. Miller
115th	Isaac Luke
116th	William H. Tyrell*
	James M. Seitzinger
	Seneca G. Willauer
	Edmund Randall
117th	Daniel Caldwell
118th	Thomas H. Mensing
	William B. Jones
	John P. Fraley
	George W. R. Carteret
119th	John Rodgers
121st	Lewis Clapper
	Malcolm Murray
	William F. Dawson
122nd	Daniel H. Heitshu
123rd	John S. Bell
	James Shaw
	Andrew S. Miller
124th	Joel Hollingsworth
125th	J. Randolph Simpson
126th	D. K. Appenzellar
127th	Henry T. Euston
128th	Henry J. Fink
129th	N. B. Robins
	William Bannan
130th	Samuel Loncks
131st	James B. Forrest
132nd	James F. Trump
	J. W. Willits
	C. H. Boone
133rd	William Slack
134th	John J. McGarvey
	James A. McMillen
135th	John Hupper
136th	Jacob Johnston

137th	John J. Shaffer
138th	Samuel Aikens
	Charles Jones
139th	David B. Warden
	George M. Gray
140th	Joseph Moody
	E. G. Emory
	Harry J. Boyde
141st	W. W. Scott
	Isaac Yetter
	Daniel Schoonover
142nd	John V. Miller
	Noah Koontz
143rd	Nathan Vosler
	J. A. Stetler
	Francis Furman
	Mark B. Perigo
145th	L. O. Eldridge
147th	Philip Fermier
	Jeremier Fisher
148th	Isaiah P. Leightly
	David W. Miller
	Alfred O. Moore
149th	H. H. Spayd*
	Robert R. Brown
150th	Henry K. Lukens
	Roe Reisinger
151st	S. B. Caveny
152nd	Charles Schlecht
	W. H. Davis
153rd	Noah Dietrick
	Stphen Romig
155th	James J. Carroll
	John C. Sias
157th	C. Baer
158th	William Martin
159th	Milton A. Gherst
160th	E. L. Vandling
161st	Charles Bowers
162nd	Jacob A. Loose
	James W. McClure
163rd	George W. Hock
165th	J. M. Kingsborough
166th	John H. Welk
167th	Harry Newman
	David Bricker
	R. M. Johnson
168th	John G. Ashbaugh
169th	Henry A. Hall
171st	N. B. Critchfield
	Reuben S. Moist
	Balaam Younkin
	Henry A. Kissinger
172nd	David Heimbach
173rd	William H. Otto
175th	Samuel O. Fernwalt
176th	Jacob B. Werley
177th	Hiram Graham

	James M. Lemon
	Daniel H. Heisey
178th	Daniel Fishel
179th	P. A. Snyder
182nd	Joseph R. Davison
183rd	William Richardson
	John V. Sailer
	George W. Hess
184th	Adam V. Miller
185th	Lewis Connor
186th	John R. Curry
	J. B. Neal
187th	S. D. Borkel
188th	Harry T. Graves
	W. H. Walters*
190th	John Wehler
191st	Charles U. Burns
192nd	Charles M. Johnson
	Charles Wylie
193rd	Homer L. McGraw, Sr.
194th	W. M. Hedden
195th	Israel Bair
198th	W. D. Kincaid
	Isaiah Wertley
	W. D. Sands
199th	August Nawman
	Henry C. Grady
200th	William Warner
201st	Frank H. Hoy
202nd	Augustus W. Mennig*
	Benjamin C. Rosh
	W. S. Knauss
203rd	Charles W. English
	William J. Tomlinson
204th	John W. Williams*
	James C. Hunker
205th	Joseph M. Owens
206th	J. M. Marshall
	J. A. Johnston
207th	Charles H. Ilgenfritz
208th	W. S. Seabold
	George H. Imboden
209th	E. J. Humphreys
	F. H. Barker
210th	William Shuye
	Joseph F. Ripley
211th	Isaac B. Brown
212th	Joseph B. Eaton
	I. J. McCandless
213th	L. S. Hatfield
	William H. Mohler
	J. C. Long
214th	George W. Ryder
	J. E. Wise
	William E. Clungeon
215th	John G. Engle
2nd Prov.Cav.	John Kirk

Chapter IV
Pennsylvania United States Colored Troops

In addition to the 350,000 white soldiers fielded by the Commonwealth during the Civil War, Pennsylvania was officially credited with 8,612 black soldiers, placing the Keystone State sixth among the states in black recruitment. The five states recruiting more blacks than Pennsylvania were Southern states; hence, Pennsylvania was first among the Northern states in black recruiting. With the exception of the 54th and 55th Massachusetts and the 29th Connecticut, all black regiments were designated as "United States Colored Troops" and not officially credited to any state.[1]

The Lincoln government was very cautious over the issue of black enlistments early in the war, wishing to preserve the loyalty of the slave-holding border states, and it was not until after the Emancipation Proclamation was issued that the government seriously considered the topic of black soldiers. Legitimate acceptance of colored regiments began in Louisiana in September 1862 and in the occupied sections of South Carolina in January 1863. Some Northern states, especially Massachusetts, received official permission in early 1863 to begin raising colored regiments. Approximately six hundred black Pennsylvanians trekked north to enlist in the 54th and 55th Massachusetts regiments. A Philadelphia Quaker, Norwood P. Hallowell, became colonel of the 55th. Hundreds of other blacks enlisted in regiments from other states as well.[2]

It was not until June 1863 that Governor Curtin was authorized to begin recruitment of black soldiers. The 1860 census counted 56,949 colored people living in the Commonwealth, approximately two percent of the total population. Of these 26,373 were male. Some 22,000 blacks lived in Philadelphia, with other centers in Lancaster and Huntingdon counties. Since more than 1,000 blacks had already gone elsewhere to enlist, Major George L. Stearns, the Recruiting Commissioner for United States Colored Troops in the middle Atlantic states, who was appointed to this position on June 17, faced the prospect of recruiting from a reduced pool of available manpower. As a result, blacks from neighboring states were enticed to enlist in Pennsylvania's eleven black regiments.[3]

The day after Stearns was appointed to supervise the recruitment of colored soldiers, the War Department granted official permission for the Commonwealth to begin active recruiting. Stearns established his headquarters in Philadelphia, where a number of patriotic citizens gathered their support to help raise black recruits. Collectively known as the Supervisory Committee for Recruiting Colored Regiments, these seventy-five Philadelphians elected businessman Thomas Webster Chairman, and set up four standing sub-committees to direct the Committee's varied activities.

Since federal responsibility for the black recruits did not begin until they were mustered into government service, the Supervisory Committee had to provide transportation and subsistence to the volunteers from the time they left home to their arrival at camp. The Committee spent almost $60,000 from organization until its disbandment in December 1864. In addition to the money spent on food and transportation, the Committee advertised extensively for recruits. Such activity carried Committee members into New Jersey, Delaware, and Maryland for recruits to fill the eleven regiments organized in Pennsylvania. Since the state provided no funds for the Committee, it had to rely on private contributions to defray all its expenses.[5]

Only a week after the drive for black recruits began in June 1863, a rendezvous camp designed exclusively for the colored regiments opened. Named Camp William Penn, the site was located eight miles north of Philadelphia on a farm owned by Lucretia Mott, a Philadelphia Quaker who was tireless in her efforts as a "noted abolitionist, pacifist, feminist and champion of causes relating to racial and social equality." The camp was on an elevated piece of ground, with streams for fresh water located nearby. The camp was only half a mile from Chelten Hills and the depot of the North Pennsylvania Railroad. Thus, Camp William Penn was ideally suited, close to the city and yet far enough away to avoid problems with the pervasive anti-black feeling in Philadelphia.[6]

Lieutenant-Colonel Louis Wagner of the 88th Pennsylvania was selected as camp commander.

Wagner had been wounded in the Second Battle of Manassas and was unfit for active field operations. He opened the camp on June 26, 1863, when the first black recruits arrived to be mustered into service. Early recruits were housed in tents. It was not until September 1863 that Secretary of War Stanton gave approval for more permanent structures to be erected. By December, barracks, officers' quarters, mess halls, and a chapel had been constructed for the soldiers. Usually, not more than two regiments at one time occupied the camp. Each regiment spent an average of only two months at the facility, since the need for troops was so great that each regiment was dispatched to the front as soon as it was organized.[7]

The War Department made an early decision to segregate blacks into separate regiments, each to be commanded by white commissioned officers. To procure officer candidates of adequate ability to command, the Supervisory Committee established the Free Military School at 1210 Chestnut Street. All white applicants wishing to gain commissions in black regiments had to attend a two-week class in military tatics and regulations. Classes began in December 1863 when the first group of thirty soldiers entered the school. Major George A. Hearns was in charge of the school, while the ex-colonel of the 12th Pennsylvania Reserves, John H. Taggart, instructed the applicants in military tactics and etiquette. An eleven-man examining board carefully scrutinized all applicants and recommended to the Examining Board in Washington those whom they felt to be qualified as officers in black units. The Free Military School thus provided a high quality in its selection of officers for Pennsylvania's colored troops.[8]

Black soldiers faced much discrimination and danger during the war. At the outset, the pay of a black private was a mere $10 per month, while white privates drew $13 per month. Black regiments were oftentimes detailed as "engineers," prison guards, and other less glamorous duties rather than combat. If used in combat, white officers knew that many Southerners advocated hanging if captured, since slaveholders viewed white officers as participating in treasonous acts against the South. Blacks captured in battle could expect to be turned over to slaveholders or possibly even killed. On more than one occasion, Confederate troops refused to take black prisoners, preferring to kill them instead. Sometimes wounded blacks who were captured were also killed in cold blood.[9]

In spite of the adverse circumstances under which they fought, Pennsylvania blacks contributed to the Union cause. While only a few of the eleven regiments fought in any major battles, each aided the Federal victory in some small way. One twentieth century historian has written that their activities "stretched from Maryland and North Carolina to western Florida and the Rio Grande. Employed as garrison troops, prison guards, border patrols, skirmishers and attack forces, they fought the enemy, boredom, homesickness, scurvy and disease until the time came for them to be mustered out."[10]

The Flags of Pennsylvania's Colored Regiments

Because the flags issued to the eleven USCT regiments from Pennsylvania no longer exist, it is very difficult to ascertain the exact details concerning the types of colors carried by the regiments. Based on the surviving evidence, it appears that the Supervisory Committee hired a very talented black artist from Philadelphia to paint regimental colors to present to each regiment as it left Camp William Penn for the war. These regimental flags were of regulation size and often contained the national arms on the reverse and an allegorical painting depicting various episodes of the newly-freed blacks in uniform. Details for each of these regimental colors can be found under the separate regimental sketches.

The artist hired by the Supervisory Committee was David Bustill Bowser, a talented artist born in 1820. He was named after his father. His grandfather was a baker for the Continental Army and later became one of the first black school teachers in Pennsylvania. David became an artist at an early age, specializ-

David Bustill Bowser

ing in emblems and banners for fire companies and fraternal organizations. A very few of his marine and landscape paintings also still remain. A portrait of President Lincoln, said to be done from life, also exists. Bowser was twice married previous to the Civil War. Although there is no direct evidence linking Bowser to the Supervisory Committee, a March 29, 1864, letter from Mr. J. W. Forney to Thomas Webster seems to indicate that Bowser was hired to paint the regimental flags. This letter reads as follows:[11]

> While in Philadelphia two days ago, I learned that an effort was being made to deprive Mr. D. B. Bowser of the work of painting the flags of the colored regiments, and I would have called upon you to make an appeal on his behalf had not the weather been so bad. He came to see me, but I was too much occupied to give him a hearing, and he writes me this morning, begging me to intercede with you—which I most earnestly and cheerfully do. He is a poor man, and certainly professes very remarkable talent. He has been active in the cause and is himself a colored man, and it seems to me there would be a peculiar hardship in taking away this little job from him and giving it to a wealthy house. Will you do your best for him, and greatly oblige."

Webster did keep Bowser's job, and all surviving photographs of the regimental flags indicate Bowser as the artist. He also designed flags for black regiments from other states as well as Pennsylvania. The designs he used varied for each flag, but all seem to have been executed in good taste. After the war, Bowser was quite active in the United Order of Odd Fellows, and he became a Mason of the thirty-second degree. He died in Philadelphia on July 1, 1900.

In addition to the flags prepared by Bowser for the Supervisory Committee, the black regiments also carried national flags and guide markers. Where these were obtained and when they were carried is extremely difficult to verify owing to the paucity of extant source materials. As each regiment returned to Camp William Penn to be mustered out of service, it left its flags at the camp. These colors were then sent to Major William B. Lane, the Chief Mustering Officer at Philadelphia, for safekeeping. They were still under Lane's jurisdiction in April 1866 when the major sent a list of colors under his care to Adjutant-General Russell. This list included the following flags:[12]

regiment	national colors	regimental colors	guidons
3rd	1	1	2
6th	1	–	2
8th	1	–	–
22nd	1	1	2
24th	1	1	1
25th	1	1	2
32nd	1	–	–
41st	–	–	–
43rd	1	1	2
45th	1	1	2
127th	1	1	–

The above list suggests that each regiment received its colors and guidons according to the Army Regulations, with one national and one regimental flag each, plus the two flank markers. It is unknown if the regimental colors on the list are the same flags painted by David Bowser.

When the Mustering Office closed in June 1866, the flags of the colored regiments were sent to the War Department for storage, since the regiments had all been designated as "United States." They remained in Washington until 1906, when they were forwarded to the United States Military Academy Museum at West Point. A year earlier, the War Department had returned all captured flags to the states and then sent all other flags in its possession to West Point. The list of identified flags forwarded to the Academy included flags for the 22nd, 25th, 32nd, 43rd, and 127th USCT. Other Pennsylvania flags may have been on this list, which included many colors which had deteriorated and were unable to be positively identified.[13]

The flags remained in the West Point Museum until sometime just prior to the American entry into World War II. By that time, the Museum had acquired hundreds of flags, and storage space had become limited. All flags that had not been restored were reclassified and those considered as expendable were destroyed. As a result, most of the colors of the United States Colored Troops were discarded. A few that remained in good condition were retained. Some of these were later transferred to other military museums. Thus, only one identified flag of a Pennsylvania colored regiment seems to have survived the years since the Civil War.[14]

In addition to the flags on the 1866 list, two other colors were furnished to the 6th and 22nd USCT. On October 11, 1864, Major-General Benjamin F. Butler issued a congratulatory order to the Army of the James to recognize the bravery of his troops in the 1864 Petersburg-Richmond area battles. The valor of his colored regiments was especially noted, and several regiments were authorized to inscribe battles on their colors. Butler also directed his quartermaster to furnish new colors for the colored troops in the Eighteenth Corps. It was February 1865 by the time Butler's request went through the proper chain of command and was approved by General Grant.

Horstmann Brothers & Company received the contract and supplied the colors at some unspecified time after February 1865. Each national color contained thirty-five stars arranged in the standard oval pattern, with the regimental, brigade, division, and corps identification painted on the center red stripe. However, all the colors were mislabelled. In September 1865, Assistant Quartermaster Captain P. P. Barnard noted that the stripes omitted the "U.S.C.T."

Advance the Colors!

designation and each was incorrectly labelled with "24th Corps" rather than "25th Corps." However, nothing was done to change the colors and the single surviving flag (that of the 37th USCT) still bears the mistaken identification.[15]

Notes

[1]*O.R.*, Series 3, volume 5, p. 662.

[2]Taylor, *Philadelphia*, pp. 186-187; Binder, "Negro Regiments," pp. 383-386.

[3]Binder, "Negro Regiments," pp. 386, 392-393.

[4]*Ibid.*, pp. 387, 389.

[5]*Ibid.*, pp. 390-392.

[6]Wert, "Camp William Penn," p. 340; N. D. Melair, Jr., "Request for Proposal. Preparation of Documentation for the Nomination of La Mott Historic District for the National Register." Copy in possession of Capitol Preservation Committee.

[7]Wert, "Camp William Penn," pp. 340-342, 345-346.

[8]Binder, pp. 401-404; Taylor, *Philadelphia*, p. 188. Officer schools were also established by other states in addition to Pennsylvania.

[9]Binder, pp. 399-400, 405.

[10]*Ibid.*, p. 416.

[11]Forney to Webster, March 29, 1864, in Free Military School Register and Scrapbook, p. 76, Historical Society of Pennsylvania. Biographical information on Bowser can be found in the following: James A. Porter, *Modern Negro Art* (New York: Dryden Press, 1943), pp. 39-42, 175; Charles H. Brooks, *History and Manual of the Grand United Order of Odd Fellows in America* (Philadelphia, 1893), pp. 246-247. Some of Bowser's papers can be found in the Moorland-Spingarn Research Center, Howard University, but these are postwar materials and of limited use for the study of his work during the Civil War.

[12]Major Lane to Adjutant-General A. L. Russell, April 20, 1866, RG 19.

[13]F. C. Ainsworth to Superintendent, United States Military Academy, February 21, 1906, enclosing list of flags forwarded, RG 94.

[14]Letter of Michael J. McAfee to Richard A. Sauers, May 15, 1985, enclosing list of flags remaining in Museum ca. 1940.

[15]For the literature associated with these flags, see the following, all in the National Archives, RG 92, Records of the Office of the Quartermaster-General, Consolidated Correspondence File, Boxes 302-304: Captain E. E. Camp to Major-General Rufus Ingalls, December 21, 1864, enclosing a copy of General Butler's October 11, 1864, order and his own list of flags needed; Captain J. D. Bingham to Captain William Myers, December 30, 1870; Captain William Myers to Lieutenant-Colonel Stewart Van Vliet, January 19, 1871. The Horstmann contract is in RG 92, Entry 2195, Book 11, page 161. I am indebted to Mr. Howard Madaus for providing copies of the above material for this study.

Bibliography

I: General References on Blacks in the Civil War

Brown, William W. *The Negro in the American Rebellion, His Heroism and His Fidelity* Boston: Lee and Shepard, 1867.

Cornish, Dudley T. *The Sable Arm: Negro Troops in the Union Army, 1861-1865.* New York: Longmans, Green, 1956.

Quarles, Benjamin. *The Negro in the Civil War.* Boston: Little, Brown & Company, 1953.

Williams, George W. *A History of Negro Troops in the War of the Rebellion.* New York, 1888; Reprint edition, New York: Negro Universities Press, 1969.

Wilson, Joseph T. *Black Phalanx.* Hartford, 1888.

II: Pennsylvania Troops

Binder, Frederick M. "Pennsylvania Negro Regiments in the Civil War." *Journal of Negro History* 37 (1952): 383-417.

———. "Philadelphia's Free Military School." *Pennsylvania History* 17 (1950): 281-291.

Davis, George L. "Pittsburgh's Negro Troops in the Civil War." *Western Pennsylvania Historical Magazine* 36 (1953): 101-113.

Wert, Jeffrey D. "Camp William Penn and the Black Soldier." *Pennsylvania History* 46 (1979): 335-346.

3rd United States Colored Troops

National Color

This colored regiment was the first to be organized at Camp William Penn. Its colonel was Benjamin C. Tilghman, who had commanded the 26th Pennsylvania until he was wounded at Chancellorsville. While the regiment remained in camp, representatives of the Supervisory Committee presented "a large and handsome American flag" to the regiment on the afternoon of July 29, 1863.[1] The regiment left Philadelphia on September 18, 1863, having been assigned to the Tenth Corps, which was attempting to recapture the city of Charleston, South Carolina. Upon its arrival, the 3rd was used in the siege of Fort Wagner, losing six men killed and twelve wounded. Early in 1864, the regiment was transferred to the District of Florida, where it was assigned to the defenses of Jacksonville, remaining there until the end of the war. While garrisoning this city, the 3rd was trained as heavy artillery and participated in an occasional foray into the surrounding countryside. After the Confederate surrender, the 3rd moved to Tallahassee and other points as garrison troops until mustered out of service on October 30, 1865.

Regimental Color

Under the aegïs of the Supervisory Committee, a committee of ladies from Philadelphia presented a regimental flag to the regiment on the evening of November 17, 1863. Since the 3rd was already on active duty at Charleston, Lieutenant-Colonel Louis Wagner, commandant of Camp William Penn, accepted the flag for the absent regiment. The presentation ceremony took place at Sansom Street Hall, and began with addresses by two local supporters. As a brass band played the "Star-Spangled Banner," the flag was brought on stage and unfurled. A newspaper reporter recorded that "the cheering became so intense that the music was scarcely heard." The flag was then officially presented to the 3rd and received by Lieutenant-Colonel Wagner.[2]

This regimental flag was painted by Mr. Bowser, and was said to cost $150.[3] Colonel Wagner briefly described the flag in a letter he wrote to Colonel Tilghman a week after the presentation: "It is a magnificent banner, regulation size, of fine blue silk, with coat-of-arms of U.S. and name of regiment on one side, and a painting, finely executed, of the Goddess of Liberty presenting a flag to a color—and colored—sergeant on the other side."[4] It is unknown exactly

Obverse, 3rd USCT Regimental Color

Reverse, 3rd USCT Regimental Color

when the regiment received this flag. Wagner was unsure where to send it and still retained it when he queried Colonel Tilghman in January 1864.[5]

Notes

[1] *Philadelphia Inquirer*, July 30, 1863.
[2] *Ibid.*, November 18, 1863.
[3] *Ibid.*
[4] Wagner to Tilghman, November 25, 1863, in National Archives, RG 110, Entry 3594 (Camp William Penn, Letters Sent).
[5] Wagner to Tilghman, January 9, 1864, *Ibid.*

6th United States Colored Troops

National Color

The 6th USCT was the second regiment formed at Camp William Penn in the fall of 1863. Assigned to the Army of the James, the regiment departed Philadelphia on October 14, 1863, arriving at Fort Monroe shortly thereafter. It went into camp near Yorktown, remaining on the Peninsula until the spring of 1864. Most of the regiment's activity during this time consisted of severe fatigue duty upon the Federal fortifications in the area, the monotony dispelled by an occasional raid into the countryside toward Richmond.

In early May 1864, the 6th was relieved from garrison duty and participated in Major-General Benjamin F. Butler's attack on Petersburg. The regiment occupied City Point, then moved nearer Petersburg and built a strong earthwork to protect a pontoon bridge across the Appomattox River. On June 15, the regiment took part in the initial assaults on Petersburg, capturing a weakly-defended Rebel battery before being relieved by white troops. The regiment remained on active duty in the siege lines near Petersburg until late August. Knowing that black troops were positioned opposite them, Confederate marksmen took a special interest in firing on the Negro regiments, causing several casualties each day the troops remained on the front line. The regiment was relieved from this service duty in early August, spending most of the next two months performing fatigue duty on Butler's Dutch Gap Canal in the general's unsuccessful attempt to change the course of the James River.

Early on the morning of September 29, the brigade to which the 6th was attached left its position, and, together with most of Major-General Edward O. C. Ord's Eighteenth Corps, moved to assault the Confederate entrenchments on New Market Heights, north of the James River. The Army of the James would attack north of the river while a strong detachment of Meade's Army of the Potomac would strike Lee's right flank southeast of Petersburg. The pincers attack might catch Lee off-guard and prohibit the Confederate general from shifting troops around to bolster any weak spots in his line.

As the Federal troops formed to attack the advance line of Rebel fortifications, the 6th found itself facing a section of earthworks manned by the veterans of Colonel Frederick M. Bass's Texas Brigade. Together with the 4th USCT, the 6th charged forward over rough ground into a withering enemy musketry

Sergeant Alexander Kelley, 6th USCT

and artillery fire. The 6th's ranks were thinned at each step. The color-guard was decimated and it was not long until the color-sergeant fell. An officer picked the national color up and fell within seconds. Lieutenant Frederick Meyer of Company B then seized the fallen staff and was instantly killed by a bullet through the heart. Lieutenant Nathan H. Edgerton, the regimental adjutant, soon came upon the scene and found the color still grasped by the dead Meyer. He pried the flag loose and carried it forward in spite of a wound to his wrist, the same bullet splintering the flagstaff. When Edgerton felt too weak to continue, Sergeant Alexander Kelley of Company F took the flag and bore it from the field.[1]

The initial assault failed and the survivors of the two colored regiments fell back to regroup. When the casualties were counted, the 6th found it had lost 41 killed, 160 wounded, and 8 missing, a total of 209 officers and men. This loss was sixty-two percent of the 367 soldiers who had begun the charge. Two companies had been deployed as skirmishers and did not take part in this attack, so the proportionate loss in the eight charging companies was extremely high. Company D, captained by John McMurray, entered the fighting with thirty men; only three came out safely. McMurray's company thus was accorded the dubious honor of having suffered the greatest reported loss by a Union company throughout the entire war.

Edgerton and Kelley both later received Congressional Medals of Honor for their valiant actions. Lieutenant Edgerton reminisced about his deed in the following way:[2]

> The earthwork immediately in front of us was strengthened by an abatis extending along its entire face. This had in front of it a sluggish stream with slimy banks and mossy bottom, about four yards wide. Just at the left of our regiment, the enemy's earthwork ran at right angle to the front we were charging and enabled him to give us an enfilading fire as we moved forward, which was terribly effective. . . . When I got over the stream, I found a level space of ground thickly covered with our dead and wounded. Among these I saw Lieutenant Meyers [sic] lying upon the flag, dead, but still holding it. I took it from him and pushed forward to bring up the colors to their proper place.
>
> All at once I went down, but jumped up immediately and tried to raise the flag, for I thought I had fallen over the dewberry vines which grew thickly there, but finding it did not come, I looked down, after trying again, to see why I could not lift it, and found my hand covered with blood, and perfectly powerless, and the flag-staff lying in two pieces. I sheathed my sword, took the flag with its broken staff and reached the abatis. Colonel John W. Ames was there, and about a corporal's guard of men, others soon appeared out of the powder smoke, which was so dense that we could only see a few feet ahead of us. After waiting a few moments to see how many we could muster, the Colonel said: "We must have more help, boys, before we try that. Fall back." When we got beyond the stream and out of the cloud of smoke, we could begin to see how terribly we had been cut to pieces.

A later assault drove the Rebels out of their position to the main line, which was breached, but enemy reinforcements and Federal bungling prevented a wider breakthrough in the direction of Richmond. The 6th reorganized and moved to occupy a portion of the captured line near Fort Harrison, and had the pleasure of helping repulse a Confederate attempt to drive the Yankees out of their hard-won gains. The regiment remained bivouacked in the area until mid-December, drilling new recruits and guarding a section of the earthworks.

In December, the brigade to which the 6th was assigned was ordered to take part in the amphibious attack that eventually captured Fort Fisher, the main fortification guarding the entrance to the port of Wilmington, North Carolina. The regiment landed with the other army troops, but was not engaged in the successful assault on the fort. After participating in several minor skirmishes, the 6th was part of the force that occupied Wilmington on February 22, 1865. The regiment then marched to Raleigh, and was camped near the city when Confederate General Joseph E. Johnston surrendered his army to General Sherman. Upon the cessation of hostilities, the 6th was returned to Wilmington for provost guard duty. It remained in the city until mustered out of service on September 20, 1865.

Regimental Color

The newly-formed 6th USCT received its regimental color on August 31, 1863, the flag presented at Camp William Penn by a deputation of colored citizens. This flag was also painted by Mr. Bowser, who designed it as follows: The obverse depicts the Goddess of Liberty holding a flag, exhorting a freedman now dressed as a soldier to do his duty. In the background, another slave applauds the black soldier. The motto "Freedom for All" is painted on a scroll above the central motif, while "6th United States Colored Troops" adorns the lower scroll. The reverse of the flag contains the national coat-of-arms, together with the presentation date of the flag. After presentation, this flag was placed on exhibit at the headquarters of the Supervisory Committee for several weeks. A newspaper reporter who noticed it wrote that "it is a most beautiful specimen of workmanship, and reflects great credit upon the donors and artist."[3]

Because of the ethnic prejudice in Philadelphia, Mayor Alexander Henry had earlier refused Lieutenant-Colonel Wagner permission to parade the 3rd USCT through the city. The city council later cautiously decided to allow the 6th USCT to parade on the afternoon of October 4, 1863. "Walnut, Pine and Broad Streets listened to the measured tread of the dusky soldiers and the staccato of a full drum corps. The Union blue, the white gloves and the glint of fixed bayonets contrasted sharply with the dark faces perspiring under the rays of a warm October sun." As the regiment passed the Continental Hotel, a city tough ran out from the crowd and snatched the color away from the sergeant, who knocked the intruder down, rescued his flag, and resumed his place in the ranks, to the cheers of many of the spectators. This was the only incident during the parade, and thereafter, other black regiments also paraded through the city to demonstrate their martial learning.[4]

This regimental flag was carried in the September 29, 1863, assault at New Market Heights. Sergeant-Major Thomas Hawkins of Company C retrieved the fallen color after the bearer was killed, and brought the torn flag off the field. He later received a Medal of Honor for this deed. To show their appreciation of the sergeant-major's action, the regimental officers presented the flag to Hawkins when the regiment mustered out of service in September 1865. The subsequent history of this flag is not exactly known.

Obverse, 6th USCT Regimental Color

Reverse, 6th USCT Regimental Color

When G.A.R. Post 1 presented its collection of flags to the Union League of Philadelphia on November 22, 1919, a flag of the 6th USCT was included. This may be the regimental color that Hawkins kept after the war. The Union League donated its collection to the William Penn Museum in 1977, but no trace of this flag can be found.[5]

Color-Bearer

Sergeant John D. West of Company D carried one of the regiment's two flags during the assault on Petersburg, June 15, 1864. On July 4, Sergeant West was reduced to the ranks for cowardice before the enemy on that date.[6]

Notes

[1]This paragraph is based on Mulholland, *Medal of Honor*, p. 516, which does not mention Kelley's role. Edgerton, in the passage quoted elsewhere in this sketch, does not mention Kelley at all. However, when Edgerton applied for a Medal of Honor, Captain Robert B. Beath of Company A wrote a letter in support of Edgerton's application. Beath wrote that Kelley picked the flag up after Meyer was killed, and Kelley was quickly wounded, letting the color fall. It was then, according to Beath, that Edgerton appeared and seized the flag. See Beath's letter of December 1, 1897, in Edgerton's Medal of Honor file, RG 94.

[2]Mulholland, *Medal of Honor*, pp. 516-517.

[3]*Philadelphia Inquirer*, September 1, 21, 1863.

[4]Binder, "Negro Regiments," pp. 397-398.

[5]Hawkins to General J. B. Kiddoo, January 22, 1870, in Hawkins Medal of Honor file RG 94. It is my conclusion that Hawkins took the regimental flag, and that Edgerton and Kelley received their medals for carrying the national color. The several documents bearing on Edgerton and Kelley alternate between using "national color" and "regimental color." Since Major Lane's 1866 list included the 6th USCT's national color, I think this is the flag Edgerton and Kelley carried, and since no regimental flag appears on the list, it is apparently the one taken by Hawkins.

[6]Special Orders #30, July 5, 1864, in Regimental Order Book, RG 94.

Bibliography

McMurray, John. *Recollections of a Colored Troop*. Brookville, 1916.
Montgomery, Horace. "A Union Officer's Recollections of the Negro as a Soldier." *Pennsylvania History* 28 (1961): 156-186.
This article draws heavily on McMurray's book listed above.

8th United States Colored Troops

National Color

Containing a number of recruits from Delaware, the 8th USCT was the third regiment formed at Camp William Penn in the autumn of 1863. Charles W. Fribley, a captain in the 84th Pennsylvania, was chosen colonel of the new regiment, which included many other officers with equal military experience. The 8th left Philadelphia on January 16, 1864, for Hilton Head Island, South Carolina, where it remained for a short time while an expedition to reinforce the Federal troops in Florida was readied.

Placed under the command of Brigadier-General Truman Seymour, the 8th landed at Jacksonville, Florida, in early February and then formed part of Seymour's expedition of about 5,500 men. This force marched inland and was initially successful in routing small detachments of Rebel troops as the Federal expedition pushed inland. On February 20, 1864, Truman's command encountered a sizeable Confederate force under Brigadier-General Joseph Finnegan at Olustee, also called Ocean Pond. Finnegan formed his men in a lightly-forested area, his position strengthened by rifle pits.

Seymour was initially surprised by the strong Rebel opposition, but soon moved his advance troops forward to engage the enemy. As the 8th USCT reached the field, Seymour ordered Colonel Fribley to deploy his men on the left of a railroad and attack the enemy. Fribley ordered his untested command forward into the face of a withering musketry fire. Surgeon Alexander P. Heichhold wrote that ". . . before we were fairly in line our men were dropping like leaves in autumn." Lieutenant Oliver W. Norton, a veteran of the 83rd Pennsylvania, bitterly recalled the first combat action of valiant but scared soldiers:

> Military men say it takes veteran troops to maneuver under fire, but our regiment with knapsacks on and unloaded pieces, after a run of half a mile, formed a line under the most destructive fire I ever knew. We were not more than two hundred yards from the enemy, concealed in pits and behind trees, and what did the regiment do? At first they were stunned, bewildered, and knew not what to do. They curled to the ground, and as men fell around them they seemed terribly scared, but gradually they recovered their senses and commenced firing. And here was the great trouble—they could not use their arms to advantage. We have had very little practice in firing, and though they could stand and be killed, they could not kill a concealed enemy fast enough to satisfy my feelings.

Soon, Confederate troops began to enfilade the 8th's left flank. Colonel Fribley then ordered his men to fall back slowly, and to maintain firing as they fell back. The colonel was soon killed and the major wounded and carried from the field. The lieutenant-colonel had recently been promoted to the colonelcy of another colored regiment, so the 8th did not have any staff officers remaining. With no overall direction, the heavy enemy musketry fire soon caused much confusion within the 8th's ranks. The regiment slowly began to break apart and drift to the rear. The sergeant carrying the national color was killed, and the man who next picked the flag up was likewise killed. The color company was almost annihilated. Of the forty-three men in this company who entered the battle, thirty were casualties. Three sergeants and five corporals of the color-guard fell while endeavoring to protect the colors.[1]

By this time, the regiment had fallen back near Battery E, 3rd United States Light Artillery. This battery had earlier taken position behind the regiment, and many officers of the 8th later complained that their own artillery had fired into them at different times during the battle. As the 8th fell back and attempted to rally near the guns, an artillery lieutenant rushed out to the retreating infantry and pleaded with Lieutenant Elijah Lewis not to abandon the battery. Lieutenant Lewis had just found the national color on the ground, the bearer having been killed. The lieutenant took the flag and planted it in the ground near one of the guns. With the help of other officers, Lewis then attempted to rally enough men to form a new line of battle. But the Rebel fire was too hot to stand, and Captain R. C. Bailey, the senior officer remaining in the regiment, ordered the survivors to fall back.[2]

During the confusion of the retreat, the national color was left on the field and apparently taken by the enemy. To explain the loss of the flag, Captain Bailey, Lieutenant Lewis, and Lieutenant Andrew F. Ely all deposited statements containing their account of its loss. Lieutenant Ely's short report best explained the situation when the color disappeared:[3]

> I was near Lieutenant Lewis when he picked up the colors and saw him carry them toward the battery on our left. I called to the men to rally around the colors and save the battery. Lieutenant Norton also attempted to rally those on my left. We succeeded in bringing up a fragment of the regiment within a few yards of the battery, when the horses of one of the guns came rushing onto our little line, throwing us into some confusion. I think at this time Lieutenant Lewis gave the colors to one of the men. I saw him strike one of the horses with his sword, and in conjunction with some others seize the horses by the bits to stop them. He

did not get the colors again, and we commenced falling back obliquely to the right in obedience to an order from Capt. R. C. Bailey, then commanding the regiment. I saw a corporal carrying our battleflag, and supposing they had the other, paid no further attention to the matter.

In the end, the Federals were defeated and fell back to Jacksonville. Seymour failed to deploy all of his troops at the same time, and Finnegan's men defeated the Yankees in detail. In addition to the loss of its national color, the 8th suffered heavy casualties—66 killed, 262 wounded, 15 missing—a total loss of 343. The regiment entered the battle with 565 officers and men.

Regimental Color

At some point prior to the Battle of Olustee, the 8th received some type of regimental flag. No photograph or presentation documentation has been located, and thus it is unknown if Mr. Bowser painted this flag for the regiment. Together with the national color, this regimental flag was carried at Olustee. As the regiment stood and fought the enemy, the sergeant carrying the flag was hit in his right hand by a ball which nearly tore off the hand. Rather than let the flag fall, the sergeant calmly seized the staff with his left hand and retained possession of the flag until he found a corporal to give the flag to for safekeeping. Lieutenant Ely saw a corporal, perhaps the same man, carry the flag from the field.[4]

The 8th USCT remained in Jacksonville until mid-April, when it was transferred to Saint John's Bluff, Florida. Here, the regiment fortified the small town and acted as the garrison, sending out an occasional raiding party into the surrounding countryside. While stationed here, Sergeant Robert Brown of Company F was appointed color-sergeant on June 13.[5]

In August 1864, the 8th was transferred to the Army of the James, part of the forces operating against Petersburg and Richmond. At first stationed in the trenches near Petersburg, the 8th took part on the Battle of New Market Heights on September 29-30, losing sixty-eight casualties in the unsuccessful attack on Fort Gilmer and the repulse of the major Confederate counterattack. On October 13, the regiment was part of the Tenth Corps attack on the Rebel entrenchments along the Darbytown Road, suffering the loss of forty men in this brisk engagement. Upon the conclusion of the autumn 1864 operations, the 8th remained north of the James River until the April 1865 attack on Petersburg, when it returned to its former position and participated in the final Yankee attack on the city.

After Lee's surrender in April 1865, the 8th, as part of the Twenty-fifth Corps, was sent to Texas, where the government concentrated a sizeable military force to watch French activities in Mexico. The regiment remained in Texas until October, when it began a slow homeward voyage that ended in its mustering out of service on December 12, 1865. During its term of service, the 8th USCT suffered more battle casualties than any other black regiment.

Color-Bearer

One of the wounded color-sergeants left upon the Olustee battlefield was Samuel Waters of Company C. He died of his wounds in Andersonville Prison on June 30, 1864.[6]

Notes

[1] *O.R.* 35.1, p. 313.
[2] *Ibid.*, pp. 313-314.
[3] *Ibid.*, p. 314
[4] Letter of Dr. Heichhold in the *Lebanon Courier*, March 17, 1864; *O.R.* 35.1, p. 314.

[5] Special Orders #23, June 13, 1864, Regimental Order Book, RG 94.
[6] Special Orders #47. November 20, 1864, deprived the absent Waters of his rank so another could be promoted in his place, Regimental Order Book, RG 94; Bates 5: 973, lists his death date.

Bibliography

Norton, Oliver W. *Army Letters 1861-1865.* Chicago: O. L. Deming, 1903.

22nd United States Colored Troops

National Color
Regimental Color

This regiment was organized at Camp William Penn in January 1864. Colonel Joseph B. Kiddoo had earlier commanded the 137th Pennsylvania. Upon organization, the regiment left Philadelphia on February 10, 1864, bound for Yorktown, Virginia. At some point prior to departure, the regiment probably received a set of national and regimental colors. The regimental color was painted by Mr. Bowser, and followed a similar pattern with the other flags he painted, with the national arms on the reverse and an allegorical scene as the central painting on the obverse side. In this case, Bowser used the Virginia state motto, "Sic Semper Tyrannis" (Thus Always to Tyrants), to highlight the painting of a black soldier bayonetting a fallen Rebel color-bearer who is trying to defend himself. In the background, other black soldiers fire on the retreating enemy troops.

The 22nd USCT remained in camp during the winter months, then was assigned to the Eighteenth Corps, Army of the James. During the first phase of the operations against Petersburg, the regiment spent most of its time constructing fortifications along the James River to protect some of the pontoon bridges across the river. On June 15, 1864, the Eighteenth Corps attacked the Rebel lines around Petersburg, and achieved some breakthroughs against the lightly-defended entrenchments. The 22nd played a prominent part in the attack, capturing two forts and seven cannon. Losses totalled 138 officers and men for the day's fighting.

After spending time in the trenches, the regiment fought in the Battle of New Market Heights on September 29-30, losing seventy-eight men in an unsuccessful attack on the enemy's works. The 22nd next fought in the engagement on the Darbytown Road on October 27. Colonel Kiddoo was wounded as the regiment emerged from a woods and charged across an open field at the enemy entrenchments. The Rebel works were sparsely manned, but the 22nd was not properly supported and the attack was repulsed. A large number of new recruits, in battle for the first time, also caused confusion in the ranks during the charge, which aided in the regiment's failure. Shortly after the regiment returned to its camp, Lieutenant-Colonel Ira C. Terry singled out the name of Corporal Nathan Stanton as the soldier who most distinguished himself in the late fighting. Corporal Stanton carried his color forward although shot through the hand, and did not leave the field until the regiment retreated.[1]

The regiment then took part in the successful attack on the Rebel lines that compelled the evacuation of Petersburg and Richmond on April 2, 1865. The 22nd was among the first units of the Twenty-fifth Corps to enter the city, and the men aided greatly in extinguishing some of the many fires burning throughout the city. Owing to its "excellent discipline and soldierly qualities," the 22nd was detailed to participate in the funeral obsequies for President Lincoln, and then aided in pursuing Lincoln's assassins on Maryland's eastern shore. In May 1865, the 22nd was sent to Texas for duty there, returning to Philadelphia for muster out on October 16, 1865.

Obverse, 22nd USCT Regimental Color

Notes

[1] Undated report of Lieutenant-Colonel Terry to Lieutenant D. L. Proudfit, A.A.G., on page 16 of the Regimental Letter Book, RG 94.

Advance the Colors!

24th United States Colored Troops

National Color
Regimental Color

Formed from blacks recruited primarily in eastern Pennsylvania, the 24th USCT was the last regiment formed at Camp William Penn. It was so designated in February 1865, but did not leave Philadelphia until May 1865. The new regiment received a national color at some point, and friends of the regiment presented a regimental color on April 14, 1865.[1] This flag was painted by Mr. Bowser. The obverse shows an unarmed black soldier standing on a mountaintop, reaching toward the heavens for a message that is suspended toward his grasping fingers. The message is a simple "Fiat Justitia" (Let Justice Be Done). The motto painted on the scroll above this motif reads "Let Soldiers in War be Citizens in Peace." The reverse contains the national coat-of-arms with the presentation date.

Upon leaving Philadelphia, the 24th USCT went to Washington, where it remained until early June, when it was assigned to guard Rebel prisoners at Camp Lookout, Maryland. After a month on this duty, the regiment was transferred to Richmond, then to Burkesville, where it engaged in provost guard duty and aided in distributing government supplies to the needy. In late September, the regiment returned to Richmond and was mustered out of service on October 1, 1865.

Notes

[1] "Presentation of a Flag to the 24th Regiment USCT," *Philadelphia Inquirer*, April 15, 1865.

Obverse, 24th USCT Regimental Color

Reverse, 24th USCT Regimental Color

25th United States Colored Troops

National Color
Regimental Color

Organized in February 1864, the 25th USCT was to be the nucleus of a brigade of three more black regiments to be raised in Texas. Colonel Gustavus A. Scroggs was to take his command to Indianola, Texas, and there recruit three new regiments. The colonel would be promoted to brigadier-general for his efforts. The regiment left Philadelphia in two detachments, Colonel Scroggs and the right wing embarking on March 31, 1864. As the regiment marched through Philadelphia to the wharf, it stopped in front of the Supervisory Committee headquarters on Chestnut Street to receive a regimental flag from the Committee. Mr. Webster presented the flag with the following speech, printed here in full:[1]

> On behalf of the Supervisory Committee, I present your regiment a flag emblematic of the cause at stake, and the men who are to determine it. Our liberties, our peace, our future welfare, self-government itself, and all the best hopes of humanity were assailed at one blow when the impious hand of Rebellion was raised against the old flag and the Union—when the giant curse of our country, Slavery, took up arms against progress and the rights of man.
>
> At last, AT LAST! the race that has been for centuries the victims of our hypocrisy and our injustice is summoned to arms to redress its own wrongs, to fight slavery and to assist in saving liberty and constitutional government. You command a select regiment of this race. I know the men; they are obedient, intelligent and patriotic. They are well trained and well officered and fit for their glorious mission. You will lead them, I hope, to victory.
>
> Take this flag, Colonel, and when it is streaming in the wind let your men catch inspirations from its emblem. Liberty is there placing a musket in the hands of a stalwart black man, and bids him "Strike! for God and Liberty." Wave this banner over the Savannahs of the South. Carry it to the Gulf. Let loyal blacks in bonds see it, and the radiant Stars and Stripes supplant the flaunting rag of their masters.
>
> Make this flag famous. Go hence with your brave black compatriots and obey its motto—"Strike for God and Liberty." Make emancipation, which is still but an unenforced paper decree, a fixed fact. Make it familiar as light, absolute as fate and eternal as time. Remember you have a noble work before you; you are not only to save liberty, but to free a race and to elevate it by the ennobling pursuit of arms. May your regiment, under your lead, prove its devotion to freedom and to the country, by endurance, by fortitude, by bravery—aye! and if necessary, by glorious death on the battle field. Earn, by heroic deeds, the title to be great. Carry dismay and terror to the enemy. Achieve for the Twenty-fifth Regiment a surname that shall live in history.

But the 25th regiment was not destined to play an important part in crushing the Rebellion. As the transport with the right wing aboard rounded Cape Hatteras, it encountered a storm and sprung a leak. It was only through the superhuman effort of its passengers that the ship was saved and managed to reach Beaufort, North Carolina, where the men abandoned the hulk. When the regiment landed, they found that the Rebels were threatening to attack the Federal defenders of the coastal area, and the regiment went to Washington, N.C., as reinforcements. It remained here until late April 1864, when it reembarked for New Orleans, arriving there on May 1, to find Lieutenant-Colonel Frederick L. Hitchcock and the left wing. Hitchcock arrived just after the end of the disastrous Red River Campaign, and the 25th was detained as reinforcements. Colonel Scroggs resigned in protest when his entire regiment was prohibited from going forward to Texas. Hitchcock then became the new colonel.

In mid-May, the 25th USCT was sent to form part of the garrison of Barrancas, Florida, across the harbor from Pensacola. While occupying Forts Barrancas and Pickens, the regiment drilled as heavy artillery and became quite proficient. It remained here until it was sent home for muster out, which occurred in Philadelphia on December 6, 1865. The regiment did

Obverse, 25th USCT Regimental Color

Advance the Colors!

take part in two small skirmishes with Rebel troops near Pensacola, but the regiment's greatest loss of life resulted from scurvy and other diseases. By June 8, 1865, the regiment lost 168 men by disease.

After the regiment returned to Philadelphia, it paraded through the streets before being disbanded. On this occasion, the regiment halted in front of the Union League headquarters and presented the regimental color to that association. President George H. Boker responded to Colonel Hitchcock's presentation "in an eloquent and impressive manner." The present location of this flag is unknown.[2]

Color-Bearers

On February 27, 1864, Sergeants George W. Davis of Company D and William Lyons of Company I were appointed color-sergeants of the regiment. The color-guard was composed of ten corporals rather than the regulation eight.[3] On July 30, 1865, Sergeant Daniel Thompson of Company A was appointed color-sergeant.[4] As the regiment's naval transport steamed north toward Philadelphia on November 23, 1865, Colonel Hitchcock appointed Sergeant Henry Key of Company H as color-sergeant.[5]

Notes

[1] "The Twenty-fifth United States Colored Troops," *Philadelphia Inquirer*, April 1, 1864. This flag was painted by Mr. Bowser. See "Flags for the Colored Regiments," *Philadelphia Inquirer*, March 24, 1864.

[2] Bates 5: 1027.

[3] Regimental Orders #9, February 27, 1864, Regimental Order Book, RG 94.

[4] General Orders #26, July 30, 1865, *Ibid*. In this order, the regulation eight corporals were appointed as color-guards.

[5] Special Orders #108, November 23, 1865, *Ibid*.

32nd United States Colored Troops

National Color
Regimental Color

The men comprising the 32nd USCT were mainly from Pennsylvania, with large contingents from New Jersey and Delaware. The regiment was organized in March 1864, and left Philadelphia in late April. Sometime before departure, the regiment received a regimental color painted by Mr. Bowser on behalf of the Supervisory Committee.[1] This color had an oil painting of John Brown on one side, and was turned over to the War Department when the regiment disbanded. This accounts for the absence of the flag on the April 1866 Philadelphia list.[2] There was a flag presentation to an unspecified regiment at Camp William Penn on April 4, 1864. Troops present included the 32nd and parts of the 25th and 43rd regiments. Since the 32nd was the only complete regiment present, it is possible that this unit received the "splendid American flag."[3]

Upon its organization, the regiment was ordered to the Department of the South, arriving at Hilton Head Island in late April 1864. It remained on this island for some time before being sent to take part in the siege of Charleston, returning to its camp in No-vember. On November 30, the 32nd USCT took part in the engagement at Honey Hill, South Carolina, as part of a force of 5,500 men under Brigadier-General John P. Hatch that was sent to break the Charleston and Savannah Railroad. By doing so, Hatch's force would help General Sherman's attack on Savannah by preventing reinforcements and supplies from reaching the city. However, Hatch's attack on the 2,000 defenders was badly managed and the Federal raid was unsuccessful. Another raid was launched soon after, and the 32nd was engaged in the sharp fighting at Deveaux Neck, South Carolina, on December 7, 1864.

After the success of this raid, the 32nd moved to James Island and participated in several skirmishes as Federal troops moved closer to Charleston, ending in the fall of the city on February 18, 1865. Thereafter, the 32nd was part of a detachment of Federal troops sent into the interior of South Carolina to intercept Confederate rail traffic. The regiment skirmished at several points along the railroad between Camden and Statesboro, meeting no appreciable opposition as the Confederacy collapsed. After the Confederate surrender, the 32nd returned to Charleston and acted as provost guards that point and at Hilton Head and Beaufort. It returned to Philadelphia and was mustered out of service on August 22, 1865.

Notes

[1]"Flags for the Colored Regiments," *Philadelphia Inquirer*, March 24, 1864.

[2]Thompson, p. 29.

[3]"Flag Presentation at Camp William Penn," *Philadelphia Inquirer*, April 5, 1864.

Bibliography

Baird, George W. *The Thirty-second U.S.C.T. at the Battle of Honey Hill.* Boston, 1887.

Thompson, Benjamin W. "Back to the South: The Benjamin W. Thompson Memoir, Part III." *Civil War Times Illustrated* 12 (November 1973): 28-39.

41st United States Colored Troops

No colors belonging to this regiment are included on any of the three lists dating from 1866, 1906, and the 1920s West Point inventory. It is assumed that this unit would have received a national and a regimental color, but there is no evidence to substantiate this hypothesis.

The regiment was organized at Camp William Penn in the autumn of 1864. Six companies participated in the fighting on the Darbytown Road on October 27, then went into camp near Chaffin's Farm. Here they were joined by the remainder of the regiment. When the Twenty-fifth Corps was organized, the 41st was assigned to the Second Division. The regiment was engaged in the April 2, 1865, assault on Petersburg, losing one killed and eight wounded. After Lee's surrender, the 41st was transferred to Texas, where it served from June through November, when the regiment was mustered out of service. It returned to Philadelphia and was officially disbanded on December 14, 1865.

43rd United States Colored Troops

National Color
Regimental Color

The 43rd USCT was organized during the spring and summer of 1864. Before the regiment could be completely formed and equipped, the first six companies, the only ones then organized, were sent to join the Army of the Potomac in April 1864. These companies were attached to the Fourth Division of the Ninth Corps. At some point, according to the West Point list, the regiment received both a national and a regimental flag. It is unknown if Mr. Bowser prepared the regimental color.

Upon joining the army, the 43rd moved south into the Wilderness, engaged in guarding the army's immense supply trains. Company G joined the regiment on June 6. The regiment was not heavily engaged with the enemy until it moved forward during the Battle of the Crater on July 30. The brigade moved to the right of the Crater, but was repulsed by enemy reinforcements and fell back into the Crater proper. Still, the regiment managed to capture some prisoners and a Rebel battleflag. While the 43rd remained in the Crater, it fought gallantly against the attacking enemy forces until compelled to retreat to the main Federal line. The chaplain of the regiment recorded the following about this portion of the battle: "As each brave color-bearer was shot down, another, and another, would grasp the National emblem, all riddled with balls, and plant it further on the enemy's line. In this terrific engagement, this battalion of the Forty-third had its colors almost entirely cut up by the fire, and the color staffs splintered and broken."[1]

The remaining companies joined the regiment in August. These companies had been delayed and placed in the defenses of Baltimore when a Confederate force invaded Maryland and threatened Washington. The united regiment then participated in the fighting on the Weldon Railroad (August 17-20) with minimal losses. Later in 1864, the regiment was transferred to the new Twenty-fifth Corps, composed entirely of colored troops. Its next action was on January 24, 1865, when the regiment fired upon Rebel gunboats steaming down the James River toward the Federal supply base at City Point. The 43rd's musketry fire was so heavy and accurate that the Rebel gunners could not open their armored portholes to use their cannon and turned back. Until the fall of Richmond in April 1865, the regiment remained in the trenches and skirmished with the opposing forces many times. After Lee's surrender, the regiment was transferred to Texas, where it served quietly until late November. It returned by sea to Philadelphia and was mustered out of service on November 30, 1865.

Color-Bearers

On May 16, 1864, Sergeant William R. Butler of Company F was selected to carry one of the colors. Five corporals were named in this order as guards.[2] On September 5, 1864, nine corporals were appointed as bearer and guards. This list does not distinguish between who the bearer was and who were the guards. The names were Samuel A. Reed, Company A; William Molson, Company B; Wesley Jackson, Company C; A. L. Coleman, Company D; M. Ray, Company E; William Brown, Company G; William H. Brewer, Company H; James H. Murray, Company I; and Sussex Broady, Company K.[3]

Notes

[1] Bates 5: 1082.
[2] General Orders #5, Regimental Order Book, RG 94.

[3] Special Orders #20, *Ibid.*

Bibliography

Mickley, Jeremiah M. *Forty-third Regiment, U.S.C.T.* Gettysburg: J. E. Wible, 1866.

45th United States Colored Troops

National Color
Regimental Color

This regiment was initially recruited during the summer of 1864. As soon as the first four companies were formed, they were rushed to Washington to join the city's defenses when Confederate General Jubal A. Early threatened the capital in July 1864. These four companies remained on duty in the city until they rejoined the regiment in March 1865. They were the only colored troops in Lincoln's second inaugural parade.

Obverse, 45th USCT Regimental Color

Meanwhile, the remaining six companies were recruited and formed at Camp William Penn. A regimental flag painted by Mr. Bowser was presented to the regiment on September 15, 1864. The presentation speech on behalf of the Supervisory Committee was delivered by Brigadier-General William Birney, and the flag was accepted by Major James T. Bates.[1] The obverse of this flag depicts a colored color-bearer standing in martial repose in front of a bust of George Washington. The sergeant's left hand grasps an American flag while his right hand rests on a sword. In the background, battle smoke partially obscures advancing black soldiers, who are firing on the enemy. The motto on the scroll above the painting reads "One Cause, One Country."

These six companies left Philadelphia in late September, and were assigned to the Tenth Corps in the Army of the James. It participated in the Battle of New Market Heights on September 29-30, losing only one man killed and three wounded. The regiment also took part in the fighting on the Darbytown Road on October 13, and at Charles City Cross Roads on October 27, with minimal casualties. It was assigned to the new Twenty-fifth Corps later in the year, and served with this corps until mustered out. Although the 43rd fought in the engagements near Petersburg that led to the fall of both that city and Richmond, it suffered few casualties. After the surrender of Lee's army, the corps was transferred to Texas, the 43rd being stationed at Edinburg and Brownsville. It was mustered out of service on November 4, returning to Philadelphia on December 13, 1865.

Notes

[1] "Flag Presentation at Camp William Penn—Speech of Brig.-Gen. Birney and Others," *Philadelphia Inquirer*, September 16, 1864.

Advance the Colors!

127th United States Colored Troops

National Color
Regimental Color

This regiment was formed at Camp William Penn during the months of August and September 1864. The 1866 list includes both a national and a regimental color of the 127th's. The regimental color was received on September 15, 1864, during the same ceremony in which the 45th USCT received a similar flag from the Supervisory Committee. Mr. Charles Gibbons presented this flag, which was received by Lieutenant-Colonel James Givin.[1] Mr. Bowser painted the flag, the obverse depicting a fully-equipped colored soldier bidding adieu to the Goddess of Liberty. A military camp can be seen in the background. The motto on the scroll above the painting reads "We Will Prove Ourselves Men."

Upon leaving Philadelphia later in September, the 127th was assigned to the Tenth Corps, Army of the James, and then to the Twenty-fifth Corps when that body of troops was formed in late 1864. The regiment primarily was used to construct fortifications and perform guard duty, and thus was not under enemy fire until April 2, 1865, when the forces under Grant captured Petersburg and Richmond. A mere three men were wounded as the regiment advanced toward the Confederate line. After participating in the Appomattox Campaign, the regiment was transferred to Texas, where it remained on duty until mustered out of service on October 20, 1865.

Obverse, 127th USCT Regimental Color

Color-Bearer

On September 10, 1864, Sergeant William Reynolds of Company D was appointed to carry one of the regiment's flags, possibly that received on September 16.[2]

Notes

[1]"Flag Presentation at Camp William Penn—Speech of Brig.-Gen. Birney and Others," *Philadelphia Inquirer*, September 16, 1864. The museum of the Philadelphia Camp, Sons of Union Veterans, includes a regimental color marked 127th USCT, but the central painting has been souvenired, making positive identification impossible.

[2]General Orders #2, Regimental Order Book, RG 94.

PART II

11th Infantry

State Color

The 11th Pennsylvania three-months regiment was mustered out of service in late July 1861. Once back in Pennsylvania, officers of the old 11th strove to have the regiment accepted for a term of three years. After some delay, they succeeded in doing so, and the regiment was reformed with Colonel Henry Coulter as commander. Before leaving Harrisburg, Governor Curtin presented the regiment with a state flag on November 20, 1861, the governor placing the silk banner in the hands of Color-Sergeant Charles H. Foulke of Company A.[1]

After a tour of duty at Annapolis, the 11th was reassigned to northern Virginia as railroad guard for both the Manassas Gap and the Orange and Alexandria Railroads. When the federal government concentrated the scattered troops in northern Virginia to form the Army of Virginia, Brigadier-General James B. Ricketts's division, to which the 11th was attached, became part of Major General Irvin McDowell's Third Corps. The 11th briefly tasted its first whiff of hostile gunpowder when Ricketts moved to cover the withdrawal of Federal troops engaged with Stonewall

State Color
Maker: EH
Size: 68" × 74¹/₂"
1985.010

Jackson's corps at the Battle of Cedar Mountain on August 9, 1862. Sergeant Foulke was accidentally wounded in the foot two days later and turned the flag over to Sergeant Robert H. Knox of Company C.[2]

Jackson then moved around General Pope's right flank, followed by General Lee with the other half of the Confederate army. Pope, waiting for reinforcements from the Army of the Potomac, played a delaying tactic in an attempt to prevent the enemy from uniting before his own reinforcements arrived. McDowell's corps brought up the rear of the retreating army, and the 11th had a sharp skirmish with the enemy at Rappahannock Station before retiring and burning the railroad bridge to delay the advance of Lee's Confederates. Pope then sent Ricketts's division to Thoroughfare Gap in the Bull Run Mountains with orders to hold the gap as long as possible to give him time to concentrate his troops. However, Longstreet's troops arrived simultaneously and pushed the outnumbered Federals out of the gap. In this action, the 11th lost more than fifty men.

Ricketts then withdrew to join the main army on the battlefield of Second Manassas. The troops were worn out from their long marches, so Ricketts was held in reserve on the first day of the battle, August 29, 1862. The men were still in reserve the following afternoon when Longstreet launched his assault on Pope's exposed left flank. His attack completely shattered the troops initially opposing the assault and thereby threatened to gain the rear of the Federal army and cut off its communications and retreat route to Washington.

When Longstreet struck, Ricketts's division was hurried to the left of the army and went into position on Bald Hill. As the regiments deployed into line, the seemingly endless mass of grayclad infantry approached and opened fire. One of the 11th's soldiers recounted his experience that day:

But it was now our time to reply, and immediately our whole line was ablaze with spiteful streams of fire as our musketry opened fiercely on the heavy gray masses that came rolling on like a huge, resistless billow ready to engulf all opposition. In the face of our fire their lines pressed forward with desperate courage, with their battle flags pushed bravely to the front. The ground had become encumbered with the dead and dying.

Great pools of clotted blood stained the trampled grass, while groaning, imprecations, and prayers mingled with the roar of battle and the hoarse voices of the combatants.

The 11th found itself in the center of this maelstrom. After the brigade commander and other colonels had become casualties, Colonel Coulter found himself in command of the brigade, which was thinning rapidly under the enemy pressure. Losses in the 11th were heavy. Sergeant Knox was wounded early in the action, and immediately after taking the state flag, Sergeant Samuel S. Bierer was likewise wounded. Lieutenant Absalom Schall picked up the fallen banner and was himself shot down. Sergeant Bierer then grabbed the flag and bore it safely from the field as the regiment retreated. After fighting on Bald Hill for only an hour, the 11th fell back to reorganize. Of the 346 men who entered the fight, 176 were killed, wounded, or captured.[3]

The beaten Union army fell back to Washington, and when Lee invaded Maryland, General McClellan was placed in command and started out in pursuit. The 11th was now attached to Major-General Joseph Hooker's First Corps, which fought briefly at South Mountain before reaching the battlefield at Antietam, where, on September 17, 1862, the bloodiest single day of the war took place.

Hooker's corps opened the battle at 5:00 a.m. by attacking the left flank of Lee's position. The action centered on a forty-acre cornfield and in the East Woods before Hooker's men fell back as reinforcements arrived to continue the fighting. Again, the 11th suffered heavy losses, amounting to over one-half of the men who entered the battle. Private Daniel Mathews, the color-bearer, fell wounded very quickly. Another private, William Welty, took the flag from Mathews's hands and was immediately killed. His place was taken by Corporal Frederick Welty, who, together with the rest of the color-guard, was shot down. The flag remained on the field for a short time when Lieutenant Edward H. Gay picked it up, only to receive two wounds. Sergeant Henry Bitner then carried the state color during the rest of the fighting.[4]

After a slight reorganization of the First Corps, the 11th found itself as part of Brigadier-General Nelson Taylor's Third Brigade, Second Division. At the battle of Fredericksburg on December 13, 1862, the division acted as a support to General Meade's Pennsylvania Reserves, which made a temporary breakthrough in Jackson's line near the railroad crossing at Hamilton's. In this battle, Taylor's brigade formed the first line of the division with the 11th as the left regiment on the line. The troops advanced across the open ground under a heavy fire from Confederate artillery. After laying down under cover of a swale, Brigadier-

General John Gibbon advanced the brigade to attack the main enemy line, then about one-half mile in front. As the troops marched forward, they were "exposed to a most galling fire of small-arms," especially the two left regiments. Coulter was wounded and three color-bearers—Corporal John V. Kuhns (thrice wounded), Private Cyrus W. Chambers (killed), and Corporal John W. Thomas (severely wounded)—were successively shot down before Captain Benjamin F. Haines picked up the flag. General Taylor then ordered the regiment to rally on its colors and as the First and Second Brigades advanced to the attack, the shattered Third Brigade withdrew.[5]

The First Corps was not heavily engaged at Chancellorsville, and next fought at Gettysburg on July 1, 1863. The Second Division of the corps was posted on the right of the line of battle, and successfully repelled many attacks on its position, in turn counterattacking and taking many prisoners. In the charge upon Iverson's North Carolina brigade, Color-Corporal John H. McKalip was wounded and the color fell for a time, later being picked up by Private Michael Kepler, who carried it until April 1864. The 11th again lost heavily, with some 140 of 212 present on the field as casualties.[6]

After participating in the fall 1863 campaigns, enough men re-enlisted to have the 11th classed as "veteran volunteers." With several hundred new recruits, the reinforced regiment, now a part of Major-General G. K. Warren's Fifth Corps, moved into the Wilderness to begin General Grant's campaign against Lee's army. During the heavy fighting in the gloomy forest, the 11th lost severely but acquitted itself well.

Grant then marched south and from May 8-18 fighting raged with various intensity around Spotsylvania Court House. Brigadier-General John C. Robinson's division of the Fifth Corps led the advance to this battle and on May 8, while pushing back the enemy, Corporal J. J. Lehman was killed as the 11th attacked. In further combat here, another bearer was wounded and the regiment again lost heavily, being reduced to a mere shadow of its former strength.[7]

The 11th then participated in the engagements along the North Anna River, at Bethesda Church, and at Cold Harbor, before settling down in front of Petersburg to engage the enemy in the lengthy siege operations before the city. The Fifth Corps moved west to strike the Weldon Railroad and fought a battle at Globe Tavern on August 18-21, 1864. In the confused fighting on August 19, Confederate regiments turned the right flank of Brigadier-General S. W. Crawford's division and attacked from the rear. To add to the chaos, Federal artillery batteries shelled both friend and foe alike for a short time. During this period Corporal William Mathews of Company C carried the

Advance the Colors!

state flag. The corporal bore the flag until December 3, when Sergeant Albert Carter was appointed bearer.[8]

After the Globe Tavern battle, the 11th next took part in another raid against the Weldon Railroad in December 1864, spending the rest of the winter resting and occupying trenches in the lines facing Petersburg. The next major battle in which the 11th fought was at Hatcher's Run on February 5-7, 1865. The regiment lost eighty-nine men in the successful fighting along the creek.

The regiment then took an active part in the battle of Five Forks (March 31-April 1, 1865), and followed Lee's retreating army to the surrender at Appomattox Court House on April 9. The surviving members of the 11th Pennsylvania returned to Harrisburg, where the regiment was mustered out of service on July 1, 1865. The tattered remnant of the state flag was returned to state care by Sergeant J. C. Scheurman of Company A, the 11th's last color-sergeant, who had been appointed to the position on May 28, when Sergeant Carter was discharged.[9]

The battered remnant of the 11th's state color vividly illustrates the pride which the rank and file attached to their flag. Rather than request a replacement flag from the state, the men resolved to keep their original, battle-worn banner. At least twice during the war, the regiment authorized emergency repairs to the flag. The first evidence of this occurred on September 8, 1863, when the regimental council of administration authorized that a part of the tax assessed on the sutler be used to make repairs to the flag.[10] A similar measure was adopted on April 29, 1864.[11] The flag shows what these repairs entailed. Replacement silk was obtained and sewn directly to the remnants of the original stripes. The added silk supporting the shredded original stripes is thought to be of a different composition as evidenced by the differential aging and fading of the two materials.

The flag also bears evidence of the Lincoln mourning period of 1865. Upon the the assassination of the President, Secretary of War Edwin Stanton ordered that all regiments drape their flags and drums with black crepe to honor the dead Lincoln. Based upon the surviving evidence, it seems that most regiments simply tied black crepe to the flagstaffs, but the men of the 11th went further than this. Strips of black crepe were used to outline the center red stripe of the flag. Crepe was also sewn around the edge of the flag directly next to the fringe. Thus the men of the regiment paid their respects to Lincoln.

Martinsburg Flag

While in the three-months service, the 11th Pennsylvania was one of the regiments that distinguished it-

Martinsburg Flag
Size: 49⁷/₁₆" × 81⁵/₈"
1985.009

self in the small but important Federal victory over Stonewall Jackson's Confederates at Falling Waters, Virginia, on July 2, 1861. After this victory, Federal General Robert Patterson's army lay inactive in the northern Shenandoah Valley, the 11th going into camp near Martinsburg. There were many loyal citizens in this section of Virginia, and several acts of gratitude were shown to the Northern soldiers while they were in the area.

Early in the evening of July 12, a gentleman from Martinsburg carrying a flag entered the 11th's camp. He was accompanied by some fifteen young ladies, one of whom, a Miss Miller, presented the flag to the regiment with the following short speech:[12]

> In behalf of the ladies of this neighborhood, I am delegated to present to you this flag as a token of their high appreciation of your courage and gallantry in leaving your quiet homes, facing danger and death, to march to the succor of those whom the rebels, the enemies of our glorious government, had placed under the reign of terrorism. May God bless you, preserve your health and lead you honorably and triumphantly through this contest for liberty and rights; and when this "Star Spangled Banner" shall in triumph wave over all sections of our once happy country, when it may be said, and repeated of Gen. Washington, that he was the Father and founder of our glorious republic, then may you be guided safely to your homes, and posterity will rise up and call you blessed, that you sacrificed comforts and pleasures and endangered your lives to perpetuate our glorious Union and handing it down to them unimpaired.

The flag presented to the regiment was a non-regulation homemade wool bunting national flag. It apparently was a 33-star flag used for local celebrations, and had a thirty-fourth star added to keep the flag current with the number of states. Kansas had been admitted to the Union on January 29, 1861, and was eligible to be placed on the flag as a star on July 4. Thus, it appears that the local women added the new star for the presentation to the regiment. A black pentagon was painted in the central large star on the flag and a small star painted within the pentagon to give

Designating Flag
Size: 58¼" × 74¾"
1985.011

the flag thirty-four stars. In addition to the "11th Rgt. P. V." on the center red stripe, the ladies added the date of the regiment's organization, "April 26, 1861," on another stripe. They also painted the presentation date in the blue canton.

This flag was carried by the regiment until the Second Battle of Manassas. During the heavy fighting on Bald Hill, Color-Sergeant William Feightner was wounded and captured. Private Samuel Coleman of the 17th Virginia seized the flag and gave it to his bri-gade commander as a tropy. The flag was retaken in 1865 and returned to Pennsylvania in 1905.[13]

Designating Flag

On December 3, 1909, Colonel Richard Coulter, Jr., turned over to Adjutant-General Thomas J. Stewart the designating flag of the 11th Pennsylvania. This banner was one of a complex system of identification flags designed by General McClellan in 1861. Each regiment was assigned one of these flags, which, by utilizing different combinations of stripes and numbers, was supposed to make the battlefield identification of each regiment a simple matter for Federal officers. This system never went inot effect for all regiments and and was abolished early in 1863. Corporal Henry B. Temple of Company K first carried this banner and at Second Manassas, Private William H. West of the same company bore it into battle.[14] The combination of the blue "4" and arrangement of stripes designated the 11th as the fourth regiment, Third Brigade, Second Division, Third Corps, Army of Virginia.

Company E Flag

The Westmoreland-Fayette Historical Society has custody of a national flag presented to Company E by the ladies of West Fairfield in 1861. It was presented to the Society in 1938.

Notes

[1]Locke, p. 42.
[2]Bates 1: 266.
[3]Phil K. Faulk, "A Month of Battles," *National Tribune*, January 4, 1906; Bates 1: 251.
[4]Bates 1: 266.
[5]*Ibid.*; *O.R.* 20, pp. 507-508.
[6]Bates 1: 257-259.
[7]*Ibid.*, p. 266.
[8]*Ibid.*
[9]*Ibid.*
[10]Special Orders #14, September 8, 1863, Regimental Order Book, RG 94.

[11]Major John B. Keenan to Captain A. C. Paul, April 29, 1864, Regimental Letter Book, Westmoreland County Historical Society.
[12]Bates 1: 108-109; *Sunbury American*, July 20, 1861.
[13]Bates 1: 109; RG 94, Entry 178, Register of Captured Flags, #237. For a Confederate account of the capture, see "Four Years in the Ranks," an unpublished memoir by Alexander Hunter of the 17th Virginia, in the Virginia Historical Society; copy in library of the Manassas National Battlefield Park.
[14]"Flag of the Eleventh Pennsylvania Volunteer Infantry," *Annual Report of the Adjutant-General of Pennsylvania, 1909*, p. 16. For the only complete study of the designating flag system, see H. M. Madaus, "McClellan's System of Designating Flags, Spring-Fall, 1862," *Military Collector & Historian* 17 (Spring 1965): 1-14.

Bibliography

Bierer, Jacob S. Papers. Pennsylvania State Archives.
Coulter, Richard. Papers. Pennsylvania State Archives; Westmoreland County Historical Society.
Cruishank, G. L. *Back in the Sixties: Reminiscences of the Service of the Company A, Eleventh Pennsylvania Regiment*. Fort Dodge: Times Job Printing House, 1892.
Faulk, Phil K. "Battle of Cedar Mountain." *Philadelphia Weekly Times*, March 31, 1883.
_____. "Battle of the Wilderness." *Philadelphia Weekly Times*, October 25, 1884.
_____. "A Month of Battles." *National Tribune*, December 28, 1905, January 4, 1906.

_____. "South Mountain." *Philadelphia Weekly Times*, August 12, 1882.
Howe, George W. "Historical Outline of the 11th Regiment Pennsylvania Volunteers." *Journal of the Lycoming County Historical Society* 15 (Fall 1979): 6-17.
Lippy, John D., Jr. *The War Dog: A True Story*. Harrisburg: Telegraph Press, 1962.
Locke, William H. *The Story of the Regiment*. Philadelphia: J. B. Lippincott & Company, 1868; New York: James Miller, 1872.
Menges, Jacob R. Memoirs. USAMHI, CWTI Collection.
Penn, R. W. Papers. Pennsylvania State Archives.

23rd Infantry

State Color

Originally a three-months regiment, most of the members of the 23rd re-enlisted and the new organization was allowed to retain its old number for its three-years term of enlistment. After reorganizing in Philadelphia, the regiment proceeded to Washington and went into camp in the Bladensburg area. While here, the regiment received the state colors on December 15, 1861, presented by Speaker of the House Galusha A. Grow on behalf of Governor Curtin. The flag was made by Horstmann Brothers & Company, and was the only state color furnished to the regiment during its term of service.[1]

The 23rd, nicknamed "Birney's Zouaves" in honor of Colonel David B. Birney, was uniformed with a dark blue zouave uniform when it first enlisted. However, as these uniforms wore out they were replaced with standard issue uniforms, and after a few months the 23rd came to look no different from most other Federal infantry regiments. While in winter camp, Colonel Birney was given permission to add five companies to his command, but in February 1862 these companies were detached and used to form part of the 61st Pennsylvania.

After spending a quiet winter, the 23rd, a part of Brigadier-General Darius N. Couch's division of the Fourth Corps, embarked with the Army of the Potomac on McClellan's Peninsula Campaign. The regiment participated in the siege of Yorktown, and when the Confederates evacuated and retreated, it was part of the force that followed and fought at Williamsburg on May 5, 1862. The 23rd was only lightly engaged but did manage to arrive on the field in time to take possession of an abandoned enemy fort and plant the regiment's flag on the parapet to signal that the Rebel defenders had retreated.[2]

On May 31, 1862, when Confederate General Joseph E. Johnston attacked the two divisions of the Fourth Corps stationed near Fair Oaks Station, Couch's troops moved to the support of their hard-pressed comrades. The 23rd was one of the regiments that moved up to delay the Rebel advance until a new line could be formed in the rear. The regiment moved

State Color
Maker: HB

Size: 72 1/8" × 78 3/8"
1985.012

into a wood and attacked some Confederate units in flank, initially surprising them and driving the enemy through the trees until the 23rd was in turn forced to retreat by superior weight of numbers. During this fighting, Color-Sergeant Samuel F. Bolton was killed, and the entire color-guard became casualties. One of the men saw the flag on the ground, picked it up, and brought it back as the regiment fell back to its camp. There, together with the 67th New York, it held the enemy at bay for one and one-half hours before retiring to the new line. During this day's battle, the 23rd lost 129 soldiers.[3]

During the Seven Days' Battles the 23rd primarily did routine picket duty, losing very few men. Couch's division was not engaged during the campaign that culminated in the Second Battle of Manassas, and arrived on the battlefield of Antietam immediately after the end of the fighting there. The division was then attached to the Sixth Corps, with which it remained until the end of the war. At Fredericksburg on December 13, 1862, the 23rd was not heavily engaged, the regiment having but two men wounded.

At the conclusion of the Fredericksburg Campaign, the regiment retired the state color. Later, the third colonel of the 23rd, John Ely, remarked that the state banner was "war torn, pierced with bullets on the bloody fields of Fair Oaks, White Oak Bridge, and Malvern Hill, Va." In January 1863, the flag was sent to the regimental adjutant's home in Philadelphia.[4] When the regiment returned home in 1864, Colonel Glenn obtained the flag and elected to retain possession of it when he found that no adequate storage facilities had been developed to take proper care of the returned colors.[5] However, he did journey to Philadelphia and gave the flag to state care on July 4, 1866.[6]

Officers' Flag

After retiring the state flag, the 23rd's officers pooled some money to purchase a new flag that the regiment used during the rest of its term of service.[7] On May 3, 1863, the 23rd was engaged in the charge of the Sixth Corps at Fredericksburg with the regiment taking part in the successful attack on Marye's Heights, even though Colonel Glenn had no such orders. The regiment arrived at Gettysburg late on July 2, and was only marginally engaged as skirmishers during the rest of this titanic struggle.

The 23rd went into winter camp near Brandy Station and then was transferred to Johnson's Island in Lake Erie, off Sandusky, Ohio, to guard the prison

Right: Sergeant Francis M. Worth, Wounded at Cold Harbor

camp there. The regiment remained here until May 9, 1864, when it was ordered to rejoin the Army of the Potomac. Shortly after arrival the unit took part in the unsuccessful charge on the enemy line at Cold Harbor on June 1. During this charge, the 23rd lost over two hundred officers and men, including Color-Sergeant Francis M. Worth, who was wounded in both legs and taken prisoner after the regiment fell back.[8]

The regiment then moved with the Sixth Corps across the James River and participated in the opening phases of the operations around Petersburg. When Confederate troops invaded Maryland and threatened Washington, the corps was sent back to bolster the garrison, arriving in the city on July 12. Thereafter, the 23rd took part in the exhausting marches of the corps as it followed the retreating enemy into the Shenandoah Valley. Although there were occasional skirmishes, nothing of any major importance occurred before late August when the enlistments of the majority of the regiment expired. Those who had re-enlisted were consolidated into three companies and attached to the 82nd Pennsylvania until the end of the war.

Philadelphia Flags

Philadelphia women presented the 23rd with several flags during its term of service. The old three-months 23rd Pennsylvania had received a flag and it is possible that this banner was carried when the unit re-enlisted for three years. After the battle of Antietam, a new stand of colors was presented to the regiment; this gift included a pair of flank guidons. Finally, in December 1863, friends of the regiment scheduled a ball in Philadelphia for the benefit of the soldiers, the proceeds being used to purchase six hundred pairs of woolen gloves and a new flag painted with the names of the battles in which the regiment had fought. None of these flags seem to have survived. A small pamphlet describing the artifacts housed in G.A.R. Post 2 in Philadelphia includes mention of at least one flag of the 23rd. Many of these flags are now owned by the Philadelphia Camp, Sons of Union Veterans, and it is quite possible that one or more of the unidentified colors are these presented flags.[9] When the regiment returned to Philadelphia on August 26, 1864, three flags, "torn and stained, and covered with inscriptions of great battles . . ." were carried in the brief parade through the city.[10] These flags may have been the officers' flag and the two presented in 1862 and 1863.

When the color guards paraded in Philadelphia on July 4, 1866, the survivors of the 23rd marched with five stands of colors—the state flag, the banner paid for by the officers, and the three flags presented by the Philadelphia women.[11]

Notes

[1]"Presentation to the Pa. Twenty-third—Speech of Speaker Grow," *Philadelphia Inquirer*, December 16, 1861; Bates 1: 307, writes the presentation occurred on December 14.

[2]Wray, pp. 40-41; *O.R.* 11.1, pp. 515, 517.

[3]Wray, pp. 45, 129, 183. According to "The Twenty-third Regiment," *Philadelphia Inquirer*, June 10, 1862, Sergeant Bolton was killed by the first volley fired by the enemy, a bullet passing under one of his eyes, killing him instantly.

[4]John Ely To Governor Curtin, September 28, 1865, RG 19.

[5]John F. Glenn to James L. Reynolds, April 21, 1866, RG 19.

[6]For Glenn's participation, see "Our Battle Flags," *Philadelphia Inquirer*, July 5, 1866.

[7]Ely to Curtin, cited in Note 4 above.

[8]Wray, p. 160.

[9]Wray, pp. 31, 109; Bates 1: 311, 315; "Recollections of an Interesting Visit," (n.p., n.d.) p. (3).

[10]The Twenty-third Regiment Penna. Vols.,"*Philadelphia Public Ledger*, August 26, 1864.

[11]"Our Battle Flags," *Philadelphia Inquirer*, July 5, 1866.

Bibliography

"Birney's Zouaves, 23rd Pa Vols. Reunion and Tablet Dedication at Gettysburg." *Grand Army Sccount and Soldiers Mail*, August 21, 1886.

Glenn, John F. "The 23rd Regiment Pennsylvania Volunteers (Birney's Zouaves)." *Philadelphia Weekly Press*, April 28, 1886.

Miller, R. J. "A Close Call." *Grand Army Scout and Soldiers Mail*, April 24, May 1, 8, 1886.

Taber, Joseph S. C. Diary, July 15, 1861-August 16, 1863. USAMHI, CWTI Collection.

Wray, William J. *History of the Twenty-third Pennsylvania Volunteer Infantry, Birney's Zouaves, Three Months and Three Years Service, Civil War, 1861-1865*. Philadelphia, 1904.

_____. "Peril of the Left Wing at Fair Oaks. *National Tribune*, January 28, 1926.

_____. . . . *Report of the First Annual Reunion of the Survivors Association, 23rd Penna. Vols., Held at Maennerchor Hall, Philadelphia, Penna., May 31, 1882*. Philadelphia: William P. Kildare, Printer, 1883.

26th Infantry

State Color

This three-years regiment was organized soon after President Lincoln's election 1860, in response to the threat of secession, but was not accepted for service until May 1861. The regiment was then sent to Washington, where it remained in camp until April 1862. While in Washington, Company B was detached to guard the quartermaster depot, and did not rejoin the regiment until February 1863. The 26th received the Pennsylvania state flag in October 1861. This color was supplied by Evans & Hassall, and was the only state flag given to the regiment.

The 26th was assigned to Major-General Samuel P. Heintzelman's Third Corps, with which it remained until the corps was broken up in the spring of 1864. This corps participated in the April-May 1862 siege of Yorktown, and followed the retreat of the enemy up the Peninsula toward Richmond. During the Battle of Williamsburg on May 5, the 26th was deployed on the right of the Federal battleline, with one wing of the regiment used as skirmishers to prevent any Confederate troops from turning their flank. During the Battle of Fair Oaks on May 31-June 1, the regiment was not engaged, remaining on the extreme left flank of the army to guard against a possible flank attack by the enemy. When the Third Corps advanced toward Richmond on June 25, the 26th supported the skir-

mish line with four companies, but these troops were not heavily engaged with the enemy. Once McClellan began to withdraw the army to Harrison's Landing, the 26th's only brisk fighting was during the Battle of Glendale on June 30 when the regiment aided in driving back Confederate troops that had penetrated between the Third Corps battleline and the Pennsylvania Reserves further to the right.

At the conclusion of the Peninsula Campaign, the Third Corps was withdrawn to Alexandria and marched to join General John Pope's Army of Virginia in the campaign of Second Manassas. During the first day of the Second Battle of Manassas (August 29), Brigadier-General Cuvier Grover, commanding the brigade to which the 26th belonged, launched a bayonet attack that broke through Stonewall Jackson's line along an unfinished railroad embankment. However, Grover's five regiments were not supported and were forced to fall back to the main Union line. The 26th was guarding the left flank of the brigade during this gallant charge, and when the brigade began to retreat, the regiment found itself almost entirely surrounded and had to fight its way out, losing about 60 soldiers. The color-sergeant was shot down and the flag was almost captured, when Sergeant George W. Roosevelt ran forward, picked the flag up, and brought it safely off the field. He would later be awarded a Medal of Honor for this deed.[1]

After this unsuccessful campaign, the Third Corps remained in Washington and rested, and thus did not take part in the Maryland Campaign. After rejoining the army, the 26th participated as skirmishers in the defeat at Fredericksburg on December 13, 1862, losing very few men. During the Battle of Chancellorsville, on May 2-3, 1863, the regiment suffered about one hundred casualties. At Gettysburg on July 2, the 26th found itself as the extreme right flank of the Third Corps, with nothing between it and Gettysburg except skirmishers. When Confederate troops attacked the corps, the division was forced to retreat to Cemetery Ridge after the rest of the Third Corps line collapsed late in the afternoon. The division retired slowly, often turning about to fire on the pursuing Confederates. At each location where the Federals

Postwar Banner and Streamers
Banner Size: 18" × 61¼"
1985.013

Advance the Colors!

Sergeant George W. Roosevelt

stopped to fire, they left scores of dead and wounded comrades behind as they retired to the main line. The 26th lost heavily, with 213 of 364 officers and men as casualties, including three color-bearers killed.[2]

After Gettysburg, the regiment took part in the Bristoe Station and Mine Run campaigns before going into winter quarters. In 1864, when the Third Corps was broken up and merged into the Second Corps, the 26th was assigned to the Third Division of that corps. The regiment fought in the battles of the Wilderness and Spotsylvania, losing slightly more than one hundred men in both engagements. After taking part in the movement of the army to the North Anna River, the regiment was relieved from duty and sent home for mustering out. Those veterans who had re-enlisted were transferred to the 99th Pennsylvania. The remnant of the 26th Pennsylvania reached Philadelphia in early June 1864 and was mustered out of service later that month. The state flag was literally shot to pieces during the war so the veterans made a small banner that they attached to the flagstaff. This, together withthe numerous battle streamers, are all that remains to honor the reigiment that protected one of Pennsylvania's battleflags.[3]

California Flags

Mrs. Frederick McCrellish, wife of the editor of the *San Francisco Alta Californian*, and her sister both had relatives who joined the 26th. To show their patriotism in an area far removed from the immediate scene of the conflict, these two women decided to present a "regulation" silk flag to the regiment. This flag was presented to the regiment on January 17, 1862, Sergeant William S. Small of Company I being detailed as bearer. The regiment carried this banner throughout the 1862 battles, and then informed the presenters that the flag was so torn and pierced by bullets that it should be laid aside if it was to be preserved for the future. The war-torn color was sent to California via Panama, then by the steamer *Ariel* to San Francisco. This ship was stopped and boarded by the C.S.S. *Alabama*, but the Rebel sailors did not know that a Federal battleflag was aboard their prey.[4] The same two ladies prepared a replacement flag, which was presented to the regiment sometime in the fall of 1863.[5] The present location of both flags is unknown.

Philadelphia Flags

On June 15, 1861, the 26th received two flags from Philadelphia friends of the regiment. One of these flags, described as a "national," was the gift of Colonel William F. Small's wife and another woman. The second, a "regimental state flag," was obtained for the regiment by the three daughters of Mr. George F. Jones, at whose Girard Street residence the presentation took place.[6] Nothing further has been located about the subsequent history of these flags.

Company B Flag

The Anderson Guards received a "splendid silk American flag" on April 25, 1861, a gift from the ladies of the Kensington District of Philadelphia.[7] Nothing else is known about this flag.

Notes

[1] See George W. Roosevelt's brief description of his rescue of the colors in a letter to Adjutant-General R.C. Drum, April 12, 1887. John Tweedale, Chief Clerk of the War Department, noted in a June 9, 1887, letter to General Drum that there were no eyewitness accounts of Roosevelt's action, but the circumstances dictated that the veteran should receive a Medal of Honor for his actions at Bull Run and Gettysburg, where he captured a Confederate flag. Both letters are in Roosevelt's Medal of Honor file, RG 94.

[2] Taylor, *Philadelphia*, p. 52.

[3] In "Historic Battle Flags," *Philadelphia Times*, May 24, 1896, it is written that "the flag itself is gone, only the flagstaff remaining. . . ." However, the article "Our Battle Flags," *Philadelphia Inquirer*, July 5,

1866, remarking on the 4 July ceremony, noted that the veterans of the 26th brought along a "tattered battle flag." This flag may have been one of the presented colors.

[4] "Female Patriotism," *Philadelphia Inquirer*, November 11, 1861; "The California Flag Presented to the Twenty-sixth Pennsylvania Volunteers," *Philadelphia Inquirer*, February 16, 1863; Regimental Orders #22, January 16, 1862, Regimental Order Book, RG 94.

[5] Bates 1: 351.

[6] "Flags Presented to Colonel Small's Regiment," *Philadelphia Public Ledger*, June 17, 1861.

[7] *Philadelphia Public Ledger*, April 27, 1861.

Bibliography

Bartlett, William H. Letters. USAMIII.

27th Infantry

State Color

The 27th Pennsylvania stemmed from a Philadelphia militia unit organized early in 1861, a majority of the soldiers being of German birth. After being organized for three years, the regiment proceeded to Washington and helped cover the withdrawal of the army after the defeat at First Manassas. The regiment remained at Washington during the winter of 1861-62, during which time it was attached to Brigadier-General Louis Blenker's division of the First Corps. The state color, which had been supplied to the state in October 1861 by Evans & Hassall, was finally presented to the regiment on March 5, 1862, by Representative Robert McKnight of Pittsburgh on behalf of Governor Curtin.[1]

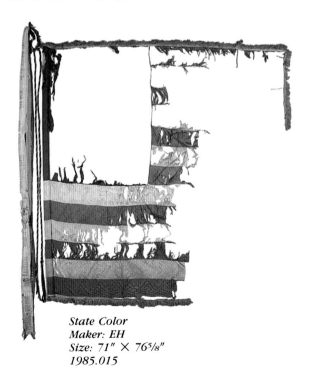

State Color
Maker: EH
Size: 71" × 76⁵⁄₈"
1985.015

In the spring of 1862, the division was transferred to Major-General John C. Fremont's command in West Virginia. Fremont fought a battle with Stonewall Jackson's Rebels at Cross Keys on June 8, 1862. The 27th lay in support of a battery during this battle which resulted in a Union defeat. Fremont began to

withdraw his regiments, but in the resulting confusion, the 27th and the battery did not receive orders to retreat. When enemy troops moved to surround the regiment, Colonel Adolph Buschbeck changed front to the rear, and in conjunction with a detachment of the 42nd Pennsylvania (Bucktails), drove the enemy back, saved the battery, and retired to the main Federal army. As the troops neared their friends, they were shelled by a Union battery, which did not cease until Colonel Buschbeck had the 27th's color-sergeant run in front of the column and wave the flag back and forth to signify that they were Federal troops.[2]

After the defeat at Cross Keys, Fremont was relieved and most of his troops incorporated in General John Pope's Army of Virginia, the 27th Pennsylvania being assigned to the First Corps. Pope's army concentrated in northern Virginia to oppose Lee's Confederates, who were on the march north after repelling the Federal attack on Richmond. Pope's smaller army was forced to retreat as the enemy moved north, the 27th forming part of the rearguard to dispute the Rebels as they attempted to cross the Rappahannock River. This campaign culminated in the Federal defeat at the Second Battle of Manassas on August 29-30, 1862. In this engagement, the color-guard had one man killed and several wounded.[3]

After the retreat to the Washington defenses, the 27th became part of the new Eleventh Corps, which did not take part in the battles of Antietam or Fredericksburg. When General Hooker embarked on the Chancellorsville Campaign in 1863, the Eleventh Corps participated in the advance to the Chancellorsville region and formed the right flank of the army. As Stonewall Jackson's surprise assault on the corps on the evening of May 2 began to rout many of the first regiments attacked, the 27th was one of a very few regiments to get into position for a show of organized resistance. But this battleline collapsed under the heavy Confederate pressure with the 27th losing fifty-six men. Among the wounded was Color-Sergeant Henry Rosengarten.[4]

After fighting in the the the Battle of Gettysburg, the Eleventh Corps was part of the reinforcements sent to Chattanooga to help lift the Rebel siege of this important city. The corps left the Army of the Potomac in late September and was moved by rail to Nashville, then to Bridgeport, Alabama. From here, the corps marched to Chattanooga to join General Grant's troops assembling at that city. Grant attacked the Rebel army in late November and gained a complete victory. The 27th was among the troops commanded by General Sherman who attacked the northern end of Missionary Ridge on November 25. A desperate bayonet charge temporarily enabled the attacking force to secure a lodgement near the summit of Tunnel Hill, but after two hours' fighting, during which time the 27th exhausted its ammunition, a Confederate counterattack drove the Federal survivors back. The 27th lost heavily in this futile assault.

Once Grant had driven the enemy away from Chattanooga, he sent Sherman with a detachment of troops to open communications with the Federal garrison at Knoxville, then also under siege by the enemy. The Eleventh Corps was part of this force, which marched most of the distance toward Knoxville before the enemy retreated, allowing the reinforcements to return to Chattanooga. After wintering near the city, the 27th participated briefly in the opening stages of General Sherman's Atlanta Campaign, which began in early May 1864. After skirmishing at Rocky Face Ridge, Dallas, and near Dalton, the remnant of the 27th was relieved from duty on May 23 and sent home to Philadelphia. There the regiment was mustered out of service on June 11. The tattered state color was returned to state care during the July 4, 1866, ceremony in Philadelphia.

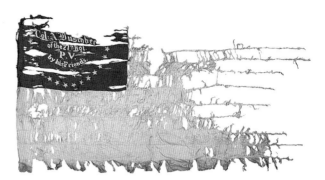

National Color
Size: 44³/₈ (-) × 84⁵/₈" (-)
1985.014

National Color

In addition to the state flag, the 27th also carried a United States flag for an unspecified period of time. The flag was inscribed for presentation to Colonel Buschbeck, who was promoted to colonel on October 2, 1861. Thus, this flag was presented to the 27th sometime after this date. When the regiment was forced to fall back after holding its position for over two hours in the unsuccessful charge at Chattanooga on November 25, 1863, the flag was one of eight colors taken by the Confederates of Major-General Patrick R. Cleburne's division.[5] The flag remained in Confederate hands until April 16, 1865. On that date, cavalry troopers of Brigadier-General Edward M. McCook's First Division of Wilson's Cavalry Corps attacked and captured the Rebel Fort Tyler at West Point, Georgia.[6] The banner was afterwards forwarded to the War Department, which returned it to Pennsylvania in 1905.

Notes

[1] "Flag Presentation to Penna. Regiments," *Philadelphia Inquirer*, March 8, 1862.
[2] *O.R.* 12.1, p. 676.
[3] Bates 1: 388.
[4] *Philadelphia Inquirer*, May 8, 1863.

[5] *O.R.* 31.2, p. 752. The official battle report by the 27th's Major August Riedt, found in *O.R.* 31.2 pp. 367-370, does not mention the loss of this flag.
[6] *O.R.* 49.1, p. 431.

Bibliography

There are no published materials on the 27th other than what is in Bates, the brief sketch in Taylor's *Philadelphia in the Civil War*, and in *Pennsylvania at Gettysburg*. As of the present writing, no unpublished letters or diaries have come to the author's attention.

28th Infantry

First State Color

The 28th Pennsylvania was raised in June 1861 by Colonel John W. Geary, already famous as the first mayor of San Francisco and one of the pre-war governors of the Kansas Territory. There were originally fifteen companies in the 28th. In November 1862, five of these were detached and used to form the nucleus of the new 147th Pennsylvania. After the defeat at Bull Run, the 28th was rushed into federal service and spent the rest of 1861 performing guard duty along the Potomac River in the vicinity of Harper's Ferry. In March 1862, the 28th crossed the Potomac and advanced into northern Virginia, occupying Leesburg and driving irregular Confederate cavalry and guerrillas out of this area.

Evans & Hassall completed the 28th's state color in early October 1861. Governor Curtin wanted to present the flag to the regiment in person, but his schedule prevented him from leaving Harrisburg. Finally, in March 1862, the Governor sent the flag to Harper's Ferry, where it was delivered to the 28th's quartermaster, who in turn took the banner to regi-

First State Color
Maker: EH
Size: 70⅞" × 76⅜"
1985.019

mental headquarters at Upperville, Virginia, on March 8.[1]

When General John Pope organized the Army of Virginia, the 28th became a part of Major-General Nathaniel P. Banks's Second Corps. The 28th took part in the advance of the corps to Front Royal in July 1862 and then, as most of Banks's troops fought Stonewall Jackson's Confederates at Cedar Mountain on August 9, guarded the vital signal station on Thoroughfare Mountain. Banks's regiments were decimated in this engagement, and Pope did not use the corps during the Second Battle of Manassas.

After the defeated Federals retreated to the safety of the Washington defenses, Banks's troops were reorganized as the Twelfth Corps, Army of the Potomac. The corps joined the army in the pursuit of Lee's troops in Maryland, the 28th arriving near Sharpsburg on September 16. During the bloody fighting on the 17th, the Twelfth Corps entered the battlefield and drove the enemy out of the East Woods into the Cornfield, where the assault by General George S. Greene's division bogged down. Greene's battered regiments managed to advance ahead of other Federal units. His thin line held for some time in the vicinity of the Dunker Church before Rebel reinforcements forced his command to retire from the field. The 28th lost 266 officers and men during Greene's attack, the second highest loss by a Federal regiment that day. All eight color-corporals were casualties, as were both color-sergeants. One soldier wrote that "we have not much of our colors to show, they being almost all carried away by the shells and balls of the enemy."[2]

Once McClellan returned to Virginia soil in leisurely pursuit of Lee, the Twelfth Corps was left in the rear to guard the army's communications, and the 28th did not take part in the defeat at Fredericksburg in December. However, when General Joseph Hooker marched part of the army to Chancellorsville in late April 1863, the Twelfth Corps was part of the general's flanking movement. On May 2, the 28th was engaged as skirmishers, and on the following day, the 28th was one of the last regiments to leave the works as the corps began to fall back after Jackson's troops threatened the right of the corps battleline. There was some momentary confusion in the ranks as contradictory orders were issued. Seeing this, General Geary dismounted and pushed his way to the front of his old regiment. Taking the colors, the general cried, "Men, follow your old commander." The regiment surged forward and helped repel a Rebel assault before retreating.[3]

After participating in the Gettysburg Campaign and in the pursuit of Lee's army back into Virginia, the corps was then transferred to Tennessee as reinforcements to the Federals besieged in Chattanooga. The 28th, after arriving at Nashville, was sent by rail to Bridgeport, Alabama, then marched overland toward Chattanooga. On November 24, 1863, the regiment took a minor part in Geary's assult on Lookout Mountain. Three days later, the 28th was part of the force that attacked the Confederate rearguard near Ringgold, Georgia, at Taylor's Ridge. The Federal commanders underestimated the defending force and the Twelfth Corps regiments were repulsed with loss.

After spending the winter near Chattanooga, the regiment took an active part in a naval expedition down the Tennessee River to destroy boats that could be used by the enemy to invade across the river. The 28th, now part of the Twentieth Corps, rejoined General Sherman's army for the Atlanta Campaign, which began in May 1864. Moving into northern Georgia, the 28th fought at Rocky Face Ridge and then was lightly engaged near Resaca and Pumpkin Vine Creek. In mid-June, the 28th was one of the regiments that charged the enemy positions on Pine Knob Mountain. Later that month, the 28th was under fire four straight days at Kenesaw Mountain until relieved by other troops. After aiding in repulsing Rebel General John B. Hood's attack on the Twentieth Corps at Peach Tree Creek on July 20, the regiment lay near Atlanta, skirmishing with the enemy until the city was occupied by the corps on September 4.

Geary's men remained in the city until early November when Sherman launched his famous "March to the Sea." The Twentieth Corps, part of the Army of Georgia, was one of the units that accompanied Sherman. The march was militarily uneventful until the army reached Savannah, which was placed under siege until the Confederate defenders evacuated in mid-December. The 28th was one of the first regiments that entered the city on December 21, marching immediately to abandoned Fort Jackson and raising the regimental flag over the works. General Geary's division remained behind as the Savannah garrison while the rest of Sherman's army marched north into the Carolinas. The division was relieved in late January 1865 and joined the army for the Carolina Campaign, which ended with the surrender of General Joseph E. Johnston's Confederates on April 26.

Second State Color
Maker: EH
Size: 72" × 79⅛"
1985.018

This campaign involved little fighting for the 28th. Once Johnston surrendered, the army marched leisurely north, reaching Alexandria in May 1865.

While the 28th lay encamped at Savannah, Colonel John Flynn requested a replacement state color from the Governor. Flynn's letter clearly expressed the feelings of reverence the men felt toward their flag:[4]

Well knowing the hearty interest felt by Your Excellency in any manner effecting the honor, or illustrating the loyal zeal and courage of the sons of the old Keystone—I take the privilege of addressing you—the 28th Penna. Vet. Vols. Inf. is at the time nearly destitute of what Genl. Meagher happily termed "the illuminated diploma of a nation's authority" viz. "a flag." The shattered and battle torn remains of the one we have, I shall be glad to place at your disposal, I think I may say without egotism that it is unsullied save by the hard hits it has received in many a well fought "field." In some day to come I trust it may have a place in the Archives of the State—a mute (as mutilated) witness of its presence where the gallant Hooker shook his sword at the Rebellion; proudly we have borne it aloft through the historic campaigns of the Glorious Sherman; on our entrance into this city at gray dawn of the 21st of December, we being the advance of Geary's command were ordered to move at once on Fort Jackson . . . the old flag frail as it was had to do duty by mounting the staff which the [enemy] had so long usurped, so with our old battle cheer up it went, there was a slight breeze blowing which nearly finished our old pet, but we kept it flying 'till the first steamer pushed up to us completing our connexion with the gulf. Should you deem proper to send us a New Flag, we are pledged in the future as in the past to carry it where the path of duty and honor may lead (unfalteringly). . . .

Second State Color

Governor Curtin requested a replacement state color for the 28th in late January 1865. The flag was sent to

Adjutant-General Russell by Evans & Hassall on February 6. Because of the difficulties of sending the flag to Sherman's troops, Russell retained the flag until April 6, when he forwarded it to James B. Nicholson in Philadelphia.[5] Mr. Nicholson went to see the regiment while it lay in camp at Cloud's Mills, Virginia, just outside Alexandria. He presented the replacement state color to the 28th on May 23.[6] The color was carried by the veterans in the 1866 parade and officially returned to state care at that time.

Philadelphia Flags

While in service, the 28th received at least two flags from Philadelphia friends of the regiment. Two of these colors were presented to the regiment on Octo-

National Color, Unidentified
Size: 68" × 71½"
1985.021

National Color, 1861 Presentation
Size: 70¾" × 70¾"
1985.016

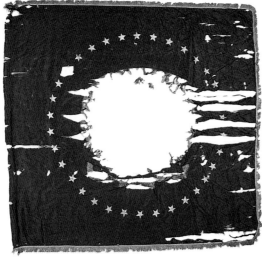

Regimental Color, 1861 Presentation
Size: 68⅞" × 72"
1985.017

ber 31, 1861. On that day, a Philadelphia committee headed by James B. Nicholson, Samuel R. Hilt, and Gilbert S. Parker, came to the 28th's Maryland camp and presented the flags. One was a 34-star national color, the other a regimental flag with the state arms on one side and the national arms on the other.[7] After receiving the two flags, the regiment paraded with them for the first time on November 28.[8]

It is not known when these flags were carried by the regiment. When the unit returned to Philadelphia for its furlough in January 1864, it paraded through the city before disbanding. A reporter noted that there were four flags all riddled with bullet holes.[9] These flags were probably the state color, the two Philadelphia flags, and the unidentified national color listed below. The two Philadelphia flags were possibly left in the city when the regiment returned to Sherman's army in 1864. When Colonel Flynn requested a replacement state color in January 1865, he also asked for a "State Flag, there being none on hand." This phraseology is mysterious, but since the colonel had already requested a state color, it is possible that Flynn meant a "state regimental" color by this last remark. If so, this would indicate that the 28th was not carrying the Philadelphia flags in January 1865.[10] The national flag presented in October 1861 was turned in to state care in 1866. The regimental flag was given to the state sometime between 1914 and 1922, when it was installed in Case #1 in the Rotunda.

National Color

The small remnant of this color makes positive identification impossible. This is probably one of the flags referred to by a reporter witnessing the parade of the veteran regiment through Philadelphia in January

Advance the Colors!

1864 (see above section). If so, the flag was certainly carried previous to the Atlanta Campaign, but it is unknown if it was carried in 1864-65. The remnant was turned over to state care in 1866.

Company A Flag

When the Pardee Guards, who would become Company A of the 28th, left Hazelton on June 25, 1861, the ladies of the town presented a "beautiful silk flag" to the men. Nothing further has been located about this flag.[11]

Color-Bearers

Names of three color-sergeants have been located. On July 10, 1862, Sergeant George Grady of Company G was appointed color-bearer.[12] The sergeant was wounded at Antietam on September 17 and discharged from service in December because of his wound. Sergeant Charles P. Kennedy of Company I was appointed bearer on January 12, 1863.[13] Kennedy was wounded at Chancellorsville on May 2. It is not known if he was still acting as bearer at that time. Sergeant Jacob G. Orth of Company D was carrying one of the regiment's colors when he was wounded at Chancellorsville on May 3, 1863.[14]

Sergeant Jacob G. Orth, Wounded at Chancellorsville

Notes

[1]John P. Nicholson Diary, March 8, 1862, Huntington Library. According to the *Philadelphia Public Ledger* of July 29, 1861, Company E was the original color company.

[2]"From the Twenty-eighth Regt., P. V.," *Pottsville Miners' Journal,* October 4, 1862.

[3]*Wilkes-Barre Record of the Times,* May 27, 1863.

[4]Colonel John Flynn to Governor A. G. Curtin, January 10, 1865, RG 25.

[5]A. L. Russell to J. B. Nicholson, April 6, 1865, Nicholson Papers.

[6]*O.R.* 47.1, pp. 725-726.

[7]Bates 1: 421; "Letter from Geary's Regiment," *Philadelphia Public Ledger,* November 4, 1861.

[8]Nicholson Diary, November 28, 1861.

[9]"Arrival and Reception of the Twenty-eighth Pennsylvania Regiment," *Philadelphia Inquirer,* January 11, 1864.

[10]Flynn to Curtin, cited in Note 4 above.

[11]"Departure of the Pardee Guards," *Wilkes-Barre Record of the Times,* June 26, 1861.

[12]Circular of July 10, 1862, Regimental Order Book, RG 94.

[13]Regimental Orders #8, January 12, 1863, Regimental Order Book, RG 94.

[14]*Philadelphia Public Ledger,* May 22, 1863.

Bibliography

Armor, William C. Papers. Pennsylvania State Archives.

Blundin, Lewis. "'Above the Clouds.' What a Pennsylvanian Knows About Lookout Mountain." *National Tribune,* October 21, 1886.

_____. "Cedar Mountain." *National Tribune,* May 13, 1886.

_____. "Cedar Mountain." *National Tribune,* August 18, 1886.

_____. "Comrade Blundin Wants Fair Play." *National Tribune,* July 8, 1886.

_____. "Lookout Mountain." *National Tribune,* December 2, 1886.

_____. "The Regiment that Supported the First Rhode Island Artillery at Antietam." *National Tribune,* March 18, 1886.

_____. "The White Star People. Comrade Blundin Again Brings His Gun into Position." *National Tribune,* January 27, 1887.

Brown, Henry E. "Lookout Mountain." *Philadelphia Weekly Press,* May 9, 1888.

_____. *The 28th and 147th Regiments in Penna. Vols. at Gettysburg.* n.p., n.d.

Cornet, J. L. "Pennsylvania Valor." *Philadelphia Weekly Times,* December 25, 1886.

_____. "The 28th Pennsylvania at Antietam." *Grand Army Scout and Soldiers Mail,* September 22, 1883.

Foering, John O. Letters. Historical Society of Pennsylvania.

Nicholson, John P. Papers. Henry E. Huntington Library.

_____. *Association of the 28th and 147th Regiments Infantry and Independent Battery "E," Light Artillery.* Philadelphia: Allen, Lane & Scott, 1882.

Stewart, James P. Letters, June 28, 1861 July 6, 1863. USAMHI, CWTI Collection.

29th Infantry

First State Color

This regiment was recruited in Philadelphia and mustered into Federal service in July 1861. After some preliminary military training, the 29th was sent to the Harper's Ferry area, and encamped through the winter of 1861-62 in Pleasant Valley, Maryland.

In the spring of 1862, the 29th, a part of Major-General Nathaniel Banks's command, crossed the Potomac and marched south to Winchester, which was occupied on March 12. Sometime during the period March 12-21, while the regiment performed picket duty near Winchester, the state color finished by Evans & Hassall in October 1861 finally reached the 29th.[1] The regiment spent some time in the Winchester area on guard duty, until Stonewall Jackson marched north with his troops to attack Banks's inferior numbers. Jackson struck Banks's retreating column just south of Winchester on May 25. More than one hundred men, including Colonel John K. Murphy, were captured as the Federal line folded and retreated through Winchester. Thereafter, a portion of

First State Color
Maker: EH
Size: 71½" × 78⅞"
1985.023

the 29th was incorporated into General Pope's Army of Virginia, and participated in the campaign of Second Manassas. Most of the regiment was detailed for provost guard duty at Williamsport, Maryland, falling back to Chambersburg when Lee's troops invaded Maryland in September.

After Lee's invasion was driven back, the 29th became part of the Twelfth Corps, which guarded the Army of the Potomac's rear during the Fredericksburg Campaign. The Twelfth Corps then wintered near Stafford Court House. While in winter camp, the state color was sent to Philadelphia to have the battle honor "Shenandoah Valley, VA.," inscribed on it. Evans & Hassall completed this additional lettering in January 1863.[2]

The corps then took part in the Chancellorsville Campaign of April-May 1863. Although the corps as a whole lost heavily, the 29th was lucky, losing only twenty-one men, as the regiment fought from the protection of breastworks until the corps was forced to retreat on May 3. At Gettysburg, the 29th took part in the heavy fighting on Culp's Hill on July 3.

After participating in the pursuit of Lee's defeated army, the Twelfth Corps was part of the reinforcements shipped to Chattanooga to help relieve the Rebel siege of that city. The 29th went by rail to Bridgeport, Alabama, then marched overland toward Chattanooga. When General Longstreet's Rebels attacked Geary at Wauhatchie on October 28, the 29th was on picket duty and delayed the enemy advance long enough for Geary to form line and repulse the more numerous attackers.

On November 24, General Hooker's forces opened the battle for Chattanooga by launching an attack on the Confederate force occupying Lookout Mountain. The 29th Pennsylvania received the honor of leading the advance against the enemy. The regiment had to contend with a forty-five degree slope cut by numerous gullies that made the ascent difficult. Colonel William Rickards, Jr., led his regiment forward through all these difficulties. His command was vying with the 111th Pennsylvania and 8th Kentucky to see who would be the first unit to reach the mountain summit in a battle that was obscured to those on

Advance the Colors!

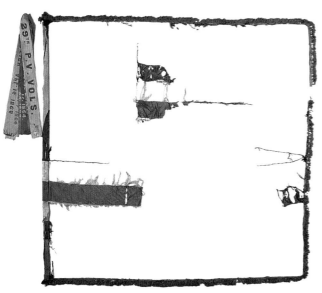

Second State Color
Maker: HB
Size: 72½" × 80¼"
1985.022

Part of the Canton from the Second State Color

the ground level by fog, an engagement said to be fought "above the clouds." After an upward assault covering over three miles, members of the 29th reached the summit and unfurled the state color to signify that Lookout Mountain, a key to Chattanooga, had fallen to men of Geary's "White Star" division.[3] Two days later, the 29th was engaged in the unsuccessful assault on the Confederate rearguard at Ringgold, Georgia.

Second State Color

During the regiment's veterans' furlough, a replacement state color was supplied by Horstmann Brothers & Company. The flag was ready for delivery on February 6, 1864, and sent directly to Colonel Rickards. The reinforced 29th left Philadelphia in March 1864 and returned to Sherman's army, encamped south of Chattanooga.[5]

The Atlanta Campaign opened in May 1864. The 29th was first engaged at Resaca on May 15, when the division charged the Rebel trenches, only to be repulsed with some loss, the 29th losing more than sixty men killed and wounded. During the fighting at New Hope Church, the 29th was under fire for eight days between May 25-June 1, sustaining few casualties. The armies next met in front of Pine Knob, where the 29th drove in the Rebel pickets and advanced to within one hundred paces of the enemy works before falling back to build breastworks. When the Twentieth Corps crossed the Chattahoochie River near Atlanta and was attacked at Peach Tree Creek on July 20, the 29th was one of the reserve regiments that was thrown into action to repulse General John B. Hood's assaults. The corps then settled down into

siege warfare, finally entering Atlanta on September 2.

Sherman began his March to the Sea on November 15, 1864. This march was devoid of any large en-

Second State Color, 1865

gagements and the 29th next lost soldiers in the brief siege operations at Savannah until that city fell to Sherman's troops. After garrisoning the city for one month, Geary's division rejoined the army and took part in the victorious northward march through the Carolinas, culminating in the April 1865 surrender of Confederate Joseph E. Johnston's army. Sherman's veterans then tramped northward to Alexandria, Virginia, where his regiments went into camp until they were disbanded. The 29th was mustered out of service in July 1865. The second state color was left at Camp Cadwalader and was officially returned to state care on July 4, 1866.[6]

Philadelphia Flags

During its term of service, the 29th received three flags from Philadelphia friends. Two of these were presented to the regiment on August 30, 1861. The presentation took place at the regimental camp in Jones Woods, near Hestonville, West Philadelphia. Lieutenant Lemuel C. Reeves of Company I presented the flags on behalf of the presentation committee. One of the flags was described as a national color, the other as a state color, quite probably a blue regimental with the state coat-of-arms.[7] These flags were carried by the regiment until June 1862, when they were sent back to Philadelphia to have battle honors painted on each.[8] Both flags seem to have been returned to the 29th and were carried in the December 1863 parade through the city.[9] At some point after the war both colors were obtained by G.A.R. Post 2 in Philadelphia, and were used during the regiment's fiftieth anniversary ceremony in 1911.[10] At present, the 34-star national color is owned by the museum of the Philadelphia Camp, Sons of Union Veterans. The regimental color is owned by a private collector.

A third color was the gift of a number of Philadelphia ladies. Mr. Henry M. Dechert travelled to the Virginia camp of the 29th and presented the flag on June 4, 1863. The gift also included a pair of general guide markers.[11] The subsequent history of these flags is unknown.

Unidentified National Color, 1865

Color-Bearers

The names of two color-bearers have been located. Both carried flags of the regiment during the fighting on Lookout Mountain on November 24, 1863. One bearer was Sergeant William Betzhold of Company H. The other was Corporal Charles H. Martin of Company F.[12]

Notes

[1]David Monat, "Three Years With Company G in the 29th Pennsylvania Volunteers." in Twenty-ninth Pennsylvania Collection, Historical Society of Pennsylvania.

[2]Evans & Hassall bills, RG 25.

[3]O.R. 31.2, p. 433.

[4]Colonel Samuel M. Zulick to A. L. Russell, May 25, 1866, and Colonel Rickards to Russell, May 30, 1866, both in RG 25.

[5]Horstmann sent the flag to the state on February 15, 1864, RG 25. According to the "Flag Memorandum" list of individuals who presented flags to regiments, RG 25, this color was delivered to Colonel Rickards in person, most likely during the regiment's 30-day furlough in Philadelphia.

[6]Zulick to Russell, May 25, 1866, RG 25.

[7]"From Colonel Murphy's Regiment," *Philadelphia Public Ledger*, September 5, 1861; David Monat manuscript cited in Note 1.

[8]"The Flags of the Twenty-ninth Regiment," *Philadelphia Inquirer*, June 12, 1862.

[9]"The Reception of the Twenty-ninth Regiment P.V.," *Philadelphia Public Ledger*, December 24, 1863. This article has the following statement: "The two flags of this regiment, the National and State Colors, were proudly borne by the color bearers and the tattered and stained silk bearing the evidences of fierce struggles, where bullets and fire were thickest, attracted the attention of all, and called for the enthusiasm of the people."

[10]David Monat to Henry M. Dechert, April 1911, in Twenty-ninth Collection.

[11]"The Twenty-ninth Pennsylvania Regiment—Presentation of a Flag," *Philadelphia Public Ledger*, June 9, 1863; Bates 1: 488; David Monat manuscript.

[12]*O.R.* 31.2, p. 433.

Bibliography

Anonymous. "Lookout Mountain." *Philadelphia Weekly Times*, August 31, 1878.

Callahan, Robert. "They Kept Going. A 29th Pennsylvania Man Tells How the "White Star" Shone on Lookout Mountain." *National Tribune*, February 19, 1885.

Leake, Adam. "The Youngest Volunteer." *National Tribune*, February 19, 1885.

Rickards, William, Jr. "Above the Clouds. The Brilliant Movement by Which Lookout Mountain was Captured." *National Tribune*, January 1, 1885.

Twenty-ninth Pennsylvania Collection. Historical Society of Pennsylvania.

The Pennsylvania Reserve Corps

The "Reserve Volunteer Corps of the Commonwealth" was created by one of the legislative acts signed into law by Governor Curtin on May 15, 1861. Curtin was fearful of the possible dire consequences of the shortage in the Pennsylvania militia caused by the mustering of twenty-five regiments into federal service. Since Pennsylvania bordered on a state of dubious loyalty, the Governor influenced the Legislature to authorize the raising and equipping, at state expense, of a force to consist of thirteen regiments of infantry, one of cavalry, and one of artillery, for defense of the Commonwealth. The men were to be enrolled for a period of three years, but if needed, the corps would be placed at the disposal of the federal government.

Accordingly, camps were established in Harrisburg, Pittsburgh, Easton, and West Chester, as the corps would represent all sections of the Commonwealth. Brigadier-General George A. McCall was placed in command of the corps, and it did not take long for the regiments to recruit more than enough men. Although the Reserves were numbered as "line" regiments, they were better known by their more popular "Reserve" designations. The thirteen infantry regiments, numbered 30th through 42nd, were known as the 1st through the 13th Reserves, and thus each regiment had two numbers. For example, the 32nd Pennsylvania was also known as the 3rd Pennsylvania Reserves. The artillery regiment, numbered 43rd, was better known as the 1st Pennsylvania Light Artillery, and the cavalry regiment, the 44th, as the 1st Pennsylvania Cavalry.

Once organized, two of the regiments proceeded to picket duty along the upper Potomac River, but the majority of the infantry regiments remained in the camps, finally moving to Camp Curtin. There, on July 22, 1861, they were mustered into the service of the federal government for three years. The corps then proceeded to Washington, where a camp was established at Tenallytown, Maryland.

On May 16, 1861, the day after the Reserve Corps was authorized, Governor Curtin signed into law a resolution authorizing him to spend the $500 given to the Commonwealth by the Society of the Cincinnati for the procurement of battleflags for Pennsylvania regiments. This money was used against the sum charged by Horstmann Brothers & Company for the state colors supplied to the Reserve Corps regiments. Since the corps represented most of the Commonwealth's sixty-six counties, and was the first organized body of three-years troops furnished to the government by Pennsylvania, Governor Curtin decided that the Society's money would be used to procure colors for the corps.[1]

The Governor also wanted to present the new flags to the Reserve Corps in person so he travelled to Tenallytown with the colors for the formal presentation on September 10, 1861. Early that morning, the nine regiments in camp were assembled in line, with the color companies formed in front, each colonel at the head of this company. At 11 o'clock, President Lincoln, Secretary of War Simon Cameron, Major-General George B. McClellan, together with a host of other dignitaries, entered the camp. Half an hour later, announced by a rousing artillery salute, Governor Curtin, his staff, and a number of distinguished Pennsylvanians rode into the camp.[2]

After exchanging greetings with the other dignitaries, the Governor proceeded down the line of regiments, handing the new flag to each colonel and stating that he was authorized to do so by the Legislature. After receiving the flags, the color companies wheeled back into line and unfurled the new flags to the September breeze. At the conclusion of the presentations, Governor Curtin returned to his carriage, stood up on the seat so all could see him, and delivered the following address, reproduced in full here because it represents the type of address that the Governor usually gave when he presented colors to other Pennsylvania regiments:

> General McCall and Men of Pennsylvania: Were it not for the surroundings, one might be struck by the novelty of this scene. Large assemblages of the people of Pennsylvania, on any occasion which calls them together for deliberation on subjects touching the general welfare and the public good, are always attended with a charm that fascinates. But when I look over the thousands of Pennsylvanians away

from the soil of their State, in arms, there is inspiration in the occasion.

I came here today on a duty enjoined by the Legislature of Pennsylvania. The remnant of the descendants of the heroes and sages of the Revolution, in the Keystone State, known as the Cincinnati Society, presented me with a sum of money to arm and equip the volunteers of Pennsylvania, who might go into public service in the present exigency. I referred the subject to the Legislature. They instructed me to make these flags and pay for them with the money of the Cincinnati Society. I have placed in the centre of the azure field the coat-of-arms of your great and glorious State, and around it a bright galaxy of stars. I give these flags to you today, and I know you will carry them wherever you appear, in honor, and that the credit of your State will never suffer in your hands.

Our peaceful pursuits in Pennsylvania have been broken. Many of our people have abandoned those arts of industry which lead to development and progress, and have been forced to bear arms. They have responded to the call of the National Government, and while you are here in obedience to that call, your fellow-citizens at home are occupying the camps you have lately vacated. All our material wealth, and the life of every man in Pennsylvania, stands pledged to vindicate the right, to sustain the Government, and to restore the ascendency of law and order. You are here for that purpose, with no hope of acquisition or vengeance, nor from any desire to be enriched by the shedding of blood. God forbid! Our people are for peace. But if men lay violent hands on the sacred fabric of the Government, unjustly spill the blood of their brethren, and tear the sacred Constitution to pieces, Pennsylvania is for war—war to the death!

How is it, my friends, that we of Pennsylvania are interrupted in our progress and development? How is it that workshops are closed, and that our mechanical and agricultural pursuits do not secure their merited award? It is because folly, fanaticism, rebellion, murder, piracy, and treason prevail over a portion of this land; and we are here today to vindicate the right, to sustain the Government, to defend the Constitution, and to shed the blood of Pennsylvanians, if it need be, to produce this result. It will do no harm to repeat here, in the presence of so many Pennsylvanians in arms, that in our State the true principles of human liberty were first promulgated to the world; and there also the Convention met that framed the Constitution; and Pennsylvania, loyal in the Revolution, now stands solidly and defiantly to arrest the treason and rebellion that would tear into pieces the sacred instrument of our Union of States.

My friends, one might regret to see so many men of Pennsylvania here in arms today. But there is a pleasure in the recollection that you have been willing to volunteer your services in the defense of the great principle of human liberty. Should the wrong prevail, should treason and rebellion succeed, we have no government. Progress is stopped, civilization stands still, and Christianity in the world, for the time, must cease—cease forever. Liberty, civilization and christianity hang upon the result of this great contest.

God is for the truth and the right. Stand by your colors, my friends, this day delivered to you, and the right will prevail. I present to you today, as the representative of the people of Pennsylvania, these beautiful colors. I place in your hands the honor of your State. Thousands of your fellow-citizens at home look to you to vindicate the honor of your

great State. If you fail, hearts and homes will be made desolate. If you succeed, thousands of Pennsylvanians will rejoice over your success, and on your return, you will be hailed as heroes who have gone forth to battle for the right.

They follow you with their prayers. They look to you to vindicate a great Government, to sustain legitimate power, and to crush out rebellion. Thousands of your friends in Pennsylvania know of the presentation of these flags today; and I am sure, that I am authorized to say that their blessing is upon you.

May the God of Battles, in His Wisdom, protect your lives, and may Right, Truth and Justice prevail.

Once Curtin finished, General McCall responded briefly and then dismissed the regiments.[3]

With few exceptions, the thirteen infantry regiments comprising the Pennsylvania Reserves all fought together as a separate division during their three-years term of service. The batteries of the 1st Artillery were dispersed and served with many different units. The 1st Pennsylvania Cavalry likewise served with the cavalry of the Army of the Potomac and thus the histories of these two regiments will be detailed separately later. What follows is a concise historical narrative of the services performed by the infantry regiments of the Pennsylvania Reserve Corps.

The corps remained in camp in the Washington area throughout the winter of 1861-62. While here, McCall divided his command into three brigades, and although regiments were occasionally shifted between brigades, this organization remained until muster-out. On December 20, 1861, Brigadier-General Edward O. C. Ord's Third Brigade, strengthened by the 13th Reserves and a battery of artillery, met a Confederate foraging party commanded by J. E. B. Stuart at Drainesville, Virginia. Ord's command drove the enemy from the field and won a small but important victory which was overplayed by the Northern press, anxious for any kind of military success.

To show the state's appreciation of the victory, Governor Curtin ordered that the colors of the 6th, 9th, 10th, 12th, and 13th Reserves be inscribed with "Drainesville, December 20th, 1861." Accordingly, the flags were sent to Philadelphia for the lettering. The flags were returned to the regiments by Speaker of the House Galusha A. Grow on January 11, 1862. The entire division formed in line to honor the regiments receiving the inscribed flags, but more than one soldier was not thrilled with the proceedings. Nathan A. Pennypacker of the 4th Reserves wrote his wife the next day, commenting that he just read the Speaker's oration in the paper, as he could not hear it from where he was standing with his company. "We did not enjoy it much as it was *so* bad underfoot. The mud was ankle deep and as we marched through the fields, the *mud* stuck to our boots, so much, that we could scarcely walk, but it was all for glory, and it is all right."[4]

When General McClellan embarked his troops for the Peninsula Campaign, McCall's division was assigned to Major-General Irvin McDowell's First Corps, charged with protecting the capital from danger. The division advanced in mid-April, occupying Fredericksburg as a prelude to McDowell's southward advance toward Richmond to draw enemy attention from McClellan's army. However, President Lincoln forced McClellan to change his plans for a two-pronged assault on the Rebel capital, and the Reserves were shipped by water to join McClellan's troops near Richmond.

McCall's regiments were attached to Major-General Fitz John Porter's Fifth Corps, occupying the army's right flank north of the Chickahominy River. McCall pushed his men forward to Mechanicsville, just a few miles from Richmond. When General Lee decided to attack Porter's isolated corps, McCall's men were the initial Federals his troops encountered. When word was received of the Rebel advance in force, including the nearness of Stonewall Jackson's command from the Shenandoah Valley, McCall pulled his regiments back into a defensive position behind Beaver Dam Creek, just east of Mechanicsville. Here, his eleven regiments (the 6th and 11th were temporarily detached elsewhere) were assaulted on June 26, the opening of the Seven Days' Battles. Every Southern charge was beaten back by a combination of effective artillery fire and the countercharges of some of the Reserve regiments, and at nightfall, McCall's men still held, having suffered less than five hundred casualties.

The division pulled back to join the rest of the Fifth Corps in a defensive position at Gaines' Mill. Lee and Jackson struck Porter's troops the next day. Late that afternoon, but only after some very stubborn and bloody fighting at close quarters, the superior numbers of Rebels broke through the valiant Federals and compelled a retreat. McCall's division was at first held as a reserve force, being sent to the front line by regiments whenever the enemy threatened to break through Porter's thin line. The 11th Reserves and the 4th New Jersey relieved other troops during the afternoon, but owing to the excessive battle smoke, failed to receive orders to retire. As a result, most of these two regiments were captured.

Porter pulled back across the Chickahominy as McClellan began to retreat to his new base of operations at Harrison's Landing on the James River. Retreat across the White Oak Swamp hindered the smooth withdrawal of the army and gave Lee the chance to interpose between some detachments of the Army of the Potomac. The Pennsylvania Reserves had been protecting the lengthy Artillery Reserve and its ammunition train on this retreat through the swamp. After getting the trains to safety, McCall's troops were detached to guard the vital New Market Cross Roads against any attack from the direction of Richmond.

McCall formed his men to guard this road junction, his twelve regiments (the 6th was still detached) fronting a large open farm surrounded by extensive pine woods. Confederate brigades commanded by General Longstreet launched a series of massed assaults against McCall's exhausted regiments on the afternoon of June 30. This encounter, known as White Oak Swamp, New Market Cross Roads, Charles City Cross Roads, Glendale, and Nelson's Farm, was the most stubbornly-contested engagement the Reserves ever fought. Longstreet's initial assaults were repulsed and the Reserves launched limited counterattacks. But, in spite of the early success of the Pennsylvanians and their artillery support, heavy Confederate numbers finally pushed the overmatched Federals off the field. Yankee reinforcements arrived as the Reserves were retiring and prevented any enemy advantage. All the Federal cannon were left on the field—most of the horses having been killed—and other Federal officers feared that the combat might again break out should the reinforcements move onto the field to remove the guns. McCall himself was captured when he blundered into Confederate pickets as he reconnoitered during the twilight. Every color-bearer in the division was either killed or wounded, but no flags fell into enemy hands.[5]

The remnant of the division was held in reserve during the remainder of the campaign. From a strength of some 8,000 men on June 26, the Reserves lost 3,067 casualties during the Peninsula Campaign. After resting for some time at Harrison's Landing, the division was moved by water to Aquia Creek and then marched to rejoin McDowell's corps, now a part of Pope's Army of Virginia. The division, now commanded by Brigadier-General John F. Reynolds, fought in the Second Battle of Manassas on August 29-30, 1862. The Reserves performed a valuable service during the Federal retreat on August 30, by making a stand on Henry House Hill and delaying Longstreet's assaults long enough for Pope's beaten troops to evacuate the battlefield.

Upon retreating to Washington, Reynolds was called to Pennsylvania to take command of the militia as Lee invaded Maryland, and Brigadier-General George G. Meade took command of the Reserves. The division, now a part of Hooker's First Corps, next fought in the battle of South Mountain on September 14, driving the defending Rebels from a strong position at Turner's Gap. Three days later, the Reserves opened the Federal attacks at Antietam, Meade's bri-

Advance the Colors!

gades driving through the East Woods and into the Cornfield before Rebel counterattacks drove them back. The Reserves lost another 1,000 casualties in these two engagements.

Still under the able command of General Meade, the division scored the only Federal success in the defeat at Fredericksburg on December 13, 1862. After waiting for the fog to clear, Meade's troops dashed forward, crossed a railroad, and hit a gap in the portion of the Confederate line held by General Ambrose P. Hill's division. Two Rebel brigades were surprised and went to pieces as the Reserves smashed through them. Advance elements of Meade's soldiers managed to reach the crest of the heights behind Hamilton's Crossing, but the Pennsylvanians failed to receive any support from other Federal units and Stonewall Jackson's counterattack pushed Meade's command out of its temporary lodgement. The Reserves lost 1,853 soldiers for this, the only Federal "success" of the day.

After the Fredericksburg Campaign, the Reserves were sent to the Washington defenses to rest and recruit. The division had seen some extremely hard fighting and needed this period of recuperation. While in the Washington area, Brigadier-General Samuel W. Crawford was assigned to command and would continue until the Reserves mustered out in 1864.

As news of Lee's invasion of Pennsylvania reached Washington, many of the Pennsylvania Reserves officers petitioned to have the division rejoin the Army of the Potomac in case there was a battle on Pennsylvania soil. After some delay, the First and Third Brigades were released to rejoin the Fifth Corps, while the Second Brigade (3rd, 4th, 7th, and 8th Reserves) remained in the Alexandria area. The division reached the Gettysburg battlefield during the morning of July 2, and was initially stationed with the Fifth Corps in reserve. As the Rebel attacks on the Third Corps opened, Federal reinforcements were sent to the left flank to prevent an enemy breakthrough. Crawford's division followed the rest of the Fifth Corps, reaching Cemetery Ridge just north of Little Round Top late in the afternoon. The general deployed Colonel William McCandless's First Brigade (1st, 2rd, 6th, and 13th Reserves) and the 11th Reserves of the Third Brigade, sending the rest of this brigade to support the left flank of the troops fighting on Little Round Top.

As Federal troops fell back to Cemetery Ridge, Crawford launched McCandless's regiments in a bayonet charge which halted pursuit of the defeated troops, the Reserves stopping along the stonewall bordering the Wheatfield. Later that night, Colonel Joseph Fisher's Third Brigade occupied the summit of Big Round Top to prevent enemy encroachment

there. On July 3, McCandless's brigade moved out late in the afternoon on a reconnaissance, driving the Rebels out of the Devil's Den-Wheatfield area, capturing many prisoners and a battleflag.

After the end of the Gettysburg Campaign, the division participated in the Bristoe Station and Mine Run campaigns, and then went into winter quarters near Brandy Station. During the opening of the Mine Run maneuvers, General Crawford wrote to Adjutant-General Russell, requesting new colors for the Reserves, noting that the colors of the regiments were "very nearly destroyed." As an added note two days later, Crawford remarked that since the 2rd and 13th Reserves had received flags presented by friends, it was not necessary to supply these two regiments with colors.[6] Evans & Hassall furnished second state colors for the 1st, 3rd, 4th, and 5th Reserves, while Horstmann Brothers & Company made the flags for the 6th, 7th, 8th, 9th, 10th, 11th, and 12th Reserves. Both companies completed these replacement state colors in December 1863.

Upon the opening of Grant's 1864 campaign against Lee's Army of Northern Virginia, the two brigades of Pennsylvania Reserves with the Fifth Corps were strengthened with the addition of the 7th and 8th regiments when the Second Brigade, still in the Washington defenses, was broken up. The 3rd and 4th Reserves were sent to the Department of West Virginia, where they took part in the Union victory at Cloyd's Mountain on May 9, 1864. After participating in the rest of General George Crook's campaign amidst the mountains of West Virginia, the two regiments were sent to Harrisburg, where they were mustered out of service on June 17.

Meanwhile, the balance of the division took part in the bloody struggle in the Wilderness on May 6. Crawford's men fought near the right flank of the confused Federal battle line, initially in support of General James S. Wadsworth's division of the Fifth Corps. Crawford's troops moved to the front and began driving the advancing Rebels back through the tangled underbrush. Soon thereafter, Crawford received orders to withdraw when officers noticed that his men had advanced too far and were in danger of being surrounded. However, not all the Reserves received the order to retreat in time. The 7th Reserves had indeed advanced too far and most of the regiment was surrounded and captured by the Georgia regiments of General John B. Gordon's Brigade.

The Reserves were next engaged at Spotsylvania on May 7-9, losing 166 officers and men in the attacks on the entrenched Confederates. During the movement of the Fifth Corps over the North Anna River fords, the Reserves took part in some heavy skirmishing against the enemy. The final battle in which the division participated was at Bethesda Church on May 30, only a few miles from Mechanicsville, where two years earlier, the division had repulsed Longstreet's attacks. On May 30, 1864, the Reserves fended off three assaults by the Southerners of Dick Ewell's Second Corps. On June 1, the three-years term of enlistment of most of the survivors of the Reserves was up, so the regiments were relieved from duty and sent to Harrisburg for muster out. About 1,200 returned home for a reception in front of the state Capitol on June 6, before they dispersed to their homes. Another 1,700 re-enlisted and were organized as the 190th and 191st Pennsylvania. All in all, the Pennsylvania Reserves acquitted themselves quite well, in spite of the initial problems with organization and election of officers.

Notes

[1]*Laws of Pennsylvania, 1861*, pp. 777-778; *A Synopsis of the Records of the State Society of the Cincinnati of Pennsylvania* (Philadelphia, 1909), pp. 120-121.

[2]Sypher, pp. 114-115.

[3]Bates 1: 542-544.

[4] Sypher, p. 141; "Flags of General Ord's Brigade," *Pittsburgh Evening Chronicle*, January 4, 1862; Nathan A. Pennypacker to wife, January 12, 1862, Pennypacker Letters, Chester County Historical Society.

[5]Sypher, p. 392.

[6]Samuel W. Crawford to A. L. Russell, November 13, 1863; November 15, 1863, RG 19, Immediately before Crawford formally requested new colors, he issued General Orders #11 to the division on November 6. This order read as follows: "The immediate attention of Brigade Commanders is called to the condition of the Regimental Colors of their respective commands. These standards borne so nobly on so many fields are identified with the history and career of each Regiment and will perpetuate its fame long after the organization has ceased to exist. The torn and tattered condition of these colors evince a degree of carelessness on the part of Regimental Commanders, that the General commanding the Division regrets very much to see and he directs immediate steps to be taken to repair these colors, so that unnecessary destruction may be prevented. Brigade Commanders will report to these Headquarters such Regiments of their commands whose colors are so far destroyed as to make further use unadvisable when efforts will be made to replace them from the State." In Regimental Order Book, RG 94.

Bibliography

Crawford, Samuel W. "The Pennsylvania Reserves at the Battle of Gettysburg." *Philadelphia Weekly Press*, September 8, 1886.

Eberhart, J. L. "The Pennsylvania Reserves. An Interesting Sketch of the Famous Crack Division." *National Tribune*, April 3, 1884.

Giles, James P. "The Pennsylvania Reserve Volunteer Corps." *Philadelphia Weekly Press*, June 2, 1886.

McCall, George A. *Pennsylvania Reserves in the Peninsula.* Philadelphia, 1862.

Patterson, Robert. "The Pennsylvania Reserves." *Philadelphia Weekly Times*, November 15, 1879.

Pennsylvania. Antietam Battlefield Memorial Commission. *Second Brigade of the Pennsylvania Reserves at Antietam; A Report of the Antietam Battlefield Memorial Commission of Pennsylvania and Ceremonies at the Dedication of the Mounments Erected by the Commonwealth of Pennsylvania to Mark the Position of Four Regiments of the Pennsylvania Reserves Engaged in the Battle.* Harrisburg: Harrisburg Publishing Company, 1908.

Pennsylvania Reserve Association. *Pennsylvania Reserve Volunteer Corps "Roundup," Wednesday and Thursday,. June 24, 25, Harrisburg, Pa., Together with a Roster of Comrades Present.* Philadelphia: Electric Printing Company, 1903.

_____ . *The Report of the Committee on the Services of the Pennsylvania Reserves at Gettysburg.* Philadelphia: J. B. Lippincott Company, 1889.

Sypher, Josiah R. *History of the Pennsylvania Reserve Corps.* Lancaster: Elias Barr & Company, 1865.

30th Infantry
(1st Reserves)

First State Color

The ten companies forming the 1st Reserves rendezvoused at a camp in West Chester before moving to Harrisburg. The day after the Federal defeat at Manassas, the regiment was ordered to Annapolis to perform guard duty until relieved in late August. Colonel R. Biddle Roberts then moved his command to Washington, where it joined the rest of the division in camp at Tenallytown, Maryland. While here, the regiment received its state color on September 10, 1861. Company H, the Carlisle Light Infantry, was the color company.[1]

After spending the winter in camp, the 1st Reserves marched with the division to occupy Fredericksburg in April 1862, then was transferred to the Army of the Potomac in June. The regiment participated in the Peninsula Campaign, fighting bravely in the engagements at Mechanicsville, Gaines' Mill, and New Market Cross Roads. Colonel Roberts received the special thanks of General McCall for his regiment's gallantry in this latter battle.

The Reserve Division then joined Pope's Army of Virginia and took an active part in the campaign that culminated in the Second Battle of Manassas, another Yankee defeat. Although heavily engaged on the second day of this battle, August 30, the 1st Reserves lost only twenty-eight men. The division immediately marched into Maryland to counter Lee's invasion of that state. At the battle of South Mountain on September 14, Colonel Roberts led his regiment in a charge against enemy troops lodged behind a stonewall in Turner's Gap. During this attack, Private Thomas McNamee of Company C carried the state flag. The assault was successful, and Colonel Roberts received the personal thanks of General Hooker for the 1st's performance in the fighting.[2] Three days later, the 1st took part in the bloody fighting at Antietam, engaging the enemy in the now-famous Cornfield. After returning to Virginia, the regiment participated in the charge of Meade's division against Stonewall Jackson's troops during the Battle of Fredericksburg on December 13, 1862.

Since the Reserves had lost heavily in the battles in which they had fought, the entire division was sent back to Washington to rest and refit. When Lee invaded Pennsylvania in June 1863, two brigades were sent to join Meade's army. The division, now directed by General Crawford, arrived at Gettysburg on July 2, 1863, and was held in reserve until late in the day. Crawford was ordered to deploy his men directly to the north of Little Round Top to prevent a Confederate breakthrough as Longstreet's Rebels drove the Federals back from the Peach Orchard line.

As the last of the retreating Yankees cleared Crawford's battleline, the general launched a charge against the pursuing enemy. Crawford later recalled that as the charge began, he found himself by the side of the color-guard of the 1st Reserves. Hoping to encourage the men, the general reached down from his horse to grasp the flagstaff from the bearer, who apparently was Color-Corporal George K. Swope, Sergeant Bertoless Slott having been wounded in the hand as the regiment started forward. Swope would not let the

First State Color
Maker: HB

Size: 69½" × 78"
1985.025

Second State Color
Maker: EH

Size: 71" × 79¼"

1985.024

general take his flag, but after Crawford reminded the corporal who he was, Swope allowed Crawford to take the flag and wave it back and forth in front of the advancing Reserves to encourage them to greater efforts. However, Swope clung to the general's trousers during the charge and reclaimed his precious banner when the regiment reached the stonewall bordering the Wheatfield. The regiment moved further to the front on July 3, clearing the enemy from the woods on the opposite side of the Wheatfield.[3]

After the conclusion of the Gettysburg Campaign, the division marched back into Virginia, taking a minor part in the maneuvers during the fall of 1863 in northern Virginia, before retiring to winter quarters near Bristoe Station.

Second State Color

Owing to the heavy fighting the Reserves had seen, Crawford recommended new colors for eleven of the regiments. The 1st Reserves received its replacement flag on December 17, 1863. This new flag was temporarily captured when an enemy force launched a surprise attack on the regiment's winter camp on March 24, 1864. Although surprised, the 1st Reserves man-

aged to rally and form a line. They counterattacked and forced the intruders to retreat across a railroad embankment. Enemy reinforcements arrived and they again charged forward, driving the chagrined Keystoners back. The regiment's color-bearer had established himself on top of the railroad and was captured in the melee as the 1st Regiment fell back. After reorganizing, the regiment again sallied forth and drove the enemy off the field. The opposition's color was almost seized, but the resourceful bearer tore it from the staff and ran to the rear, occasionally turning to defiantly wave the flag in the face of the attackers. By this time, both sides had spent their energy and declared a truce. It was only then that the men of the 1st Reserves definitely ascertained that their opponents were the hardy men of the 11th Reserves. However, this giant snowball fight had shown observers that the Reserves could fight in all types of weather.[4]

When Grant commenced his 1864 campaign against Lee's army, the 1st fought well but lost heavily in the battles of the Wilderness and Spotsylvania. On May 31, the regiment fought its last battle at Bethesda Church, and was relieved from duty the following day. Those who had not chosen to re-enlist were then sent to Harrisburg, where the regiment was mustered out of service on June 13. Both state colors were deposited in Harrisburg and were officially returned to state care on July 4, 1866.

Annapolis Flag

While the regiment was on guard duty in this Maryland city, it received a color presented by the loyal Union ladies of Annapolis. No more information is available about this flag.[5]

Company Flags

On June 25, 1861, two of the Lancaster County companies in the regiment received "national colors" from a committee of Lancaster citizens. These two companies were the Union Guards (Company B) and the Lancaster Guards (Company E). No further information has been found about these flags.[6]

Notes

[1]*Adams Sentinel*, July 31, 1861.

[2]*O.R.* 51. 1, p. 143.

[3]This information is from Crawford to Peter F. Rothermel, March 8, 1871, Rothermel Papers, Pennsylvania State Archives. However, a letter from J. R. Dobson to Crawford, June 16, 1882, Crawford Papers, Library of Congress, has a different account. Dobson recalled that the general

took the flag from Sergeant Slott, not from Swope.

[4]*Lancaster Daily Evening Express*, March 29, 1864.

[5]Spyher, p. 101.

[6]"Presentation at Camp Wayne," *Lancaster Daily Evening Express*, June 25, 1861.

Bibliography

Dennis, J. "The Fight on the Left of the Line at Gettysburg." *Grand Army Scout and Soldiers Mail*, October 4, 1884.

Flick, Henry. Memoirs, 1861-1864. USAMHI, HbCWRT Collection.

Gilbert, Charles E. *A Sketch of the Seven Days' Fight in Front of Richmond*. Gettysburg: J. E. Wible, Printer, 1880.

Minnigh, Henry N. *History of Company K, 1st (Inft.), Penn'a. Reserves, "The Boys Who Fought at Home."* Duncansville: Home Print, 1891.

Rupert, Alfred. Papers. Chester County Historical Society.

Swope, George K. "Pennsylvania Reserves." *National Tribune*, October 15, 1885.

Turner, John P. Company "A" History. Chester County Historical Society.

Urban, John W. *Battle Field and Prison Pen; or, Through the War, and Thrice a Prisoner in Rebel Dungeons*. Philadelphia: Hubbard Brothers, 1882.

_____. *My Experience Mid Shot and Shell and in Rebel Den*. Lancaster, 1882.

_____. *Through the War and Thrice a Prisoner in Rebel Dungeons*. Philadelphia: J. H. Moore & Company, 1892.

Way, Joseph. Papers. Chester County Historical Society.

31st Infantry
(2nd Reserves)

State Color

Recruited in Philadelphia, the 2nd Pennsylvania Reserves trained at the Easton camp before moving to Harrisburg to be equipped by the state. The regiment then was transported to Baltimore, but the commanding officer there refused to accept the regiment, because it had not been officially mustered in by the state. The 2nd then moved to Harper's Ferry and spent time there guarding the Potomac River. Owing to the muster problems in the command, four companies were disbanded in August 1861. Subsequently, three new companies were added, but the regiment never contained more than nine companies.

The regiment was on this picket duty and was not present at Tenallytown when Governor Curtin presented colors to the Reserve Corps regiments, but Woodward writes that the color-guard was sent to receive the state flag in lieu of the regiment's absence. The 2nd joined the division in late September and remained in camp during the winter. When McCall's command marched south to occupy Fredericksburg, the 2nd was one of the regiments involved, thereafter being transferred to the Peninsula with the division.

At the battle of Mechanicsville on June 26, 1862, the 2nd Reserves held the right of McCall's line and was heavily engaged in repulsing several Confederate attacks. During the fighting at Gaines' Mill the next day, the 2nd lost one of its color-corporals, who was mortally wounded. Two days later, the 2nd took part in the stand of the division at New Market Cross Roads. The regiment was one of those which counter-attacked the oncoming Rebels, the 2nd's battleflag approaching very near a Rebel flag as the two forces crashed together.

At the end of the Peninsula Campaign, the division was sent to join Pope's troops in northern Virginia. During the climactic struggle on August 30, the division was on the left of the Federal line, performing heroic service in holding the enemy attacks until other troops could reinforce them. After the division fell back to Henry House Hill, it launched limited counterattacks to drive back the triumphant regiments commanded by General Longstreet. As the 2nd attacked, Colonel William McCandless, although wounded in the thigh, took the flag and attempted to lead his men forward, but his wound was serious enough to have other men carry him off the field. The regiment also retired.[1]

The regiment next was engaged at Turner's Gap, South Mountain, on September 14, 1862. During the bloody struggle in the Cornfield at Antietam, Color-Sergeant William J. Fulton, Company H, was wounded.[2] Three months after the battle of Antietam, the 2nd fought at Fredericksburg, taking part in Meade's unsuccessful attack at Hamilton's Crossing. As the regiment lay prone in line of battle prior to this attack, an artillery shell cut the flagstaff in two. Color-Sergeant William Derr still carried the colors forward, but as the regiment crossed a wooden fence at the enemy line, the sergeant was shot down with a mortal wound, and two of the guards were wounded. Rather than be taken to the rear by caring comrades, Ser-

State Color
Maker: HB

Size: 71" × 77¼"
1985.026

Fredericksburg Battle Damage on Staff of State Color

Captain P. J. Smith took the flag from the fallen sergeant and planted it at the stonewall. One color-guard was killed and another wounded in this attack.[4]

The 2nd Reserves participated in the campaign in northern Virginia during the autumn of 1863, then went into winter camp near Bristoe Station. At the opening of the 1864 campaign, the 2nd fought in the bloody engagement in the Wilderness and at Spotsylvania. After some skirmishing at the North Anna River, the 2nd fought at Bethesda Church on May 31, after which the regiment was relieved and sent home for muster out, which was done at Philadelphia on June 16. Colonel McCandless kept the state flag in his

Obverse

Reverse

1864 Cooper Shop Presentation
Maker: HB
Size: 73″ × 74⅛″
1985.027

geant Derr insisted that others take the flag and lead the 2nd forward.[3]

After the heavy losses suffered by the division in 1862, it was sent to Washington to rest. When news was received of Lee's invasion of Pennsylvania, two brigades were sent to join the Army of the Potomac for the battle that would be fought on Pennsylvania soil. The 2nd Reserves arrived on the Gettysburg battlefield early on July 2, and was held in reserve until late in the day, when the division was sent to reinforce the left of the Federal line. After deploying north of Little Round Top, the regiment participated in the charge down the slope and across Plum Run Valley, to the stonewall at the Wheatfield. During this charge, Color-Sergeant James Toomey was wounded.

possession but turned it over to state care during the July 4, 1866, ceremony.[5]

Presented Flags

During its term of service, the regiment received two flags presented by friends. The first was on May 29, 1861, a gift of several ladies from Philadelphia.[6] On March 16, 1864, a committee from the Cooper Shop Volunteer Refreshment Saloon visited the 2nd's winter camp and gave the regiment a flag and a set of flank markers. Color-Sergeant Joseph F. Sweeton received this flag for the regiment.[7] This last flag was turned over to the state on July 4, 1866. The location of the other is unknown.

Notes

[1] See Woodward, pp. 175-188, for Second Manassas.

[2] *Ibid.*, p. 331

[3] *Ibid.*, p. 245. Captain P. J. Smith took the flag and bore it through the remainder of the battle. See "Philadelphia Heroes," *Philadelphia Inquirer*, December 19, 1862.

[4] Sypher, p. 472.

[5] McCandless to J. L. Reynolds, April 16, 1866, RG 19,

[6] Woodward, p. 31.

[7] *Ibid.*, pp. 303-304. However, the presentation plaque on the staff is marked September 1863, but the color was not delivered until March 1864. Since the regimental historian was careful to include reference to the flags of the regiment, and he does *NOT* include any September 1863 presentation, I believe the Cooper Shop's gift was not delivered until 1864. See "Flag Presentation," *Philadelphia Public Ledger*, March 17, 1864.

Bibliography

Hamilton, William. Papers. Library of Congress.

Woodward, Evan M. *Our Campaigns; or, the Marches, Bivouacs, Battles, Incidents of Camp Life and History of Our Regiment During Its Three Years Term of Service*. Philadelphia: John E. Potter and Company, 1865.

32nd Infantry
(3rd Reserves)

First State Color

Primarily from Philadelphia, Bucks, and Berks counties, the 3rd Pennsylvania Reserves was formed at the Easton camp in June 1861. The new regiment moved to Washington in July, remaining in the Tenallytown camp most of the winter. Together with most of the division, the 3rd received its first state color on September 10, 1861, from Governor Curtin in person.

After participating in McCall's advance to and the occupation of Fredericksburg, the 3rd was transferred to the Army of the Potomac in June 1862. The regiment fought in the battles of Mechanicsville, Gaines' Mill, and New Market Cross Roads, losing nearly two hundred men in these three engagements. In this last battle, the 3rd recaptured the state color of the 7th Reserves, which had been taken when the Rebel troops temporarily seized Cooper's Battery B, 1st Pennsylvania Light Artillery.

First State Color
Maker: HB
Size: 71½" × 65⅛" (-)
1985.028

The division was then moved to Aquia Creek and marched to join Pope's Army of Virginia. It was engaged at the Second Battle of Manassas on August 29-30, 1862, helping to stem the Rebel assaults long enough for the beaten Federals to retreat from the field. During the Maryland Campaign which followed immediately, the 3rd was not engaged at South Mountain, but fought at Antietam, where the regiment lost over fifty men as casualties. The regiment then participated in Meade's attack at Fredericksburg, the 3rd being the last of the Reserves to retreat from the hill crest the division temporarily occupied.

After Fredericksburg, the division was sent to Washington to rest. The Second Brigade, to which the 3rd belonged, was stationed in the defenses of Alexandria. Owing to the excessive battle damage, the regimental historian described the state color as "so torn and damaged by the enemy's balls that it was necessary to carry them with the covers on, except in battle."[1]

Second State Color

As a result of such heavy battle damage, the 3rd received a replacement flag on December 17, 1863. In January 1864, having been stationed in Alexandria for almost a year, the 3rd and 4th were detached from the brigade and sent to West Virginia for duty. The regiment went by rail to Martinsburg, where it performed guard duty between there and New Creek for about three months. In April, the regiment was concentrated near Charlestown as one of the regiments detailed to participate in Brigadier-General George Crook's raid up the Kanawha River Valley.

Crook started on May 2, 1864. After many miles of relatively uneventful marching, the expedition fought an engagement with Rebel troops at Cloyd's Mountain on May 9. While other Federal regiments worked their way around the enemy flanks, Colonel Horatio G. Sickel's brigade launched a frontal assault on the enemy position. Although exposed to a heavy fire of both musketry and artillery, in which three

Second State Color
Maker: EH

Size: 71⅝" × 77⅞"
1985.029

3rd marched back to the expedition's starting point, then went via steamer to Pittsburgh, and by rail to Philadelphia, where the regiment was mustered out of service on June 16. Sergeant T. Watson Bewley of Company C was the regiment's last color-bear.[2] Both state colors were turned over to the adjutant-general and included in the July 4, 1866, ceremony in Philadelphia.

Notes

[1]Woodward, pp. 228-229.
[2]"Returned Soldiers," *Bucks County Intelligencer*, July 5, 1864.

Bibliography

Boyer, John H. Letters. USAMHI, CWMisc Collection.
Briner, Albert. Letter, November 23, 1861. USAMHI, HbCWRT Collection.
[Leake, William H.] "The Chaplain of the 3rd Pennsylvania Reserves." *National Tribune*, December 25, 1884.
Woodward, Evan M. *History of the Third Pennsylvania Reserve*. Trenton: MacCrellish & Quigley, Printers, 1883.
Wright, Albert A. 1864 Diary. In George J. Fluhr Collection, USAMHI.

color-bearers were shot down, the brigade reached the enemy works just as they began to retreat. After marching several more days, the 3rd's term of enlistment expired. In company with the 4th Reserves, the

33rd Infantry
(4th Reserves)

First State Color
Maker: HB

Size: 72¼" × 78"
1985.030

First State Color

The 33rd Pennsylvania Volunteer Infantry, organized at Easton, initially proceeded to Baltimore for duty. The regiment reported at the division camp at Tenallytown in late August. The 4th was on picket duty when Governor Curtin presented the state colors on September 10, but the 4th's color-guard marched to the ceremony and Corporal M. H. Vanscoten of Company H received the state flag from Curtin.[1]

After marching to Fredericksburg in April-May 1862, the division was transported by water to join McClellan's troops in front of Richmond. When Lee opened the Seven Days' Battles by attacking the Reserve Division at Mechanicsville on June 26, the 4th Reserves was held in reserve and did not take an active part in the battle. However, the Battle of Gaines' Mill on June 27 resulted in a heavy loss to the regiment. After supporting other sectors of the Federal line, the 4th was ordered to the extreme left of the line. Here, it repulsed several Rebel attacks before being overwhelmed and forced to retreat across the Chickahominy River to avoid being captured.

During the heavy fighting at New Market Cross Roads on June 30, the 4th Reserves supported Ran-

dol's Regular Army battery, repulsing several charges before a determined Confederate attack forced its way into the battery, where some desperate hand-to-hand fighting took place. In the words of General Mc-Call: "It was here my fortune to witness one of the fiercest bayonet fights that perhaps ever occurred on this continent. Bayonet wounds, mortal or slight, were given and received. I saw skulls crushed by the butts of muskets, and every effort made by either party in this life-or-death struggle, proving indeed that here Greek had met Greek." Captain Thomas F. B. Tapper personally rescued his regiment's flag during one of these enemy attacks. Seeing the color in danger of capture, the captain rushed headlong into the fray with drawn sword. After striking down a Southern officer who had just seized the flag, Tapper retrieved the banner and carried it to the rear in safety.[2] The regiment lost two hundred of six hundred men in these two battles.

After being transferred to northern Virginia, the 4th Reserves next was in action on August 29-30, in the Second Battle of Manassas, but escaped with slight loss. The regiment fought at South Mountain on September 14, and then advanced with the division into the Cornfield at Antietam on September 17, losing about fifty soldiers in this action. In its final battle action of 1862, the 4th charged with the division against Jackson's line at Fredericksburg on December 13. Shortly after the conclusion of this campaign, the division was transferred to Washington to rest, the 4th Reserves being stationed in Alexandria.

Damage to Staff of First State Color

Second State Color
Maker: EH

Size: 71" × 77½"
1985.031

Second State Color

The Second Brigade of the Reserves, to which the 4th was attached, remained in the Washington defenses until early 1864. While here, the regiment received a replacement state color on December 17, 1863. A few weeks later, both the 3rd and 4th Reserves were detached and sent to West Virginia. First stationed in the Martinsburg area, the two regiments then were marched to a point near Charlestown where an expedition was being formed to operate against railroads supplying Lee's army. This expedition fought a small engagement against Confederate troops at Cloyd's Mountain on May 9, 1864. The brigade to which the two regiments belonged launched a frontal assault against the enemy during which two color-bearers of the 4th were shot down. Shortly after this battle, the 4th's enlistment time expired. The unit was transported by river to Pittsburgh, then by rail to Philadelphia where the 4th was mustered out on June 15. Lieutenant-Colonel Thomas F. B. Tapper kept both state colors when the regiment was disbanded, explaining later that he was told to be in no hurry to turn them in, since they could not receive proper care.[2] However, the colonel turned them in on July 4, 1866.

First and Second State Colors, 1865

Presented Flag

The War Library and Museum has custody of a presented flag of the 4th Reserves. It is a crudely-made replica of the state battle flag, but no documentation for this color exists. It was housed in the Samuel K. Zook G.A.R. Post in Norristown for an undetermined period of time and then was obtained by two different collectors before being purchased by MOLLUS.

Color-Bearer

During the Battle of Cloyd's Mountain on May 9, 1864, it seems that the 4th Reserves carried both state colors. One of the bearers was wounded and his place was taken by Sergeant C. W. Whiteman of Company G, who was instantly killed, "but the colors were again raised triumphantly." Colonel Tapper remarked that the first state color was pierced with eight shots, the second with nine.[4]

Notes

[1]Statement of Corporal Vanscoten, in *Second Brigade at Antietam*, p. 62.

[2]Bates Alexander, "Pennsylvania Reserves," *Hummelstown Sun*, November 2, 1894.

[3]Tapper to J. L. Reynolds, April 16, 1866, RG 19.
[4]*O.R.* 37.1, p. 32.

Bibliography

Henry, William H. Letters of July 15, 1861, and October 16, 1862. USAMHI.

Pennypacker, Nathan A. Letters. Chester County Historical Society.

Vanscoten, M. H. *The Conception, Organization and Campaigns of Company H," 4th Penn. Reserve, Volunteer Corps, 33 Regiment in Line, 1861-5* Tunkhannock: Baldwin & Chapman, 1885.

Advance the Colors!

34th Infantry
(5th Reserves)

First State Color

Recruited in the Commonwealth's central counties, the 5th Reserves was formed at Camp Curtin in June 1861. The regiment, in company with the 13th and an artillery battery, was then sent to Cumberland, Maryland, where it performed garrison duty until relieved in late July. The 5th proceeded to the Tenallytown camp, and when Governor Curtin arrived to present colors to the division, the regiment was given the honor of escorting the Governor into camp.

After the April-May 1862 occupation of Fredericksburg, the regiment moved with the division to join McClellan's army near Richmond. At the battle of Mechanicsville on June 26, the regiment lost some fifty casualties while repulsing several Confederate attacks on the Federal position. After participating in the fighting at Gaines' Mill on June 27, the 5th lost heavily at New Market Cross Roads on June 30. Colonel Seneca G. Simmons was killed as the regiment

Pieces of the First State Color

counterattacked and drove back one of the many Rebel assaults of the day. During this fighting, the flagstaff was shot in two while in the color-sergeant's hands. Spying a small sapling growing nearby, the guards cut it down, stripped the bark, and attached the flag to it. This staff has lasted to the present day.[1] The flag was apparently lost to the enemy for a short time because Colonel James T. Kirk of the 10th Reserves reported later that his regiment recaptured a stand of American colors, said to be that of the 5th Reserves. As this regiment retreated after repulsing an enemy attack, it returned the flag to the 5th.[2] When the regiment finally retired from the field, Captain Frank Zentmyer of Company I took the torn flag from yet another bearer and carried it from the field. A corporal of the Slifer Guards tersely wrote home that ". . . the spear and tassels are gone, and the flag is full of holes."[3]

The division joined General Pope's army in northern Virginia, seeing action during the Second Battle of Manassas on August 29-30, 1862. After more battle action at South Mountain and Antietam, where the 5th lost very few men, the regiment took part in Meade's attack at Fredericksburg on December 13. The 5th held the left of the line during the attack,

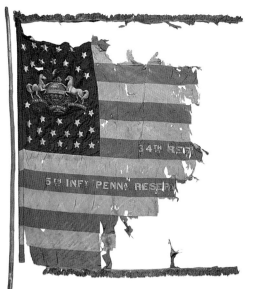

First State Color Size: 70⅞" × 71¾" (-)
Maker: HB 1985.033

Second State Color
Maker: EH

Size: 70½" × 77⅜"
1985.032

conclusion of the autumn maneuvers in northern Virginia, the regiment was stationed at Alexandria to guard the railroad against Confederate guerrillas.

Second State Color

While in Alexandria, the regiment received a replacement state color in December 1863. The 5th was relieved from guard duty and rejoined the division, now a part of the Fifth Corps, in time to participate in the battles of the Wilderness, Spotsylvania, the North Anna River, and Bethesda Church. Its term of enlistment then expired and the 5th was sent to Harrisburg, where it was mustered out on June 11. Both state colors were left with the state's military department and officially returned to state care on July 4, 1866.

Company C Flag

On May 1, 1861, the Washington Cadets received a "beautifully embellished silk banner" from Miss Sophia McLeod. The presentation took place in front of the armory in Clearfield. Judging from the presentation speech, it appears that this flag was some type of stars and stripes, but nothing further has been located concerning its subsequent history.[5]

Color-Bearer

Corporal William Kohler of Company H was mentioned as one of the regiment's color-bearers on a list of men to receive passes for the 1866 parade. According to Bates, Corporal Kohler was wounded at Spotsylvania on May 12, 1864, and was absent in the hospital at muster out.[6]

losing more than 150 officers and men. The color-sergeant was shot down during the fighting, whereupon Corporal James C. Voris seized the fallen color. Voris, a twenty-two year old from Sunbury, soon received a mortal wound, but continued to wave the flag until he collapsed. The young soldier's courage and bravery in the face of death was an act which inspired all who witnessed it.[4] The division was then transferred to the Washington defenses to rest. When Lee invaded Pennsylvania, the First and Third Brigades of the division were sent to rejoin the army. On July 2, 1863, at Gettysburg, the 5th was one of the regiments that occupied the summit of Big Round Top during the evening of that same day. Upon the

Notes

[1]"An Hour Among the Battle-Flags," *Harrisburg Daily State Journal*, September 22, 1873.

[2]*O.R.* 11.2, p. 425.

[3]*Bellefonte Central Press*, July 25, 1862; *Union County Star and Lewisburg Chronicle*, July 15, 1862.

[4]*Sunbury Gazette*, February 7, March 14, 1863.

[5]"Flag Presentation—Interesting Ceremony," *Clearfield Republican*, May 8, 1861.

[6]Bates 1: 686; Note from Colonel J. W. Fisher, July 3, 1866, RG 25.

Bibliography

Treziynlny, J. Frank. 1862 Diary, August 23 - September 3. In Dawson Flinchbaugh Collection, USAMHI, HbCWRT Collection.

35th Infantry
(6th Reserves)

First State Color

Organized in June 1861, the 6th Pennsylvania Reserves was first moved to Washington, taking up camp at Tenallytown, Maryland. The regiment was one of those which received its state color on September 10, 1861, during the presentation by Governor Curtin. When Brigadier-General Edward O. C. Ord's Third Brigade marched out the Leesburg Pike to Drainesville on December 20, 1861, it met and defeated a Confederate foraging party of similar size, a small victory but nevertheless a morale-boosting event for the Northern press, which played the engagement for more than it was worth. Governor Curtin, in recognition of the Reserves' victory, ordered that ''Drainesville, December 20, 1861,'' be inscribed on the colors of the five regiments that participated in this small engagement. The entire division was drawn up for a review when these flags were returned from Washington on January 11, 1862.[1]

After the May 1862 occupation of Fredericksburg, the division joined McClellan's army on the Penin-

sula. The 6th Reserves was detached from McCall's command and posted as guards at Tunstall's Station and White House, the main Federal supply base. Thus, the regiment missed the hard fighting in which the rest of the division participated. The 6th's first major engagement with the enemy was at the Second Battle of Manassas, August 29-30, 1862. As the division made a stand on Henry House Hill on the second day of the battle, the flagstaff was hit and broken as Major Henry J. Madill carried it while leading his men. Immediately after this happened, Brigadier-General John F. Reynolds, in command of the division, grabbed the splintered staff and rode up and down in front of the division battle line, waving the colors back and forth to encourage his men to greater efforts.[2]

Following Second Manassas, the 6th next contested with the enemy at South Mountain on September 14, and three days later was engaged at Antietam, losing well over one hundred men on the war's bloodiest day. At Fredericksburg on December 13, the 6th again lost heavily, its casualties numbering one-third of those engaged.

The division then was rotated to Washington to rest and refit. As news arrived of Lee's invasion of the Keystone State, officers petitioned to release the division for combat on its native soil. Two brigades were sent and joined the army in time to fight at Gettysburg. As the 6th Reserves marched through Drainesville en route to join Meade's Army of the Potomac, the state color, now bearing the inscription earned there in 1861, was unfurled to the breeze so the townspeople could see that those same hated Yankees were still alive.[3] At Gettysburg, the 6th was part of the force that charged down the slope of Little Round Top to cover the retreat of other Federal regiments on July 2.

Second State Color

Subsequent to the ending of the autumn campaign in northern Virginia, the regiment went into camp near Brandy Station. A second state color was received in

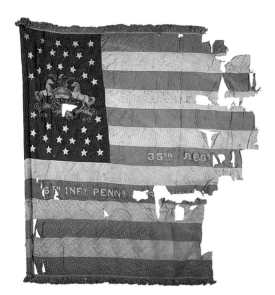

First State Color　　*Size: 70 1/2" × 71 5/8" (-)*
Maker: HB　　*1985.034*

December 1863. This color was carried in the opening stages of the 1864 campaign, prior to the regiment's relief from duty on June 1. The regiment fought in the Wilderness, at Spotsylvania, on the North Anna River, and at Bethesda Church, and was then sent to Harrisburg for muster out later in June. Both state colors were left in Harrisburg and officially returned to state control on July 4, 1866.

Second State Color
Maker: HB
Size: 73¼" × 76¾"
1985.035

Notes

[1] January 11, 1862, entry in Jacob Heffelfinger Diary, USAMHI (Heffelfinger was a member of the 7th Reserves).
[2] Bates 1: 697.

[3] Benjamin Ashenfelter to father July 29, 1863, Ashenfelter Letters. The flag may have been carried by Sergeant George W. Deen of Company E, who is listed as bearer in Special Orders #2, January 13, 1863, Regimental Order Book, RG 94.

Bibliography

Ashenfelter, Benjamin F. Letters. USAMHI, HbCWRT Collection.
Crocker, Silas W. "Fredericksburg. The Charge of the Pennsylvania Reserves." *National Tribune*, January 10, 1889.
———. "Gettysburg. The Part Taken by the 6th Pennsylvania Reserves." *National Tribune*, October 15, 1885.

———. "The Horrors of Salisbury Prison." *National Tribune*. September 16, 1882.
Janeski, Paul. *A Civil War Soldier's Last Letters*. N.p., n.d. (Member of Company H, killed September 16, 1862).
Wheaton, Francis E. Letter, May 17, 1862. USAMHI, CWMisc Collection.

36th Infantry
(7th Reserves)

First State Color

Organized at West Chester in June 1861, the 7th Pennsylvania Reserves first moved to a temporary camp outside Washington, and entered the Tenallytown camp on August 2. The regiment received its state color on September 10, and spent the winter of 1861-1862 training for the cam-

First State Color

First State Color
Maker: HB

Size: 72¼″ × 76⅝″
1985.036

paigns ahead of them. Private Adam Wray of Company F, the only Danville native in the regiment, was selected as bearer. Although a private, Wray had been a color-bearer in the Mexican War and was chosen as bearer for his experience.[1]

After the occupation of Fredericksburg in May 1862, the entire division was transferred by water to the Army of the Potomac near Richmond. First engaged with the enemy at Mechanicsville on June 26, the regiment fought again the next day at Gaines' Mill, where the 7th was moved about to three different places in line to reinforce threatened breakthroughs. On June 30, the regiment battled superior numbers of the enemy during the heavy combat at New Market Cross Roads. During this confused and bloody struggle, all members of the color-guard were either killed or wounded. Private Wray was so severely wounded that he was discharged from service. He went home to Danville and soon died from his wounds. He is buried in Danville's Fairview Cemetery.[2] Captain Robert M. Henderson of Company A, though wounded, took the fallen flag and bore it safely from the field of bat-

99

Sergeant Reuben W. Schell

tle.[3] The regiment lost about three hundred soldiers during the Peninsula Campaign.

Owing to the destruction of the color-guard, Private Reuben W. Schell of Company D was promoted to corporal and given the honor of bearing the state color. Schell would later be promoted to sergeant and remain as bearer until his capture on May 5, 1864.[4] The division joined Pope's army in time to participate in the Second Battle of Manassas on August 29-30, 1862. Losses were heavy, including Lieutenant-Colonel Henderson, who was wounded.

The regiment then marched with the rest of the division in pursuit of Lee's army, which had invaded Maryland. After a successful engagement at Turner's Gap on South Mountain (September 14), the 7th struck the Rebels in the Cornfield at Antietam on September 17. Corporal Schell passed through the battle without a scratch, but men on both sides of him were killed and the flag received some damage from the eight bullets that passed through its folds. Schell realized that he had a dangerous assignment, but he considered it the post of honor and continued to carry the flag.[5]

Upon the army's return to Virginia, the regiment next battled with the enemy at Fredericksburg on December 13. During the division's charge on Jackson's line, the 7th Reserves was on the left of the line. As the 7th reached a railroad during the advance, Corporal Schell was struck by a bullet that luckily hit his belt buckle. However, the breath was knocked out of him and he fell, later finding his stomach and side very bruised. Private Henry Dilman immediately took the flag but had not gone more than ten steps when a Rebel bullet pierced his heart. The regiment suffered eighty-six casualties in this unsuccessful charge.[6]

After the Fredericksburg Campaign was over, the division was sent to Washington to rest and recuperate. The 7th was stationed in Alexandria for most of its period of duty behind the lines.

Second State Color

While in Alexandria, the regiment received a replacement state color in December 1863. The first state color was apparently retained and was given to the adjutant-general's office in late June 1864.[7] It was officially returned to state care on July 4, 1866. Now a part of the Fifth Corps, the regiment rejoined the Army of the Potomac in time for General Grant's campaign that began in May 1864.

The 7th skirmished briefly during the fighting in the Wilderness on May 4. The next day, Colonel William McCandless, commanding the First Brigade of the Reserve Division, advanced his command to the support of another Fifth Corps division. Together with the 2nd and 11th Reserves, the 7th plunged into the tangled undergrowth in search of the elusive enemy forces. McCandless met a Rebel force, drove it back through the woods, and advanced in pursuit. As the regiments pushed on, General Crawford, the division commander, sent word to retire immediately as the brigade had advanced too far and was in danger of being surrounded. McCandless withdrew the 2nd and 11th, but the 7th had veered slightly from the other units and could not be located immediately. As the 7th continued to struggle through the woods, Confederate troops suddenly appeared in both the front and rear. The regiment moved to the left, then to the right, seeking escape, but encountered only enemy soldiers. Rather than risk annihilation of his isolated command, Colonel Henry C. Bolinger surrendered the entire regiment to the 61st Georgia of Brigadier-General John B. Gordon's Brigade. One of his captains took the flag from Sergeant Schell and sent it to

Advance the Colors!

the rear for safekeeping. Schell later would return from Southern prisons, but the flag has since disappeared. Thereafter, the survivors of the regiment, primarily Company B, remained with the division and fought at Spotsylvania, North Anna River, and Bethesda Church before being relieved and mustered out in June 1864.[8]

Company A Flag

In 1861, Mrs. Samuel Alexander of Carlisle made a flag that she presented to Company A. The staff upon which the flag was fastened was taken from a Revolutionary War flag used by Carlisle soldiers. The flag was kept by Captain John I. Faller after the war. Its present location is unknown.[9]

Notes

[1]*Carlisle American Democrat*, October 2, 1861.

[2]Information from Randy Hackenburg, USAMHI.

[3]*O.R.* 11.2, p. 404.

[4]On Schell's promotions, see his letter to his father, June 4, 1863, Schell Letters. This date differs from that listed in Bates.

[5]Schell to father, September 24, 1862.

[6]Schell to father, December 17, 1862; Benneville Schell, Jr., to father, December 28, 1862.

[7]Captain S. B. King to A. L. Russell, May 24, 1866, RG 19.

[8]For the Confederate account of the capture of the 7th Reserves, see G. W. Nichol, *A Soldier's Story of his Regiment* (n.p., 1898), pp. 142-144. Sergeant David Runkle, commander of the 7th Reserves Re-enactment Unit, has communicated with all likely repositories in Georgia in an unsuccessful attempt to locate the flag if it still remains.

[9]Civic Club of Carlisle, *Carlisle Old and New* (Harrisburg: J.H. McFarland Company, 1907, reprinted 1973), pp. 44, 46.

Bibliography

Alexander, Bates. "Pennsylvania Reserves." *Hummelstown Sun*, August 25, 1893-September 24, 1897?. In possession of Richard H. Hartwell, Hummelstown, copy in USAMHI, Save the Flags Collection.

Faller, Leo and John I. Letters. USAMHI, HbCWRT Collection.

Flower, Milton E. (editor). *Dear Folks at Home: The Civil War Letters of Leo W. and John I. Faller*. Harrisburg: The Telegraph Press for the Cumberland County Historical Society and the Hamilton Library Association, 1963.

Harrison, Huldah. Letters. USAMHI.

Heffelfinger, Jacob. Papers. USAMHI, CWTI Collection.

Hinch, Lowry. Letters. USAMHI.

Holmes, William R. April 1863 letter. USAMHI, CWMisc Collection.

McLaughlin, Florence C. (editor). "'Dear Sister Jennie—Dear Brother Jacob'. The Correspondence Between a Northern Soldier and His Sister in Mechanicsburg, Pa., 1861-1864." *Western Pennsylvania Historical Magazine* 60 (1977): 109-143, 203-240.

Ryan, William. Letters. USAMHI.

Schell, Benneville, Jr., and Reuben W. Letters. In possession of Robert S. Ulrich, Montoursville, Pennsylvania.

Strock, William E. 1862 Memoir. USAMHI, HbCWRT Collection.

37th Infantry
(8th Reserves)

First State Color

Recruited in western Pennsylvania, the 8th Reserves was organized at Camp Wright, near Pittsburgh, and moved from there by rail to Washington in late July. The regiment remained in camp near the city throughout the winter of 1861-62. The first state color was received on September 10, 1861.

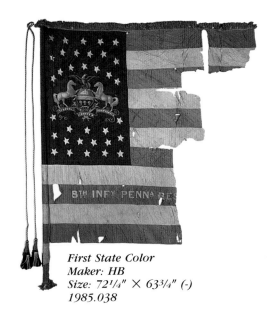

First State Color
Maker: HB
Size: 72¼" × 63¾" (-)
1985.038

First State Color at Muster Out

After participating in the division's march to Fredericksburg in May 1862, the 8th was shipped by water to join the Army of the Potomac near Richmond in June. The regiment first engaged the Rebel troops at Mechanicsville on June 26, the unit supporting Easton's battery of the 1st Pennsylvania Light Artillery. Several attacks on the battery were repulsed, but in the retreat to the Gaines' Mill position most of Company F was cut off and captured. During the ensuing struggle at Gaines' Mill on June 27, the 8th moved about the field in support of other units and lost heavily as a result. Three days later, the regiment fought at New Market Cross Roads, again losing many gallant soldiers.

The division then went to northern Virginia and joined General Pope's Army of Virginia in time to take an active role in the Second Battle of Manassas. The regiment again suffered heavy casualties, almost one-half of the number engaged. Two weeks later, the 8th Reserves was part of the attacking force at Turner's Gap on South Mountain on September 14, 1862. During the attack on Rebel troops posted behind a stone wall, the right flank of the regiment reached the wall

Advance the Colors!

first, drove the defenders back and brought an enfilade fire to bear on the 17th South Carolina, driving it back and forcing the entire Rebel line to give way. During the bloody fighting at Antietam on September 17, the regiment engaged the enemy in the Cornfield, suffering heavy casualties. The 8th's final 1862 action was at Fredericksburg on December 13, as the division charged the enemy and temporarily broke through before being forced to yield when reinforcements failed to arrive.

Upon the conclusion of the Fredericksburg Campaign, the division was sent to Washington to rest and refit. It remained in the Alexandria defenses until April 1864 and did not take part in the Gettysburg Campaign.

Second State Color

The regiment received a replacement state color in December 1863. This flag was carried by the regiment in its final campaign, which included the fighting in the Wilderness, May 4-5, 1864, and at Spotsylvania, May 8-15. The 8th's term of service was up on May 17. Proceeding to Pittsburgh, the 8th was mustered out of service on May 24. Both state flags were kept by D. Macferron, who forwarded them to Harrisburg on April 27, 1866, for inclusion in the July 4 ceremony in Philadelphia.[1] In 1889, a member of the 8th Reserves Regimental Association sent the cord and tassels from one of the flags, which had been kept by Corporal A. J. Bisset as a war souvenir, to Adjutant-General Daniel H. Hastings for reattachment to the tattered banner, which was then in the Flag Room.[2]

Company B Flag

The Jefferson Riflemen received an "elegant silk flag" from the ladies of Pittsburgh's Eighth Ward on May 23, 1861, while the regiment was organizing at Camp Wilkins. No other information has been located.[3]

Second State Color
Maker: HB
Size: 73⅞" × 76⅛"
1985.037

Company C Flag

The Anderson Cadets received a silk flag from Mrs. George Gallup of Pittsburgh on May 30, 1861. Nothing else is known about the flag.[4]

Company K Flag

On April 27, 1861, the ladies of Washington presented a "beautiful flag" to the Hopkins Infantry. The ceremony took place in fromt of the Washington County Court House. No other information has been found.[5]

Color-Bearer

Corporal John M. Oliver of Company K was listed as one of the bearers for the 1866 parade, the corporal having been one of the bearers during the war.[6]

Notes

[1]D. Macferron to J. L. Reynolds, April 27, 1866, RG 19.
[2]John M. Kent to D. H. Hastings, April 1, 1889, RG 19.
[3]"Flag Presentation at Camp Wilkins," *Pittsburgh Post*, May 24, 1861.

[4]"Flag Presentation,"*Pittsburgh Post*, May 31, 1861.
[5]"Flag Presentation to the Hopkins Infantry," *Washington Reporter and Tribune*, May 2, 1861.
[6]Note from William Gray, July 4, 1866, RG 25.

Bibliography

Darby, George W. *Incidents and Adventures in Rebeldom, Libby, Belle Isle, Salisbury*. Pittsburgh: Press of Rawsthorne Engraving and Printing Company, 1899.

Hill, Archibald F. *Our Boys, the Personal Experiences of a Soldier in the Army of the Potomac*. Philadelphia: John E. Potter, 1864.

38th Infantry (9th Reserves)

First State Color
Maker: HB
Size: 71³/₈″ × 76¹/₂″
1985.040

First State Color

Another of the Reserve regiments recruited in western Pennsylvania, the 9th, after organizing at Pittsburgh, proceeded to Washington in late July, where it remained all winter. During Governor Curtin's presentation of colors to the division on September 10, the 9th was on picket duty at Great Falls, but the color-guard did report to camp and received the colors from the Governor in person. The regiment was engaged in the "battle" of Drainesville on December 20, which was painted on the state color soon thereafter.

The regiment took part in the divisional march to Fredericksburg and then was transferred to the Army of the Potomac outside Richmond in June 1862. During the engagement at Mechanicsville on June 26, the 9th was formed in support of the left flank of McCall's division, and the following day at Gaines' Mill, fought in support of the 62nd Pennsylvania and 9th Massachusetts. On June 30, McCall's division was attacked by Longstreet's Confederates at New Market Cross

Roads. In this heavy fighting, the 9th acted as a support to Cooper's Pennsylvania battery, then marched to the left flank of the line to aid repulsing the enemy there. During this movement Cooper's battery was captured by an enemy attack, but upon returning the 9th charged and retook the guns. Color-Sergeant Henry W. Blanchard was wounded during this battle but insisted on returning to duty as soon as his wounded arm was bandaged.[1]

After the end of the Peninsula Campaign, the division went to northern Virginia and joined Pope's army in time to participate in the Second Battle of Manassas. The regiment then fought at South Mountain on September 14, before entering the war's bloodiest day at Antietam on September 17. As the 9th fought in and around the nowfamous Cornfield, Sergeant Blanchard was again wounded, so severely

Sergeant Henry W. Blanchard, Wounded at New Market Cross Roads and Antietam

Advance the Colors!

that he was forced to leave the field and could not continue to carry the flag. Private Walter Beatty of Company I took the banner and was immediately struck down by a Rebel bullet. Another private in the same company, Robert Lemmon, also was killed shortly after he took up the colors. At this point, Adjutant Robert Taggart ordered Private Edward Dorien to take the flag, "and he did so with and alacrity and look of pride that showed an appreciation of the honor." For his gallantry, Dorien was promoted to corporal.[2]

Second State Color   Size: 72³/₈″ × 76″
Maker: HB   1985.039

The 9th Reserves then participated in the Fredericksburg charge on Jackson's enemy position, the regiment suffering heavily. After this battle, the division was sent to Washington to rest, the 9th being stationed on the Orange and Alexandria Railroad as guards. The regiment rejoined the Army of the Potomac and reached the battlefield at Gettysburg on July 2, 1863. It was part of the force that occupied Big Round Top, suffering minimal casualties.

Second State Color

A second state color was received in December 1863, but this flag was never carried in combat. As the regiment prepared to enter the Wilderness fighting on May 4, its term of enlistment expired and it was relieved for muster out, which occurred on May 13, 1864. Both state colors were returned to Adjutant-General Russell in late April 1866 by D. Macferron in time for the July 4 Philadelphia ceremony.[3]

Company A Flag

On June 1, 1861, the Pittsburgh Rifles received a flag from a delegation of Pittsburgh women from the area of 3rd and Grant Streets, where the men were recruited. No other information has been located.[4]

Company C Flag

The Iron City Guards received a silk flag from a number of Pittsburgh women on May 7, 1861. Nothing else is known about this flag.[5]

Notes

[1]Sypher, p. 392
[2]*Ibid.*; Robert Taggart, "Civil War Recollections," p. 55, in Taggart Papers. Taggart spells the name Dorien, Bates has Dorian, and Sypher writes it Doran. Which is correct?

[3]D. Macferron to J. L. Reynolds, April 27, 1866, RG 19.
[4]"Flag Presentation," *Pittsburgh Gazette*, June 4, 1861.
[5]"Flag Presentation," *Pittsburgh Post*, May 8, 1861.

Bibliography

Beale, Anna M. Papers. Western Pennsylvania Historical Society. Includes letters from E. S. Alter, August 1861-February 1862, and F. J. Logan, May 1861-July 1862.
McQuaide, John D. Letters. USAMHI, CWTI Collection.
McQuaide, Joseph L. Letters. Western Pennsylvania Historical Society.
Murdoch, Alexander. "The Pittsburgh Rifles and the Battle of Drainville."

Western Pennsylvania Historical Magazine 53 (1970): 299-304.
Taggart, Robert. Papers. Pennsylvania State Archives.
Truxall, Aida C. (editor). *"Respects to All," Letters of Two Pennsylvania Boys in the War of Rebellion*. Pittsburgh: University of Pittsburgh Press, 1962. Includes letters, July 1861-April 1864, of Adam S. Bright.

39th Infantry (10th Reserves)

First State Color

Organized at Camp Wilkins near Pittsburgh, the 10th Pennsylvania Reserves moved to Washington in late July and remained near the capital throughout the winter of 1861-62. The state color was presented in person by Governor Curtin during the ceremony on September 10. At the Battle of Draineville on December 20, the regiment supported the Federal artillery, and did not suffer any casualties. However, owing to its presence on the field, Governor Curtin authorized the inscription of "Dranesville, December 20, 1861," on the regiment's flag.

In May 1862, the division occupied Fredericksburg and then was moved via water to join McClellan's army near Richmond in June. At Mechanicsville on June 26, the regiment repelled several enemy assaults against its position, then fought again the next day at Gaines' Mill, where the 10th was shuttled about in support of the Federal front line. When the division

was attacked at New Market Cross Roads on June 30, the 10th, near the left of the line, counterattacked briefly to drive back one of many charges against the battle line, suffering heavily in the combat, which was hand-to-hand at times.

The regiment moved to northern Virginia and fought at Second Manassas on August 29-30. Then, marching into Maryland to counter Lee's invasion, the 10th battled the enemy at Turner's Gap on South Mountain, September 14. Three days later, while most of the division charged through the Cornfield at Antietam, the 10th was detached to guard the right flank of the First Corps battleline. In its final action of 1862, the regiment participated in the charge at Fredericksburg, losing heavily.

In February 1863, the division was removed to Washington to refit, the 10th Reserves being stationed at Upton's Hill. As part of the Third Brigade of the division, the 10th was released to rejoin the main army in time to fight briefly at Gettysburg. The regiment deployed in the hollow between the Round

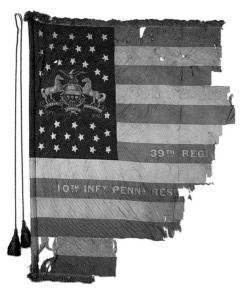

First State Color
Maker: HB
Size: 71⅝" × 58¼" (-)
1985.041

Second State Color
Maker: HB
Size: 72⅝" × 76½"
1985.042

106

Advance the Colors!

Tops late on July 2, protecting this area on the following day. After the minor campaigns in northern Virginia during the months of October and November, the regiment went into camp near Brandy Station.

Second State Color

A second color from the state was received in December 1863. This flag was borne by the regiment in its last campaign. As part of the Fifth Corps, the 10th fought in the Wilderness, at Spotsylvania, along the North Anna River, and at Bethesda Church before being sent to Pittsburgh, where the regiment was mustered out of service on June 11. The two state colors were forwarded to Adjutant-General Russell in late April 1866 to be included in the formal July 4 ceremony in Philadelphia.[1]

Company K Flag

The Wilson Rifles of New Galilee, Beaver County, received a silk flag from the ladies of that town on June 20, 1861. It was evidently some type of national color. The subsquent history of this flag is unknown.[2]

Notes

[1]D. Macferron to J. L. Reynolds, 27 April 1866, RG 19.

[2]*Beaver Weekly Argus*, June 26, 1861.

Bibliography

Casey, James B. (editor). "The Ordeal of Adoniram Judson Warner: His Minutes of South Mountain and Antietam." *Civil War History* 28 (1982): 213-236.

Furst, Luther C. Reminiscences. USAMHI, HbCWRT Collection. Furst was detached to the Signal Corps in late 1861.

Roy, Andrew. *Recollections of a Prisoner of War.*. Columbus, Ohio: J. L. Trauger Printing Company, 1905; revised edition, 1909.

Warner, A. J. Papers. Western Reserve Historical Society.

40th Infantry
(11th Reserves)

First State Color

One of the Reserve regiments recruited in western Pennsylvania, the 40th Pennsylvania was organized at Pittsburgh, proceeded to Washington and eventually went into camp at Tenallytown, Maryland. The regiment was given its first state color by Governor Curtin in person on September 10, 1861. After spending the winter in the camps near the capital, the 11th marched south to occupy Fredericksburg in May 1862 and then was transferred by water to the Army of the Potomac in June.

McCall's division was assaulted by Confederate troops on June 26 at the Battle of Mechanicsville. The 11th was only marginally engaged, with one company deployed as skirmishers. During the opening stages of the Battle of Gaines' Mill on June 27, the regiment was again held in reserve. But, as enemy pressure continued along the thin Federal battleline, the 11th was moved forward to bolster one of the weakest parts. Owing to the heavy musketry smoke

Second State Color
Maker: HB
Size: 73¼" × 75¾"
1985.044

on this part of the field, neither the 11th Reserves nor the 4th New Jersey received the order to retreat when the line fell back, and the majority of both regiments were captured. Only Company B, which was detached as pioneers, escaped. The 11th's state color was taken to Richmond, retaken by Federal troops in 1865, and transferred to War Department control. Tagged as #86 on the register of captured Federal flags, it was returned to state care in 1905.

Unidentified Flag

During the period from June 1862 to December 1863 it is unknown what colors the 11th carried into battle. After the capture of most of the regiment, the survivors were attached to the 7th Reserves during the Battle of New Market Cross Roads. The prisoners were exchanged in August 1862, and by the Second Battle of Manassas the 11th had been reconstituted. During this battle, Color-Sergeant James L. Hazlett was severely wounded while carrying an unspecified flag.[1]

First State Color
Maker: HB
Size: 70½" × 77¼"
1985.043

Advance the Colors!

Two weeks later, another color-bearer was killed as the regiment fought at South Mountain.[2] During the December 13 Battle of Fredericksburg, Private James J. Fritz carried the regimental colors.[3] The regiment then was sent to the Alexandria area to rest, but rejoined the army in time to fight at Gettysburg on July 2, taking part in the charge of the First Brigade to the stonewall at the Wheatfield. After the autumn maneuvers in northern Virginia, the regiment went into camp near Bristoe Station.

Second State Color

A replacement state color was received in December 1863. This flag was carried by the regiment during the fighting in the Wilderness, at Spotsylvania, North Anna River, and Bethesda Church, after which the 11th was relieved from duty as its term of service had expired. It returned to Pittsburgh and was disbanded in June 1864. The state flag was apparently given to the Adjutant-General's Office and was officially returned to state care on July 4, 1866.

Notes

[1] J. T. Stewart, *Indiana County, Pennsylvania*, 2 volumes (Chicago: J.H. Beers & Company, 1913), 1: 111.

[2] Thomson and Rauch, *History of the Bucktails*, p. 205.
[3] Stewart, *Indiana County*, 1: 111.

Bibliography

Barton, Michael (editor). "The Civil War Letters of Captain Andrew Lewis and His Daughter." *Western Pennsylvania Historical Magazine* 60 (1977): 371-390.

Bell, David. Letters. USAMHI.

Christy, H. F. "The 'Reserves' at Fredericksburg." *National Tribune*, September 19, 1901.

Fry, Jesse. Diary, February-August 1863. USAMHI, CWTI Collection.

Jackson, Frank W. "Colonel Samuel M. Jackson and the Eleventh Pennsylvania Reserves." *Western Pennsylvania Historical Magazine* 18 (1935): 45-47.

Jackson, Samuel M. *Diary of General S. M. Jackson for the Year 1862*. Apollo, 1925.

Lantzy, Philip A. Letters, July 27, 1861-August 24, 1862. USAMHI, HbCWRT Collection.

Lewis, Andrew. Letters, September 8, 1861-July 24, 1862. USAMHI, HbCWRT Collection.

McIlwain, James H. Letters. USAMHI, Lewis Leigh Collection.

41st Infantry
(12th Reserves)

First State Color

Organized at Camp Curtin from ten companies that had rendezvoused there, the 12th Reserves remained in Harrisburg until mid-August 1861 when it joined the division at the Tenallytown camp. The regiment received its first state flag on September 10, in company with the other regiments of McCall's division. As part of Brigadier-General E. O. C. Ord's Third Brigade, the 12th was present at the engagement at Drainesville on December 20, but lost only one man wounded. The regiment's presence on the field entitled it to have the battle inscribed in gold letters on the state color, which was done in January 1862.

After the occupation of Fredericksburg in May 1862, the division joined McClellan's forces near Richmond. McCall's regiments were attacked at Mechanicsville on June 26, the beginning of the Seven Days' Battles. The 12th was posted on the left of the line and repulsed the several attacks on its position.

First State Color
Maker: HB
Size: 71¼" × 78¼"
1985.046

The next day, during the Battle of Gaines' Mill, the regiment supported an artillery battery, suffering very few casualties. However, at New Market Cross Roads on June 30, the regiment lost heavily, as one wing was advanced in front of the main line, and was driven off the field by a large enemy force.

The division moved to northern Virginia in August, taking part in the Second Battle of Manassas on August 29-30. The color-guard lost heavily in the fighting withdrawal, and when the regiment finally retired, Lieutenant Edward Kelly of Company E took the flag safely from the field.[1] After this campaign, the regiment moved into Maryland, fighting at South Mountain and Antietam, losing many soldiers in both battles. During the heavy struggle in the Cornfield at Antietam, the color-bearer, Private David H. Graham, was killed and the entire color-guard was wounded. One of them, although bleeding from two wounds, crawled off the field, dragging the torn battleflag with him.[2] In its final 1862 engagement at Fredericksburg on December 13, the regiment took part in the charge and repulse of Meade's division against the Confederate troops commanded by Stonewall Jackson.

The depleted Reserve Division was then sent back to Washington to rest. After the news was received of Lee's invasion of Pennsylvania, the First and Third Brigades of the division were permitted to rejoin the army in time to fight at Gettysburg on July 2-3. The 12th was one of the regiments that scaled the steep slope of Big Round Top during the evening of July 2, fortifying the eminence and guarding it the next day. The division then took a minor part in the Bristoe Station and Mine Run campaigns during the autumn of 1863 before going into winter camp near Bristoe Station.

The 12th Reserves took part in the opening stages of Grant's 1864 campaign against Lee's army of Northern Virginia. After the fierce struggle in the Wilderness, the regiment fought at Spotsylvania on May 10. During the charge on the enemy works that day, the colors were saved from certain capture by Orderly-

Advance the Colors!

Sergeant James Johnson of Company E. Lieutenant J. C. Fackenthal recalled this incident:[3]

On the day . . . mentioned the regiment occupied an entrenched position at the edge of a woods, while the Confederates were just as nicely fixed on the opposite side of the woods, about a half a mile distant, with an open field in their front and batteries in position to harrow and cross harrow the ground at the same time. Late in the day we received notice that a grand charge, all along the line, would be made about sundown. . . . The Twelfth advanced by division, Companies 'E' and 'F' forming the centre division, and having in charge the colors. Before leaving the woods the troops on our right commenced to yell, giving the enemy timely notice of our approach, and he replied vigorously with shot, shell, grape and canister. The roar of cannon and rattle of musketry was deafening, and when we reached the clearing those fellows who yelled so lustily in the start broke and ran for dear life, and no power on earth could stop them, and 'the jig was up.'

Color-Sergeant William H. Weaver,[4] of the Twelfth, was hit by a grape and fell upon his flag. The regiment was swept back like chaff before a hurricane, and the rout was complete. Sergeant Johnson, seeing the colors drop, ran to Weaver and pulled the flag from under him, and vainly attempted to rally the men, but it was too hot. Waving the old tattered and torn flag in their teeth, he gave them three bucks and a ball and skedaddled for our side of the woods with the Johnnies close upon his heels. In the meantime (and a mean time it was) our boys got home, and seeing Johnson coming through the brush, mistook him for a Rebel sergeant, and, of course opened fire on him. Seeing the danger, he dodged behind a tree until the shower passed, and the next minute was safe within our works. . . .

Johnson had bravely saved our old battle flag, and if the Lieutenant in command did then and there kiss him under a scorching fire of shot and shell, what of it; it is the only recognition he has ever received for the gallant act, notwithstanding members of Congress have been informed of the facts and a suitable reward requested.

Second State Color
Maker: HB

Size: 72¼" × 76½"
1985.045

After the fighting at Spotsylvania, the 12th then took part in the North Anna River crossing and on May 30 repulsed an attack near Bethesda Church. The regiment then was relieved and returned to Harrisburg for muster out.

Second State Color

The 12th did receive a replacement state color in December 1863, but, judging from the way Lieutenant Fackenthal described Sergeant Johnson's rescue of the "old tattered and torn flag," it appears that the regiment continued to carry its first flag as well. Both were returned at muster out and were a part of the 1866 ceremony.

Notes

[1] *O.R.* 51.1, p. 131.
[2] *Ibid.*, p. 155.

[3] Quoted in Hardin, pp. 214-215.
[4] Bates 1: 894, has Weaver as captain from February 10, 1863.

Bibliography

Hardin, Martin D. *History of the Twelfth Regiment Pennsylvania Reserve Volunteer Corps (41st Regiment of the Line), from Its Muster into the United States Service, August 10th, 1861, to its Muster Out, June 11th, 1864, Together with Biographical Sketches of Officers and Men and a Complete Muster-out Roll.* New York: the author, 1890.

———. Papers. Chicago Historical Society.

McCallister, W. A. "A Singular Fatality." *National Tribune,* March 22, 1888. Concerns Second Manassas battle.

42nd Infantry
(13th Reserves)

State Color

Thomas L. Kane, a Pennsylvanian already famous for his successful mediation between the federal government and the Mormons, conceived the idea of raising a rifle regiment from the rugged mountaineers living in the northern mountains of the Commonwealth. After some delay, ten companies of troops moved to Harrisburg and were organized as the 13th Pennsylvania Reserves. This regiment, perhaps Pennsylvania's most famous Civil War unit, was more popularly known as the "Bucktails," since the men in the companies from the western counties wore a buck's tail in their caps as a symbol of their marksmanship. In honor of Kane's efforts to raise the regiment, it was also known as the "Kane Rifle Regiment of the Pennsylvania Reserve Corps," and also as the 1st Pennsylvania Rifles.

Shortly after organization, the 13th, together with the 5th Reserves and an artillery battery, was sent to Cumberland, Maryland, for guard duty. The regiment then joined General Banks's troops near Harper's Ferry, where it remained until early October. Thus, the Bucktails were not present when Governor Curtin presented the state colors to the Reserve Division, although the color-guard may have been sent to receive the 13th's flag. Colonel Kane's regiment took part in the engagement at Drainesville on December 20, 1861, and this battle was inscribed on the regiment's flag by order of the Governor.

After the division moved south to occupy Fredericksburg in May 1862, the regiment was divided into two detachments. Colonel Kane, by personal request, had Companies C, G, H, and I, detached under his command and was sent to the Shenandoah Valley to operate with the Federal troops there. Major Roy Stone took command of the remaining six companies, which were then transferred with the division to the Army of the Potomac, operating on the Peninsula near Richmond.

Major Stone's command first engaged the enemy during the Battle of Mechanicsville on June 26. His marksmen, posted at one of the bridges over Beaver Dam Creek, repelled every assault against their position until the division withdrew that night. During the darkness and the confusion in the retreat, Company K was cut off and retired into a swamp to avoid capture, but eventually emerged hungry from the swamp after four days and surrendered.

As the division retired, parts of Companies D and E did not receive the order and were also surrounded. Captain Alanson E. Niles of Company E had the state color with his command, and his men retreated into one of the swamps along the Chickahominy River to avoid surrendering the banner. However, after more and more enemy troops began combing the swamp for the elusive Yankees, Niles was forced to give up. Rather than lose the flag, his men buried it in the swamp, and so reported after the war when Adjutant-General Russell inquired about the missing color.[1]

However, Niles's men apparently did not do a good job of hiding the flag for the Confederates did discover it. When Federal troops occupied Richmond in 1865, the flag was found rolled up within a large U.S. garrison flag located in the attic of the Capitol building.[2] Major-General Edward O. C. Ord, commanding the Army of the James, and a former brigade commander of the Reserves, saw the flag and took it home with him. In 1899, his daughter, Mrs. John Mason, loaned the color to the Smithsonian Institution, where it has remained ever since.[3]

Company I Flag

In April 1861, when word was received of Kane's recruiting for the regiment, the companies that eventually became C, G, and I, gathered on the upper reaches of the Susquehanna River and floated by raft to Lock Haven, and then took trains to Harrisburg. Before leaving home, the men of Company I, recruited in McKean County, received a wool bunting flag to take with them. The lead raft carried this flag.[4] When Kane divided the regiment into two wings, this banner was taken by Kane's four companies into the Shenandoah Valley. The detachment engaged Jackson's troops at Harrisonburg on June 6, 1862, at Cross Keys on June 8, and again at Cedar Mountain on August 9. The detachment was present at Catlett's Station when the famed Rebel cavalry leader Jeb Stuart raided General Pope's headquarters there on August 22. Kane's men attacked during the night and succeeded in driving off the Rebel raiders before more damage was done to Pope's wagon train.

The detachment then fought in the Second Battle of Manassas on August 29-30, and was the last of the Federal troops to cross Bull Run as the army retreated to Washington. The companies under Major Stone's command also fought in this battle as part of the Reserve Division, and as the column retreated to Washington the regiment was finally united as one body of men. Owing to the loss of the state color, Company I's flag was briefly used as the regimental color. The flag was given to Colonel Kane when the Bucktails mustered out of service, and he forwarded it to state care in time for the July 4, 1866, ceremony.[5]

Company K Flag

When the Raftsmen Rangers left Curwensville on May 9, 1861, Mrs. William Irvin presented the men with a "beautiful silk flag."[6] This flag was apparently carried in the battles of South Mountain and Antietam, and at Fredericksburg on December 13, 1862. In this latter engagement, Corporal John Looney of Company G bore the flag, and during the charge against Jackson's Confederates, Looney was mortally wounded, his life

Company I Flag
Size: 47¹/₂″ × 81¹/₂″
1985.047

149th Regiment Presentation Color
Size: 71¹/₂″ × 74¹/₂″ (-)
1985.048

blood spurting over the flag. The flag was badly damaged and the staff was broken. This is the last mention of this particular color, and thus it is unknown if it was carried in any other engagements. It was given to the Irvin family after the war and carried in reunion parades.[7]

Presented Color

In late 1862, Major Stone resigned to become colonel of the new 149th Pennsylvania, styled the "bogus Bucktails" by the original Bucktails in disdain for what they considered to be Stone's recruiting of another rifle regiment. The bad feelings that surfaced between the two commands would later be smoothed, and on May 15, 1863, the 149th presented a new flag to the 13th Reserves. This was a national color, and contained the names of the twelve battles in which the Bucktails had fought, and also included the inscription "Presented to the First Rifle Regiment by the 149th Penna. Vol." in the midst of the blue canton.[8]

This banner seems to have been carried by the Bucktails in all subsequent engagements, including the fighting at Chancellorsville, Gettysburg, the Wilderness, Spotsylvania, North Anna River, and Bethesda Church. When the Bucktails were relieved for muster out, those who had re-enlisted were assigned to the 190th Pennsylvania, also known as the 1st Veteran Reserves. Major William R. Hartshorne of the 13th, destined to become colonel of the 190th, took this flag as the new regiment's color until the state could provide a new flag.[9]

The 190th apparently carried this flag during the battle of Cold Harbor and the Petersburg assaults of June 1864. During the engagement at the Weldon Railroad on August 19, the 190th was flanked by a hidden Confederate force, and many officers and men were captured. This presented color was also taken, and was returned to Pennsylvania by the War Department in 1905. Upon its reception by the Adjutant-General's Office, there was some confusion at first, because the flag was tagged by the War Department as belonging to the 149th Pennsylvania. After some letter-writing, the true story of the flag was uncovered and it was deposited in the Flag Room beside the Bucktails' other banner.[10]

Company F Flag

The members of Company F, recruited in Mauch Chunk, Carbon County, received a flag from the local ladies before the command entrained for Camp Curtin, The subsequent history and disposition of this flag is unknown.[11]

Maryland GAR Flag

In December 1906, the Adjutant of Maryland G.A.R. Post 1 in Baltimore wrote to Adjutant-General Stewart, informing him that a flag marked as belonging to the Bucktails had been found when the Maryland Civil War flags were removed from the cellar of the State House in Annapolis to the present display cases on the main floor. This banner was sent to Stewart, but its present location is unknown.[12]

Notes

[1] W. R. Hartshorne to A. L. Russell, May 26, 1866, RG 19.

[2] "Our Richmond Correspondence," *Philadelphia Inquirer*, May 6, 1865.

[3] F. D. Beary, "Battle Flag History," in 42nd Regiment Collection, Pennsylvania State Archives.

[4] Thomson & Rausch, p. 12; Glover, p. 22.

[5] Kane to Adjutant-General, October 1, 1873, RG 25.

[6] "For the War," *Clearfield Republican*, May 15, 1861.

[7] Thomson & Rausch, p. 234; "The Bucktail Battle Flags," 1891 newspaper article in Bucktail scrapbook owned by Ronn Palm.

[8] Thomson & Rausch, p. 249; Adjutant-General Stewart to H. H. Spayd, April 29, 1907, RG 25.

[9] Thomson & Rausch, p. 325.

[10] Stewart to Spayd, in Note 7 above. The color was listed as captured by Colquitt's Brigade. See National Archives, RG 94, Entry 178, Register of Captured Flags, #64.

[11] Thomson & Rausch, p. 44

[12] G. Hubert Schmidt to Adjutant-General Stewart, December 12, 1906, RG 25.

Bibliography

Annual Reunion of the Regimental Association of the Bucktails; or First Rifle Regiment, P.R.V.C. 1 (1887), 2 (1888), 3-4 (1889-1890), 10 (1896), 12 (1898), 16 (1902).

Bard, John P. "The 'Old Bucktails,' 42d Regiment Pennsylvania Volunteers at the Battle of Gettysburg." *Philadelphia Weekly Press*, May 19, 1886.

"The Bucktails, The Famous Rifle Regiment of Pennsylvania." *Grand Army Scout and Soldiers Mail*, January 6,13,20, 1883.

Crapsey, Angelo. Letters. Potter County Historical Society.

Dedication of Monument and 20th and 21st Annual Reunions of the Regimental Association of the "Old Bucktails" or First Rifle Regiment P.R.V.C., Driftwood, Penna., September 14th and 15th, 1906; and April 27th, 1908. n.p., n.d.

Deming, A. J. "Bucktails at Gettysburg." *National Tribune*, February 4, 1886.

Eberhart, Gilbert R. "Something Further About the Bucktails." *National Tribune*, May 1, 1884.

42nd Regiment Collection. Pennsylvania State Archives.

Glover, Edwin A. *Bucktailed Wildcats, A Regiment of Civil War Volunteers.* New York: Thomas Yoseloff, 1960.

Hobson, Charles F., and Shankman, Arnold. "Colonel of the Bucktails: Civil War Letters of Charles Frederick Taylor." *Pennsylvania Magazine of History and Biography* 97 (1973): 333-361.

Hoffsammer, Robert D. "The Pennsylvania Bucktails." *Civil War Times Illustrated* (January 4, 1966): 16-27.

Johnson, Wallace W. "About the Bucktails. The Famous Regiment of Pennsylvania Rifle-men. The Hardy Woodsmen. . . . Up the Shenandoah. . . . ." *National Tribune*, January 7, 1886.

Jones, N. Y. "The Pennsylvania Reserves at Gettysburg." *Grand Army Scout and Soldiers Mail*, November 3, 1883.

McNeil, Hugh W. Papers. Pennsylvania State Archives.

Presley, William. Memoirs. USAMHI, HbCWRT Collection.

Reinsberg, Mark. "Descent of the Raftsmen's Guard: A Roll Call." *Western Pennsylvania Historical Magazine* 53 (1970): 1-32.

_____ (editor). "A Bucktail Voice: Civil War Correspondence of Pvt. Cordello Collins." *Western Pennsylvania Historical Magazine* 48 (1965): 235-248.

Thompson, James D. Memoirs. USAMHI.

Thomson, Osmund R. H., and Rausch, William H. *History of the "Bucktails," Kane Rifle Regiment of the Pennsylvania Reserve Corps (13th Pennsylvania Reserves 42nd of the Line).* Philadelphia: Electric Printing Company, 1906.

1st Artillery
(43rd Regiment)

State Color

Organized as part of the Reserve Corps, the 1st Pennsylvania Light Artillery comprised eight original batteries mustered into service in June 1861. A ninth company, Battery I, was formed in March 1865 from the surplus recruits of the other batteries. A state color was provided to the regiment in September 1861, presumably when Governor Curtin presented colors to the infantry regiments of the Reserve Corps on September 10, 1861. In all probability, this flag was never used in combat, serving instead as the regimental headquarters flag. As mentioned in Chapter Two, the War Department order of April 2, 1863, reduced the headquarters personnel of each light artillery regiment to reflect the tactical separation of the batteries. Thus, the wartime history of this state color is uncertain. It was probably returned to the state on July 4, 1866, although it does not appear in any of the extant lists.

Battery Guidons

The eight original batteries never acted as a unified force, being parcelled out to artillery battalions and brigades in different divisions and corps. As a result, the individual batteries saw much varied action with both the Army of the Potomac and the Army of the James. Each battery probably carried some type of guidon secured either from the federal government or by local presentation. The existence of two battery guidons has been verified. On May 24, 1861, the ladies of Mount Jackson, Lawrence County, presented a guidon to the Mount Jackson Guards, who became Battery B. The presentation notice indicates that this guidon was some type of stars and stripes arrangement, probably a swallowtail national flag.[1]

A guidon of Battery F is owned by the Wyoming County Historical and Geological Society in Wilkes-Barre. This flag was presented to the Society in 1957 by the daughter of the battery's commander, R. Bruce Ricketts. The exact wartime history of this particular

State Color
Maker: HB

Size: 71" × 78¼"
1985.049

guidon is uncertain, but it may have been the one carried by the battery at Gettysburg. On July 2, 1863, Ricketts's battery was posted on Cemetery Hill and was attacked by a Confederate brigade of Louisiana troops just as it was growing dark. An artillery battery's weapons were designed primarily for long-range fire, but canister was used when attacking troops came close. Should the canister fail to repulse the attackers, the cannoneers would have problems defending the battery because most were unarmed. On this occasion, the supporting infantry retreated, leaving Ricketts's command alone for a short time. Lieutenant Charles B. Brockway described the desperate plight of the gunners before reinforcements arrived:[2]

> We, therefore, bore the brunt of the attack *alone*, our left piece, which was close to the stone wall, was spiked by the enemy, but only after they had killed, wounded, or taken prisoners every man belonging to it. Some of the drivers were bayonetted on their horses. Still, our men stood at their posts—the officers and drivers supplying the places of those who had fallen. Our canister failing, "rotten shot" was used; that is, shrapnel without fuse, the shell bursting at the

Guidon of Battery F

muzzle of the gun. By the time the enemy got in the Battery it was quite dark.

A rebel First Lieutenant attempted to seize our Battery guidon which was planted in one of the central earthworks, but while in the act of grasping it, the bearer, James H. Riggin, rode up and with his revolver shot the officer through the body. Seizing the colors, he wheeled his horse, but at the same moment was shot himself, and died soon after.

A Sergt. of the [Louisiana] "Tigers" got clear back to the limbers, and there caught Riggin's horse, and picked up the fallen colors. While leading back the horse he was encountered by Sergt. [Richard] Stratford, who, unable to recognize him in the dark, demanded to know "where he was going with that horse." The rebel brought his musket to his shoulder and demanded Stratford's surrender. At this moment I walked up, and a glance showed me the true state of affairs. Having no sidearms by me I picked up a stone, and in a most unmilitary manner broke the fellow's head. He tumbled to the ground, but Stratford, not knowing the cause, seized his musket and shot him through the abdomen. Fearing he had missed him in the darkness, he clubbed the musket and broke the fellow's arm, whereupon he asked for "quarter," which of course was given. I don't think he lived long. (As I raised the fallen colors, the staff was shot in two in my hands.)

The scene was now one of the wildest confusion. Friends and foes were indiscriminately mixed, and our brave men, though outnumbered and without arms, by means of handspikes, rammers, stones, etc., made a sturdy resistance, animating each other with shouts and cries, "to conquer on the soil of our native state or perish."

Federal infantry soon came up and drove the enemy back.

Notes

[1]"Flag Presentation, &c.," *Lawrence Journal*, May 25, 1861.

[2]Lieutenant Brockway to David McConaughy, March 5, 1864, Peter F. Rothermel Papers, Pennsylvania State Archives.

Bibliography

Orwig, Thomas G. "First Pennsylvania Light Artillery. A Grand Array of Splendidly Efficient Batteries." *National Tribune*, March 31, 1904.

Battery B

Alloway, John W. 1863 Diary. Historical Society of Pennsylvania.

Battery B Collection. Pennsylvania State Archives.

"Cooper's 'Battery B' Before Petersburg." *Blue and Gray* 4 (1894): 41-44.

McClelland, William. "A Brave Battery." *Philadelphia Weekly Times*, June 18, 1887.

Stewart, John Q. "An Address Delivered by John Q. Stewart at the Twenty-second Annual Reunion of the Association of Battery B, First Artillery, Pennsylvania Reserve Corps, at Mount Jackson, Lawrence County, Penn'a., Monday, June 8, 1891." New Castle: New Castle News, 1891.

_____. "Address of John Q. Stewart at the Thirty-first Annual Reunion of Battery B, First Pennsylvania Light Artillery, P.R.V.C., Mount Jackson, Lawrence County, Penna., Friday, June 8, 1900." N.p., n.d.

Battery F

Brockway, Charles B. "Charge of the 'Tigers'." *Philadelphia Weekly Times*, April 16, 1881.

"One of Our Fighting Batteries. Brief History of Rickett's Battery F, 1st Pennsylvania." *Grand Army Scout and Soldiers Mail*, January 27, February 3, 1883.

"Ricketts and His Battery." *Gettysburg Compiler*, October 12, 1886.

Sweet, O. F. "Ricketts' Battery. It was One of Those at Gettysburg Which Came to Stay." *National Tribune*, April 29, 1909.

Battery G

Moore, L. E. C. "Charge of the Louisiana Tigers at Gettysburg, July 2, 1863." *National Tribune*, August 5, 1909.

Rudisill, James J. *The Days of Our Abraham, 1811-1899*. York: York Printing Company, 1936.

Advance the Colors!

1st Cavalry (44th Regiment)

First State Standard

The 1st Pennsylvania Cavalry was the single cavalry regiment raised as part of the Reserve Volunteer Corps, and was thus alternately known as the 15th Reserves. George D. Bayard, a Regular Army officer, was the regiment's first colonel. The state standard was apparently presented to the regiment on September 10, 1861, the day Governor Curtin presented colors to the infantry regiments of the Reserve Corps. The standard was a part of the initial Horstmann contract, which included ten company guidons for the regiment.

Five companies of the 1st Cavalry were present at the Battle of Drainesville on December 20, 1861. Thereafter, the regiment was separated from the Reserve Corps and performed duty in northern Virginia. Colonel Bayard led the regiment south as the advance of Major-General Irvin McDowell's occupation of Fredericksburg in April 1862. The regiment was then detached and sent to the Shenandoah Valley, where it skirmished constantly with Stonewall Jackson's retreating column. After this exhausting duty, the regiment rested for two weeks at Manassas, then joined the new Army of Virginia. One corps of the army attacked Jackson's troops at Cedar Mountain on August 9. As twilight drew near and the beaten Yankees began to withdraw, the 1st Battalion of the regiment charged a large body of Confederate infantry and aided in delaying any Rebel advance. The regiment then was engaged at Thoroughfare Gap on August 28, and helped protect the army's retreat after the defeat at Second Manassas on August 29-30.

With most of its horses broken down after almost four months of constant campaigning, the 1st Cavalry remained at Washington for six weeks to refit. It then joined the Army of the Potomac during that army's advance through Virginia to Fredericksburg. During the battle there on December 13, the regiment was held in reserve and was not heavily engaged. After spending the winter of 1862-63 on picket duty, the

regiment remained behind in the Falmouth area when the Cavalry Corps departed on a raid behind Lee's army as part of the Chancellorsville Campaign. The regiment continued to picket the Rappahannock River until relieved from that duty on May 9.

As the opening stages of the Gettysburg Campaign unfolded, the regiment took part in the Battle of Brandy Station on June 9, then acted as rearguard for the Federal cavalry during the fighting at Aldie and Middleburg on June 22. During the Battle of Gettysburg, the regiment was temporarily detached from the corps to act as army headquarters guards. Upon the return of the army to Virginia, the 1st Cavalry took part in the Bristoe Station and Mine Run campaigns during the fall of 1863 before going into winter quarters near Warrenton.

Soon after the opening of General Grant's 1864 campaign, the new commander of the Cavalry Corps, Major-General Philip H. Sheridan, took most of the corps on a raid toward Richmond. His troopers moved steadily toward the Rebel capital and were met by increasing opposition as the Yankees got nearer to the city. The 1st Pennsylvania formed part of Sheridan's rearguard, and fought a lively engagement with Rebel cavalry on May 9 near Childsburg. As a retreating regiment fell back through the ranks of the 1st, Colonel John P. Taylor formed his men to meet the pursuing Gray cavalry. One of the enemy troopers dashed forward, seized the regimental stan-

First State Standard
Maker: HB
Size: 27¼" × 32¼"
1985.050

Second State Standard
Maker: HB
Size: 25⅞" × 30¼"
1985.051

dard, and demanded its surrender. The reply was a volley that killed him and saved the flag.[1] Sheridan's troopers ended their raid on May 25, when the cavalry rejoined the army near the James River.

Upon the end of the raid, the cavalry was immediately detailed as the advance guard of the army, and fought at Haw's Shop on May 28. Sheridan's troopers were soon detached for a raid against the Virginia Central Railroad. The raid lasted until June 24, and the 1st Cavalry was heavily engaged both at White House on the twenty-first and at Saint Mary's Church on the twenty-fourth. By that time, the army had reached Petersburg and had begun siege operations. The division to which the 1st was attached fought in several of the battles around Petersburg, including those at Reams' Station (July 12), Malvern Hill (July 28), Lee's Mills (July 30), Gravel Hill (August 14-15), and Reams' Station (August 23-25). Shortly after this last engagement, those troopers who had not re-enlisted were relieved from duty and sent to Philadelphia, where they were mustered out of service on September 9. The state standard was taken along home and was included on the February 1865 quartermaster return list. It was officially returned to state care on July 4, 1866.

Second State Standard

The soldiers remaining with the regiment after the majority went home were consolidated into a battalion of four companies. This detachment participated in most of the cavalry engagements in the Petersburg area until Lee's surrender in April 1865. The state issued a cavalry standard to the battalion in December 1864. Shortly after the end of the war, the battalion was consolidated with the survivors of the 6th and 17th Pennsylvania Cavalry as the 2nd Provisional Cavalry. This new regiment remained in service until August 1865. When this unit was formed, the 1st Cavalry sent its state standard to Harrisburg, where it was received in July 1865. It was included in the 1866 parade.

Presented Standard

In recognition of the gallantry of the 1st Battalion's charge at Cedar Mountain on August 9, 1862, the ladies of Kishacoquillas presented the unit with a national flag.[2] Its subsequent history during the war is unknown. It is presently owned by the War Library and Museum, Military Order of the Loyal Legion of the United States, Philadelphia.

Company G Guidons

The Chester County Historical Society has custody of both the state and federal guidons of Company G. The state-issued guidon, manufactured by Horstmann Brothers & Company, appears to be the only survivor of the 112 guidons made for the state by this company.

Company K Guidon

The ladies of Bridgeville, Allegheny County, presented a national flag to the local company which became Company K, 1st Pennsylvania Cavalry. The flag was presented to the unit in August 1861 prior to their departure for Harrisburg. Since company flags were discouraged by the War Department, this flag was sent home and was owned by two members of the company until 1911, when it was given to the Captain Thomas Espy Post 153 of the G.A.R., Carnegie, where it still remains.[3]

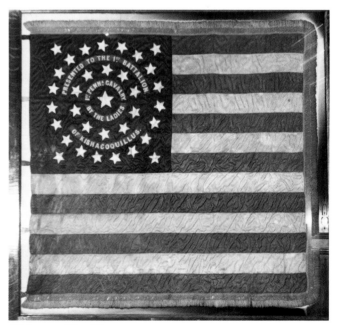

Kishacoquillus Flag

Notes

[1] Bates 1: 1023.

[2] The acceptance letter can be found in the *Lewistown Gazette*, October 8, 1862.

[3] *Catalogue of Relics in Memorial Room, Capt. Thos. Espy Post No. 153, G.A.R. Library Building, Carnegie, Penna., 1911* (n.p., n.d.), p. 21.

Bibliography

Bachman, Aaron E. "My Experience During the Civil War." Typescript reminiscences. Historical Society of Western Pennsylvania; copy in USAMHI, HbCWRT Collection.

Carson, J. Harvey. "The 1st Pennsylvania Cavalry." *Grand Army Scout and Soldiers Mail*, August 28, 1886.

Feather, Jacob. "The Sloop Captured by Cavalry." *National Tribune*, November 8, 1883.

Hall, Wilmer C. Papers. Pennsylvania State Archives.

Holbrook, Warren L. "Davies's Brigade. The Services of Those Gallant Troopers in the Last Campaign." *National Tribune*, June 9, 1887.

Jones, Owen. In Jones Family Papers. Historical Society of Pennsylvania.

Lloyd, William P. Diaries. Southern Historical Collection, University of North Carolina, Chapel Hill.

———. "The First Pennsylvania Cavalry in the Gettysburg Campaign." *Philadelphia Weekly Press*, May 26, 1886.

———. *History of the First Reg't. Pennsylvania Reserve Cavalry, from its Organization, August, 1861, to September, 1864, ...* Philadelphia: King & Baird, Printers, 1864.

Miller, Charles B. Letters, June 29, 1862; July 18, 1864. USAMHI, HbCWRT Collection.

Moyer, William F. "Brandy Station." *National Tribune*, March 20, 1884.

Smoyer, Edward B. Letters. Historical Society of Pennsylvania.

Thomas, Hampton S. "Brandy Station." *Philadelphia Weekly Times*, November 10, 1877.

———. *Some Personal Reminiscences of Service in the Cavalry of the Army of the Potomac.* Philadelphia: L. R. Hammersly & Company, 1889.

"The Twin Regiments. 1st Penna. and 1st New Jersey Cavalry." *Grand Army Scout and Soldiers Mail*, December 16, 23, 30, 1882.

45th Infantry

First State Color

The companies forming the 45th Pennsylvania were recruited in the counties of Tioga, Lancaster, Centre, Mifflin, and Wayne. Three days after the final organization of the 45th, Governor Curtin visited Camp Curtin and presented the state color to the new regiment on October 22, 1861.[1] The color was apparently given to Sergeant Joseph Reigle of Company E, who carried it until February 1864.[2] The regiment then entrained for Washington, where it remained until mid-November when it was transferred to Fort Monroe.

In early December, the 45th was assigned to a division commanded by Brigadier-General Thomas W. Sherman, who moved his troops by sea to Beaufort, South Carolina. Here the 45th was divided between Otter and Hilton Head Islands as garrison troops. The regiment remained in this area until July 1862, several of the companies taking part in minor expeditions into Rebel-held territory.

The 45th was then transferred to Virginia and was attached to the Ninth Corps, with which it remained until it was disbanded in 1865. After arriving at Newport News in mid-July, the regiment moved to Aquia Creek, where it guarded the railroad and supply depot until shortly after the Federal defeat at Second Manassas. It then moved by water to Washington to rejoin the corps. The 45th took part in the Battle of South Mountain on September 14, suffering a loss of 134 men. Three days later, the regiment participated in the Battle of Antietam, losing thirty-eight soldiers. Most of the Ninth Corps remained in reserve during the disastrous Battle of Fredericksburg on December 13, and the 45th suffered no casualties.

After remaining in camp near Newport News until mid-March 1863, the Ninth Corps was transferred to the Department of the Ohio. The 45th moved by rail to Cincinnati, and then marched south into Kentucky, occupying Covington and Paris in April. The 45th then moved to Hustonville, where it stayed until early June, when a large detachment of the corps was sent to reinforce General Grant's army at Vicksburg, Mississippi. The troops arrived near the besieged city on June 19, and were assigned as part of the force that guarded the rear of the Federal army. After the surrender of Vicksburg, Major-General William T. Sherman commanded an expedition sent to capture Jackson, the capital of Mississippi. The Ninth Corps was a part of this force and entered the city on July 17. Shortly thereafter, the corps returned to Kentucky.

At first stationed in Covington, the 45th began an epic march of over two hundred miles to Knoxville on September 10, arriving there on the twenty-sixth. The regiment participated in the fighting at Blue Springs on October 10, and then helped the retreating army repulse an enemy attack at Campbell's Station on November 16. Burnside withdrew his outnumbered forces to Knoxville, which was besieged by Confederate General James Longstreet until December 6. The regiment spent most of the winter in camp at Blaine's Cross Roads, where a majority of the regiment re-enlisted for another three years. Those who did so were granted a furlough, and the 45th arrived in Harrisburg on February 8, 1864. A local reporter saw the returning veterans and noted the following about the state color: "The flag of the 45th has half a

First State Color
Maker: EH
Size: 72¼" × 65¼" (-)
1985.052

Advance the Colors!

dozen fields emblazoned on its stripes, and is in tolerable good repair, but the loose end is mostly frayed out by balls and by storms." The flag was left in Harrisburg and officially returned to state care on July 4, 1866.[3]

Second State Color

When the regiment reassembled at Annapolis in March 1864, it received a new state color. Now a part of the First Brigade, Second Division, Ninth Corps, the strengthened 45th entered the Battle of the Wilderness on May 6. During the confused and fragmented struggle in the tangled undergrowth, the regiment suffered a loss of 143 officers and men. The bearer of the state color was shot down as the regiment assaulted a portion of the Confederate line. As the regiment was forced to retreat and reform, a corporal found the flag and carried it to safety.[4] This act resulted in the rallying of the regiment as described in the introduction to this volume.

The regiment was next engaged in the Battle of Spotsylvania, which lasted from May 8-21. The regiment was fighting on the eighteenth when the bearer was shot down. Corporal John Kinsey seized the flag and safely took it from the field as the regiment again was repulsed. Kinsey later received a Medal of Honor for his heroic action.[5] After marginally participating in the fighting at the North Anna River, the 45th suffered heavy casualties at Cold Harbor on June 1-3. During the June 17 assault at Petersburg, Corporal Thomas Evers of Company D, then the bearer of the state color, was either slightly disabled or became exhausted from the heat and was forced to relinquish

Third State Color
Maker: HB
Size: 71³/₈″ × 77¹/₂″
1985.053

his banner. Corporal Charles T. Kelley of Company G then bore the flag safely until Evers returned to duty sometime in July.[6]

After Grant's failure to capture Petersburg, his army settled down into siege warfare to wear down the Confederate defenders. The 45th's next action was on July 30, when the tunnel dug by the 48th Pennsylvania was completed and a section of the Rebel earthworks was blown up. The Federal attack was bungled and thrown back with heavy losses. Of the 220 men remaining with the regiment, one hundred were acting as skirmishers, leaving only 121 with the colors as the regiment joined in the attack. About one-third of the men became casualties, and the state color was captured by the enemy.[7] Upon its capture, the flag seems to have disappeared and was not among the identified flags returned to the states in 1905.

National Color

During the 1864 campaign, the 45th carried some type of national color alongside the state color. Sergeant Reigle, bearer of the first-issue state color, carried this national flag until he was wounded at Cold Harbor on June 3. Corporal Justus D. Strait of Company I then took the flag until Reigle returned to duty on June 19. Reigle bore the flag into the Battle of Poplar Springs Church on September 30, where the regiment was almost annihilated. The brigade was flanked by a Rebel counterattack and fell to pieces very quickly. Lieutenant-Colonel Theodore Gregg managed to rally about seventy men around Sergeant Reigle, but when Rebel troops threatened to surround the small band of Yankees, Gregg told everybody to scatter and save themselves. Sergeants Reigle (suffering from a flesh wound) and Strait ran through the woods toward the rear. As they emerged from the underbrush, the two men were confronted by by a dismounted group of the 10th Virginia Cavalry, which took them prisoner. The official report of the remnant of the 45th, reduced to a strength of less than one hundred men, mentioned that the flag had been torn from the staff and destroyed to prevent capture, but the exchanged prisoners later refuted this story. Once captured, the national color disappeared from history.[8]

Third State Color

Sometime prior to December 24, 1864, the 45th received a replacement state color.[9] Meanwhile, the shattered regiment was rebuilt with conscripts and volunteers. Its first action with the new banner was its participation in the assault on Petersburg on April 2,

1865, which resulted in the capture of the city. Color-Sergeant Andrew J. Goodfellow of Company A was cited in Ninth Corps reports for his personal valor during the capture of Confederate Fort Mahone that day.[10] After the surrender of General Lee, the 45th moved with the corps to Alexandria, participated in the Grand Review on May 23, and was then mustered out of service on July 17. The third state color was retained by Colonel Curtin, who wrote Adjutant-General Russell that he would have it painted with battle honors in time for the 1866 parade. However, only two battles were added to the color previous to the parade, when Curtin officially returned the flag to the Commonwealth.[11]

Notes

[1]Albert, p. 18, writes that the state color was presented on October 22. However, the story "Flag Presentation," *Pennsylvania Daily Telegraph*, October 21, 1861, indicates the flag was received that same day.

[2]Albert, p. 165. The names of the bearers in the regimental history are conflicting on the dates each carried one of the flags. All names in this sketch are the author's reconstruction, and there may be some mistakes.

[3]"Harrisburg Correspondence," *Union County Star and Lewisburg Chronicle*, February 12, 1864. Captain E. Beauge wrote that the first state color was retained by the regiment until late October 1864, when it was returned to Harrisburg. For this see Albert, p. 167.

[4]*Ibid.*, pp. 121-122. Roberts, in *As They Remembered*, p. 122, writes that Corporal John Heberford was the man who rescued the flag. There is no man by this name in the regimental roster in Bates. There is a Private J. G. Heberling in Company E, who may not be the same man.

[5]See Colonel F. C. Ainsworth to John Kinsey, March 2, 1897, in Kinsey's Medal of Honor file, RG 94.

[6]Albert, p. 140.

[7]Colonel Curtin to General A. L. Russell, June 15, 1866, RG 19.

[8]*O.R.* 42.1, 585; *O.R.* 42.3, pp. 479-480; Albert, pp. 164-165.

[9]This color was finished by Horstmann Brothers & Company on December 12. A soldier writing home on December 24 mentioned that the flag had been received recently. See "From the 45th Pa. Regt.," *Wellsboro Agitator*, January 11, 1865.

[10]*O.R.* 46.1, p. 1034.

[11] Curtin to Russell, cited in Note 7.

Bibliography

Albert, Allen D. *A Grandfather's Oft Told Tales of the Civil War, 1861-1865*. Williamsport: Grit Publishing Company, 1913.

_____. *History of the Forty-fifth Regiment Pennsylvania Veteran Volunteer Infantry, 1861-1865*. Williamsport: Grit Publishing Company, 1912.

Button, Warner. Letters, January 3, 28, 1862, May 1864. USAMHI, HbCWRT Collection.

Carroll, Robert. Diary, September 30, 1864-April 9, 1865. Lancaster County Historical Society.

Catlin, James E. "White and Black. A Novel Review of Prisoners in the Streets of Petersburg." *National Tribune*, March 10, 1887.

Gregg, Theodore. Papers. Pennsylvania State Archives.

Decker, George. Letters, November 1861-April 1863. In George Miller Collection, USAMHI.

Myers, Ephraim E. *A True Story of a Civil War Veteran*. York, 1910.

Roberts, Agatha L. *As They Remembered*. New York: William-Frederick Press, 1964.

46th Infantry

First State Color

The 46th Pennsylvania Volunteer Infantry was formed from ten different companies that rendezvoused at Camp Curtin in September 1861. Three of these companies had served as three-months units, Company A being the Logan Guards of Lewistown. Governor Curtin presented the new regiment with the state flag early on the evening of September 17, the day before the 46th left Camp Curtin for the front. The ceremony took place in back of the Capitol. Lieutenant-Colonel James L. Selfridge received the flag on behalf of absent Colonel Joseph F. Knipe.[1]

After leaving Harrisburg, the regiment was assigned to the command of Major-General Nathaniel P. Banks, headquartered at Harper's Ferry. Banks's corps crossed the Potomac and occupied the upper Shenandoah Valley in February and March 1862. After spending some time on garrison duty, the 46th participated in the Battle of Winchester on May 25, when Confederate General Stonewall Jackson's troops struck Banks's reduced command and forced Banks to retreat in haste across the Potomac. During the fighting that day, Color-Sergeant James McQuillan of Company D was wounded in the calf of his leg by a rifle bullet. The sergeant dropped to the ground for a moment and then sprang to his feet. With one hand raised above his head cheering the regiment onward, Sergeant McQuillan waved the state color with his other hand, apparently forgetting his painful wound. Two more bullets passed through the flag before the 46th retired from the field. Including casualties suffered during the retreat, the regiment lost 110 soldiers.[2]

Upon the organization of Federal troops in northern Virginia into the Army of Virginia, the 46th found itself as part of Banks's Second Corps. Banks pushed southward from Culpeper and attacked Jackson's corps at Cedar Mountain on August 9. Together with the rest of its brigade, the 46th charged forward through a wheatfield and encountered superior numbers of Rebel infantry. After a severe combat, the state flag was temporarily captured by the enemy. However, the regiment rallied and in some desperate hand-

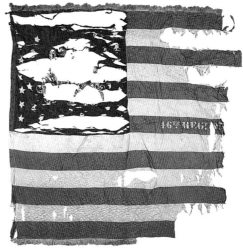

First State Color
Maker: EH
Size: 64¼" × 65¼" (-)
1985.055

to-hand fighting retook their prized banner, which was "completely riddled with balls."[3] Of the 504 officers and men who entered the fight, the 46th suffered a loss of 31 killed, 102 wounded, and 111 captured or missing, a total of 244. Banks's corps was so decimated by this battle that it took only a minor part in the campaign that resulted in the Second Battle of Manassas later in August.

Banks's corps then became the Twelfth Corps, Army of the Potomac, and participated in the Battle of Antietam on September 17. Here, the 46th was engaged but suffered only a slight loss. The corps was not engaged during the Battle of Fredericksburg on December 13. During this time, the flag was carried by Sergeant Charles A. Row of Company E.[4] The Twelfth Corps advanced to join the main army and went into winter quarters near the town of Falmouth, across the river from Fredericksburg.

The 46th next fought in the Battle of Chancellorsville in May 1863. Stonewall Jackson's surprise attack on May 2 completely routed the Eleventh Corps, and when that corps fell back, the position of Major-General Henry W. Slocum's Twelfth Corps was in danger. Slocum was forced to refuse his line to defend his rear, and in the maneuvering during the night of

May 2, the 46th was ordered out of its entrenchments and then ordered to reoccupy the old line. However, Rebel troops had silently occupied the Yankee earthworks, and as the 46th moved back on the double-quick, the advance of the regiment ran into the enemy line before the identity of the opposition was discovered. A hand-to-hand fight broke out, and soon, the fighting attracted the attention of nearby Federal artillerymen, who opened fire on friend and foe alike. Over eighty soldiers of the 46th were captured, including the color-sergeant and his state flag.[5] The capture of the flag was credited to Private J. S. Webber of the 12th North Carolina, a unit of Brigadier-General Alfred Iverson's Brigade of Rodes's Division.[6] This flag was recaptured in 1865 and retained by the War Department until 1905, when it was returned to Pennsylvania.

National Color

Sometime after the loss of its state color, the 46th received a national flag from an unidentified source. The regiment carried this flag throughout the remainder of its term of service. After the Chancellorsville Campaign, the regiment marched north to fight at Gettysburg on July 2-3, 1863. In October, the Eleventh and Twelfth Corps were detached from the Army of the Potomac and sent to Tennessee as reinforcements for the Federal troops in Chattanooga. The First Division of the corps was entrusted with the task of guarding the railroad from Tullahoma, Tennessee, to Bridgeport, Alabama, and thus did not take part in the November Battle of Chattanooga. The regiment re-enlisted as a veteran organization over the

National Color
Size: 70½" X 79"
1985.054

winter and returned to the Commonwealth for a month to rest and recruit.

Strengthened to 763 officers and men, the 46th left its camp near Chattanooga in early May to participate in General Sherman's successful campaign that resulted in the capture of Atlanta on September 2, 1864. The regiment fought in the Battle of Resaca on May 15, and then in the series of engagements collectively titled New Hope Church from May 25 through June 4. On June 22, the 46th helped repulse a Rebel assault on the position of the Twentieth Corps near Kenesaw Mountain. The Confederate attack on the corps at Peach Tree Creek on July 20 was also repulsed. Thereafter, the 46th remained with the corps in the siege line around Atlanta until the Confederates evacuated the city on September 1.

During the long and arduous marches and incessant fighting and skirmishing of the Atlanta Campaign, Sergeant William Baron of Company E carried the national color. Although but little remains of the flag, the staff bears evidence of the hard service seen by the 46th. A minie ball took a small chunk out of the staff. Near the bottom of the pole, a shot fractured the wood, which was wrapped with some type of cord. The staff was also shot completely through in the middle, which was repaired with a brass band. This band has inscribed on it Sergeant Baron's name as well as the names of three battles—Resaca, Dallas, and Kenesaw.

After the fall of Atlanta, the 46th was part of the force that accompanied Sherman on his famous march to the sea through Georgia. Savannah was captured on December 21, 1864, and after a short rest, Sherman's victorious army marched north through the Carolinas. Confederate General Joseph E. Johnston surrendered his army to Sherman on April 26, 1865, and shortly thereafter, most of Sherman's troops tramped north, finally reaching Alexandria, Virginia, in May. The 46th was mustered out of service here on July 16. The national flag carried by the regiment during the 1864-65 campaigns was officially given to state care on July 4, 1866.

Unidentified National Color

The museum of the Philadelphia Camp, Sons of Union Veterans, has custody of the remnants of a 34-star national color attributed to the 46th Pennsylvania. Nothing else is known about this flag.

Second State Color

This flag was supplied to the state by Horstmann Brothers & Company in March 1864. The flag was originally inscribed for the 48th Pennsylvania, but

Advance the Colors!

was altered as the replacement flag for the 46th. Judging from its condition, this flag was never carried by the regiment, which may not have obtained the flag until it reached Alexandria. It was carried in the 1866 parade and turned over to state care at that time.

Pittsburgh Flag

During the May-June 1864 Pittsburgh Sanitary Commission Fair, a voting competion was held for participants to determine a winning regiment to present a national color donated to the fair by the ladies of the First United Presbyterian Church of Allegheny City. The 46th received the most votes, and the color was forwarded to the unit sometime in June 1864. The subsequent history of the flag is unknown, although it is quite possible that one of the two national colors described above is this Pittsburgh flag.[7]

Second State Color
Maker: HB

Size: 70⅞" × 76⅝"
1985.056

Notes

[1]"Interesting Ceremony," *Pennsylvania Daily Telegraph*, September 18, 1861.

[2]"The Forty-sixth Pennsylvania Regiment," *Harrisburg Patriot and Union*, May 31, 1862.

[3]"The Forty-sixth Pennsylvania Regiment," *Reading Daily Times*, August 14, 1862.

[4]"List of Officers of Co. E, 46th Regiment," *Reading Daily Times*, November 14, 1862.

[5]Colonel James L. Selfridge to Governor Curtin, November 13, 1863, Folder 23, Regimental Papers, RG 19; William T. Shimp to Annie, May 14, 1863, Shimp Letters.

[6]*O.R.* 25.1, p. 990.

[7]"The Prize Colors," *Pittsburg Gazette*, June 21, 1864.

Bibliography

Barret, C. N. "With the Red Star Division at Chancellorsville." *Grand Army Scout and Soldiers Mail*, January 3, 10, 17, 24, 31, 1885.

Brooks, George A. 1862 Diary. Southern Historical Collection, University of North Carolina, Chapel Hill.

Caldwell Family Correspondence. USAMHI, CWTI Collection. This collection includes letters, 1861-September 1864, of William and Thomas Caldwell.

"Chancellorsville. A Private Criticizes the Generals and Tells His Own Story of That Battle." *National Tribune*, July 23, 1885.

Crosby, John W. "Cedar Mountain." *National Tribune*, June 21, 1888.

Garrett, John S. Letters, 1861-1863. Pennsylvania State Archives.

Patton, James H. 1865 Diary. USAMHI.

Shimp, William T. Letters, December 1861-January 1865. USAMHI, CW-Misc Collection.

Stewart, Jerome B. 1862 Letters. Potter County Historical Society.

47th Infantry

First State Color

Composed of seven companies recruited in the Lehigh Valley and three from Perry and Northumberland counties, the 47th Pennsylvania was organized at Camp Curtin in early September 1861. On Friday afternoon, September 20, Governor Curtin visited the camp and presented a state color to the new regiment.[1] The regiment left camp the next day for Washington, where it remained for about four months. While stationed near the capital, the 47th's chief duties were drilling and occasional stints as outpost guards.

In late January 1862 the 47th was chosen to be part of an expedition led by Brigadier-General John M. Brannan. The general took his troops to Key West, Florida, to serve as garrison troops in the area. The 47th was assigned to Fort Taylor, remaining there until mid-June, when it was included as reinforcements for a projected attack on Charleston, South Carolina. This assault never took place, and after a bout of guard duty at Beaufort, South Carolina, the 47th was detailed as part of an expedition that captured Jacksonville, Florida, and pushed up the St. John's River. This minor foray compelled local Confederate forces to retreat into the interior of the state.

After the conclusion of this brief campaign, the 47th was attached to an expedition that attempted to interdict rail transportation between Charleston and Savannah by destroying the bridge over the Pocotaligo River. The major engagement of this expedition took place on October 21, 1862, as Federal regiments collided with Confederate defenders deployed near the bridge. After a series of unsuccessful attacks, the Federal expedition retreated to its ships. Of the six hundred officers and men taken into this engagement, the 47th suffered a loss of 18 killed and 94 wounded, one-third of the entire Yankee casualty list.

Upon returning to Hilton Head from the failure at Pocotaligo, the 47th recuperated for a few weeks before returning to Key West in mid-November. The regiment was divided in half, garrisoning Forts Taylor and Jefferson, serving in this capacity from November 1862 through February 1864. During the winter of

First State Color   Size: 54½" (-) × 62⅜" (-)
Maker: EH   1985.057

1863-64, most of the soldiers in the 47th re-enlisted for another term of service, and thus were allowed furloughs before rejoining the regiment.

In February 1864 the 47th was relieved from the onerous garrison duty and sent to Louisiana to join the Nineteenth Corps, Department of the Gulf. Major-General Nathaniel P. Banks, commanding the department, was preparing to advance up the Red River to seize the cotton crop said to be in great abundance in northwest Louisiana. Banks's troops started the advance on March 10, and the Federal expedition managed to approach near Mansfield before Confederate defenders counterattacked. In an engagement known as the Battle of Sabine Cross Roads on April 8, Banks's lead elements were attacked and driven back. Banks withdrew his small army a few miles and set up a defensive position at Pleasant Hill.

The pursuing enemy troops attacked on April 9, and for most of the afternoon the outcome of the struggle was uncertain. Finally, the Yankees counterattacked and drove the enemy from the field. In the course of the latter stages of the battle, the 47th charged forward and recaptured a Massachusetts battery. Color-Sergeant Benjamin F. Walls of Company C rushed forward and planted the state color on one of the battery's caissons. As he did so, a bullet pierced his left shoulder and the sergeant fell wounded. Sergeant William Pyer of the same company then took the flag and was also wounded.[2]

The wound to Sergeant Walls spelled the end of his army service. Walls, a wealthy farmer from Juniata County, was sixty-five years old when he enlisted as a private in 1861. When Walls appeared before an army surgeon for the required physical examination, the surgeon pronounced the elderly Walls unfit for service. "By the Lord!" Walls responded, "I have yet to learn that a man ever becomes too old to serve his country!" Intimidated by this outburst of patriotism, the surgeon passed Walls. He was promoted to sergeant and carried the colors until wounded at Pleasant Hill. Walls was not permitted to re-enlist when his original term expired in September 1864. He retired to his farm and died in 1877.[3]

Even though Banks defeated the Rebels at Pleasant Hill, he abandoned the campaign and retreated to New Orleans. In July, the Nineteenth Corps was detached from the Department of the Gulf and ordered to Washington, which was threatened by a Rebel force in the Shenandoah Valley. Upon its arrival in Maryland, the corps became part of Major-General Philip H. Sheridan's command, which pushed into the Valley and defeated the enemy at Winchester on September 19, 1864. The 47th played a minor role in the victory at Fisher's Hill on September 21-22. The regiment suffered its heaviest loss in the Battle of Cedar Creek which occurred on October 19. In this battle the Nineteenth Corps bore the brunt of some of the heaviest Rebel assaults, the 47th suffering a loss of 154.

After the successful conclusion of the Shenandoah Valley campaign, the regiment spent the winter guarding the railroads near Charlestown, Virginia. This was the last action seen by the 47th, for the Virginia hostilities effectively ended when General Lee surrendered on April 9, 1865. In the spring of 1865 the 47th received a new state color (see below) but seems to have retained the original flag until May 11, when it was sent to the State Agency in Washington.[4] It was officially returned to Commonwealth on July 4, 1866.

Second State Color

Owing to the heavy battle damage suffered in Louisiana and Virginia, a replacement color was supplied to the regiment by Horstmann Brothers in February 1865. Horstmann sent the flag to Sunbury, where Captain Daniel Oyster obtained it on March 7, 1865. The captain was home on leave and took the new state color to the regiment when he returned. This new flag contained the names of all the battles in which the 47th had participated.[5] Upon the conclusion of the war, the 47th encamped near Washington until June, when it was ordered to Savannah for garrison duty. A month later, the 47th moved to Charleston, where it remained until January 1866. Its services no longer needed, the regiment returned to Pennsylvania and was mustered out of service in Philadelphia on January 9. The 47th was the only Keystone unit to fight west of the Mississippi River and was perhaps the longest serving Federal unit. The second state color was officially returned to state care on July 4, 1866.

Second State Color	Size: 72½" × 78¾"
Maker: HB	1985.058

Notes

[1]"Presentation of Colors," *Pennsylvania Daily Telegraph*, September 20, 1861.

[2]Bates 1: 1154; "Letter from the Sunbury Guards," *Sunbury American*, May 7, 1864.

[3]Bates 1: 1154.

[4]The cost for shipping the flag to Washington was $1.50. See "Proceedings of the Council of Administration of the 47th Regt. Pa. Vols.," Wyoming Historical and Geological Society, Wilkes-Barre.

[5]"A Beautiful Flag," *Sunbury Gazette*, March 11, 1865.

Bibliography

Albert, George W. Diary, 1863-64. USAMHI, HbCWRT Collection.

"The Forty-seventh Pennsylvania Regiment," *Grand Army Scout and Soldiers Mail*, February 10, 17, 1883.

Gardner, Reuben S. Papers. Pennsylvania State Archives.

Geety, William W. Papers. USAMHI, HbCWRT Collection.

Marshall, Charles L. "The Battle of Cedar Creek," *National Tribune*, September 13, 1888.

Schmidt, Lewis G. *A Civil War History of the 47th Regiment of Pennsylvania Veteran Volunteers*. Allentown: the author, 1986.

48th Infantry

First State Color

Recruited exclusively in Schuylkill County, the 48th Pennsylvania was organized at Camp Curtin in September 1861. Governor Curtin visited the camp on September 20 to present the new regiment with a state color.[1] A few days later, the regiment left Harrisburg and went into camp near Fort Monroe, Virginia. It remained here, drilling and training, until November 11, when it was transported to Hatteras Inlet, North Carolina. Here, the 48th acted as part of the garrison until March 1862. Six companies were then detached to join the expedition commanded by Brigadier-General Ambrose E. Burnside, which captured New Bern on March 14. Although not engaged in the battle, the portion of the 48th with the Federal division transported ammunition to the battlefield. Burnside considered this reserve supply of ammunition so important that he allowed "New Bern" to be placed on the 48th's color.[2]

The remainder of the regiment soon joined the companies at New Bern, and the entire regiment remained camped near the city until early July 1862. At this time, most of Burnside's troops were withdrawn

Second State Color
Maker: HB
Size: 72" × 67¼" (-)
1985.059

Regimental Colors at Muster Out, July 1865
Second State Color at Left, National Color at Right

to Virginia upon General McClellan's failure in the Peninsula Campaign. Burnside's command became the Ninth Corps, with which the 48th continued to serve until it was disbanded in 1865. The 48th first engaged enemy forces at the Second Battle of Manassas on August 29-30, 1862. Here, the Second Division

128

of the corps suffered heavy losses while unsuccessfully attempting to drive Stonewall Jackson's Confederates out of a railroad cut. The 48th was then slightly engaged at Chantilly on September 1 during the retreat to Washington.

The corps then moved into Maryland as the Army of the Potomac countered General Lee's invasion of that state. After fighting at South Mountain on September 14, the 48th took part in the Battle of Antietam three days later, suffering sixty casualties. The army then returned to Virginia, where the 48th was next engaged at Fredericksburg on December 13. In February 1863, the Ninth Corps was detached from the Army of the Potomac and sent with Burnside to the Department of the Ohio. The 48th moved to Lexington, Kentucky, where it remained as the garrison from April through mid-September 1863. At this time, the regiment was transferred to eastern Tennessee, fighting at Blue Springs (October 10), Campbell's Station (November 16), and the Siege of Knoxville (November 17-December 5). The regiment then went into winter camp near Knoxville, where most of the men re-enlisted for another three years. It was relieved for furlough and arrived in Pottsville on February 3, 1864. The tattered state color was apparently left in the city when the regiment returned to the front. The remnant may have been included with the flags given to the Historical Society of Schuylkill County in 1913; if so, not enough remains to positively identify it.

Second State Color

A replacement state color was sent to the regiment soon after it reported to the Ninth Corps rendezvous camp at Annapolis. The strengthened regiment then participated in the 1864 campaign, including the fighting in the Wilderness (May 6-7), Spotsylvania (May 8-18), North Anna River (May 23-26), Totopotomoy River, Bethesda Church (May 28-31), and Cold Harbor (June 3-6). The army then crossed the James River and attacked the Confederate defenses of Petersburg in fighting lasting from June 16-18. The two armies then settled down behind their trenches into siege warfare that lasted until the city was taken on April 2, 1865.

Since many of the 48th's soldiers had been coal miners before the war, Lieutenant-Colonel Henry Pleasants devised a plan whereby his regiment would tunnel under the opposing enemy defenses and blow them up, thus leaving the way open for a successful attack. The plan was approved and the tunnel was dug and packed with explosives from June 25 to July 28. Two days later, the mine was detonated but the

Federal attack was bungled and repulsed. Still, the 48th won enduring fame by its tunnelling operation, which was thought impossible by many of the professional military engineers.

The regiment next fought in the Battle of Poplar Springs Church on September 30, suffering fifty-four casualties. Thereafter, the regiment remained in the trenches, taking its turn of duty until the successful April 2, 1865, assault on Petersburg. Sergeant John Taylor of Company A carried the state color through the attack, in which ninety-nine Pennsylvanians became casualties, including Colonel George W. Gowen, who was killed as the troops surged forward.[3] After Lee's surrender, the 48th marched to Alexandria and remained in that area until mustered out of service on July 17, 1865. The battered state color was left in Harrisburg and returned to the Commonwealth on July 4, 1866.

1861 Pottsville Flag

Shortly after the 48th left Harrisburg for Fort Monroe in September 1861, Mr. John T. Werner of Pottsville sent the regiment a "fine American flag." This banner cost $60, and was painted with the name and number of the regiment, together with the motto "In the Cause of the Union We Know No Such Word as Fail" in the midst of the blue canton.[4] This flag was apparently carried by the regiment until it returned to Pottsville in February 1864. It was left in the city and was given to the Historical Society of Schuylkill County in 1913. The small remnant of a blue canton, containing a few gold stars and a bit of gray paint, may be all that remains of this flag.

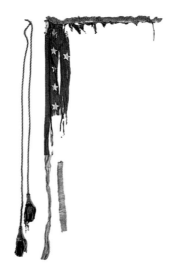

Possible Remnant of 1861
Pottsville Flag
S1984.001

Sergeant Samuel A. Beddall, Company E

National Color
Size: 71¹/₂" × 72¹/₂"
1985.060

Regimental Color, 1864 Pottsville Presentation
Size: 69¹/₂" × 78¹/₄"
S1984.008

1864 Pottsville Flags

When the regiment reached Port Carbon en route to Pottsville on February 3, 1864, the veterans stopped at the Mansion House to receive a flag obtained for the regiment by Mrs. E. R. Bohannon and Miss Miesse of Pottsville. Representative James H. Campbell delivered the presentation speech. The flag was furnished by Evans & Hassall and was a blue regimental color, with the state arms on one side and the national arms on the reverse. Scrolls containing the names of Bull Run, Chantilly, Antietam, and Fredericksburg surrounded each coat-of-arms. The ladies also presented four guidons, one red, one white, one blue, and one a small American flag. These flags were carried by the regiment until it disbanded in July 1865. Sergeant John Roarty of Company C carried the regimental color until October 2, 1864, when he was relieved as bearer by Sergeant Samuel A. Beddall of Company A, who carried it through July 1865. The flag was taken home to Pottsville and was given to the Historical Society in 1913. One of the monocolor guidons was in the possession of Philip Richards of Company A when it was photographed in 1899. The photograph then appeared in a 1903 newspaper article. Its present location is unknown.[5]

National Color

This unmarked 35-star national color was apparently carried by the 48th at the end of the war and left in Harrisburg when the unit disbanded. Nothing further is known about the history of this flag.

Advance the Colors!

Company A Flag

On January 1, 1863, the ladies of Port Clinton presented a national flag to Company A, the Port Clinton Artillery. This flag contained the names of New Bern, Bull Run, Chantilly, South Mountain, Antietam, and Fredericksburg. Its subsequent history and disposition is unknown.[6]

Flank Markers

These two markers were part of the 1984 Historical Society of Schuylkill County's donation to the flag program. Their history cannot be verified at this time.

Record Banner

Since the colors of the 48th were so tattered and torn as to prevent the battle honors from being painted on them, a special record flag was prepared. Captain Edward S. Harty designed the flag, which was painted by Pottsville resident James Mudey. This banner was carried in the 1866 Philadelphia parade and deposited in the Flag Room. When the flags were moved into the new room in the Executive Library and Museum Building, the banner was not placed on display and the veterans complained about this oversight. Apparently, nothing was done with the banner until it was placed in Case #5 in 1914.[7]

Below: Flank Marker
Size: 27¹/₄" × 32¹/₂"
S1984.003

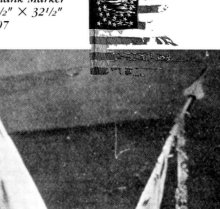

Above: Flank Marker
Size: 27¹/₂" × 32¹/₂"
S1984.007

Record Banner
Size: 53¹/₄" × 70¹/₄"
1985.166

Unidentified Colors of the 48th

Notes

[1] Bosbyshell, pp. 18-19; Bates 1: 1191.

[2] Bosbyshell, p. 47.

[3] Gould, p. 300.

[4] Bosbyshell, pp. 18-19; Wallace, *Schuylkill County*, p. 86.

[5] Bosbyshell, pp. 142-143; Gould, pp. 158-159, 342; Wallace, *Schuylkill County*, pp. 297-298; "Concluding Chapter of Colonel George W. Gowen's Army Career," *Germantown Independent-Gazette*, March 20,

1893; "Brilliant Reception of the Forty-eighth Regiment, P.V.," *Pottsville Miners' Journal*, February 6, 1864.

[6] Gould, p. 108.

[7] "Return of Battle Flags to the State," *Pottsville Miners' Journal*, July 7, 1866; O. C. Bosbyshell to Military Board of the State of Pennsylvania, May 29, 1895, RG 25.

Bibliography

Bausum, Daniel F. "Personal Reminiscences of Sergeant Daniel F. Bausum, Co. K, 48th Regt., Penna. Vol. Inf., 1861-1865." *Publications of the Historical Society of Schuylkill County* 4 (1914): 240-249.

Bosbyshell, Oliver C. *The 48th in the War, Being a Narrative of the Campaigns of the 48th Regiment, Infantry, Pennsylvania Veteran Volunteers, During the War of the Rebellion*. Philadelphia: Avil Printing Company, 1895.

———. "The Petersburg Mine." *Maine Bugle* 3 (1896): 211-223.

Featherston, John C. ". . . The Work of the 48th Regiment, Pennsylvania V.V.I., at Petersburg Mine, and Which Resulted in the Great Battle of the Crater, as detailed by John C. Featherston, Late a Captain in the Alabama Brigade of General Mahone's Division, Which Recaptured This Important Point in the Confederate Lines. A Lecture Delivered at Pottsville, Schuylkill County, the Home of the 48th Regiment, by Capt. John C. Featherston." N.p., [1906].

Gould, Joseph. *The Story of the Forty-eighth, A Record of the Campaigns of the Forty-eighth Regiment Pennsylvania Veteran Volunteer Infantry During the Four Eventful Years of Its Service in the War for the Preservation of the Union*. Philadelphia: Alfred M. Slocum Company, 1908.

Heisler, H. C. Papers. Library of Congress.

"An Incident of Camp Life on Hatteras." *Grand Army Scout and Soldiers Mail*, April 21, 1883.

Pleasants, Henry, Jr. *The Tragedy of the Crater*. Boston: Christopher Publishing House, 1938.

Watson, John. "About Fort Mahone." *National Tribune*, August 11, 1887.

Wren, James. Diary, February 20-December 18, 1862. Antietam National Battlefield Park.

49th Infantry

First State Color

This infantry regiment was formed from ten independent companies at Camp Curtin in September 1861. Shortly after formation, Governor Curtin came to the camp and presented the state color to Colonel William H. Irwin on September 20.[1] The 49th entrained for Washington the next day, going into winter camp on the Virginia side of the city. While in this camp, the regiment was formed with three other regiments into a brigade command by Winfield Scott Hancock, who would later become one of the best Federal corps commanders. The brigade was initially assigned to the Fourth Corps but was shifted to the Sixth Corps when that command was formed in late May 1862. Thereafter, the 49th's history was part of that corps.

The command was transported by water as part of McClellan's campaign against Richmond, which began in March 1862. After the siege of Yorktown, the 49th joined the pursuit of the retreating enemy forces. Elements of the two armies fought a sharp engagement at Williamsburg on May 5, 1862. As Hancock's brigade advanced on the flank of the enemy

First State Color
Maker: EH
1985.062

battleline, some fortifications were seen ahead of the troops. Unsure where the enemy was, Hancock ordered Color-Sergeant Theodore D. Hoffman of Company D to take the colors and a squad of men into a nearby abandoned fort and raise them, hoping to draw enemy fire and thus locate the foe. Hoffman did this, and Hancock quickly formed his regiments into line and repulsed several attacks on his position.[2]

After marching with the army to within a few miles of the Confederate capital, the 49th took part in the Seven Days' Battles, being actively engaged on June 27th and 28th, in the fighting at Garnett's Hill and Golding's Farm, losing very few men to enemy fire. Otherwise, the regiment suffered little, although scores of soldiers became sick from the unhealthy climate on the Peninsula, and the 49th was much reduced in strength because of all the men in the hospitals.

McClellan's troops were transferred to northern Virginia in August 1862 to reinforce General Pope's Federal army, but most of the Sixth Corps arrived too late to take part in the Second Battle of Manassas. As Lee's victorious Confederates invaded Maryland, the corps was part of the troops that McClellan led to intercept the enemy. The two armies met at Antietam on September 17, 1862, in the war's bloodiest day. Hancock's brigade was engaged toward the close of the fighting on the northern section of the battlefield, but the 49th was only marginally in the battle. Thus, the new color-sergeant, John M. Thompson, escaped injury.[3]

After the end of the Maryland Campaign, both armies returned to Virginia, and next clashed at Fredericksburg on December 13. Again, the Sixth Corps was not heavily engaged and the 49th suffered the loss of a single wounded man. Shortly thereafter, owing to its reduced strength through sickness, the regiment was consolidated into a battalion of four companies. The reorganized 49th then participated in the Chancellorsville Campaign, fighting at Salem Church on May 3.

The 49th then took part in the Gettysburg Campaign but was not engaged in that important battle.

Sergeant Henry Entriken with the Remnant of the First State Color

Sergeant Samuel H. Irvin, Company C

Together with the rest of the corps, the soldiers of the 49th marched thirty-two miles with only one brief stop, arriving on the battlefield late on July 2, in time for part of the corps to be used as reinforcements. Upon the return to Virginia, the regiment was in the brief campaigns in northern Virginia, including the charge on the enemy entrenchments at Rappahannock Station on November 7, which resulted in the capture of two Southern brigades. After the Mine Run Campaign, the 49th went into winter camp near Brandy Station.

Over the winter, enough volunteers and drafted men were received to form five new companies and thus the 49th Pennsylvania entered the 1864 campaign greatly strengthened. Sergeant John J. Hight of Company D was appointed color-bearer on March 7.[4] After fighting in the Battle of the Wilderness on May 5-6, the 49th entered the sanguinary combat at Spotsylvania. It was one of twelve regiments chosen by

Colonel Emory Upton to charge the Confederate breastworks late in the afternoon of May 10. Three companies were acting as skirmishers and only six companies participated in this desperate attack, which was initially successful but failed when reinforcements did not bolster the original attacking troops. The 49th paid a fearful price in this assault. Together with the minor casualties suffered during the next two days, the regiment suffered a casualty rate of sixty-three percent of the 470 officers and men in the battle. Both the colonel and lieutenant-colonel were killed. All the color-corporals were either killed or wounded, and Sergeant Hight himself was slightly wounded but retained the flag.[5]

The depleted regiment then participated, with slight loss, in the engagements at the North Anna River, Cold Harbor, and the fighting around Petersburg. On July 7, 1864, the corps began to leave Petersburg and was taken to Washington to protect the

Advance the Colors!

capital from a small Confederate army commanded by Jubal Early. The corps followed the retreating enemy and fought with Early's men at Winchester on September 19, the 49th losing forty-five men in this battle. Shortly afterwards, the 49th was detached as part of the garrison of Winchester and thus did not participate in the Battle of Cedar Creek in October.

Second State Color

While in camp at Winchester, a replacement state color was issued to the 49th. The new color was presented by the brigade commander, Colonel Oliver Edwards, on October 26, being received for the regiment by Captain James T. Stewart. Sergeant Hight, who had carried the old state color since March, had been replaced as bearer by Sergeant Henry Entriken on October 19. When Sergeant Entriken received the new stand of colors, the old was given to Corporal Theodore H. McFarland for safekeeping until it could be returned to the adjutant-general's office.[6]

The 49th remained in the northern Shenandoah Valley until early December when the corps returned to Petersburg. After spending an uneventful winter, the regiment aided in the assault that finally captured Petersburg, losing very few men. The regiment's final engagement with the enemy was at Saylor's Creek on April 6, 1865, where fifty officers and men became

Second State Color
Maker: HB
Size: 71 1/8" × 76 1/2"
1985.061

the 49th's last battle casualties. After Lee's surrender at Appomattox, the regiment remained on guard duty in Virginia until it was mustered out of service in July. The second state color was then returned to Harrisburg, and both were officially given to state care during the July 4, 1866, ceremony.

Notes

[1] Westbrook, p. 89.

[2] *Ibid.*, pp. 106-108.

[3] Thompson was appointed color-sergeant on September 3, 1862, and was promoted to 2nd lieutenant on October 24, *Ibid.*, p.33.

[4] *Ibid.*, p. 46. It is not known who Hight replaced as color-bearer. A photograph of Sergeant Stephen Transue of Company D identifies him as

color-bearer but includes no dates. Since Transue was promoted to 1st sergeant in March 1864, it is possible that he carried the colors during 1863.

[5] *Ibid.*, pp. 189-201.

[6] *Ibid.*, pp. 224-225. At some point during 1864, Sergeant Samuel H. Irvin of Company C was color-bearer, *ibid.*, p. 14.

Bibliography

Arnold, John C. Papers. Library of Congress; USAMHI.

Clarkson, B. F. (edited by John M. Priest). "Vivid in My Memory." *Civil War Times Illustrated* 24 (December 1985): 20-25. Recollections of the Battle of Antietam.

Hutchinson, A. B. "Rappahannock." *National Tribune*, January 8, 1885.

Jones, B. F. "Sailor's Creek. What a Pennsylvania Soldier Saw and Did There." *National Tribune*, April 28, 1887.

Russ, William A., Jr. (editor). "Civil War Letters. Four Letters Reflecting

the Experiences of Company I, Forty-ninth Regiment, Pennsylvania Volunteer Infantry, in the Summer Campaigns of 1864." *Snyder County Historical Society Bulletin* 3, #9 (1955): 929-935 of volume 2 reprint.

Stewart, James T. "An Incident of the Battle of Antietam." *National Tribune*, December 19, 1889.

Westbrook, Robert S. *History of the 49th Pennsylvania Volunteers.* Altoona: Altoona Times Print, 1898.

50th Infantry

First State Color

Formed from companies recruited in a range of counties from Bradford and Susquehanna in the north, to Lancaster in the south, the 50th Pennsylvania was organized at Camp Curtin in late September 1861. Governor Curtin presented the state color to the new regiment on October 1. The color was handed to Color-Sergeant Richard Herbert of Company E, which was the color-company of the regiment.[1] After packing up all equipment, the 50th was transported to Washington, D.C. Remaining here only one week, the regiment then moved to Annapolis, where it was assigned to the expeditionary corps commanded by Brigadier-General Thomas W. Sherman.

First State Color　　　Size: 54¾" (-) × 79⅝"
Maker: EH　　　　　1985.065

Sherman's command soon embarked on naval transports and steamed south to occupy Hilton Head Island, South Carolina, whose Confederate forts had just been captured by a naval force. The 50th landed on the island and proceeded to occupy Beaufort, remaining on Hilton Head until mid-July 1862. During the regiment's tour of garrison duty, it skirmished with Confederate forces in several small engagements. One of these, a minor affair at Port Royal

Ferry, occurred on January 1, 1862. The regiment suffered only two men wounded as it attacked and destroyed an unfinished Rebel fort on the mainland. One of the wounded was Sergeant Herbert, who was hit in the leg by a spent piece of artillery shell. Another piece struck the flagstaff.[2]

In mid-July 1862, the brigade to which the 50th was attached was transferred to Virginia, where it became a part of Major-General Ambrose E. Burnside's Ninth Corps, remaining with this corps for the rest of its term of service. After debarking at Fort Monroe, the regiment moved to Fredericksburg, then skirmished with the advance guard of General Lee's army along the Rappahannock and Rapidan rivers. The 50th then fought in the Second Battle of Manassas, August 29-30, 1862, and in the succeeding engagements at Centreville and Chantilly as the beaten Federal army retreated to Washington.

Lee then invaded Maryland, and the Ninth Corps was part of McClellan's army that marched out to intercept the invasion. The 50th was marginally engaged in the Battle of South Mountain on September 14, suffering only two casualties. Three days later, on September 17, the regiment participated in the bloody struggle at Antietam, losing nine killed and thirty-one wounded during the advance of Burnside's corps on the left flank of the army. The regiment was present on the battlefield of Fredericksburg, Virginia, on December 13, but was not engaged with the enemy.

Upon the conclusion of the 1862 Virginia campaigns, the Ninth Corps was transferred to the Department of Ohio, arriving in northern Kentucky in March 1863. The 50th was initially stationed as garrison troops at Camp Dick Robinson, Stanford, and Somerset, Kentucky. When General Grant needed reinforcements to aid in his siege of Vicksburg, Mississippi, several regiments from the Ninth Corps, the 50th among them, were moved by rail and steamboat to join Grant's troops in early June. After the fall of Vicksburg, the regiment was part of General Sherman's force that attacked and captured Jackson, the capital of Mississippi. Although the 50th suffered very few casualties to enemy fire, the Mississippi campaign was particularly hard on the regiment, which was greatly reduced in strength as a result of the diseases contracted in the hot southern weather.

The regiment returned to Kentucky in August 1863. In September, Burnside's troops assembled for a march into eastern Tennessee, which culminated in the capture of Knoxville later that month. Again, although the 50th was engaged in several minor skirmishes, it escaped with few casualties. Confederate troops under General James Longstreet were sent into Tennessee to recapture Knoxville, but, after a siege lasting from November 17 to December 5, the Rebel troops failed to capture the strongly-fortified city. The regiment wintered in eastern Tennessee, where enough men re-enlisted for the regiment to be credited as a veteran volunteer unit. After a severe march across the mountains to Kentucky, the 50th arrived at Camp Curtin on February 4, 1864, for a one-month veteran's furlough. The torn and tattered state color was left in Harrisburg so the regiment could obtain a new flag. This old flag remained in Harrisburg until early May 1865, when Colonel William H. Telford sought temporary loan of the old flag so the 50th could carry their original banner in the May 23 Grand Review in Washington. Colonel Telford's request was granted, and he returned the flag to Harrisburg in early August.[3] Since only one state flag was carried in the 1866 ceremony, this color may have been the one not used owing to its battered condition.

Second State Color

Together with many new recruits and drafted men, the veterans of the 50th assembled at Camp Curtin in early March 1864, and then moved to Annapolis, where Burnside's Ninth Corps was gathering. While in camp near Annapolis, the regiment received a replacement state color sometime in April. Burnside's corps entered Grant's 1864 campaign against Lee's Army of Northern Virginia by engaging the enemy in the Battle of the Wilderness on May 6, 1864. During the confused struggle in the woods, the 50th lost sixty-nine officers and men. Three days later, the regiment lost sixty men as the Third Division of the corps drove Rebel troops away from the crossing of the Ny River as the Federal army advanced toward Spotsylvania Courthouse.

The 50th's heaviest loss during the war occurred on May 12, during the titanic engagement at Spotsylvania. Burnside's troops constituted the left flank of the Army of the Potomac and throughout the day his men participated in a number of attacks on the enemy line to prevent reinforcements from being sent to oppose the major Federal assault of the day. While attacking through a pine woods, the 50th was suddenly hit in the left flank by Confederate brigades

Second State Color
Maker: EH
Size: 71⁵⁄₈″ × 77¹⁄₄″
1985.063

commanded by Generals James H. Lane and William Mahone. The Federal attack went to pieces as Rebels swarmed in from what seemed to be all sides, and the struggle became hand-to-hand. A small portion of the 50th rallied around the colors and fought its way out of the situation, "contending hand-to-hand in many instances with bayonets and butts of guns."[4]

Sergeant James H. Levan of Company C wrote home soon after the battle and described what happened as the regiment fell back and attempted to re-form:[5]

> I soon found the Captain of Co. B [George A. Yeager]. We got eight men together, when the Lieut.-Colonel [Edward Overton, Jr.] came, and we formed a line and rallied the stragglers. Gen. Burnside came up, and said, "Boys, don't go back, but go and support those guns," meaning a battery that had no support, which the rebels attempted to take, "and hold it at any cost." We had just taken our position

How the 50th Repaired the May 12, 1864, Damage to the Staff

Regimental Color
Maker: HB
Size: 72¹/₈″ × 76¹/₄″
1985.064

when Capt. [George W.] Brumm came to us with both our flags. It infused new life into us. Brumm deserves the greatest credit. He took the new flag out of the rebel hands. Our Color Sergeants were shot.

In a letter home, another soldier described the state color as follows: "Our new colors are completely riddled, having 26 holes in them and the staff cut in two." Two bearers had been wounded and one killed in the successful struggle to save the flag from capture.[6] But the cost was high for the 50th. Casualties totalled 20 killed, 46 wounded, and 114 captured or missing.

After the fighting around Spotsylvania ended, the 50th was engaged in the succeeding battles with the enemy as Grant's troops pressed southward and eventually settled down to besiege Petersburg. The 50th fought at Cold Harbor (June 3-7), participated in the unsuccessful initial assaults on Petersburg (June 17-

18), was present at the Battle of the Crater on July 30, and fought at Poplar Springs Church on September 30. By this time, the regiment was greatly reduced in strength and was thus withdrawn from active operations for two weeks, during which time many new recruits were received and drilled.

The strengthened regiment thereafter took part in the fighting at Hatcher's Run on October 27. After spending the winter of 1864-65 garrisoning part of the trench system around Petersburg, the regiment participated marginally in the recapture of Fort Stedman on March 25, 1865, and was present when the Ninth Corps attacked the Confederate line at Petersburg on April 2. The Ninth Corps did not take part in the pursuit of Lee's army that ended in his surrender at Appomattox. Shortly after the surrender, the 50th moved to Washington, where it remained until late June 1865. The regiment was then chosen by General Grant to represent the infantry of the Army of the Potomac at the ceremony of the laying of the cornerstone of the Soldiers' National Monument in the cemetery at Gettysburg on July 4. The 50th then returned to Washington where it was mustered out of service on July 30. The second state flag was returned to Harrisburg and was officially received by the state on July 4, 1866.

Regimental Color

This flag was probably obtained by the 50th solely for the May 23, 1865, Grand Review in Washington. It contains the names of all battles and skirmishes in which the regiment participated. The flag was carried in the 1866 Philadelphia parade.

Company C Flag

In early 1864, the citizens of Schuylkill Haven presented a flag to the men of Company C. No other information about this flag is available.[7]

Notes

[1]"Regimental Flag Presentation," *Pennsylvania Daily Telegraph*, October 1, 1861; Wallace, *Schuylkill County*, pp. 87-88. The story "50th Regiment," in the October 1, 1861, *Reading Daily Times*, mentions Company E as the color company, but has the name of William Herbst as the color-sergeant. According to Bates, Herbst did not enlist until February 1864.

[2]Wallace, p. 435.
[3]Telford to [Adjutant-General A. L. Russell], May 12, 1865, RG 25.
[4]*O.R.* 36.1, pp. 969-970.
[5]Wallace, p. 353.
[6]"From the Army," *Reading Daily Times*, May 23, 1864.
[7]Wallace, p. 496.

Bibliography

Ayers, Ashman, 1862 Diary. Susquehanna County Historical Society.
Beardsley, Harrison M. Letters, October 26, 1861; August 16, 1862. In Flinchbaugh Collection, USAMHI.
Campbell, Harry E. Family Papers. Cornell University.

Crater, Lewis. *History of the Fiftieth Regiment, Penna. Vet. Vols., 1861-65*. Reading: Coleman Printing House, 1884.
Tyson, William H. Letters, April-August 1864. In USAMHI, CWMisc Collection.

Advance the Colors!

51st Infantry

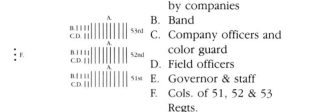

First State Color

Most of the soldiers who enlisted in the 51st Pennsylvania were members of the 4th Pennsylvania three-months volunteers. This unit was under the able command of Colonel John F. Hartranft, who also led the 51st. He would later become governor and commander of the Pennsylvania National Guard. Six of the regiment's companies came from Montgomery and Northampton counties while the other four were recruited in Union, Snyder, and Centre counties. The regiment was organized at Camp Curtin during the fall of 1861. Governor Curtin came to the camp and presented state colors to the 51st, 52nd, and 53rd Regiments in the same ceremony on November 5. Lieutenant-Colonel Thomas S. Bell of the 51st described the ceremony in a letter to a friend the next day:[1]

> The afternoon was a lovely one, and the view from where we stood could hardly have been more beautiful than it was. On our right, through the valley, the broad beautiful Susquehanna was foaming. From its banks rose up the bold mountains all gorgeously bedecked in their "coat of many colors." Before us were the tents of the camp, that shelter over 6000 Pennsylvania soldiers. Beyond, with the river sweeping round it, Harrisburg lay, quiet and peaceful. The air was quiet soft and balmy, and it was almost like an evening in June. At 4 o'clock we were drawn up in the following order:

A. The reg'ts in close column by companies
B. Band
C. Company officers and color guard
D. Field officers
E. Governor & staff
F. Cols. of 51, 52 & 53 Regts.

The Governor and staff drove on the ground, bringing with them the three flags in their cases, and took position as above (E). Then the three Colonels were ordered to the front (F) and with heads uncovered stood while the flags were unfurled and the presentation speech made. Governor Curtin, you know, is a brilliant speaker, and certainly on this occasion his address was most beautiful, patriotic and touching. When, with his tall form, shining above all others, he told us with all the force of oratory, what was expected of us when we took those standards, it did indeed seem a terrible responsibility, a task one must give his life rather than not fulfill. Each Colonel then in turn answered briefly. Then the color guards were called to the front, and the standard bearers received the flags and facing with them to their regiments, the colors were for the first time saluted. Then with our virgin flags flying and the bands playing, we marched in review past the Governor and the ceremony was ended.

In addition to the state color, the regiment carried throughout the war two additional flags presented by the ladies of Norristown. The 51st was one of a very few regiments to carry three colors simultaneously.

The 51st left Harrisburg on November 18 and went by rail to Annapolis, where it became a part of the force gathered by Brigadier-General Ambrose E. Burnside for an expedition to unknown shores. Burnside's troops left Annapolis in early January, bound for Hatteras Inlet, North Carolina. With assistance from the navy, Burnside's troops landed on Roanoke Island and forced the garrison to capitulate on February 8, 1862. Burnside then turned south to New Bern, capturing that city after a hard fight on March 14. The 51st was only marginally engaged in each of these two battles, suffering very few casualties. Thereafter, the regiment camped outside New Bern until early July. The monotony of camp life was interrupted by an expedition against the canal locks at South Mills,

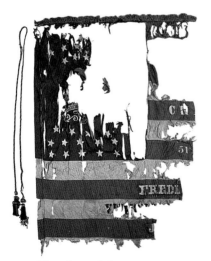

First State Color
Maker: EH
Size: 65³/₄" (-) × 48¹/₂" (-)
1985.072

highlighted by a small firefight at Sawyer's Lane on April 19.

Most of Burnside's troops were then withdrawn from North Carolina and sent as reinforcements to Virginia. These troops became the Ninth Corps, with which the 51st remained throughout its term of service. The corps was engaged in the Second Battle of Manassas on August 29-30 and fought again at Chantilly on September 1 during the retreat to Washington. Although present in both battles, the 51st sustained few losses. The corps then joined the Army of the Potomac, which marched into Maryland to bring Lee's Confederates to battle. The 51st briefly engaged the enemy at South Mountain on September 14, suffering thirty casualties.

The Battle of Antietam, fought on September 17, earned a bit of historical immortality for the 51st. During the initial stages of the battle, Burnside's Ninth Corps, on the left of the line, unsuccessfully attempted to cross Antietam Creek over a stone bridge. In mid-afternoon, the 51st was ordered to attack and capture the bridge. Supported by the 51st New York, Colonel Hartranft led the regiment on the run over the open ground toward the bridge, as enemy troops posted on the hill behind the span shot down the Federals as they neared the bridge. Captain William

First State Color in 1864

Allebaugh, commanding Company C, together with all three color-bearers, one of the guards, and a sergeant, were the first to reach the opposite shore.[2] The flags carried by the 51st were "much abused" in this charge. The flagstaff of the state color was badly damaged.[3] The regiment suffered casualties of 21 killed and 99 wounded.

After the army returned to Virginia, the regiment took part in the Battle of Fredericksburg on December 13, suffering ninety-one casualties. The Ninth Corps then spent the winter of 1862-63 near Newport News. In March 1863, the corps was sent to the Department of the Ohio as reinforcements. The 51st arrived in Kentucky and garrisoned places such as Stanford and Crab Orchard until early June. At the time, a portion of the corps was sent to Vicksburg, Mississippi, to bolster General Grant's siege of that Southern post. The 51st helped guard the western approaches to Grant's rear, then marched with Sherman's expedition to capture Jackson, which was entered on July 18. Although the regiment suffered few battle casualties, the hot, dusty Mississippi summer broke many a soldier's health.

The corps then returned to Kentucky. After resting and refitting at Crab Orchard, the 51st, together with most of the corps, marched south across the Appalachians to Knoxville. Hartranft's regiment played an important part in the engagement at Campbell's Station on November 16, as Burnside's outnumbered troops withdrew into the Knoxville defenses. His men were besieged from November 17 to December 5 by a Confederate army commanded by General James Longstreet. After the end of the siege, most of the regiment re-enlisted for another term of three years and received a veterans' furlough. After a hard winter march from Knoxville to Camp Nelson, the regiment finally returned to Harrisburg on February 8, 1864. The remnant of the state color was deposited in the city sometime before the regiment returned to the front and was included in the 1866 ceremony.

Second State Color

A replacement state color was provided to the strengthened 51st while it lay in camp at Annapolis in April 1864. Burnside's Ninth Corps joined the Army of the Potomac and participated in the Battle of Spotsylvania, which lasted from May 8-18. On May 12, the brigade to which the 51st was attached launched an attack on the Rebel entrenchments in its front. The Federal regiments advanced over the broken terrain and drove the enemy skirmishers back to the main line. As the Federals attacked, two Confederate brigades moved out and struck the assaulting column on its exposed left flank. Forming under cover of an oak

Second State Color
Maker: EH
Size: 71¹/₄" × 77³/₄"
1985.069

Third State Color
Maker: HB
Size: 70¹/₂" × 77¹/₄"
1985.066

woods, Brigadier-General James H. Lane's North Carolinians drove the surprised Yankees back and temporarily captured an artillery battery. At times the fighting was hand-to-hand.

The 51st was one of the regiments that was struck and thrown into confusion by the Rebel attack. Color-Sergeant Nathan H. Ramsey of Company C received two severe wounds during the close fighting. When another bearer was killed, Captain Allebaugh seized the state color and attempted to rally a portion of the disorganized 51st about him. However, the flag attracted the attention of a number of enemy soldiers, and Allebaugh was forced to surrender.[4] Lieutenant O. A. Wiggins of the 37th North Carolina was officially credited with the capture of the 51st's state color.[5] Including the entire operations at Spotsylvania, the 51st suffered a loss of 8 killed, 91 wounded, and 32 captured or missing, a total of 131.

The captured state color was retaken in 1865 and retained by the War Department until 1882. Sometime during the previous year, a Norristown lady visiting Washington happened to see the flag and so informed Colonel William J. Bolton. Bolton wanted the flag returned to the 51st Regimental Association, and enlisted the aid of General Hartranft, the state adjutant-general, and the Montgomery County congressmen. However, nothing came of Bolton's effort. The colonel then went to see Senator J. Donald Cameron, a member of the influential Cameron Family. The Senator introduced a joint resolution into Congress that was passed and signed into law on August 4, 1882, authorizing that the two colors lost at Spot-

sylvania be returned to the 51st Pennsylvania. The flags were indeed sent to Norristown later that month. The Regimental Association gave both colors to the Commonwealth on October 10, 1887.[6]

Third State Color

Colonel Bolton wrote to Adjutant-General Russell on June 22, 1864, explaining the circumstances surrounding the loss of the state color and seeking a replacement stand. Russell soon ordered a new flag from Horstmann Brothers & Company, which was sent to the State Agency in Washington and received by the regiment on July 29.[7] The third state color was first unfurled in combat on July 30, when the 51st participated in the Battle of the Crater. Thereafter, the 51st fought at the Weldon Railroad on August 19 and at Hatcher's Run on October 27-28 before settling down into winter quarters. The regiment was not actively engaged in the assault on Petersburg on April 2, 1865. Upon Lee's surrender, the regiment returned to the Washington area, where it was mustered out of service on July 27. This last state color was officially returned to state care on July 4, 1866.

1861 Norristown Flags

The 51st Pennsylvania carried six colors presented by the citizens of Norristown during its term of service. The first two were presented by Judge Daniel G. Smyser in front of the Montgomery County Court House on April 20, 1861. These flags—one a national color with the thirty-three stars arranged in a giant star pat-

National Color, 1861 Presentation
Size: 54½" × 63¾" (-)
1985.067

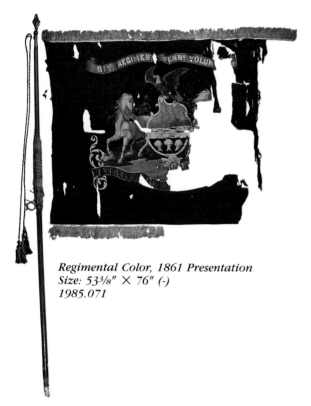

Regimental Color, 1861 Presentation
Size: 53⅜" × 76" (-)
1985.071

shell broke the staff in half. The men found an empty box of army hardtack and used strips of wood from the lid to repair the staff.[11] This repair can still be seen. Both flags were given to the state on October 10, 1887.

1862 Norristown Flags

Upon hearing of the damage to the flags at Antietam, citizens of Norristown sought and easily obtained subscriptions to purchase a new stand of colors for the 51st. One of these flags was a national color, the other a regimental color. The remnant of the regimental color indicates that it was a standard infantry regimental flag with local inscriptions added. A committee of citizens headed by Benjamin E. Chain went to the regimental camp, where they presented these flags on September 29. Both colors were carried in service until the 51st returned to the state for its furlough in February 1864. Both flags were deposited in Norristown and retained by the Regimental Association. On October 10, 1887, the remnant of the regimental color was included with the six flags the Association presented to the state. At an unspecified time, the national color was obtained by Mr. Levi Bolton, who decided that since the flag was a gift of the ladies of Norristown it should remain in the city. G.A.R. Post 11 owned the flag until 1917, when the Regimental Association obtained possession and presented it to the Montgomery County Historical Society on September 17, the fifty-fifth anniversary of the Battle of Antietam. This flag is still owned by the Historical Society.[12]

tern, the other a state regimental color—were given to the 4th Pennsylvania three-months volunteers.[8] When most of the regiment re-enlisted to become the 51st, the state regimental was repainted for this unit. The faint outline of "Fourth" can be discerned beneath the "51st" on the scroll above the state arms. The flags were carried until the Battle of Antietam. Corporal George W. Foote carried one of these flags at New Bern on March 14, 1862. Colonel Bolton recalled that Foote's color was the first planted on the enemy breastworks on that part of the line as the Federals drove the defenders from their works.[9] The state regimental color was badly damaged at Antietam. An artillery shell tore through the blue field as the regiment advanced after capturing the bridge.[10] Another

Regimental Color, 1862 Presentation
Size: 70" × 73" (-)
1985.070

Advance the Colors!

1864 Norristown Flags

On March 10, 1864, the citizens of Norristown presented a new stand of colors to the veterans of the 51st before they left the city for Camp Curtin. The flags included a national color emblazoned with the names of eleven battles in which the 51st had participated, a state regimental color, and a set of guide markers.[13] The national color was captured at the same time the state color was lost during the fighting at Spotsylvania on May 12, 1864. Corporal James Cameron of Company I, the bearer, was also seized by the enemy.[14] Leonidas H. Dean of the 12th Virginia was credited with the flag's capture, although the evidence is strong that North Carolinians of Lane's Brigade more likely took the flag. As the prisoners were sent to the rear, they were taken into custody by Virginians of Mahone's Brigade, some of whom claimed credit for the capture.[15] This flag was one of two obtained by the Regimental Association in 1882. Both flags were given to the state on October 10, 1887.

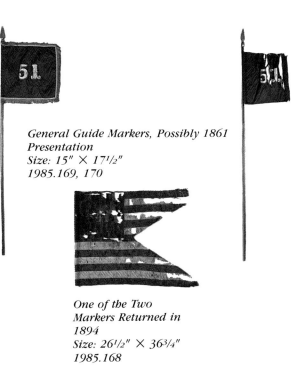

*Regimental Color, 1864
Presentation
Size: 70½" × 54¾" (-)
1985.068*

General Guide Markers

The 51st was one of many regiments to use left and right general guide markers. A set of these markers was prepared by friends of the regiment and received by Lieutenant-Colonel Bell on December 29, 1861.[16] The subsequent history of these markers is unknown. The two markers given to the state in 1887 may be these same flags. A set was presented to the regiment on March 10, 1864, by the citizens of Norristown. These were presumably carried until the end of the war. By some mistake, these markers were left in Al-

exandria when the 51st was mustered out of service. S. J. Gates of the 195th Ohio found them lying alongside one of the roads leading to Washington. Having been taken off their staffs, they were rolled up in a small package. Gates kept them and forgot about them for many years after the war. In 1890, he managed to locate Colonel Bolton, then the Inspector of Customs in Philadelphia. Gates returned the guidons to the colonel, who forwarded them to Adjutant-General W. W. Greenland in September 1894.[17]

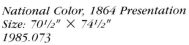

*National Color, 1864 Presentation
Size: 70½" × 74½"
1985.073*

*General Guide Markers, Possibly 1861
Presentation
Size: 15" × 17½"
1985.169, 170*

*One of the Two
Markers Returned in
1894
Size: 26½" × 36¾"
1985.168*

Notes

[1] Bell to Doctor and Cass, November 6, 1861, Bell Papers.
[2] Parker, p. 234.
[3] Colonel Hartranft to George Shorkley, October 1, 1862, Shorkley Papers.
[4] Bolton Journal, p. 595.
[5] O.R. 36.3, pp. 802, 806.
[6] Bolton Journal, pp. 1267-1268.
[7] Ibid., pp. 640, 651-652, 658. The original letter from Bolton to Russell is in the Regimental Papers in RG 19.
[8] Bolton Journal, p. 32.
[9] Ibid., p. 55.

[10] Parker, p. 239.
[11] Bolton Journal, p. 274.
[12] Ibid., p. 276; Chain, "Presentation of Flag," pp. 71-72, 74-75.
[13] Bolton Journal, p. 553.
[14] Ibid., p. 595.
[15] Related correspondence about the captures of flags on May 12 is found in O.R. 36.3, pp. 802-807. See also General Lane's unpublished report of September 16, 1864, in the James H. Lane Papers, Library of Congress.
[16] Bell to Doctor and Cass, December 19, 29, 1861, Bell Papers.
[17] Bolton to Adjutant-General W. W. Greenland, September 25, 1894, and accompanying newspaper clipping "Lost Guidons of the Fifty-first," RG 25.

Bibliography

Barrett, Eugene A. "John Frederic Hartranft: Life and Services." Ph.D. Dissertation, Temple University, 1950.

Bell, Thomas S. Papers. Chester County Historical Society.

Benfer, [Daniel]. Diary, January 1863-January 1865. USAMHI.

Bolton, William J. "War Journal." War Library and Museum, Military Order of the Loyal Legion of the United States, Philadelphia.

Chain, B. Percy. "Report of Presentation of Battle Flag of the 51st Regiment, Penna. Volunteers." *Historical Sketches, A Collection of Papers Prepared for the Historical Society of Montgomery County, Pa.* 6 (1929): 71-75.

Davis, Thomas P. Letters, June 1862. USAMHI, CWTI Collection.

Hartranft, John F. "The Stone Bridge at Antietam. How It was Carried and at What Cost." *Grand Army Scout and Soldiers Mail*, November 22, 1884.

Linn, James M. Papers. Bucknell University.

_____. "The 51st Regiment Pennsylvania Volunteers at Newberne." *Philadelphia Weekly Press*, September 1, 1886.

Parker, Thomas H. *History of the 51st Regiment of P.V. and V.V., from Its Organization at Camp Curtin, Harrisburg, Pa., in 1861, to Its Being Mustered Out of the United States Service at Alexandria, Va., on July 27th, 1865.* Philadelphia: King & Baird, Printers, 1869.

Parsons, Phyllis V. (editor). "The Schillich Diary." *Bulletin of the Historical Society of Montgomery County* 13 (Fall 1962): 195-238.

Reed, M. G. "How the 51st Pa. Took the Bridge." *National Tribune*, June 10, 1886.

Roach, Harry. "Images of the 51st Pennsylvania Infantry." *Military Images* 3 (January-February 1982): 10-13.

_____. "John F. Hartranft, Defender of the Union." *Military Images* 3 (January-February 1982): 4-9.

Schall, Edwin. "A Soldier's Story. The Battle of Roanoke Island." *Philadelphia Weekly Times*, July 14, 1877.

Shorkley, George. Papers. Bucknell University.

Society of the 51st Regiment Pennsylvania Veteran Volunteers. *Record of Proceedings of the First Annual Reunion, Held at Norristown, Pa., Sept. 17, 1880.* Harrisburg: Lane S. Hart, Printer, 1880.

_____. *Record of Proceedings of the Second Annual Reunion, Held at Lewisburg, PA., Sept. 14, 1881.* Harrisburg: Lane S. Hart, Printer, 1882.

_____. *Sixth Annual Meeting of the Association of the 51st Regiment P.V. Dedication of Monument at Antietam Bridge, October 8th, 1887.* N.p., n.d.

Advance the Colors!

52nd Infantry

First State Color

The 52nd Pennsylvania Volunteer Infantry was organized at Camp Curtin in October 1861. Most of the men forming the regiment were recruited in counties bordering the main branch of the Susquehanna in the northeastern portion of the Commonwealth. Governor Curtin presented the state colors in person to the 51st, 52nd, and 53rd during a ceremony at Camp Curtin on the afternoon of November 5, 1861.[1] Three days later, the 52nd entrained for Washington and went into winter camp near the city. The regiment was attached to Brigadier-General Silas Casey's division of the Fourth Corps.

First State Color   *Size: 72¼" × 74¼" (-)*
Maker: EH   *1985.074*

At the beginning of General McClellan's Peninsula Campaign, the 52nd was transported by water to Fort Monroe, and then marched with the division toward Yorktown. Casey's command participated in the Siege of Yorktown and in the pursuit of the retreating Confederate force toward Richmond. The regiment's first casualties occurred as several men were killed or wounded by "torpedoes" planted in the roads by the retiring enemy troops. Throughout the month of May

1862, the regiment engaged in several minor skirmishes with the enemy as McClellan's advance reached to within twelve miles of Richmond. The regiment's first and only major battle with Confederate forces was the Battle of Fair Oaks, May 31–June 1, 1862. Casey's division was attacked in its position just west of Seven Pines. The division was forced back by overwhelming numbers, but not before the Federals put up a valiant delaying action, allowing reinforcements to reach the battlefield. Casualties in the 52nd totalled 119. Color-Sergeant Henry A. Mott of Company K emerged unscathed.[2]

During the climactic series of battles known as the Seven Days, McClellan's army retreated from its menacing position near Richmond to his base at Harrison's Landing on the James River. Casey's division, mauled severely at Fair Oaks, did not take a prominent part in

Sergeant Henry A. Mott (shown here as a lieutenant) Carried the State Color in 1862

Corporal Philip G. Killian Briefly Carried the State Color in 1864

After a number of minor skirmishes with the enemy, as well as the hard labor of constructing the siege works, many of the original members of the 52nd re-enlisted and the unit was credited as a veteran volunteer regiment. On January 27, 1864, Niram A. Fuller of Company F was appointed color-sergeant, a post he retained until April 1, 1865.[3] Early in July 1864, after remaining in the siege for one year, the 52nd took part in a boat attack on Fort Johnson, in the hopes of capturing the fort as a prelude to a general attack on Charleston. However, many problems cropped up as the regiment rowed toward its objective, and the Rebels became aware of the Federal boats. Many turned back rather than continue after surprise was lost, but five boats landed. The men who attacked captured a small battery and fought their way into Fort Johnson before surrendering to superior numbers. Almost 150 officers and men were thus taken prisoner, including Colonel Henry M. Hoyt, later a governor of Pennsylvania.

The regiment then remained in the besieging force outside Charleston until the Confederates evacuated the city on the evening of February 17, 1865. Early the next morning, the Federals noticed that the enemy seemed unusually quiet, and some deserters soon spread the news of the Rebel retreat. Major John A. Hennessy of the 52nd immediately procured a boat and rowed over to Fort Sumter. At precisely 9:04 a.m. on February 18, the major raised the state color of the 52nd Pennsylvania over the now-silent ruins, the first Union flag in the fort since April 1861. The major then rowed to Fort Ripley and again raised his regiment's flag on the ramparts. Shortly afterwards, the

the retreat, serving as guards on the left flank of the army. Thereafter, the division remained behind as the rest of the Army of the Potomac moved to northern Virginia. The division garrisoned the Yorktown defenses until late December, when most of the troops were transferred temporarily to join the Department of North Carolina.

The sojourn in North Carolina was very brief, and the regiment was soon transported to Saint Helena Island, opposite Port Royal, South Carolina. Major-General David Hunter, commanding the Department of the South, hoped to launch an April attack on Charleston, but the proposed land assault was cancelled after the navy failed to break through the forts defending the harbor. Federal infantry and artillery soon landed on the islands near the harbor, and began a series of movements toward the city that ended in its capture in 1865. The 52nd debarked on Folly Island in July 1863 and remained as part of the attacking force through most of the rest of its term of service.

Second State Color
Maker: HB
Size: 72" × 77"
1985.075

Advance the Colors!

men of the 52nd won a friendly boat race with the 3rd Rhode Island Heavy Artillery for possession of Castle Pinckney, and for a third time the 52nd's flag was the first to wave over a deserted enemy fortification. Finally, Major Hennessey's boat was the first to reach the main dock at Charleston, and the state color was the first American flag to float over the city.[4]

Second State Color

Shortly after the Federal occupation of Charleston, Lieutenant-Colonel John B. Conyngham of the 52nd wrote to Adjutant-General Russell to request a replacement state flag. With this letter, the colonel forwarded the old state color for safekeeping.[5] A replace-

ment flag was ordered from Horstmann Brothers & Company, which delivered the finished product to the Pennsylvania State Agency in Washington on April 26, 1865. It is unknown when the regiment received this replacement flag. In the meantime, the 52nd was transferred from Charleston to New Bern, North Carolina. From this point, the regiment marched to Goldsboro to join the 23rd Corps of General Sherman's advancing army. After remaining on provost guard duty in and around Salisbury, the 52nd was relieved for mustering out of service, which occurred in Harrisburg on July 12, 1865. Both state colors were left in Harrisburg and officially returned during the July 4, 1866, ceremony.

Notes

[1]Thomas S. Bell to Dr. Haas, November 6, 1861, Bell Papers, Chester County Historical Society.

[2]Mott is mentioned as color-sergeant in Colonel C. Dodge, Jr., to Adjutant-General A. L. Russell, October 11, 1862, Regimental Letter Book, RG 94.

[3]For Fuller's appointment as color-sergeant, see Regimental Orders

#151, January 27, 1864, and see Regimental Orders #24, April 1, 1865, for his relief. Both orders are in the Regimental Order Book, RG 94. Corporal Philip G. Killian of Company A was color-bearer on July 5, 1864. See Regimental Orders #50, July 5, 1864, *Ibid.*

[4]*O.R.* 53, pp. 60-61; Wallace, *Schuylkill County*, pp. 396-397.

[5]Conyngham to Russell, March 4, 1865, RG 25.

Bibliography

Bannatyne, R. W. "Entering Charleston." *National Tribune,* February 2, 1888.

52nd Pennsylvania Collection. Historical Society of Pennsylvania.

Fourth Reunion of the Survivors of the 52d Regt. Pa. Vols., (Known as the Luzerne Regiment), Held in the G.A.R. Memorial Hall, Wilkes-Barre, Sept. 25, 1891. N.p., n.d.

Fuller, Frederick. *Frederick Fuller, Late Lieutenant in the Civil War, 52d Reg't. P.V. and Signal Officer, U.S.A., 1861-1865.* Philadelphia, n.d.

Mott, Smith B. *The Campaigns of the Fifty-second Pennsylvania Volunteer Infantry, First Known as "The Luzerne Regiment," Being the Record of Nearly Four Years' Continuous Service, from October 7, 1861, to July 12, 1865, in the War for the Suppression of the Rebellion.* Philadelphia: J. B. Lippincott Company, 1911.

Powell, W. George. *Sumter Regained. Dedicated to the Fifty-second Regiment, Pennsylvania Volunteers, and Read at Their Second Annual Re-union, Held at Scranton, Pa., September 25, 1889.* n.p., n.d.

_____. The 52d Pennsylvania. The First to Enter Charleston, S.C. A Graphic Account of the Evacuation." *National Tribune,* August 19, 1886.

Taylor, S. W. "Naglee's Old Brigade. Its Splendid Services in the Peninsular Campaign." *National Tribune,* August 19, 1886.

_____. "Swamp Angel Battery." *National Tribune,* March 15, 1888.

The Third Annual Meeting of the 52d Regimental Association, Held at Tunkhannock, Wyoming County, Penn'a., Thursday, Sept. 25, 1890. N.p., n.d.

53rd Infantry

First State Color

Representing soldiers drawn from thirteen Keystone counties, the 53rd Pennsylvania was organized during the fall of 1861. The officers elected as colonel John R. Brooke, a Pottstown area native who had already served in the three-months volunteers. Brooke would ultimately become a brigadier-general and continue in the Regular Army after the war. Shortly after the regiment was organized, it received its state color from the governor at Camp Curtin on November 5, 1861. Sergeant Dewalt S. Fouse of Company C was selected to bear the color.[1] The 51st and 52nd regiments received their flags during the same ceremony.

Two days after obtaining its color, the 53rd was shipped to Washington, where it remained during the winter of 1861-62, constantly drilling in routine camp duty. The new regiment was attached to the First Division, Second Corps, Army of the Potomac, with which it remained during its entire term of service. After the occupation of Manassas in March 1862, the corps was transported by water to the Yorktown Peninsula, being held primarily in reserve during the Siege of Yorktown. The 53rd's initial taste of combat occurred on the second day of the Battle of Fair Oaks, June 1, 1862. The corps was rushed as reinforcements across a rickety bridge over the flooded Chickahominy River to aid the hard-pressed Yankees south of the river. Although thrown into confusion at first, the regiment rallied and fought well, suffering ninety-four casualties. Thereafter, the regiment performed rearguard duty as McClellan's army fell back from Richmond during the Seven Days' Battles.

The Second Corps was then returned to Washington and covered the withdrawal of the beaten army after the Second Battle of Manassas. During the Battle of Antietam on September 17, 1862, the 53rd protected the right flank of the division as it assaulted the Rebel position along the now-famous Sunken Road. At Fredericksburg on December 13, the corps was in the forefront of the unsuccessful, bloody assaults on the strong Confederate position on Marye's Heights. Here, the 53rd entered the attack with 283 officers and men and suffered a loss of 155. Color-Sergeant John M. Harvey was among the severely wounded.[2]

After spending the winter of 1862-63 in camp near Falmouth, the regiment took part in General Hooker's Chancellorsville Campaign of April-May 1863. Although the First Division was actively engaged during the battle on May 3, the 53rd escaped with a loss of only eleven men. The much-reduced regiment then marched north with the army to Gettysburg. Three companies were detached as provost guards and the other seven companies could only muster 135 officers and men. On July 2, the First Division of the Second Corps went into action in the Wheatfield. Colonel Brooke, commanding the Fourth Brigade of the division, was held in reserve until the counterattacking Federals needed more impetus. Brooke's troops then launched a bayonet charge across the Wheatfield, driving the enemy from the southern end of the contested field. After repelling several attacks on their new position in the woods beyond the Wheatfield, the outnumbered Yankees were forced to retreat. The 53rd lost eighty men of

First State Color
Maker: EH
Size: 67⅝" (-) × 64⅝" (-)
1985.076

Advance the Colors!

the 135 who entered the fight, the casualties including the color-bearer.[3]

Upon the army's return to Virginia in pursuit of General Lee's army, the 53rd took part in the minor campaigns of Bristoe Station and Mine Run, then went into winter camp near Stevensburg. Most of the soldiers re-enlisted for another three years and the regiment was sent to Harrisburg for its furlough in late December 1863. A reporter who witnessed the 53rd's arrival commented on the appearance of the tattered state color: "The regimental flag exhibits the danger through which it has passed, it being completely riddled and torn with bullets. Four sets of color bearers were killed—the last having fallen at Gettysburg. The first bullet which pierced the flag went immediately through the upper circle of the figure '3'."[4] The remnant of the first state color, without a staff, was apparently left in Harrisburg when the regiment returned to the front. A replacement staff was supplied prior to the 1866 ceremony, when the flag was officially returned to Commonwealth.

Second State Color

A replacement state color was sent to the state by Horstmann Brothers in February 1864. Colonel Brooke took the flag to the 53rd sometime prior to the opening of the 1864 campaign. The regiment sufferd a mere four casualties during the fighting in the Wilderness on May 5-6. During the titanic struggle at Spotsylvania on May 8-18, the Second Corps was heavily engaged with the enemy. On May 12, the entire corps surged forward and captured a portion of the Rebel earthworks. The resulting counterattack neutralized General Hancock's breakthrough and the two armies remained locked in a stalemate. The 53rd lost 177 officers and men during this heavy fighting. After being lightly engaged during Grant's crossing of the North Anna River, the 53rd next fought at Cold Harbor on June 3. Here, Grant launched a series of attacks on Lee's position, but the attackers were repulsed with heavy losses. The 53rd's casualties totalled sixty-nine.

Grant then transferred the Army of the Potomac south of the James River to attack Petersburg. During the June 16 assaults and on the next few days, the 53rd suffered battle casualties of ninety-nine soldiers. Repulsed in his attempt to capture Petersburg, Grant settled down into a period of siege warfare that lasted until April 2, 1865. The 53rd generally remained in the siege lines during this period. The First Division of the corps took part in the Battle of Reams' Station on August 25, where the 53rd suffered light casualties.

The regiment next fought in the Battle of Five Forks, when the Second Corps was rushed to aid the

Second State Color Size: 72¹/₈″ × 74¹/₂″ (-)
Maker: HB 1985.078

hard-pressed Fifth Corps. During the Appomattox Campaign, the 53rd aided in the capture of part of Lee's wagon train on April 6. After Lee surrendered, the regiment camped at Burkesville a short time, then proceeded to Alexandria. It took part in the Grand Review on May 23, where a reporter noted that only about one-third of the state color remained.[5] The regiment was mustered out of service on June 30, 1865. This second state color was offically returned to state care on July 4, 1866.

Third State Color

Colonel William M. Mintzer ordered this flag sometime in May 1865. The flag was delayed in reaching

Third State Color Size: 73″ × 77″
Maker: HB 1985.077

the regiment, and although Colonel Mintzer wrote letters of inquiry, the regiment disbanded before the flag was received. It was therefore sent to Adjutant- General Russell's office for safekeeping. The flag was present in the 1866 parade, when it was officially given to the state.[6]

Notes

[1]"Muster Roll of Company C," *Huntingdon Globe*, November 12, 1861.

[2]"Killed and Wounded in the Fifty-third Pennsylvania Volunteers," *Philadelphia Inquirer*, December 25, 1862.

[3]"Our Harrisburg Letter," *Philadelphia Inquirer*, January 1, 1864.

[4]"Arrival of the Fifty-third Reg., P.V.," *Pennsylvania Daily Telegraph*, December 30, 1863.

[5]"Home from the Wars," *Philadelphia Inquirer*, May 24, 1865.

[6]Mintzer to General A. L. Russell, May 23, 1866, RG 19.

Bibliography

Cushing, Benjamin J. 1863 Diary. Potter County Historical Society.

Claussen, W. Edmunds. "Civil War Correspondence of Samuel Hockley Rutter." *Bulletin of Historical Society of Montgomery County* 19 (Spring 1975): 320-351.

Lucas, William. Letters, November 1861-March 1863. USAMHI.

Mann, Arthur. Letters, 1861-1864. Potter County Historical Society.

Roberts, R. Z. 1862 Letters. Potter County Historical Society.

Yeager, Thomas. Letters, 1861-1862. Lehigh County Historical Society.

Advance the Colors!

54th Infantry

First State Color

The 54th Pennsylvania was recruited in August and September 1861, under authority granted to Colonel Jacob M. Campbell of Johnstown. The companies rendezvoused at Camp Curtin, where they remained until February 27, 1862, when the regiment was ordered to Washington. On the day prior to departure, the regiment marched to the State Arsenal, where, in company with the 56th, 101st, and 103rd Regiments, it received a state color from Governor Curtin.[1]

First State Color
Maker: EH
Size: 71½" × 38⅝" (-)
1985.079a

After a month in Washington, the 54th was assigned as guards for the Baltimore and Ohio Railroad between Cumberland, Maryland, and Martinsburg, Virginia, a distance of fifty-six miles. Colonel Campbell distributed his ten companies along the line as he saw fit, and for the next two years, the regiment was engaged in this arduous duty. The railroad was constantly under attack by Confederate irregular guerrilla troops and cavalry raids. On occasion, Confederate

raiders managed to capture entire companies of the 54th while they were isolated at different stations along the railroad. Companies B and K were taken prisoner on October 4, 1862, and were exchanged in December.

During an attack on the position at North Mountain, the state color was badly damaged by fire, and was reported as lost. The Legislature passed Joint Resolution #6 on February 14, 1863, authorizing the governor to procure a replacement color for the regiment.[2] The remnant of the original state color was given to the state sometime between 1887 and 1896. This color was not on Fox's 1887 photograph list, but does appear on the list in the 1896 adjutant-general's report. When returned, it was listed as an "other" when placed in Case #1 in the Rotunda. A framed piece of this flag is owned by the museum of the Philadelphia Camp, Sons of Union Veterans. The inscription with the piece indicates that Captain G. W. P. Davis of Company F rescued it from the fire.

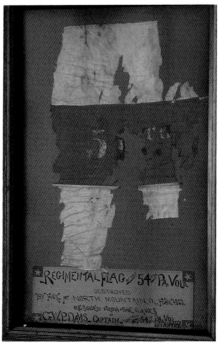

Remnant of First State Color Rescued by Captain G. W. P. Davis

National Color
Size: 46" × 80½"
1985.079b

Second State Color

The replacement color authorized by the Legislature was completed in May 1863, and was altered from a color originally painted for use by the 154th Regiment. This latter unit never completely organized as a full-strength regiment and was thus not allowed to carry a flag according to Army Regulations. The 54th carried this second color until April 1865. The 54th was relieved from its duty as railroad guards in the

spring of 1864. It marched into the Shenandoah Valley and fought its first major battle with the enemy at New Market on May 15, 1864, suffering a loss of almost two hundred men in this Federal defeat. Thereafter, it took part in the fighting at Piedmont (June 5), Winchester (July 24-25 and September 19), Fisher's Hill (September 21), and Cedar Creek (October 19). In December 1864, the regiment was transferred to the Petersburg area, and took part in the April 2, 1865, assault on Petersburg. On April 6, as the army pursued Lee's retreating army, the 54th was part of a force sent to burn High Bridge in order to delay the enemy retreat. However, as the expedition approached its objective, it encountered a much superior force of Southern infantry and cavalry. After a short fight, the Federal troops were forced to surrender. The 54th was captured as a unit, and its flag was taken and never appeared again. In 1894, survivors of the regiment finally admitted to losing the color.[3]

National Color

This unidentified color was found rolled up within the remnant of the 54th's first state color, which was returned to the state sometime prior to 1896.

Notes

[1]"Military—Presentation of Flags," *Harrisburg Patriot and Union,* February 27, 1862.

[2]*Laws of Pennsylvania, 1863,* p. 607.

[3]William H. Rose to Adjutant-General W. W. Greenland, November 17, 1894, Regimental Papers, RG 19.

Bibliography

Barr, Augustus. 1862 Letters. USAMHI, HbCWRT Collection.

Campbell, Jacob M. Papers. West Virginia University.

Hamer, John and Samuel. Papers. USAMHI, HbCWRT Collection.

Hummel, J. R. "The Record of a Live Regiment. Some Things the 54th Pennsylvania Saw and Did in the War of the Rebellion." *National Tribune,* April 19, 1900.

Leonard, Albert C. *The Boys in Blue of 1861-1865, a Condensed History Worth Preserving.* Lancaster: Press of New Era Printing Company, 1904.

Storey, H. W. *History of Cambria County, Pennsylvania.* 3 volumes. New York: Lewis Publishing Company, 1907. Volume 2, pages 77-171, contains a history of the regiment.

Suter, John. Papers. USAMHI, HbCWRT Collection.

55th Infantry

First State Color

This regiment was recruited under the authority granted to Richard White of Indiana County. White raised the new unit during the summer and fall of 1861 and was elected colonel. On the afternoon of November 18, 1861, the regiment marched from Camp Curtin to the rear of the Capitol. The new 76th Pennsylvania also assembled there, and both regiments received a state color from Governor Curtin, who delivered a rousing address to the men. The governor told the troops that both regiments would be sent south to join in the attack on Charleston. Curtin hoped that the native sons of Pennsylvania would be there when the city was laid waste for its part in precipitating the Rebellion. This address was met with wild cheers from both the soldiers and the large crowd of local citizens who witnessed the scene.[1]

Less than a week later, the 55th left Harrisburg for Fort Monroe, where it remained until early December. In company with several other regiments, the 55th became part of the garrison of Port Royal Harbor, spending most of its time on Hilton Head and Edisto islands. The regiment's only major action with the enemy came on March 29, 1862, when three companies repulsed a Confederate reconnaissance expedition against Edisto Island.

The 55th left its garrison station in October as part of the expedition to destroy the railroad between Charleston and Savannah. It took part in the Battle of Pocotaligo on October 22, losing thirty men in the unsuccessful attack. Thereafter, the regiment was sent to Beaufort, South Carolina, where it remained as part of the garrison until April 1864. During its garrison duty here, Color-Sergeant James Miller of Company E died of disease. Miller, a twenty-eight year old native of Scotland, had served in the British Army in the Crimean War. A resident of Minersville in Schuylkill County, Miller left behind a wife and child.[2]

After most of the regiment re-enlisted and was furloughed, the 55th was finally taken from garrison duty and assigned to the Tenth Corps, Army of the James. Commanded by Major-General Benjamin F.

First State Color
Maker: EH
Size: 49⅞" (-) × 62" (-)
1985.080

Butler, this army would threaten Richmond and Petersburg from the south while General Grant's troops attacked Lee's Confederates in northern Virginia. Butler concentrated his 40,000 men near Yorktown and advanced toward Richmond along the south bank of the James River in early May 1864. Butler's troops encountered stiff resistance from General P. G. T. Beauregard's outnumbered defenders, who delayed the Federal advance long enough for some reinforcements to arrive. Beauregard counterattacked on May 16 in an action known as the Battle of Drewry's Bluff. Aided by a dense morning fog, the Rebel assault overlapped the Yankee left flank and pushed the invaders back. Posted near the extreme left, the 55th Pennsylvania put up a spirited resistance until almost surrounded when other troops fell back. Colonel White and more than one hundred others were captured. Total losses for the 55th, including the advance preceding the battle, numbered almost 350.

After the failure of Butler's attack, the 55th was transferred to the Eighteenth Corps, which was sent to join the Army of the Potomac at Cold Harbor. The reinforcements participated in the unsuccessful assault on June 3, the 55th suffering a loss of 151 men. Color-Sergeant Michael Murray of Company E was among the wounded.[3] The regiment then took part in the initial assaults on the Petersburg defenses on June

Second State Color
Maker: HB

Size: 71³/₄″ × 77¹/₈″
1985.081

15-18, suffering a further loss of 156 officers and men. As the two armies settled down into protracted siege warfare, the 55th remained on duty south of the James River in the trench lines.

On September 30, the regiment was part of the expedition that moved north of the river and attacked the Rebel defenses on Chapin's Bluff. It was held in reserve during the initial Federal assaults, then was called upon to charge and capture Fort Gilmer. The regiment, now reduced to a field strength of 155, gallantly pressed forward into the face of a withering enemy musketry and artillery fire. Sergeant Augustin Flanigan of Company A, who had been promoted to color-sergeant on September 1, was wounded as he rushed forward ahead of the regiment to inspire the men. He later received a Medal of Honor for his heroism. As Flanigan fell, Sergeant Hezekiah Hammer of Company K seized the state color and took it from the field as the regiment faltered and retreated. Losses totalled eighty-two, more than fifty percent of the regiment's strength.[4]

After the repulse at Fort Gilmer, the 55th remained nearby as part of the garrison of some of the captured enemy earthworks. In November, the term of service of those who did not re-enlist expired. When Adjutant James H. Miller returned to Harrisburg on December 23, he brought with him the remnant of the state color. Hundreds of rents made by enemy bullets were visible, as were the bloodstains of its bearers. A list of battles attached to the remaining shreds included the names of eight engagements in which the 55th had fought.[5] This flag was officially returned to state care on July 4, 1866.

Second State Color

Owing to the heavy battle damage sustained in 1864, the regiment received a replacement state color sometime late that year. The flag was furnished to the state by Horstmann Brothers & Company on October 3 and forwarded to the State Agency in Washington. It was sent to the regiment sometime later. The small remnant of the 55th remained north of the James River until March 1865. In December 1864, the regiment was assigned to the new Twenty-fourth Corps. It took part in the final attack on Petersburg on April 2, suffering light casualties. The corps then aided in the pursuit of Lee's retreating army, getting astride Lee's route of withdrawal and hastening his decision to surrender on April 9. Thereafter, the 55th returned to the Richmond-Petersburg area as part of the garrison until the regiment was relieved and mustered out of service on August 30. The replacement state color was returned to the Commonwealth on July 4, 1866.

Notes

[1]"Flag Presentation," *Harrisburg Patriot*, November 19, 1861.

[2]"From the Fifty-fifth Regiment, P.V.," *Pottsville Miners' Journal*, January 9, 1864.

[3]*Pottsville Miners' Journal*, June 18, 1864.

[4]Regimental Orders #36, [September 1, 1864], Regimental Order Book, RG 94; "Gallantry of Pennsylvania Soldiers," *Philadelphia Inquirer*, October 26, 1864.

[5]"Return of the Flag of the Fifty-fifth Penna. Regiment," *Pennsylvania Daily Telegraph*, December 23, 1864.

Bibliography

"History of the Operations of the 55th P. V." *Bedford Inquirer*, December 9, 1864.

Hughes, Joseph W. Papers. USAMHI, HbCWRT Collection.

Hunt, Jerome L. "The History of the 55th Pennsylvania Volunteer Infantry Regiment." Master's Thesis, Illinois State University, 1979; copy in USAMHI.

Missong, Josiah. "The 55th Pennsylvania. What It Did and Suffered at Fort Harrison." *National Tribune*, July 21, 1887.

White, Richard. Papers. In White Family Collection, University of Virginia.

56th Infantry

First State Color

Organized during the fall of 1861, the 56th Pennsylvania was composed of men from at least a dozen counties. The regiment remained at Camp Curtin throughout the winter of 1861-62. In early March 1862, with the regimental organization still incomplete, the 56th was ordered to Washington. The new unit left Harrisburg on March 8, after receiving its state color from Governor Curtin in person. Sergeant Archibald C. Bruce was the regiment's first color-sergeant, appointed by Colonel Sullivan A. Meredith on March 7. However, Bruce became the regiment's first casualty when he died of disease on March 20. His replacement's name in unknown.[1]

After spending several weeks in the Washington defenses, the 56th spent most of the summer repairing a railroad and as guards in the Fredericksburg area. The 56th was assigned to Brigadier-General Abner Doubleday's brigade, a part of Brigadier-General Rufus King's division, Major-General Irvin McDowell's Third Corps, of the new Army of Virginia. In the meantime, Sergeant Josiah Yohe of Company C was appointed as color-sergeant on July 19.[2]

Upon its assignment to the main army, the 56th marched to Culpeper, and from there to Rappahannock Station, where the regiment first heard hostile artillery fire on August 21. One week later, the 56th received its first baptism of fire when the division was attacked by Stonewall Jackson's Confederates at Brawner Farm, near the Manassas battlefield. During the evening struggle, Colonel Meredith was painfully wounded and Lieutenant-Colonel J. William Hofmann took command. An able officer, Hofmann would retain command of the regiment, and often times the brigade, throughout the remainder of the war.

After the inconclusive fight ended the division retreated and rejoined the army on the battlefield of Second Manassas the next day, August 29. Owing to the lengthy marches of the division's weary men, King remained in reserve most of the day. Near dusk, the division was ordered forward to attack the enemy, who were supposed to be retreating. However, Confederate reinforcements had already arrived and

First State Color
Maker: EH

Size: 72¼" × 76½"
1985.082

King's attack was driven back. The 56th retired after the regiments on its left gave way. As the regiment fell back, the wooded terrain and growing darkness dispersed the men. Hofmann collected all the survivors he could and the reduced command helped cover the Federal retreat on August 30.

Together with the regimental loss of 4 killed, 84 wounded, and 99 captured or missing, Colonel Hofmann reported that his state color had been captured, together with much of the color-company. The dispirited colonel was unable to gather much information about the loss of his flag, but, when some of the captured men who had been released on parole passed the regiment on their way to Washington, Hofmann learned that the flag had been torn into small pieces and distributed among those captured. In fact, one of these men showed the colonel a small piece of blue silk from the flag. Many years after the war, Hofmann had the opportunity to read through a list of Federal colors taken by the Confederates during the war and then in possession of the War Department, pending their return to the states. Since the 56th's was not listed among the captured flags, Hofmann assumed that the story of the flag's destruction was true.[3]

But there is more to the story of the loss of the 56th's colors than at first appears. Hofmann wrote his official report of the Manassas Campaign on September 5, addressing the report to Adjutant-General Russell, and included a brief comment on the loss of the state color. The tone of the report indicated that the colonel was generally pleased with the conduct of the regiment in its first engagement with the enemy. In spite of the long marches and irregular rations, Hofmann wrote that the officers and men had performed their duty as best they could.[4] But, the very next day, Hofmann issued Regimental Orders #89, reducing Color-Sergeant Yohe and seven of the color-corporals to the ranks, "having been guilty of disgraceful conduct in the presence of the enemy by deserting the color, thus proving themselves unworth of the sacred trust that the commanding officer of the regiment had confided to their hands."[5]

The missing state color suddenly reappeared in 1887. In January of that year, Samuel Walters, a Pennsylvania veterinarian, happened to visit the residence of Norman Lewis, a Thomson, Illinois, grain, lumber, and salt dealer. While in Mr. Lewis's home, Walters spied the color of the 56th. He wrote a letter to Adjutant-General Daniel H. Hastings, advising him that a Pennsylvania flag was in Illinois and should be returned. After some apparent negotiation, Lewis gladly returned the flag to Pennsylvania and explained how he received it. Lewis had been an officer in the 92nd Illinois Mounted Infantry, one of the first units of General Sherman's army to enter Raleigh, North Carolina, on April 13, 1865. Lewis found the captured flag, together with several others, in the State House. The card attached to the 56th's flag indicated that a member of the 6th North Carolina had captured it during the Second Battle of Manassas. Lewis took the flag home with him as a souvenir, seemingly forgot about it, but returned it in July 1887. The flag was placed in the Flag Room in the South Executive Building, alongside the other two colors of the 56th.[6]

Officers' Flag

Soon after the retreat to Washington, the 56th was assigned to the First Corps, Army of the Potomac, which moved into Maryland to counter General Lee's invasion of that state. Owing to the heavy losses of the Virginia Campaign, Hofmann directed the brigade on this new campaign. The regiment was engaged in the Battle of South Mountain on September 14, and during the titanic struggle at Antietam three days later, the brigade guarded the right flank of the army and did not suffer heavy casualties.

Soon after the loss of the state color, Hofmann and the line officers in the regiment decided to share

the cost of a replacement flag. This flag was apparently received in November 1862, since a new color-sergeant was appointed on November 15, when Hofmann placed the new color in the hands of Sergeant Wallace Early of Company A, who was chosen for his "meritorious conduct."[7] The next day, Hofmann ordered Company H to be the color-company, apparently replacing Company C.[8] A new color-guard was announced on November 22.[9]

The regiment carried this new flag into the Battle of Fredericksburg on December 13, 1862. Even though other regiments of the division lost several men from Rebel artillery fire, the 56th escaped without loss. After camping for the winter near Pratt's Landing on the Rappahannock River, the regiment took part in the Chancellorsville Campaign of April-May 1863, but was not engaged in battle. Shortly after this campaign, Hofmann had the flag sent to Philadelphia to have battle honors painted on it. Thus, the flag was not carried by the regiment during the Gettysburg Campaign.[10]

The flag was returned to the regiment shortly after the Gettysburg battle and was carried in the autumn campaigns of Bristoe Station and Mine Run, where the 56th was engaged with very slight loss. During this time, the flag seems to have been carried by Corporals Winfield S. Carr and Ira Knapp.[11] When the new state color was issued to the 56th, Hofmann kept the officers' flag in his possession, where it remained until the mid-twentieth century. It then passed through the hands of at least two Civil War collectors before being acquired by the War Library and Museum, Military Order of the Loyal Legion of the United States, Philadelphia.

Gettysburg Flag

While the officers' flag was in Philadelphia being painted with the battle honors, the 56th embarked on the Gettysburg Campaign. Needing a color to identify the regiment, Hofmann had a camp color carried as the regimental flag until the larger, more proper, flag could be returned. This camp color, probably of regulation size, was made of wool bunting, dyed dark blue, with the red disk corps badge designating the First Division, First Corps, and in white muslin letters, the words "56th Regt. P.V."[12] The corps reached Gettysburg on July 1. As the 56th deployed and marched across the fields just north of the railroad cut through McPherson's Ridge, enemy troops were seen approaching. Acting under Brigadier-General Lysander Cutler's orders, Hofmann wheeled his men into line and opened fire on the Rebels. By so doing, the 56th was the first infantry unit to fire a volley in that memorable battle.

Second State Color   Size: 72¹⁄₈″ × 76¹⁄₂″
Maker: EH   1985.084

During the course of the day's fighting, Color-Sergeant Henry Eby of Company H was wounded, whereupon Corporal Patrick Burns took the banner. After the valiant stand of the corps on July 1, the depleted regiments were stationed south of the town. On the evening of July 2, when enemy troops threatened to seize Culp's Hill from the hard-pressed Federal defenders, the 56th was one of the units sent as reinforcements. As the regiment lay behind breastworks on the hill, firing at the oncoming enemy, Corporal Burns, bravely waving the flag over the works to taunt the enemy, was wounded. The young corporal was shot through the hand and received buckshot through a shoulder. The latter wound did not prove serious but Burns did not regain full use of his hand for more than two years.[13]

In December 1863, Colonel Hofmann, acting on the consent of the 56th's officers, wrote to the Union League of Philadelphia, offering the flag used at Gettysburg to the League for safekeeping. The officers considered the flag of some importance because the 56th had fired the first volley of the battle. Writing on December 28, League Secretary George Boker informed Hofmann that the flag had arrived safely and would be kept with other war souvenirs the League had been given. Boker went on to write: "But when we receive a flag that led the van through the flame and smoke of Gettysburg, that fluttered through those three immortal days over the heads of the most distinguished of our regiments and emerged from the terrible battle crowned with historic glory, we strive in vain with tongue or pen to make clear the emotions that passes our hearts."[14]

The present location of this flag is unknown. It does not seem to have been included in the Union League's flag collection which was donated to the Pennsylvania Historical and Museum Commission in 1977.

Second State Color

After spending the winter of 1863-64 near Culpeper, during which the regiment re-enlisted, the unit returned from furlough and was now attached to the Fifth Corps. The 56th fought in the Battles of the Wilderness, Spotsylvania, North Anna River, Bethesda Church, and Cold Harbor, thereafter moving with the corps to take part in Grant's operations around Petersburg. During this time, a second state color was furnished to the state by Evans & Hassall in late May. It was sent from the Adjutant-General's Office in Harrisburg to the Pennsylvania State Agency in Washington, and then to the 56th at an unspecified date.

Owing to the constant marching and fighting throughout the spring and summer operations of 1864, many regimental letter and order books are quite sparse when compared to other operations, and the 56th's books are no exception. As a result, there are few orders concerning the colors, and the brief official battle reports shed no light on any actions involving the use of the flag in 1864. Colonel Hofmann appointed a new color-guard on March 7. On April 25, Hofmann specified the company order in line of battle, making Company I the new color-company.[15] Other than these two specific actions, nothing else is known about the colors during the 1864 campaign.

After the siege operations around Petersburg began the 56th took its turn in the trenches, interspersed with occasional engagements as Grant's army slowly occupied the city's southern supply lines. The regiment fought in the Battle of Weldon Railroad on August 18-20, and again at Hatcher's Run in October. After enduring the winter of 1864-65, the regiment took an active part in the Battle of Hatcher's Run on February 5-6, 1865, and participated in the campaign that resulted in Lee's surrender at Appomattox on April 9. As the regiment camped in the Washington area prior to muster out, two new color-sergeants were appointed. One was John Y. Earhart, formerly one of the color-guard. The other was Sergeant Hugh Logue of Company I. As a sixteen-year-old Philadelphia buttonmaker in 1861, Logue had enlisted as a drummer, and had by now worked his way up through the ranks to carry one of the regiment's flags.[16] The regiment returned to Philadelphia in late June and was mustered out of service on July 1, 1865. The second state color was left at Camp Cadwalader and was officially returned to state care on July 4, 1866.

Regimental Color

This infantry regimental color may possibly have been acquired in mid-1865, suggested by Regimental Orders #31, when two color-sergeants were appointed, one to carry the state color, while the other may have been appointed for this regimental color.

Regimental Color
Size: 70½" × 76⅛"
1985.083

Union League Flag

One of the fragmentary colors received by the Pennsylvania Historical and Museum Commission from the Union League in 1977 is tagged as belonging to the 56th Pennsylvania. It is a blue silk state regimental, containing the arms of the Commonwealth on both sides. This is probably the same flag that was formerly owned by G.A.R. Post #1 in Philadelphia, which turned it over to the Union League in 1919.[17]

General Guide Markers

The 56th Pennsylvania was one of many regiments to utilize general guide markers. Colonel Meredith's March 7, 1862, appointment list included the names of Sergeant Stephen F. Garlow of Company A as Right General Guide, and Sergeant Albert A. Kuhn of Company B as Left General Guide.[18] Sometime prior to the Second Battle of Manassas, Sergeant Kuhn was replaced by Corporal Sylvester G. Gettys as Left General Guide. Gettys was reduced to the ranks on September 6, 1862, for deserting his flag.[19] Three 56th Pennsylvania general guide markers are now owned by the War Library and Museum, Military Order of the Loyal Legion of the United States, Philadelphia. One is painted with the regimental battle honors, covering the regiment's term of service through Mine Run. The other two, acquired when the museum obtained the officers' flag, are devoid of such painted honors.

Notes

[1]Bates in 2: 216, writes that a Sergeant Gordon was the regimental color-bearer and first death. However, I cannot locate any Sergeant Gordon in the muster rolls. Sergeant Bruce, appointed by Regimental Orders #26, in Regimental Order Book, RG 94, died on March 30, and this would indicate that Bates was in error with Gordon's name.

[2]Regimental Orders #75.

[3]Hofmann to D. H. Hastings, May 6, 1887, RG 25.

[4]*O.R.* 12.2, pp. 374-375.

[5]Regimental Orders #89.

[6]See the following correspondence, all in RG 25: Samuel Walters to D. H. Hastings, January 12, 28, 1887, and Norman Lewis to Hastings, July 2, 1887.

[7]Regimental Orders #94.

[8]Regimental Orders #95.

[9]Regimental Orders #96.

[10]J. William Hofmann, "The Fifty-sixth Regiment Pennsylvania Volunteers in the Gettysburg Campaign," *Philadelphia Weekly Press*, January 13, 1886.

[11]This information comes from a woodcut of the 56th's officers' flag contained in Volume 56, page 2773, Military Order of the Loyal Legion of the United States, Commandery of Massachusetts, Civil War Photograph Albums, U.S. Army Military History Institute. The woodcut lists the names of the bearers.

[12]Hofmann, "56th in the Gettysburg Campaign."

[13]*Ibid.*; *O.R.* 27.1, p. 289.

[14]Hofmann to President of the Union League, December 5, 1863, and George H. Boker to Hofmann, December 28, 1863, both in Regimental Letter Book, RG 94. The originals are in the archives of the Union League, Philadelphia.

[15]Regimental Orders #16 and #21.

[16]Regimental Orders #31. The personal information is from the company muster roll, RG 19.

[17]*Union League of Philadelphia, Annual Report 1919*, p. 98, archives of the Union League.

[18]Regimental Orders #26.

[19]Regimental Orders #89.

Bibliography

Hill, Jacob R. Papers. Pennsylvania State Archives.

Hofmann, J. William. "The Fifty-sixth Regiment Pennsylvania Volunteers in the Gettysburg Campaign." *Philadelphia Weekly Press*, January 13, 1886.

_____. "The 56th Pennsylvania at Gettysburg." *National Tribune*, March 20, 1884.

_____. *Military Record of Brevet Brigadier General John William Hof-mann, United States Volunteers (Late Colonel of the Fifty-sixth regiment Pennsylvania*. Philadelphia: A. W. Auner, Printer, 1884.

_____. "Remarks on the Battle of Gettysburg. Operations on the Right of the First Corps, Army of the Potomac. First Day of the Fight. By Bvt. Brig. Genl. J. Wm. Hofmann. . . . Read Before the Historical Society of Pennsylvania, March 8th, 1880." Philadelphia: A. W. Auner, Printer 1880.

Advance the Colors!

57th Infantry

First State Color

The 57th Pennsylvania was organized at Camp Curtin during the fall of 1861. The recruits came primarily from Mercer, Crawford, Susquehanna, and Bradford counties. Governor Curtin came to the camp on December 14, 1861, and presented the state color to the regiment.[1] Sergeant Edgar Williams of Company E may have been the initial color-sergeant. He was promoted to captain of his company and mortally wounded at Spotsylvania. Williams was described as being a color-bearer for a "long time," and since he was promoted to lieutenant in February 1863, it is apparent that he carried the colors throughout most, if not all, of the 1862 campaigns.[2]

The day after receiving its state color, the 57th was sent to Washington, where it remained throughout the winter of 1861-62. When the Army of the Potomac's corps were organized, the 57th was assigned to a division in Samuel P. Heintzelman's Third Corps. The corps embarked by water for the Yorktown Peninsula in March 1862 and participated in the resulting Siege of Yorktown. Although the regiment took part in a few skirmishes, its first battle was at Fair Oaks on May 31-June 1. The Third Corps was rushed into the fighting as reinforcements, the 57th suffering heavy casualties on May 31. During the Seven Days' Battles, the regiment was engaged at Glendale on June 30 and again at Malvern Hill on July 1.

After the unsuccessful conclusion of the Peninsula Campaign, most of the army was shipped to northern Virginia to join General John Pope's Army of Virginia. The Third Corps joined this army in time to take an active part in the Second Battle of Manassas on August 29-30. It took a further part in the engagement at Chantilly on September 1, but suffered few casualties in this operation. Having suffered heavy losses during the two 1862 campaigns, the corps remained behind in Washington and did not take part in the Maryland Campaign. During the final 1862 battle, that of Fredericksburg on December 13, the division to which the 57th was attached aided in repulsing a Confederate attack as the Pennsylvania Reserves fell back from their unsuccessful charge.

After spending the winter near Falmouth, the 57th took part in the Chancellorsville Campaign of April-May 1863. The regiment was engaged with the enemy on May 2-3, suffering seventy-one casualties. Two months later, the 57th took position in the Peach Orchard at Gettysburg and sustained heavy casualties on July 2 before retreating. Losses totalled more than fifty percent of those present. Thereafter, the 57th took part in the Bristoe Station and Mine Run campaigns before going into winter camp near Brandy Station. Most of the regiment re-enlisted for another three years and was granted a furlough. This leave occurred during January-February 1864. The state color, "torn by the bullets of many battles," was left in Harrisburg and officially returned to state care on July 4, 1866.[3]

Second State Color

A replacement flag was sent to Colonel Peter Sides in February 1864 when the regiment returned to Virginia. Sergeant Cyrus P. Slaven of Company I was appointed as bearer on April 23.[4] The strengthened regi-

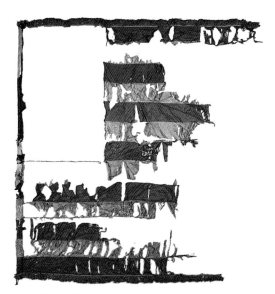

First State Color
Maker: EH
Size: 72" × 72" (-)
1985.087

Second State Color
Maker: HB
Size: 71³/4" × 78"
1985.088

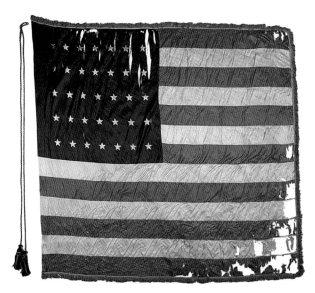

National Color
Maker: A. Brandon
Size: 71⁵/8" × 76¹/2"
1985.086

ment entered the Battle of the Wilderness as part of the Second Corps. During the fighting on May 5-6, the regiment suffered 157 casualties. Sergeant Slaven was among those wounded on the sixth.[5] The army then moved south and various intensities of combat occurred around Spotsylvania from May 8-18. After the inconclusive struggle in this last battle, Grant continued to move southward. Fighting took place at the North Anna River on May 23, at Haw's Shop on May 28, and at Totopotomoy Creek on May 29-31.

The 57th was heavily engaged during June 1864. At Cold Harbor, while the regiment lay behind breastworks waiting to attack the enemy, an artillery shell struck the furled color, piercing the staff and "tearing out one entire stripe right in the center of the flag."[6] After being repelled at Cold Harbor, Grant crossed the James River and attacked the Petersburg defenses. The 57th was engaged in the assaults of June 16 and 18. During the latter attack, a minie ball pierced the flagstaff about eight inches above the sergeant's head.[7]

Having failed to capture Petersburg by assault, Grant settled down into siege warfare to wear down Lee's army. While the armies lay in close contact with each other, several major engagements took place as the Federals tightened their grip on the supply lines feeding the Rebels. The 57th took part in the fighting along the Weldon Railroad (June 22), Deep Bottom (July 27-29, and August 16-18), Reams' Station (August 25), Poplar Springs Church (October 2), and the Boydton Plank Road (October 27). The 1864 campaign season then ended and the 57th spent a quiet winter, although it did take part in the raid on the Weldon Railroad on December 7-12.

In January 1865, having become weakened in strength, the regiment was reduced to six companies. The 84th Pennsylvania was limited to four companies and both regiments were consolidated as the 57th. The new 57th took a minor part in the closing campaign that resulted in Lee's surrender on April 9, 1865. After spending some time near Washington, the

Two Views of the Bullet Damage from June 18, 1864, Showing the Effect One Ball Could Have on a Wooden Staff

Advance the Colors!

57th was mustered out of service on June 29, 1865. The second state color was returned to Harrisburg and was included in the 1866 parade.

National Color

This 35-star national color was manufactured by A. Brandon of New York. The sleeve contains this imprint as well as that of J. W. Duncan, a federal inspector. Judging from its condition, it is probable that the regiment requisitioned this color to carry in the May 1865 Grand Review.

Regimental Color

This unmarked regimental color was possibly obtained at the same time as the national color listed above. Nothing else is known about the subsequent history of this flag.

Regimental Color   1985.085
Size: 71¹/₄" × 73⁵/₈"

Notes

[1] "Flag Presentation," *Pennsylvania Daily Telegraph*, December 14, 1861.
[2] Martin, p. 114.
[3] *Ibid.*, p. 105.
[4] Special Orders #33, April 23, 1864, Regimental Order Book, RG 94.

[5] Martin, p. 110.
[6] *Ibid.*, p. 116. Martin writes that this damage occurred on June 2. Captain E. C. Strouss, in his address printed in *Pennsylvania at Gettysburg* 1: 335, said the date was June 3.
[7] Martin, p. 118.

Bibliography

Baker, Joseph D. Letters, October 1861-November 1863. USAMHI.
Hunter, William (editor). "The Civil War Diaries of Leonard C. Ferguson." *Pennsylvania History* 14 (1947): 196-224, 289-313.
Martin, James M., et al. *History of the Fifty-seventh Regiment, Pennsylvania Veteran Volunteer Infantry, First Brigade, First Division, Third Corps, and Second Brigade, Third Division, Second Corps, Army of the Potomac.* Meadville: McCoy & Calvin, Printers, 1904.

Sallada, William H. *Silver Sheaves Gathered through Clouds and Sunshine.* Des Moines: Mills & Company, Printers, 1879.
Strouss, Ellis C. Letters, 1861-1865. USAMHI, CWTI Collection.
Whiting, W. J. "The 57th Pennsylvania at Fair Oaks." *National Tribune*, March 13, 1884.

58th Infantry

First State Color

The 58th Regiment was organized when two incomplete regiments were consolidated as one at a camp near Philadelphia in March 1862. Recruiting had begun for each unit in the fall of 1861, but neither regiment could muster enough soldiers. Governor Curtin visited Philadelphia on December 6, 1861, and presented state flags to the 58th, 67th, 90th, 91st, and 6th Cavalry. The ceremony took place at a large vacant field on Islington Avenue near the Ridge Avenue Railroad Depot.[1]

Upon final organization of the 58th, it was ordered to Fort Monroe in March 1862. After arrival, the regiment was stationed near the fort and remained in camp, drilling and performing picket duty until May 10. On that date, the 58th was included in an expedition that was transported across Hampton Roads to occupy Norfolk, which was being evacuated by the Confederates. On May 11, the 58th was the first regiment to enter the deserted city, and its flag was unfurled from the roof of the customs house.[2] The regiment encamped near the city until October,

occasionally participating in raids upon Rebel forces operating outside the Federal entrenchments.

In October 1862, the 58th was transferred to the Suffolk garrison, remaining here until January 1863. The regiment took part in the skirmish at Zuni (December 8) and at the Black Water River (December 12). It was then transferred to North Carolina where it remained until April 1864. Initially, the 58th was stationed near New Bern and took part in several raids into enemy-held territory. Skirmishes at Core Creek (February 13 and April 20), Sandy Ridge (April 27), and Bachelor's Creek Station (May 22-23) highlighted the regiment's many engagements with Confederate cavalry and irregular forces. In June 1863, the 58th moved to Washington, North Carolina, where it remained as the garrison until ordered to Virginia in 1864. One of the bearers during this period was Sergeant Charles Harman of Company A.[3]

When the 58th was transferred to Virginia, it became part of the Eighteenth Corps. The regiment was engaged in the fighting on May 9, 1864, as the Army of the James moved toward the Richmond-Petersburg Railroad, and at Drewry's Bluff on May 16. After participating in the Battle of Cold Harbor on June 1 and 3, the corps moved south of the James River and attacked Petersburg on June 15. Shortly thereafter, the 58th was relieved from duty and sent to Pennsylvania for its veterans' furlough, returning to the army in late August. Sergeant John Hoffa of Company K was color-bearer during this period, having been appointed to the position on April 14.[4]

One month after returning to the front, the 58th was engaged in the Battle of Chaffin's Farm on September 29. The brigade led the assault on Confederate-held Fort Harrison. Charging forward across open terrain for several hundred yards, the 58th scaled the parapet, entered the fort, and drove out the defenders. However, the 58th suffered casualties of almost fifty percent. The state color was severely damaged. The staff was broken in two near the middle and the spearpoint shot entirely off.[5]

After the capture of Fort Harrison, the 58th remained in the area as part of the garrison. It took part in the October 27 fighting along the Fair Oaks and

First State Color
Maker: EH
Size: 71¼" × 50⅝" (-)
1985.090

Advance the Colors!

Members of the 58th Used Iron Clamps to Repair the Broken Staff of the First State Color After the Action on September 29, 1864

Darbytown Roads and on December 8 at Spring Hill. During this time, a replacement state color was obtained because of the heavy damage to the original flag. The first-issue color remained with the regiment until February 1865. Lieutenant Thomas Birmingham of Company I, while on leave, went to Harrisburg and presented the original color to Governor Curtin on February 8.[6] It was officially given to state care on July 4, 1866.

Second State Color

A replacement state color was completed by Evans & Hassall in late October 1864. Captain Robert C. Redmond acknowledged receipt of this "regimental flag and equipments" on November 23, 1864.[7] This flag was carried by the regiment during its last campaign that culminated in Lee's surrender in April 1865. The 58th suffered few casualties in the final days of fighting in Virginia. After the Confederate surrender, the 58th was assigned as provost guards in southern Virginia, remaining in the state until January 24, 1866,

when it was mustered out of service at City Point, Virginia. The second state color was carried in the July 1866 parade.

Roxborough Flag

Bates writes that the ladies of Roxborough presented a regimental color to the 58th on February 21, 1862.[8] No confirming evidence can be located about this presentation. Scharf and Westcott, in their history of Philadelphia, recorded that the ladies presented a flag to the regiment on October 12, 1861, but did not elaborate on the type of flag.[9] However, the *Philadelphia Inquirer* reported that the flag presented on that date was about sixteen feet long, which indicates that it was some type of garrison flag and thus was probably never carried into combat.[10]

Second State Color
Maker: EH
Size: 72⁵/₈" × 74¹/₄"
1985.089

Notes

[1] "Grand Military Review. Four Thousand Men in the Field. Presentation of State Flags by the Governor," *Philadelphia Inquirer*, December 7, 1861.

[2] Bates 2: 285-286.

[3] Lieutenant Morgan Carr to Thomas J. Ingraham, September 25, 1863, Regimental Letter and Endorsement Book, RG 94.

[4] Special Orders #36, April 14, 1864, Regimental Order Book, RG 94.

[5] "The Old Flag of the Fifty-eighth Pa. Vols.," *Philadelphia Inquirer*, February 7, 1865.

[6] "Presentation of a Battle Flag To Gov. Curtin," *Pennsylvania Daily Telegraph*. February 9, 1865.

[7] Captain Redmond to Governor Curtin, November 23, 1864, Regimental Letter and Endorsement Book, RG 94.

[8] Bates 2: 285.

[9] Scharf-Westcott 1: 784.

[10] "Flag Presentation at Camp Roxborough," *Philadelphia Inquirer*, October 16, 1861.

Bibliography

Blair, William H. "Fort Harrison Again." *National Tribune*, July 26, 1888.

Clay, Cecil. "Assault and Repulse. Hoke's Charge at Fort Harrison." *Philadelphia Weekly Times*, November 5, 1881.

_____ . "Colonel J. R. Jones in Carolina." *Philadelphia Weekly Times*, September 20, 1879.

_____ . "Fort Harrison. How It was Taken, and the First Three Union

Men on the Ramparts." *National Tribune*, March 22, 1888.

_____ . "Fort Harrison. Comrade Clay Again Makes Claim to Planting the First Flag." *National Tribune*, May 2, 1889.

_____ . Papers. Historical Society of Pennsylvania.

Webster, William S. "The Capture of Norfolk." *National Tribune*, September 20, 1883.

2nd Cavalry
(59th Regiment)

First State Standard

This cavalry regiment was recruited during the fall of 1861, rendezvousing in a camp near Philadelphia. Governor Curtin presented a state standard to the regiment on March 19, 1862, at the camp, located near Point Breeze Park.[1] The flag was apparently borne by a Sergeant Fowler of Company A, who carried it through forty-three battles and skirmishes until January 1865.[2]

With its organization still incomplete, the 2nd Cavalry was rushed to Washington in April 1862. It remained in camp near the capital until June, when the 2nd finally marched into Virginia, where it was assigned to the new Army of Virginia. The regiment made a daring reconnaissance to Aldie on September 17-18. When the Army of the Potomac returned to Virginia after the Maryland Campaign, the 2nd Cavalry joined the mounted force of the army and took part in the numerous skirmishes and engagements with the Rebel cavalry until after the Battle of Freder-

First State Standard
Maker: HB
Size: 27" × 31⅞"
1985.172

icksburg. On December 28, the regiment suffered heavy losses when a much larger enemy cavalry force surprised the regiment near its camp on the Occoquan River.

After spending the winter in camp near the same area, the regiment was assigned to a cavalry division in the defenses of Washington, and thus did not take part in the Chancellorsville Campaign. This division joined the army during the Gettysburg Campaign, and the 2nd Cavalry was detached at army headquarters, helping to gather up stragglers and conduct Rebel prisoners to the rear. Thereafter, the regiment fought in many of the skirmishes during the Bristoe Station and Mine Run campaigns of October-November 1863. It then went into winter quarters near Warrenton.

During Grant's 1864 campaign, the regiment participated in the many battles and raids of the Cavalry Corps, Army of the Potomac, including the Wilderness, Todd's Tavern (May 5-7), Sheridan's Richmond Raid (May 9-24), Haw's Shop (May 28) and the Trevilian Raid (June 7-26). The cavalry then rejoined the main army. During the many battles around Petersburg, the 2nd was engaged at Deep Bottom (August 14), Charles City Cross Roads (August 16), Weldon Railroad (August 18-19), and Boydton Plank Road (October 27). The first state standard was taken along home for recruiting service by Sergeant Fowler in January 1865, when a Pittsburgh newspaper reporter noted the war-torn appearance of the flag.[3] The standard was then returned to state care and mislabeled as the standard for the 2nd Provisional Cavalry. Although little remains, the fragments of the painted area clearly show this as the 2nd Cavalry's standard.

Second State Standard

On January 21, 1865, Major G. L. McCabe requested a new standard for the regiment.[4] A replacement standard was sent to the regiment in February 1865 by Horstmann Brothers & Company. This banner was carried in the Federal victory at Five Forks on April 1,

1865, which led to the subsequent attack and capture of Petersburg and Richmond. After Lee's surrender, the regiment participated in the Grand Review on May 23. It was consolidated with the 20th Cavalry to form the 1st Provisional Cavalry on June 17, and was mustered out of service on July 13, 1865. The second state standard was taken home by Colonel William W. Sanders. The colonel was contacted in June 1866 about returning the standard. He wrote General Russell that he would send it to anyone designated by the general or come to Philadelphia on July 4 and return it in person.[5] However, he did not return the standard. After the colonel's death in 1883, his younger brother, Dallas Sanders, sent the flag to the adjutant-general's office.[6]

Second State Standard
Maker: HB
Size: 26½" × 30"
1985.005

Notes

[1]"Presentation of Flags," *Philadelphia Inquirer*, March 20, 1862.

[2]"Our Army Correspondence," *Pittsburgh Evening Chronicle*, January 31, 1865. Bates's roster for the 2nd Cavalry is very deficient and no Sergeant Fowler is included in the Company A roster.

[3]This is from the newspaper article cited in Note 2.

[4]Major G. L. McCabe to Adjutant-General Russel, January 21, 1865, RG 25.

[5]Colonel W. W. Sanders to Adjutant-General Russell, June 5, 1866, RG 19.

[6]Dallas Sanders to Adjutant-General, March 21, 1883, RG 25.

Bibliography

Anderson, John. Papers. Pennsylvania State Archives.

Powell, J. C. "Hatcher's Run." *National Tribune*, May 13, 1886.

Walker, Campbell. "At Gettysburg." *National Tribune*, March 22, 1888.

3rd Cavalry
(60th Regiment)

First State Standard

The 3rd Pennsylvania Cavalry was organized during the summer of 1861 as an independent cavalry regiment and was not officially credited to the state until October when it was numbered as the 3rd Cavalry. After organization, the regiment proceeded to Washington and went into camp south of the Potomac River. The first state standard, furnished by Horstmann Brothers & Company, was sent to the State Agency on November 4 and presented to the regiment at some unspecified time after this date.

In March 1862, the regiment participated in the advance to Manassas, then moved by water to Fort Monroe. After skirmishing during the Siege of Yorktown, the 3rd Cavalry was marginally engaged in the Battle of Williamsburg on May 5. During the Seven Days' Battles, the regiment fought at White Oak Swamp on June 29 and formed part of the army's rearguard during the retreat to Malvern Hill. The regiment remained actively engaged with the enemy skirmishers until the army was withdrawn from the Peninsula in August. After arriving at Alexandria, the 3rd was temporarily assigned to First Corps headquarters and remained on this duty during the September Maryland Campaign. The unit then actively skirmished with Rebel cavalry during the Army of the Potomac's advance through Virginia to Fredericksburg.

After the disastrous Battle of Fredericksburg, the regiment went into winter quarters near Falmouth. It took part in the cavalry fight at Kelly's Ford on March 19, 1863, then participated with most of the Cavalry Corps in the raid across the rear of Lee's army during the Chancellorsville Campaign. At Gettysburg on July 3, the 3rd Cavalry fought in the cavalry battle east of the main armies, helping to defeat an attempt by the Rebel cavalry to attack the rear of the Army of the Potomac. During this battle, the color-guard and state standard remained in reserve near the Howard House as the remainder of the unit attacked the oncoming Southern horsemen.[1] After returning to Virginia, the regiment took an active part in the Bristoe Station and Mine Run campaigns before settling into winter quarters near Warrenton.

On February 26, 1864, the regiment was detached from the Second Division of the Cavalry corps and assigned to duty in the Provost Guard. Although this detail did not involve active combat duty, the varied duties of the provost guard required long hours. The regiment acted as army headquarters guards and orderlies, provided cavalry escorts for the generals, accompanied prisoners to the rear, and guarded the army cattle and wagon trains. The regiment performed this duty until late July 1864, when the term of service of most of its members expired. The survivors were consolidated into a battalion of three companies. The remnant of the state standard was apparently sent to the State Agency shortly after the consolidation. William Brooke Rawle described it thus: "It was in a very delapedated condition, nothing I believe, but the fringe remaining."[2] It was officially returned to state care in July 1866.

First State Standard
Maker: EH
Size: 38¹/₂" 45¹/₂"
1985.092

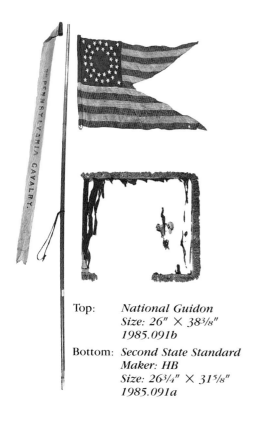

Top: *National Guidon*
         Size: 26" × 38³/₈"
         1985.091b
Bottom: *Second State Standard*
         Maker: HB
         Size: 26³/₄" × 31⁵/₈"
         1985.091a

Second State Standard

The remaining three companies continued to serve with the Provost Guard. During the months of September, October, and November 1864, enough recruits were assigned to the regiment to form five new companies. As the regimental strength increased, the commander asked Colonel Frank Jordan of the State Agency for a new flag. Jordan relayed this request to Adjutant-General Russell on October 17.[3] The replacement standard was forwarded to the 3rd Cavalry in mid-November. This banner was carried by the regiment in the closing operations around Petersburg. The regiment fought at Hatcher's Run on February 5-7, 1865, and at Five Forks on March 29. When Generals Grant and Meade entered Petersburg, elements of the 3rd Cavalry provided their escort. After Lee's surrender, the regiment acted as military police in Richmond until June 1865. During that time, four companies were mustered out of service and the survivors merged with the 5th Pennsylvania Cavalry on June 7. The men remained in service until early August, when they were sent home and returned to civilian life. The second standard was left in Philadelphia and returned to state care on July 4, 1866.[4]

Newhall Memorial Standard

In December 1863, Mr. Clement S. Barclay of Philadelphia visited the regimental camp near Warrenton and presented a standard to the regiment to honor the

memory of Captain Walter S. Newhall. The captain had drowned while attempting to cross the Rappahannock River on December 18. This flag was carried by the regiment and veteran battalion until the end of the war. On July 21, 1865, the officers of the regiment voted unanimously to give the flag to Mrs. Thomas A. Newhall, the deceased captain's mother, then living in Germantown. When the regimental history was published in 1905, the flag was still in the family's possession.[5]

Company A Guidon

A militia cavalry company, the Philadelphia Merchant Troop, became Company A of the 3rd Cavalry. The Historical Society of Pennsylvania has custody of a company guidon carried by this unit at some unspecified period. The guidon was presented to the Historical Society by George M. Newhall in 1915.

Company H Guidon

A guidon carried by the Big Spring Adamantine Guards was owned after the war by Captain William E. Miller of Carlisle. Nothing further has been located about this flag.[6]

National Guidons

There are two remaining federal guidons for the 3rd Cavalry. One, an unmarked flag, was found rolled up beneath one of the state standards in the state collection. A second is owned by the War Library and Museum, Military Order of the Loyal Legion of the United States, Philadelphia. It is painted with battle honors and is identified as that carried by Company C, which became Company B of the veteran battalion in 1864.

Reverse, Newhall Standard

Notes

[1]Regimental history, p. 304.

[2]William Brooke Rawle to Adjutant-General Russell, May 23, 1866, RG 19.

[3]Colonel Frank Jordan to Adjutant-General Russell, October 17, 1864, RG 25.

[4]Regimental history, p. 454.

[5]*Ibid.*, pp. 393, 454, 512.

[6]Civic Club of Carlisle, *Carlisle Old and New* (Harrisburg: J. H. McFarland Company, 1907, reprinted 1973), p. 46.

Bibliography

Constitution and By-Laws of Company H, Third Pennsylvania Cavalry, With a Brief History and Muster Roll. Shippensburg: D. K. and J. C. Wagner, Printers, 1878.

Edmonds, Howard O. *Owen-Edmonds, Incidents of the American Civil War, 1861-1865, Prepared from Family Records*. Chicago: Lakeside Press, 1928.

Hale, Charles R. "Sketches of Civil War Recollections." *National Tribune*, March 25, April 1, 1926.

History of the Third Pennsylvania Cavalry, Sixtieth Regiment Pennsylvania Volunteers in the American Civil War, 1861-1865. Philadelphia: Franklin Printing Company, 1905.

Hunterson, John C. "The First Cavalry Fight of the War." *Philadelphia Weekly Times*, March 1, 1879. (Kelly's Ford)

Miller, William E. "The Cavalry Battle Near Gettysburg." *Battles and Leaders* 3: 397-406.

_____. *War History. Operations of the Union Cavalry on the Peninsula, in Which Some Cumberland County Soldiers Took Part*. Carlisle, 1908.

_____. "The Third Pennsylvania Cavalry in the Gettysburg Campaign." *Philadelphia Weekly Press*, May 12, 1886.

Newhall, Walter S. Papers. Historical Society of Pennsylvania.

Rawle, William B. "With Gregg in the Gettysburg Campaign." *Philadelphia Weekly Times*, February 2, 1884; Reprinted separately, Philadelphia: McLaughlin Brothers, 1884.

_____. Rawle Family Papers. Historical Society of Pennsylvania.

Speese, Andrew J. "How Comrade Andrew J. Speese, Commander of the Cavalry Post 35, Delayed Gordon's Brigade of Rebel Cavalry." *Grand Army Scout and Soldiers Mail*, February 10, 1883. (October 1863 operations)

_____. "A Perilous Ride. How a Squad of the 3d Pa. Cavalry Rode Into and Out of an Ambush." *Grand Army Scout and Soldiers Mail*, May 26, 1883. (June 30, 1862, incident)

_____. *Story of Companies H, A and C, Third Pennsylvania Cavalry at Gettysburg, July 3, 1863*. Germantown, 1906.

Warren, E. Willard. Papers. Duke University.

Wister, Sarah. *Walter S. Newhall, a Memoir*. Philadelphia: Press of C. Sherman Son & Company, 1864.

61st Infantry

First State Color

The 61st Pennsylvania was recruited in Pittsburgh during the early fall of 1861. Owing to the demand for troops in Washington, the regiment was sent to the nation's capital before it was fully manned. Four companies were detached from the 23rd Pennsylvania to bring the 61st up to the required ten-company strength in February 1862. A state color was presented to the regiment on January 5, 1862, by state Military Agent James H. Puleston. This officer travelled to the regiment's camp some four miles outside of Alexandria, Virginia, to present the flag.[1]

While in the Washington area, the 61st was attached to the First Division of the Fourth Corps. It remained in camp until March 1862, when the corps was part of the force sent to the Yorktown Peninsula. The regiment participated in the Siege of Yorktown and then advanced up the Peninsula toward Richmond. When Confederate troops attacked the Fourth Corps on May 31 (the Battle of Fair Oaks), the First Division moved to the support of the hard-pressed Second Division, the 61st attacking superior numbers of enemy soldiers in the woods on the right of the line of battle. The 61st fought with "extraordinary bravery," losing 263 of the 574 officers and men who entered the battle. Sergeant John Davis of Company E, bearer of the state flag, escaped with out a scratch, although his banner was completely riddled with bullets. An eyewitness thought it a miracle that the sergeant escaped unhurt.[2] After suffering heavy losses on May 31, the regiment was held in reserve and did not take part in the successful conclusion of the battle on June 1.

During the Seven Days' Battles, the 61st, together with most of the Fourth Corps, guarded the left flank of General George B. McClellan's retreating army. The 61st did participate in the Battle of Malvern Hill on July 1, supporting an artillery battery and suffering twenty-three additional casualties. The First Division then embarked for Alexandria in late August and acted as rearguard when the retreating Federal army fell back from its defeat at Second Manassas. When the army marched into Maryland to counter General

Lee's invasion of that state, the division arrived on the Antietam battlefield the day after the bloody fighting. The division was then transferred to the Sixth Corps, where it remained until the end of the war. During the Battle of Fredericksburg on December 13, the division was held in reserve, then settled into winter camp near Falmouth.

Because of the heavy battle and weather damage, the regiment requested a replacement state color. The initial flag was returned to the state in April 1863 and remained in the adjutant-general's office until June 1866. At that time, Colonel Robert L. Orr borrowed the flag to have a Sixth Corps badge added. He returned it in time for the July 4, 1866, ceremony, at which time it was formally given to state care.[3]

Second State Color

A replacement state color was finished by Horstmann Brothers & Company in March 1863. The flag had originally been designed for the 144th Pennsylvania, a regiment that was never completely organized. The flag was altered for use by the 61st. It was probably received by the regiment sometime in April, when the first state color was sent to Harrisburg.

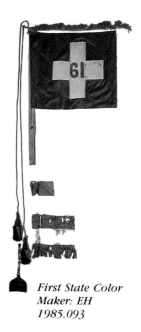

First State Color
Maker: EH
1985.093

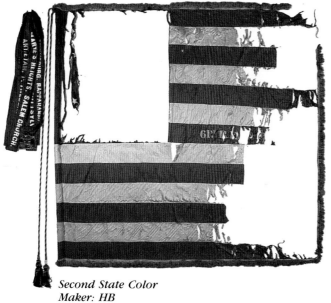

Second State Color
Maker: HB
Size: 70⅞" × 77½"
1985.094

The new flag was first used in combat on May 3, 1863. The Sixth Corps assaulted the Rebel positions on Marye's Heights at Fredericksburg that day. Colonel George C. Spear of the 61st was selected to lead one of the attacking columns. His men were to rely on the bayonet and were cautioned not to stop to fire on the enemy, posted behind a stonewall at the foot of the heights. At 11 a.m., the columns started forward over the open ground. Colonel Spear was killed shortly after the regiment began to advance and Color-Sergeant David H. Ford was wounded, causing a momentary wavering of the regiment. But Colonel Alexander Shaler of the 65th New York galloped up to rally the men and the charge proved successful. The regiment then pursued the enemy toward Chancellorsville, taking a minor part in the fighting around Salem Church before withdrawing across the Rappahannock River at Banks' Ford.[4]

During the Gettysburg Campaign, the Sixth Corps protected the right flank of the Army of the Potomac, arriving on the field by late afternoon on July 2. The 61st was stationed on Wolf's Hill and did not take an active part in the battle. After participating in the Bristoe Station and Mine Run campaigns, the regiment went into winter camp near Brandy Station.

The 61st entered the 1864 campaign well-rested and reinforced. It led its brigade into the Battle of the Wilderness on May 5. After fighting against a concealed foe for over two hours, the 61st assaulted the Rebel entrenchments but was repulsed. The enemy attacked in turn at 4:30 a.m. on May 6 but was repelled, the corps then advancing and attacking until late morning, when the Federals went over to the de-

fensive. During this struggle, Color-Sergeant Hugh Gorman was killed, the bullet first splintering the flagstaff before plunging into his body. As he fell, Sergeant Gorman asked, with his expiring breath, "Are the colors safe?"[5]

Later that same day, Confederate General John B. Gordon's troops crushed the right flank of the Sixth Corps and the 61st was part of the troops sent to bolster the retreating defenders. Many of the regiment were swept to the rear as panicked soldiers fled through the ranks of the 61st, but Colonel George F. Smith managed to keep about 250 men with the colors. General Shaler then rode up, inquired what regiment the command was, and then ordered the colors forward, admonishing the Pennsylvanians not to desert their flag. The regiment then advanced and helped stop any further Rebel gains. The 61st lost 151 casualties during these two days of fighting.[6]

The army then moved to Spotsylvania Court House where fighting raged until May 21. On May 8, the 61st advanced in the early evening and had just emerged from a swale when the regiment encountered an advancing Rebel line of battle in the darkness. An enemy officer grabbed the flagstaff and demanded surrender, but the bearer held on and in the ensuing hand-to-hand struggle, the 61st drove back the Confederate force and held its advanced position. The regiment was also heavily engaged on May 12 when the Sixth Corps attacked the Rebel earthworks as a support to other Yankee assaults.[7]

After Spotsylvania, the 61st was engaged at Cold Harbor and Petersburg before the corps was sent to Washington to help repel Confederate General Jubal A. Early's attack on the city. It then marched into northern Virginia as Early retreated up the Shenandoah Valley. The corps was enroute to Petersburg when Early turned about and defeated the Federal troops remaining in the Valley. The corps thus was

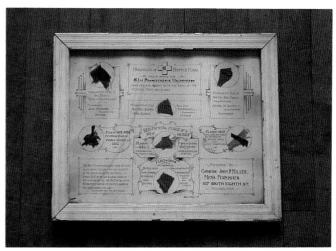

Pieces of the 61st's Flags, Collected by Colonel Orr

Advance the Colors!

Corporal John C. Matthews   Sergeant Joseph Fisher   Major Robert L. Orr

returned to the Valley. After a short but sharp skirmish at Opequon Creek on August 21, the corps bivouacked near Berryville. Here, all non-veterans of the 61st were sent home for mustering out, and the remainder of the regiment was consolidated into a battalion of seven companies. Colonel Smith, one of those who went home, took along the second state flag. He returned it to state care on July 4, 1866.[8]

Third State Color

Horstmann Brothers & Company had completed a new flag for the 61st in February 1864, forwarding it to the State Agency in Washington. However, the flag was not delivered until after the non-veterans went home in September. A January 1865 letter indicates that this replacement color was not received until late December 1864, after the Sixth Corps returned to the Petersburg area.[9]

While the regiment rested after the 1864 campaigns, three new companies were added to complete the regimental organization. The unit's final engagement took place on April 2, 1865, the day when the Army of the Potomac broke through the Confederate lines to force the evacuation of both Petersburg and Richmond. The Sixth Corps formed behind the trenches in the shape of a wedge, with the Second Division at the apex. Anticipating that this assault might well succeed, Major Robert L. Orr told both color-sergeants that he wanted the 61st to be the first regiment to plant its flags on the enemy line. When he would give the word, Orr wanted both bearers and the guard to dash forward in advance of the regiment

to encourage an all-out effort by the troops.[10] When the advance began, Lieutenant-Colonel John W. Crosby was shot and killed as the Rebel defenders of Harry Heth's division played havoc with the 61st. Sergeant William Coon, bearing the state color, was wounded shortly after the regiment began its attack. Before the flag touched the ground, Corporal John C. Matthews, carrying a flag presented by Philadelphia ladies, grabbed the flag and carried both forward for a few minutes. Then, Major Orr took the state flag and

Third State Color
Maker: HB
Size: 71¹⁄₈" × 77¹⁄₈"
1985.095

helped restore the confidence of the regiment, which had fallen into some disorder after Crosby was killed.

Orr then gave the state flag to Sergeant Joseph Fisher, who took the color and advanced some fifty yards ahead of the 61st, urging the troops forward. Fisher was soon wounded by a bursting artillery shell that shattered his arm and left a gash in his side. Even so, the plucky sergeant attempted to crawl into a Rebel fort with his flag but fainted from pain and exhaustion. Corporal Matthews received a flesh wound but continued on and planted the Philadelphia flag on the fort, aided by Lieutenant A. B. Davis of Company C. Orr, Matthews, and Fisher each received a Medal of Honor for gallantry in this assault.[11]

The regiment then took part in the Appomattox Campaign and on April 17 was honored by being detailed to escort captured Confederate flags to army headquarters. After performing provost guard duty in Danville, Virginia, the 61st moved to Washington and was mustered out of service on June 28, 1865. The third state color was left in Harrisburg and borrowed temporarily by Colonel Orr, who returned it in time for the July 1866 ceremony.[12]

Pittsburgh Flag

Just before its departure for Washington in September 1861, the regiment received a flag from the citizens of Pittsburgh. This banner was carried by the regiment into the Battle of Fair Oaks on May 31, 1862. When the regiment began to fall back and collided with Rebel troops moving toward its rear, there was some heavy fighting over the flag. Sergeant William H. Ronntree of Company D was killed. The staff was hit and broken in two. As the flag fell, a Rebel dashed forward to seize it, but Corporal James Milligan clubbed his opponent across the head with his musket and retrieved the banner. Since the flag had been given to the regiment through Colonel Oliver H. Rippey, who was killed at Fair Oaks, the regiment sent the flag to Pittsburgh along with the colonel's body. No further details have been located about this flag.[13]

Philadelphia Flag

During the winter of 1864-65, citizens of Philadelphia presented Major Orr with a flag for the 61st. This color was made of heavy blue silk, with the state arms on the obverse and the national arms on the reverse. It was inscribed "Presented by the Citizens of Philadelphia to Sixty-first Regiment Pennsylvania Volunteers for Gallant Conduct Throughout the War." The names of the major battles in which the regiment had fought were also inscribed on this color. The flag was carried in the April 2, 1865, Petersburg assault as described above. Sergeant Joseph C. Matthews received a Medal of Honor for his gallantry in the successful assault. This banner is now in the museum of the Philadelphia Camp, Sons of Union Veterans.[14]

Notes

[1]"Flag Presentations to Pa. Troops," *Philadelphia Press*, January 6, 1862. Brewer, p, 15, writes that Representative H. B. Wright presented the state color in December 1861.

[2]"How the Sixty-first Got Cut Up in the Late Battle," *Pittsburgh Evening Chronicle*, June 7, 1862.

[3]Robert L. Orr to Adjutant-General Russell, June 21, 1866, RG 19.

[4]Brewer, pp. 54-55; *O.R.* 25.1, pp. 625-627. Private James Robb of Company H seized the flag after Ford was shot. Color-Corporal William Taylor then took the flag.

[5]George F. Smith to Adjutant-General Russell, June 11, 1866, RG 19; Brewer, pp. 82-84.

[6]Brewer, pp. 85-86. Jacob Sanders, quoting from his diary, mentioned this incident as occurring on May 9. He wrote that a Michigan regiment fell back through the 61st's line, and a Confederate officer came up and tried to dupe the bearer into letting him have the flag to rally the retreating soldiers. See the *Wilkes-Barre Record of the Times*, June 1, 1864.

[7]Brewer, p. 89.

[8]Robert L. Orr to Adjutant-General Russell, June 6, 1866; George F. Smith to Russell, June 11, 1866, both in RG 19.

[9]*Wilkes-Barre Record of the Times*, January 4, 1865.

[10]Brewer, pp. 137-138.

[11]*Ibid.*, pp. 134-135; Robert L. Orr to Secretary of War Lewis A. Grant, November 28, 1893, Joseph Fisher Medal of Honor File, RG 94, National Archives; Beyer-Keydel, p. 507.

[12]Robert L. Orr to Adjutant-General Russell, June 21, 1866, RG 19.

[13]Brewer, pp. 24-26; "How the Sixty-first Got Cut Up in the Late Battle," *Pittsburgh Evening Chronicle*, June 7, 1862; "The Sixty-first P.V. At Fair Oaks," *Philadelphia Press*, June 25, 1862. Bates lists Sergeant Ronntree as wounded, but casualty lists in the *Pittsburgh Post* (June 10, 1862) and the *Pittsburgh Evening Chronicle* (June 7, 1862) both list him as killed.

[14]Brewer, pp. 135, 157-158, expanding upon statements made in Bates 2: 414-415. However, on page 135 Brewer writes that the flag was presented in November 1864, while on page 157 he has the date as January 1865.

Bibliography

Adams, Ida B. (editor). "The Civil War Letters of James Rush Holmes." *Western Pennsylvania Historical Magazine* 44 (1961): 105-127.

Blair, F. L. "That Incident in the Battle of the Wilderness." *Grand Army Scout and Soldiers Mail*, February 9, 1884.

Brewer, Abraham T. *History Sixty-first Regiment Pennsylvania Volunteers, 1861-1865*. Pittsburgh: Art Engraving and Printing Company, 1911.

_____. *Oration Delivered July 24th, 1888, on Wolf's Hill, Gettysburg, by A. T. Brewer, at Dedication of Battle Monument in Memory of the Sixty-first Pennsylvania Volunteers*. Cleveland: Cleveland Printing and Publishing Company, 1888.

_____. Memoir of Fair Oaks. USAMHI, CWTI Collection.

Clark, Samuel. "Some Recollections of Antietam." *Grand Army Scout and Soldiers Mail*, November 15, 1884.

Fairchilds, John. 1863 Diary. Pennsylvania State Archives.

"J.K.D." "One Company." *Philadelphia Weekly Press*, June 20, 1888.

Kilmer, George L. "Nineteen Heroes. The Officers Killed in Battle of the 61st Pennsylvania." War Department Pamphlet v. 270.

Lookhart, D. A. "Chancellorsville." *National Tribune*, August 30, 1883.

_____. "The 61st Pennsylvania at Fair Oaks." *National Tribune*, February 25, 1886.

Miller, W. G. "Fair Oaks." *National Tribune*, February 3, 1887.

Oehmler, Herman. Diary, January-September 1864. Soldiers and Sailors Memorial Hall, Pittsburgh.

Orr, Robert L. "Before Petersburg." *Philadelphia Weekly Press*, December 15, 1886.

Robinson, James. "Chancellorsville." *National Tribune*, September 13, 1888.

62nd Infantry

State Color

The 62nd Pennsylvania was primarily recruited in Pittsburgh in July 1861. This twelve-company regiment was raised under authority given to Colonel Samuel W. Black, a Mexican War volunteer officer and Nebraska Territory governor. After spending a few weeks at Camp Cameron, near Harrisburg, the new regiment moved to Washington, where it remained throughout the winter of 1861-62. Senator Edgar Cowan presented state colors to the 62nd and 83rd on December 21, 1861. Colonel Black responded to the Senator's presentation with the following speech, which illustrates the high regard in which the American flag was held:[1]

> In the name and in behalf of the regiment . . . I accept these colors of our country, a gift from the Commonwealth of Pennsylvania, our mother.
>
> Past memories and present troubles combine to increase and make more intense our devotion to the national flag. We witness today, and will witness with uplifted hands, and hearts unchanged, that perfidy and rebellion at home, either alone, or aided by habitual arrogance and pretension abroad, shall serve only to gather us more closely around the standard of our country.
>
> When the sky is clear, and the winds are still, it leans upon its staff in patriarchal and peaceful repose—an object of calm and contented love.
>
> But when it trembles in the storm, a nation assembles at its silent call; battalions people every hill; the mighty hosts of the mountains hasten to the field; squadrons sweep over every plain; and sovereign States, sensible that loyalty is the sign of independence, form themselves into one solid squadron for its defense.
>
> We turn with pride to the great Pennsylvania sentiment of patriotism embraced in her flags now unfurled before us. Behold and admire the beauty of the glowing thought that shines upon the standard! The arms of the State are inlaid amongst the stars of the Union! Her shield, her buckler, and her strength are there. Her own star is there; but which one is hers? Who, by searching, can find out or declare? The utmost art of astrology employs its mystic power in vain, and reveals only that which a child can see—that one differeth not from another star in glory, but shall shine together in the same heaven and with the same original and independent luster. . . .
>
> Sir, you have our thanks for the act of presentation gracefully performed, for your sentiments of kind feeling and generous confidence. . . . You do not misunderstand us.

State Color
Maker: EH
Size: 69³/₈" (-) × 78"
1985.006

> We have dedicated ourselves . . . to the service of the country, the defense and vindication of its flag, the restoration of the Constitution in all its power, and the preservation and perpetuity of the American Union in every part of its wide and great dominion. . . .
>
> But, sir, of the great result, we entertain not a single doubt, nor the slightest apprehension. The flag of the Union is our flag as it was our fathers', and we receive from them, though dead, their living faith that it shall not perish. . . .
>
> In closing, I offer no pledge nor promise. But when this battle of national existence is fought and won, as fought and won it will be, and these two standards shall reappear, within the gates of peace, as in God's good providence they may, not a star less bright than now, nor any stripe stained with dark dishonor, though the blood of many sons may crimson every inch of white, I beg you, on that day, to remember and believe, that not accident, but design, and the brave purpose of these battalions is fulfilled in that future of the flag.

In March 1862, the 62nd participated in the Army of the Potomac's advance to Manassas, then was transferred by water to the Yorktown peninsula. After taking part in the Siege of Yorktown, the regiment was assigned to the new Fifth Corps, with which it remained until the expiration of its three-years term of service. The regiment's first major engagement with the enemy occurred on May 27, 1862, as the Fifth

Corps skirmished with a Rebel force at Hanover Court House.

The 62nd next fought in the Battle of Gaines' Mill on June 27. The Fifth Corps was attacked by General Robert E. Lee's Confederates and fell back late in the day after successfully repelling most of the enemy assaults on its isolated position. Colonel Black was killed as the regiment counterattacked. Five men were shot down while carrying the state color.[2] After taking part in the army's withdrawal to Malvern Hill, the regiment fought in the battle at this place on July 1, again suffering heavy casualties. Including the loss suffered on June 27, the 62nd lost 283 officers and men.[3]

Although the Fifth Corps was heavily engaged in the Second Battle of Manassas, the 62nd was part of the reserve force and lost few men. The corps remained in reserve during the Battle of Antietam on September 17, and the 62nd was not engaged in this battle. During the Battle of Fredericksburg on December 13, the 62nd was one of the regiments that unsuccessfully stormed the Rebel defenses on Marye's Heights, suffering seventy casualties.

After spending the winter of 1862-63 in camp near Falmouth, the regiment participated in the Chancellorsville Campaign. Although the Fifth Corps was part of the force engaged in extensive marching and maneuvering during this campaign, it was not heavily engaged in the battle. At Gettysburg on July 2, 1863, the brigade to which the 62nd was attached fought in the Wheatfield. A Confederate force outflanked the Yankee line along the southern edge of this field and the combat was hand-to-hand at times before the 62nd managed to extricate itself and withdraw, having suffered a loss of more than one-third of those present. The bearer of the state color was bayonetted and wounded while defending his banner.[4] After following the defeated Rebels back to Virginia, the regiment took part in the Bristoe Station and Mine Run campaigns before going into winter quarters near Warrenton.

When the 1864 campaign opened, the 62nd fought in the Battle of the Wilderness on May 5-7, suffering sixty-one casualties. It then took part in the fighting around Spotsylvania Court House, including the climactic fighting there on May 12. The regiment also engaged the enemy at the North Anna River and at Cold Harbor before the army crossed the James River and attacked the defenses of Petersburg. The 62nd was engaged in the June 18 assault, then took part in minor skirmishing during the next few days. In early July, the regiment was relieved from duty and sent home to be mustered out of service, which occurred in Pittsburgh on July 13. Two companies remained at the front and served until early August, when their term of service expired and they also went home. The remnant of the state color was deposited in Harrisburg and officially returned to the state on July 4, 1866.

Pittsburgh Flag

Before the regiment left Pittsburgh in August 1861, a "beautiful silk flag" was presented to Company A by the ladies of the Liberty Street Methodist Episcopal Church. This flag was presented to the regiment to be used as a regimental flag with the provision that it be returned to the company when the regiment disbanded.[5] The subsequent history of this flag is unknown. The regiment carried two flags at Gettysburg, losing one to the enemy during the fighting in the Wheatfield.[6] However, it cannot be determined if this captured flag was the one presented in 1861. The Erie County Library System building contains a color marked as belonging to the 62nd. No specific information is available about the identity of this flag.

Company H Flag

A local militia company near Pittsburgh, the Upper Saint Clair Guards, purchased a flag in 1860 at a cost of $46.25. When this company entered the 62nd Pennsylvania as Company H, the flag was taken to Harrisburg, where it was found that company flags were not allowed to be carried. It was sent to Captain Thomas Espy's family, which retained it until 1907, when it was given to Captain Thomas Espy Post 153 of the G.A.R., Carnegie, where it remains.[7]

Color-Bearers

The two men carrying the 62nd's flags at Gettysburg were Sergeants Thomas H. Budlong of Company I and Jacob B. Funk of Company A. Budlong was killed and Funk was wounded in the right shoulder.[8]

Notes

[1]Undated newspaper article in Black Papers. The article "From Colonel Black's Regiment," *Pittsburgh Post*, December 30, 1861, is a brief description of the ceremony.

[2]"The Sixty-second Vindicated," *Pittsburgh Evening Chronicle*, July 21, 1862.

[3]Bates, in volume 2, page 454, writes that the color-bearer, Sergeant Smith, saved the flag from capture at Malvern Hill. Temporarily cut off from the regiment during the fighting, the sergeant tore the flag from the staff and secreted it under his uniform, then hid in a stable until Federal troops drove the enemy away. Smith was promoted to lieutenant for this act of daring. However, Bates has no Sergeant Smith in his roster and this story cannot be documented or verified.

[4]Letter of John R. Garden in the *Altoona Tribune*, August 26, 1863.

[5]"Colonel Black's Regiment," *Pittsburgh Gazette*, August 22, 1861.

[6]Garden letter cited above.

[7]*Catalogue of Relics in Memorial Room, Capt. Thos. Espy Post No.* *153, G.A.R. Library Building, Carnegie, Penna., 1911* (n.p., n.d.), p. 11.

[8]Gettysburg Casualty List, in RG 19, Civil War Service, Miscellaneous Box 2.

Bibliography

Black, Samuel W. Papers. Historical Society of Western Pennsylvania.

"The Death of Colonel Black at Gaines's Mill." *National Tribune*, June 11, 1885.

Horst, Louis. Diary, August 3, 1862-May 10, 1863. USAMHI.

McFadden, Janice R. Typescript. Historical Society of Western Pennsylvania. Includes reminiscences of James L. Graham of Company H.

Monks, Zerah C. Papers. Emory University.

63rd Infantry

First State Color

Primarily recruited in Pittsburgh during August 1861, the regiment was rushed directly to Washington before it was completely organized. By late September the 63rd was fully organized and went into camp about four miles outside Alexandria, where it remained during the winter of 1861-62. On January 5, 1862, Representative James K. Moorhead of Pittsburgh visited the regimental camp to present the state color, which was received with an appropriate speech by Colonel Alexander Hays.[1]

In March 1862, the 63rd, a part of the Army of the Potomac's Third Corps, was transported to the Yorktown Peninsula. After the Siege of Yorktown, the army advanced closer to the Rebel capital. The 63rd's first engagement with the enemy was at the Battle of Fair Oaks on May 31-June 1, in which the untried regiment suffered over a hundred casualties. After skirmishing with the enemy at Seven Oaks on June 25, the regiment was heavily engaged in the Battle of Glendale on June 30, again suffering heavy losses.

First State Color
Maker: EH
Size: 69³/₈″ × 75⁵/₈″
1985.096

During the enemy attacks that day, the 63rd supported an artillery battery and successfully repelled every attempt to capture the guns.

When the army was withdrawn from the Peninsula to northern Virginia, the Third Corps took an active part in the Second Battle of Manassas on August 29-30. During the unsuccessful attacks on Stonewall Jackson's Confederates on August 29, the 63rd charged and was repulsed three times. Losses totalled 120 of the slightly more than three hundred men taken into the fight. Color-Sergeant William W. Weeks of Company H was cited in the official battle report for his bravery. Captain James F. Ryan wrote that Weeks, "notwithstanding the fearful shower of bullets rained upon us by the enemy from their cover, gallantly carried our colors to the front, and remained with them until wounded when one of the guard, Corporal John Hoffman, Company I, caught them up and bravely maintaining his position received a shot which forced him to relinquish his charge to another of the color-guard, Corporal George Lang, Company E, who carried them safely off the field."[2]

The Second Battle of Manassas was another defeat for the army, which retreated to Washington. The Third Corps remained behind as most of the troops advanced into Maryland to counter General Robert E. Lee's invasion of that state. During this time, Corporal Lang, promoted to sergeant immediately after Manassas, carried the state color. The corps rejoined the army in time to participate in the Battle of Fredericksburg on December 13, another Yankee defeat. The regiment went into winter camp near Falmouth.

During the Chancellorsville Campaign, the Third Corps figured prominently in the fighting on May 2 and 3, 1863. The corps held the center of the Federal battleline and was almost cut off from the army when Stonewall Jackson's attack routed the Eleventh Corps. The corps counterattacked during the night of May 2-3 and rejoined the main line. On May 3, Color-Sergeant George W. Fitzgerald of Company K was wounded as the regiment attacked the Rebel breastworks. He refused to give up the flag until wounded a second time, when Corporal George F. House of Company B took the banner and planted it on the

Sergeant George F. House Carried the State Colors for a Year Until Wounded

The Staff of the First State Color was Broken by Rebel Bullets on May 3, 1863

First State Color as it Hung in the Flag Room, ca. 1900

enemy line. The corporal stood by the flag even though the staff was broken in two by enemy bullets. When the regiment retired, House took the flag with him safely. House received a coveted Kearny Medal for his bravery and was promoted to sergeant.[3]

The regiment then took part in the Gettysburg Campaign. It fought in the battle on July 2, acting as skirmishers and suffering comparatively few losses. After returning to Virginia, the 63rd took part in the Bristoe Station and Mine Run campaigns before erecting winter quarters near Brandy Station. On September 10, Major John A. Danks requested a replacement state color from Governor Curtin.[4] The initial state flag eventually remained in Major Danks's possession. He kept it until 1866, when he went to Philadelphia to officially present it to the state.[5]

Second State Color

The replacement state flag was sent to the State Agency in Washington in early December 1863. It was first carried into combat on May 5, 1864, when the regiment, now a part of the Third Division, Second Corps, attacked the enemy in the Battle of the Wilderness. In two days of fighting, the 63rd suffered 191 casualties, more than fifty percent of the regiment's strength. Sergeant House, still the regimental color-sergeant, was wounded on May 5.[6] The depleted regiment fought at Spotsylvania on May 12-14, then engaged the enemy along the North Anna River on May 23-24. It was not heavily engaged in the unsuccessful charges at Cold Harbor.

The army then crossed the James River and assaulted the Petersburg defenses, the 63rd being engaged on June 21-22. As the two armies settled down

Advance the Colors!

into protracted siege warfare, the 63rd took its turn in the trenches, suffering light casualties. The regiment's term of service expired on August 1, but it was retained at the front until September 9 when the majority of the regiment was sent home for muster out. Those who chose to re-enlist were consolidated with the 105th Pennsylvania. This small band of men continued to carry the 63rd's state color until the fighting along the Boydton Plank Road on October 27. There, the regiment encountered a much larger force of the enemy and in the ensuing confusion of a rapid retreat, the flag was captured by the enemy.[7] Tagged as #66 on the War Department's list of captured flags, this banner remained in the department until June 11, 1886, when Secretary of War William C. Endicott authorized its return to the 63rd Regimental Association, which had requested it.[8] This flag appears on the 1887 Fox list of photographed flags, so the regimental association must have given the color to the state shortly after obtaining it from the War Department.

Second State Color
Maker: EH
Size: 71¹/₂" × 72⁷/₈"(-)
1985.097

Notes

[1]"Flag Presentations to Pennsylvania Troops," *Philadelphia Press*, January 6, 1862; Hays, pp. 49-54.

[2]*O.R.* 12.2, p. 424.

[3]*O.R.* 25.1, pp. 418-419; Special Orders #29, May 25, 1863, in Regimental Descriptive, Letter, and Order Book, RG 94.

[4]Danks to Curtin, September 10, 1863, RG 25.

[5]John A. Danks to Adjutant-General Russell, June 1, 1866, RG 19.

[6]Hays, p. 303.

[7]*O.R.* 42.1, p. 349. Brigadier-General Gersham Mott, commanding the Third Division, Second Corps, investigated the loss of the colors of both the 63rd and the 105th and found that the consolidated regiment had "behaved well, and the loss of the colors was owing to being attacked suddenly as they were forming into line by a very much superior force."

[8]Adjutant-General Richard C. Drum to Governor Robert E. Pattison, June 12, 1886, RG 25; Captured Flags Document, p. 8.

Bibliography

Draher, George M. Papers. Historical Society of Western Pennsylvania.

Dunham, Samuel. "Spotsylvania." *National Tribune*, June 10, 1886.

Hays, Gilbert A. *Under the Red Patch, Story of the Sixty-third Regiment Pennsylvania Volunteers, 1861-1864*. Pittsburgh: Press of Market Review Publishing Company, 1908.

_____. Papers. Historical Society of Western Pennsylvania.

Marks, James J. *The Peninsula Campaign in Virginia; or, Incidents and Scenes on the Battle-fields and in Richmond*. Philadelphia: J. B. Lippincott & Company, 1864.

4th Cavalry
(64th Regiment)

First State Standard

The 4th Pennsylvania Cavalry was organized during the months of August, September, and October 1861, under authority granted to David Campbell of Pittsburgh. The companies began to rendezvous at Camp Curtin but were sent to Washington in mid-September. Governor Curtin went to Camp Campbell and presented a state standard to the unit on February 15, 1862.[1] After remaining in camp near Washington during the winter of 1861-62, the regiment was assigned to Major-General Irvin McDowell's corps and participated in the advance to Fredericksburg in May 1862. During this time, the standard was borne by Sergeant Amos S. Bolton of Company F. On May 27, Bolton was reduced to 4th Sergeant of his company for disobedience of orders. He was replaced as bearer by Sergeant William Hazlett of Company G.[2]

In June 1862, the regiment, now temporarily attached to the Pennsylvania Reserves, was transferred to the Peninsula and joined the Army of the Potomac. The regiment took part in the battles of Mechanicsville (June 26), Gaines' Mill (June 27), New Market Cross Roads (June 30), and Malvern Hill (July 1), suffering few casualties. When the army was transported to northern Virginia, the regiment arrived too late to fight at Second Manassas. Its next skirmishing was during the Battle of Antietam on September 17, where the cavalry supported an artillery battery and was not heavily engaged. The regiment then engaged in several skirmishes in Virginia as the army advanced to Fredericksburg. During the battle at that place on December 13, the regiment remained north of the Rappahannock River and was not engaged.

After spending the winter helping to guard the western flank of the army, two squadrons of the 4th took part in the cavalry fighting at Kelly's Ford on March 17, 1863. During the Chancellorsville Campaign, most of the Cavalry Corps, the 4th Cavalry included, participated in the raid behind enemy lines. Devoid of any major engagements with the Rebel cavalry, the raid accomplished little of importance. As the Gettysburg Campaign opened, the cavalry of the two contending armies fought a pitched battle at Brandy Station on June 9. The 4th arrived late in the day and took a minor part in the fighting. It next engaged the enemy cavalry at Aldie (June 17), Middleburg (June 17-18), and Upperville (June 21), as the mounted forces parried each other in the move north. At Gettysburg, the regiment was present on the field but not engaged.

After General Lee's defeat at Gettysburg, both armies returned to Virginia, and again the cavalry units frequently skirmished with each other. As the armed forces maneuvered for position in Virginia, Private William McDowell of Company D was appointed standard-bearer of the 4th Cavalry on August 14.[3] In October, Lee attempted to move between General George G. Meade's troops and Washington. This maneuver forced Meade to hastily withdraw to keep his troops in front of the capital. As the cavalry again skirmished, the 4th sustained heavy casualties on October 12. A large enemy force attacked the pickets in overwhelming force near Warrenton and the regiment suffered a loss of more than two hundred men. Thereafter, the decimated regiment was detached to guard the Orange and Alexandria Railroad, a duty which lasted through the winter of 1863-64.

Second State Standard

Owing to the heavy damage suffered by the initial standard through almost two years of constant ser-

State Standard
Maker: HB
Size: 26¼" × 30⅛"
1985.098

Advance the Colors!

State Standard
Maker: HB
Size: 26⅝″ × 30½″
1985.099

vice, a replacement standard was supplied to the regiment in November 1863. This standard was carried by the regiment throughout the strenuous 1864 campaign, which began with the Battle of the Wilderness (May 5-6), where the regiment engaged in minor skirmishing. Most of the Cavalry Corps then moved toward Richmond on a raid, and the 4th was heavily engaged on May 12 as the Yankee troopers briefly tangled with Rebel defenders outside the enemy capital. After rejoining the army, the regiment next fought at Haw's Shop on May 28. Shortly afterwards, the Cavalry Corps embarked on the Trevilian Raid, highlighted by a general engagement with the enemy at Saint Mary's Church on June 24, where the 4th lost heavily.

When the Army of the Potomac crossed the James River and began the siege of Petersburg, the 4th participated in several of the flank movements as the forces under General Grant attempted to interdict the Rebel lines of supply. During the brief movement

north of the James on July 27-30, the regiment was engaged with the enemy several times but suffered few casualties. After fighting on August 16 as part of another flank movement north of the James, the regiment next fought at Poplar Springs Church on September 29-30 and at Boydton Plank Road on October 27. As winter approached, the regiment took an active part in the fighting at Hatcher's Run on December 1, and then again on February 5-7, 1865. The regiment then participated in the fighting at Five Forks and in the short but victorious Appomattox Campaign. After Lee's surrender, the regiment remained at Lynchburg on guard duty until it was mustered out of service on July 1, 1865.

Third State Standard
Maker: HB
Size: 27″ × 29″
1985.003

Third State Standard

This final standard for the regiment was completed in late April 1865 and sent to the State Agency in Washington. It was still there in April 1866, and thus it is apparent that the regiment never received the flag.[4] All three standards were officially returned to state care on July 4, 1866.

Company F Guidon

On October 16, 1861, a committee of young ladies from Lebanon went to Camp Curtin and presented a silk guidon to Company F. Nothing further has been located about this flag.[5]

Notes

[1]*Raftsman's Journal*, February 26, 1862.

[2]Orders #49, December 25, 1861, Regimental Orders & Miscellaneous Book, RG 94; Special Orders #40, May 27, 1862, *Ibid.*

[3]Special Orders #97, August 14, 1863, *Ibid.*

[4]Colonel Frank Jordan to Quartermaster-General Reynolds, February 10, 1866, RG 25.

[5]"Flag Presentation," *Lebanon Courier*, October 24, 1861.

Bibliography

A Brief History of the Fourth Pennsylvania Veteran Cavalry, Embracing Organization, Reunions, Dedication of Monument at Gettysburg and Address of General W. E. Doster, Venango County Battalion, Reminiscences, Etc. Pittsburgh: Ewens & Eberle, Printers, 1891.

Doster, William E. *Lincoln and Episodes of the Civil War.* New York: G. P. Putnam's Sons, 1915.

Grant, James R. Papers. Historical Society of Western Pennsylvania.

Hyndman, William. *History of a Cavalry Company, A Complete Record of Company "A," 4th Penn'a. Cavalry, as Identified with that Regiment, and with the Second Brigade, Second Division, Cavalry Corps, in All the Campaigns of the Army of the Potomac, During the Late Civil War.* Philadelphia: James B. Rodgers Company, Printers, 1872.

Keller, William S. Letters, 1863-1865. USAMHI, CWTI Collection.

Yard, W. C. "A Bee-Hunting Expedition." *National Tribune,* July 9, 1885.

———. "Feeding the Army Under Difficulties." *National Tribune,* September 3, 1885.

5th Cavalry
(65th Regiment)

State Standard

Organized in July and August 1861, the 5th Cavalry, better known as the Cameron Dragoons, rendezvoused in Philadelphia before proceeding to Washington. It remained in the Washington area throughout the fall of 1861 and the winter of 1861-62. A state standard was sent to the State Agency sometime in December 1861 and was presented to the regiment at some unspecified date.

State Standard
Maker: HB
Size: 26⅞″ × 29⅝″
1985.101

In May 1862, the regiment was transferred to the Yorktown Peninsula to join the Army of the Potomac. The 5th Cavalry did not take part in the Peninsula Campaign, being used instead to garrison the fortifications at Williamsburg. When the army embarked for northern Virginia, the 5th was part of the force left behind to occupy the Peninsula. On September 9, 1862, a large body of Confederate cavalry attacked the camp of the 5th near Williamsburg, completely surprising the occupants. In the ensuing confusion and retreat, the state standard was captured by members of Brigadier-General Wade Hampton's cavalry. The regiment suffered a loss of over one hundred troopers, most of them captured. In March 1889, Wade Hampton, then a United States senator, returned the standard to fellow Senator Matthew S. Quay. The Pennsylvania senator in turn forwarded the banner to the state. The standard was attached to a 5th Cavalry staff in the old Flag Room. This staff contained three streamers containing the names of

the 5th's battles. The standard was probably added for the 1914 ceremony.[1]

Philadelphia Standard

On September 10, 1861, Mr. Alfred T. Jones led a delegation of Philadelphia citizens to the regimental camp near Washington to present a standard to the unit.[2] It is not known when this standard was carried or what its design looked like. Evidently, the regiment never received a replacement standard from the state and perhaps carried this local presentation throughout its term of service.

After the debacle at Williamsburg, the 5th Cavalry remained on the Peninsula, taking part in numerous small expeditions into Confederate territory. Its major engagements with the enemy were at Olive Branch Church (February 7, 1863) and Williamsburg (April 11, 1863). In September 1863, the regiment was transferred to Norfolk, remaining there as part of the garrison until early 1864. It then returned to the Peninsula as part of the Cavalry Division of the Army of the James. With the division, the 5th took part in several of the engagements around Petersburg and Richmond. Its most important service was in Brigadier-General James H. Wilson's cavalry raid of June 22-30, 1864. Wilson's foray proved disastrous for many of his regiments when his two divisions were almost surrounded by Confederate forces as the cavalry attempted to interdict the railroads south of Petersburg. The Federal raiders were forced to abandon their artillery and retreat through a swamp to avoid capture. The 5th lost more than two hundred men in this affair. Lieutenant-Colonel Christopher Kleinz later reported that the regiment lost its state standard on June 29 as the regiment retreated.[3] Since the original state standard had been captured in 1862, Kleinz must have referred to another standard, possibly that presented by Philadelphians in 1861.

Thereafter, the regiment remained with the army and skirmished with the enemy on numerous occasions. It suffered heavy casualties on October 7, when

Advance the Colors!

it was assailed by Rebel infantry and cavalry and compelled to give ground. In the spring of 1865, the 5th participated in the Appomattox Campaign and then remained in the Richmond area on guard duty until mustered out of service in August 1865.

Company Guidons

The swallowtail stars and stripes guidon was captured at Williamsburg on September 9, 1862, and was returned by Wade Hampton in 1889. The pre-1862 unmarked red and white guidon was apparently one of two also captured at Williamsburg and acquired by the War Department in 1865. Marked as #55 on the list of captured flags, both were returned to the state in 1905. The survivor of these two guidons was placed in Case #5 in 1914 and was marked as a battery guidon, although the paper label on the staff listed it as possibly belonging to the 5th Cavalry. The 1914 inventory list included a hand-written note that this red and white guidon was possibly 5th Cavalry, judg-

Company Guidon
Size: 28″ × 39″
1985.100

Company Guidon
Size: 26¹/₂″ × 37¹/₄″ (-)
1985.171

ing from legend on the envelope in which it was stored.

Notes

[1] Wade Hampton to Matthew S. Quay, March 19, 1889, RG 25; Quay to Adjutant-General D. H. Hastings, May 21, 1889, RG 25, enclosing the standard and guidon. For the reference to the streamers on the staff, see "Historic Battle Flags," *Philadelphia Times*, May 24, 1896.

[2] "Flag Presentation to the Cameron Dragoons," *Philadelphia Inquirer*, September 19, 1861.

[3] Lieutenant-Colonel Christopher Kleinz to Adjutant-General A. L. Russell, May 29, 1866, RG 19.

Bibliography

Longacre, Edward G. "The Most Inept Regiment in the Civil War." *Civil War Times Illustrated* 8 (November 1969): 4-7.

McClelland, George C. "The Burning of William and Mary College." *National Tribune*, June 21, 1883.

67th Infantry

State Color

This regiment began formation in August 1861 but was not completely organized until March 1862. During that time, the regiment lay in camp outside Philadelphia. While here, the regiment received a state color on December 6, 1861. Governor Curtin and his staff came to Philadelphia and presented state colors to the 58th, 67th, 90th, and 91st Infantry, and a standard to the 6th Cavalry. The ceremony took place in a large field fronting Islington Lane, near the Ridge Avenue Railroad.[1]

Once the regimental formation was complete, the 67th was sent to Baltimore, where it performed various guard duties until relieved in February 1863. The regiment went by rail to Harper's Ferry and then moved south to Winchester. Here, it was assigned to the Eighth Corps division of Major-General Robert H. Milroy. The division remained as garrison in the Winchester area until June 1863. As Robert E. Lee's army headed north toward Pennsylvania, his Second Corps moved in advance to drive Milroy's men out of the Shenandoah Valley. Confederate troops reached the city and began to cut off the Federal escape routes. Milroy retreated early in the morning of June 15 but Southern infantry struck the retreating column at Stephenson's Depot, three miles north of Winchester. In a confused engagement just before dawn, Milroy's division was broken and more than 4,000 of his men were captured. The 67th attacked, was repulsed, and then was surrounded. Its casualties totalled 17 killed, 38 wounded, and 791 captured or missing; only 117 men escaped the debacle.

In his battle report, Southern Colonel J. M. Williams remarked that the 2nd Louisiana took a stand of colors belonging to the 67th Pennsylvania.[2] Although the identity of this flag is uncertain, it is quite probable that it was the state color. The color in the state collection marked "state" on the staff lacks its canton, and the designating stripe contains "67th Penn'a. V—," which is not the usual way the state colors were marked. The April 20, 1866, list of flags includes three for the 67th. One was marked "state," but a pencilled addition crossed out the state color and listed two

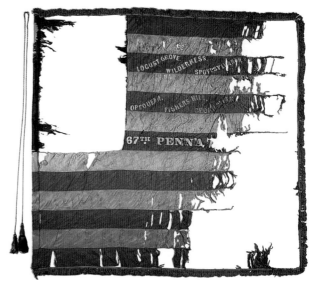

First National Color
Size: 72" × 78⅛"
1985.104

"national" colors. Owing to a lack of information, the identity of either flag cannot be firmly established.

First National Color

There are two national colors for the 67th in the state collection. One, missing its canton, bears the words "67th Penn'a. V—" on the center red stripe, as well as several battle honors painted on the stripes. The staff is marked as a "state," but the missing canton precludes positive identification. If the state color was indeed taken by the enemy at Winchester, then this flag was probably a national color acquired to replace the loss.

When the division reorganized after the defeat at Winchester, Milroy's men were assigned to the Army of the Potomac's Third Corps, taking part in the Bristoe Station and Mine Run campaigns before going into winter quarters near Brandy Station. In the spring, the division was transferred to the Sixth Corps. When the veterans returned from furlough in late April 1864, the regiment was temporarily detached and used to guard the army's supply train, although the new recruits remained with the division and fought in the 1864 battles as Grant advanced toward Richmond. The regiment was united in mid-June at Petersburg.

In July, the Sixth Corps was transferred to Washington to defend the capital from a Confederate attack. The corps then moved into the Shenandoah Valley. The 67th took part in the fighting at Winchester (September 19), Fisher's Hill (September 21-22), and Cedar Creek (October 19). In December, the corps rejoined the army at Petersburg. The 67's last major fighting with the enemy occurred on March 25, 1865, when the division charged and captured the Rebel

Regimental Color
Size: 71¹/₂″ × 78³/₄″   *1985.103*

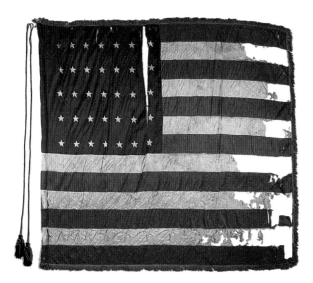

Second National Color
Size: 68¹/₂″ × 74⁷/₈″
1985.102

picket line in its front. During the attack, Color-Sergeant William A. Rager of Company E was cited for his bravery. The staff was shot off close to his left hand and twenty-two bullets passed through the silken folds.[3] After Lee's surrender, the 67th eventually returned to Washington and was mustered out of

service on July 14, 1865. This flag was carried in the July 4, 1866, parade.

Second National Color

This 35-star national color may possibly be an 1864 A. Brandon manufacture, although it is not marked as such. It bears strong resemblance to the marked Brandon national color for the 57th Infantry. No evidence has been located to indicate when this flag was carried by the 67th. It was officially given to the state on July 4, 1866.

Regimental Color

The remnant of this blue regimental indicates that it is a federal-issue infantry regimental color. Like the national color, there is no surviving evidence that has come to the author's attention to prove when it was used by the regiment.

Notes

[1]"Grand Military Review. Four Thousand Men in the Field. Presentation of State Flags by the Governor," *Philadelphia Inquirer*, December 7, 1861.

[2]*O.R.* 27.2, p. 512.
[3]*O.R.* 46.1, pp. 314-315.

Bibliography

"That Morning at Cedar Creek." *Grand Army Scout and Soldiers Mail*, October 4, 1884.

68th Infantry

State Color

A regiment numbered as the 68th was not formed until August 1862. Composed primarily of Philadelphians, the new unit was nicknamed the "Scott Legion" because a large number of its officers had served under General Winfield Scott in the Mexican War. Soon after organization, the 68th was sent to Washington when the Federal army was defeated at the Second Battle of Manassas. The regiment was assigned to the Third Corps, Army of the Potomac, remaining with this body of troops until the corps was discontinued in early 1864. In October 1862, the regiment moved to Poolesville, Maryland, and spent a few weeks doing picket duty along the Potomac River. While in camp near Poolesville, Colonel Samuel B. Thomas, one of Governor Curtin's aides, arrived and presented a state color to the 68th on October 23.[1]

The 68th first engaged the enemy at Fredericksburg on December 13, 1862, suffering few casualties. After spending the winter of 1862-63 near Falmouth, the regiment played an active role in the Chancellors-

National Color
Size: 71³/₈" × 78¹/₄"
1985.106

ville Campaign, sustaining a loss of seventy-five soldiers. Two months later, the regiment took position in the now-famous Peach Orchard at Gettysburg on July 2, 1863, and suffered its heaviest battle casualties. Late that day, the Peach Orchard was attacked by two Confederate brigades, and in the resulting confusion, the 68th was forced to retreat. The color-sergeant was killed but before the flag touched the ground, Corporal James McLarnon seized the staff and carried it safely to the rear. The corporal was eventually promoted to sergeant and bore the color until the regiment disbanded in 1865.[2]

When the armies returned to Virginia after Gettysburg, the 68th took part in the fighting at Wapping Heights on August 23 and then participated in the Bristoe Station and Mine Run campaigns before settling into winter quarters near Brandy Station. When the Third Corps was broken up and merged with the Second Corps in April 1864, the 68th was detached and assigned to the Provost Guard at army headquarters. It remained in this duty until the close of the war. Thus, the regiment escaped the bloody battles of Grant's 1864 campaign in Virginia. The Provost Guard brigade was assigned to round up stragglers,

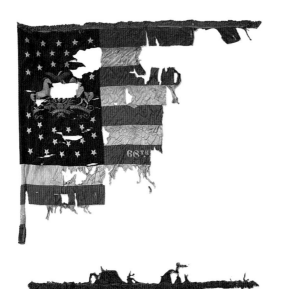

State Color
Maker: HB
Size: 61⁵/₈" (-) × 75" (-)
1985.107

Advance the Colors!

Regimental Color
Size: 72" × 78"
1985.105

mained here until mustered out of service in June 1865. The state color was returned during the 1866 ceremony.

National Color

This unmarked 34-star national color is labelled as belonging to the 68th. Nothing has been located to indicate its history.

Regimental Color

This federal regimental color is painted with both the regimental number and its popular nickname, the "Scott Legion." Judging from its condition, it does not appear to have been carried in battle and was probably obtained in 1864 or 1865.

Company C Flag

On August 25, 1862, Company C was the recipient of an American flag, presented to the company by the ladies of Oxford, Bridesburg, and Whitehall townships. Nothing else has been found about this flag.[3]

guard Confederate prisoners, furnish guards for army headquarters and supply trains, and perform other less glamorous duties. Soon after Lee's surrender in April 1865, the 68th was sent to Hart's Island, New York, to guard enemy prisoners camped there. It re-

Notes

[1]"From the Scott Legion, 68th P.V.," *Philadelphia Public Ledger*, October 29, 1862.

[2]*Pennsylvania at Gettysburg* 1: 367. In addition to Corporal McLarnon's name the author has located the name of Sergeant Charles H. Haber, whose G.A.R. business card identifies him as color-bearer for the 68th Pennsylvania. This card is located in the 84th Pennsylvania's regimental correspondence in RG 19. According to Bates 2: 681, Haber was promoted to sergeant on April 1, 1864. It is not known which flag he carried.

[3]*Philadelphia Inquirer*, August 26, 1862.

Bibliography

Schaffer, Lewis. Letters. In Brake Collection, USAMHI. Main collection of Schaffer material is housed at West Virginia University.

69th Infantry

First State Color

The 69th Pennsylvania was recruited in Philadelphia and was organized in August 1861. A large number of the soldiers were Irish. After the new regiment was formed in camp near the city, it was sent to Washington, where it remained until early October. The regiment then moved into Maryland and set up camp near Poolesville, where it remained most of the winter. A state color was furnished to the Commonwealth in November, and was sent to the State Agency in Washington to be forwarded to the 69th.

First State Color
Maker: HB
Size: 71¹/₄" × 76⁵/₈" (-)
1985.108

As part of the Philadelphia Brigade, the 69th took a brief part in some maneuvers in the northern Shenandoah Valley, then moved with the Army of the Potomac to the Peninsula, where it took part in the Siege of Yorktown in April-May 1862. It was then slightly engaged in the Battle of Fair Oaks (May 31-June 1). During the Battle of Glendale, the 69th helped protect the left flank of the Pennsylvania Reserves. At the Battle of Malvern Hill on July 1, the regiment was present on the field but not directly en-

gaged with the enemy. After the withdrawal of the army to northern Virginia, the 69th fought at Chantilly on September 1 as the beaten Federal troops retreated to Washington. At Antietam on September 17, the regiment suffered ninety-two casualties in the sanguinary fighting near the Dunker Church. During its final combat action of 1862, the regiment fought at Fredericksburg on December 13, suffering sixty-five casualties during one of the fruitless attacks on the Confederate position on Marye's Heights.

After spending the winter of 1862-63 near Falmouth, the regiment took a minor part in the Chancellorsville Campaign, where the Second Division of the Second Corps helped recapture Fredericksburg and then withdrew across the Rappahannock River at the conclusion of the fighting. The 69th then marched north and fought at Gettysburg on July 2-3, 1863. Here, on July 3, the regiment occupied a position in front of the now-famous clump of trees. As the Virginia troops commanded by General George Pickett surged across the stonewall to climax Pickett's Charge, the 69th was the only regiment of the brigade to maintain its position throughout the fighting, which was hand-to-hand at times. Every field officer was shot down and the 69th suffered a loss of fifty-five percent of its strength.

After the victory at Gettysburg, the army returned to Virginia. The 69th participated in the Bristoe Station and Mine Run campaigns of October-November, and then settled into winter camp near Stevensburg. The first state color, worn out through weather and battle damage, was retired in December, when a replacement color was provided. The flag was officially returned to state care on July 4, 1866.

Second State Color

This color was received sometime in December 1863, and was carried by the regiment during the 1864-65 campaign. The 69th fought in the Battle of the Wilderness (May 5-6, 1864), at Spotsylvania (May 8-18), North Anna River, Bethesda Church, and Cold Harbor (May 18-June 12). The army then crossed the James River and attacked the Confederate defenses of Petersburg on June 16-18. Four days later, the regiment

Advance the Colors!

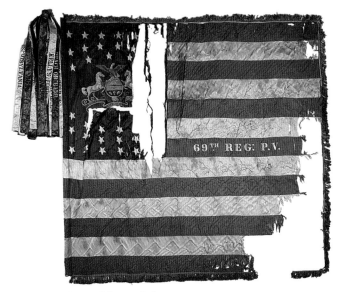

Second State Color
Maker: EH
Size: 72¹/₄″ × 77¹/₄″
1985.109

to break the Confederate lines of communication around Petersburg. After the winter of 1864-65 passed, the 69th fought again at Hatcher's Run on February 5 and yet a third time on March 29. During the ensuing Appomattox Campaign, the 69th engaged the enemy for the final time at High Bridge on April 7, two days before General Lee surrendered his army. Thereafter, the 69th returned to Washington and was disbanded on July 1, 1865. The second state color was returned to state care in 1866.

Irish Flags

During its term of service, Philadelphia friends of the 69th presented the regiment with two green Irish flags. The 69th was the only Pennsylvania unit to carry such flags. Each banner was composed of a green field. One side contained the state coat-of-arms, while the other depicted three Irish symbols—the wolfhound, round tower, and sunburst.[1] The first Irish flag was presented to the regiment on March 13, 1862, while the 69th lay in camp near Winchester, Virginia.[2] It was carried side-by-side with the state color until March 1864, when the regiment returned to Philadelphia for its veterans' furlough. It was then placed in the museum housed in Independence Hall, where it remained "for many years," then mysteriously vanished.[3]

A replacement Irish flag was given to the regiment when it departed for Virginia in April 1864. This flag

was severely mauled in the fighting along the Weldon Railroad. A Southern attack on the exposed left flank of the Federal line resulted in large numbers of prisoners being captured. The 69th suffered a loss of 8 killed, 26 wounded, and 173 captured or missing.

The regiment next engaged the enemy at Reams' Station on August 25, and then at Hatcher's Run on October 27-28, as General Grant's troops attempted

Field and Staff Officers of the 69th Pennsylvania, June 1865. Second State Color on Left, Irish Flag on Right

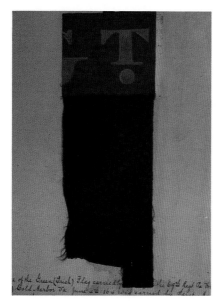

Piece of Second Irish Flag

was carried until the end of the war and then disappeared from history. During the fighting at Cold Harbor on June 4, 1864, Sergeant Henry O'Neill of Company D carried this flag. An artillery shell burst within a few feet of the sergeant's face, badly shattering the banner. O'Neill himself was lucky to survive the explosion. His left arm was torn off above the elbow. Another fragment ripped through his nose and gouged out one of his eyes. As a reward for his bravery, the color-guard gave O'Neill a piece of the flag to take home with him. It is the only known surviving fragment of this second Irish color.[4]

Color-Bearers

Names of several bearers exist, but it is not known whether they carried the state or Irish colors. Sergeant John King of Company H carried a flag until relieved by Sergeant Patrick Murphy on May 22, 1862.[5] Murphy was wounded at Fredericksburg on December 13 and discharged from the army on March 5, 1863. His place was taken by Corporal Michael Dougherty of Company C, who was promoted to sergeant on March 23, 1863.[6] Finally, Sergeant Michael Brady of Company C carried one of the colors at Gettysburg.[7]

Notes

[1] *Pennsylvania at Gettysburg* 1: 378.

[2] "Reception of a Flag by the Sixty-ninth Pennsylvania Regiment," *Philadelphia Inquirer*, March 20, 1862.

[3] "A Battleflag for Independence Hall," *Philadelphia Inquirer*, April 26, 1864; McDermott, p. 38.

[4] Inscription on framed flag fragment, owned by John Stanchak.

[5] Special Orders #151, May 22, 1862, Regimental Letter, Indorsement, Furlough, Order, and Casualty Book, RG 94.

[6] Special Orders #7, March 23, 1863, *Ibid*.

[7] Undated list of names, in folder marked "Battle of Gettysburg, Historical Notes," Peter F. Rothermel Papers, Pennsylvania State Archives.

Bibliography

McDermott, Anthony W. *A Brief History of the Sixty-ninth Regiment of Pennsylvania Veteran Volunteers, From Its Formation Until Final Muster Out of the United State Service.* Philadelphia: D. J. Gallagher & Company, Printers, 1889.

"Sixty-ninth Pennsylvania has Glorious Record." *Philadelphia Record*, May 1, 1904.

6th Cavalry
(70th Regiment)

First State Standard

This cavalry unit was recruited primarily in Philadelphia under authority granted to Richard H. Rush, its first colonel. The regiment was initially armed with ten-foot lances and was nicknamed "Rush's Lancers." It was not until May 1863 that the regiment gave up this weapon in favor of carbines. Governor Curtin visited Philadelphia on December 6, 1861, to present flags to five new Pennsylvania regiments, among which was the 6th Cavalry. The ceremony took place in a large field on Islington Lane, near the Ridge Avenue Railroad.[1]

Shortly after receiving the standard, the 6th Cavalry moved to Washington and went into winter camp near Columbia College. It remained here until March 1862, when the regiment took part in the occupation of Manassas by the Army of the Potomac. It then accompanied the army to the Yorktown Peninsula, where it first engaged the enemy on May 25 near Hanover Court House. The regiment was actively engaged in various activities during the months of June and July, suffering seventy-four casualties during the Seven Days' Battles. Divided into several detachments, the 6th fought in the battles of Mechanicsville (June 26), Gaines' Mill (June 27), and Glendale (June 30). Upon the transfer of the army to northern Virginia, the 6th Cavalry went into camp near Alexandria and did not take part in the Second Manassas Campaign.

The regiment then took part in the Maryland Campaign which culminated in the Battle of Antietam on September 17, the regiment suffering few casualties. In October, the regiment was part of the force that unsuccessfully tried to intercept Confederate cavalry leader James E. B. Stuart's raid around the Army of the Potomac. The regiment remained near Frederick, Maryland, until early December, when it rejoined the army. Although present on the Fredericksburg battlefield, the 6th was not engaged.

After wintering near Falmouth, the regiment took part in the cavalry raid behind General Lee's army during the Chancellorsville Campaign of April-May

1863. On June 9, the regiment suffered its heaviest wartime loss during the cavalry fight at Brandy Station. During the several charges and countercharges that day, the 6th lost more than one hundred troopers, including one of the color-bearers, who was shot from his horse. The standard was caught before it fell and was carried from the field.[2] During the advance northward to Gettysburg, the 6th fought at Aldie (June 17) before reaching Gettysburg on July 3. It took a minor part in the battle that day, being used as skirmishers on the army's left flank. However, the regiment was heavily engaged in numerous cavalry engagements during Lee's retreat to Virginia.

During the fall of 1863, the regiment took part in the Bristoe Station and Mine Run campaigns before going into winter quarters near Culpeper. When the 1864 campaign opened, the 6th Cavalry accompanied the First Cavalry Division and fought in the Wilderness (May 7), and then was part of Major-General Philip H. Sheridan's first cavalry raid, which lasted from May 9-24. After the cavalry rejoined the army, the 6th fought at the North Anna River and Cold Harbor before riding off to participate in Sheridan's Trevilian Raid (June 7-24). During this raid, the 6th was heavily engaged at Trevilian Station on June 11-12. After rejoining the army in front of Petersburg, the 6th remained in camp until it moved with the division to fight at Deep Bottom on July 27-29, suffering few casualties.

Most of the Cavalry Corps was then transferred to the Shenandoah Valley, the 6th fighting near Winches-

Albumen Photograph of the First State Standard

Second State Standard
Maker: HB
Size: 27" × 30¼"
1985.110

1861 Presentation Guidon of
Company E
Size: 24" × 35"

ter on August 11 and at Smithfield on August 29. After this last skirmish, the regiment was relieved from duty and sent to a remount camp in Pleasant Valley, Maryland. The regiment remained in its Maryland camp until late January 1865, when it moved to Winchester and rejoined the division. Sheridan's cavalry then moved up the Valley and swept it clear of organized resistance. The cavalry eventually marched overland and rejoined Grant's troops at Petersburg. The 6th Cavalry took part in the fighting on the White Oak Road (March 31, 1865) and at Five Forks the next day. After Lee's surrender at Appomattox, the regiment moved to Washington and was mustered out of service on June 17. The state standard was never returned to the Commonwealth and its eventual disposition is unknown.

Second State Standard

Horstmann Brothers & Company finished a replacement standard for the state on April 10, 1865. This standard was probably forwarded to the 6th and was carried until it disbanded in June. It was presented to the state on July 4, 1866.

National Standard

On July 15, 1886, the War Department, acting upon the request of Lieutenant-General Sheridan, gave a flag tagged as #94 to Colonel F. C. Newhall.[3] It is now owned by Howard M. Madaus of Milwaukee.

National Standard

Germantown Flags

On October 30, 1861, a deputation of Germantown women presented a standard and ten company guidons to the regiment in its camp near Philadelphia. Nothing further is known about the history of these flags.[4] Recently, the museum of the First City Troop acquired the standard (a federal-style design with "Rush's Lancers" painted on the red scroll) and Company E's guidon from the Germantown Historical Society.

Company I Guidon

The War Library and Museum, Military Order of the Loyal Legion of the United States, Philadelphia, has custody of a guidon of Company I.

Notes

[1]"Grand Military Review," *Philadelphia Inquirer*, December 7, 1861; Gracey, pp. 27-33.
[2]Gracey, p. 160.

[3]Captured Flags Document, p. 8.
[4]"The Presentation at Camp Meigs," *Philadelphia Inquirer*, October 31, 1861; Bates 2: 741; Gracey, pp. 21-25.

Bibliography

Dedication of the Monument of the Sixth Penna. Cavalry "Lancers" on the Battlefield of Gettysburg, October 14, 1888. Philadelphia: James Beale, Printer, 1889.
Geisel, Christian. Papers. Pennsylvania State Archives.
Gracey, Samuel L. *Annals of the Sixth Pennsylvania Cavalry*. Philadelphia: E. H. Butler & Company, 1868.
Knight, Sue Clark. Papers. State Historical Society of Wisconsin. Contains letters of Robert Milligan.

Newhall, Frederic C. *With General Sheridan in Lee's Last Campaign, by a Staff Officer*. Philadelphia: J. B. Lippincott & Company, 1866.
Smith, Thomas W. Letters. Historical Society of Pennsylvania.
Strang, Edgar B. *General Stoneman's Raid; or, the Amusing Side of Army Life*. Philadelphia: E. B. Strang, 1911.
_____. *Sunshine and Shadows of the Late Civil War*. Philadelphia, 1898.
Todd, Frederick P., and Larter, Harry G. "6th Pennsylvania Cavalry (Rush's Lancers), 1862." *Military Collector & Historian* 6 (1954): 102.

71st Infantry

National Color

The 71st Pennsylvania was recruited in April 1861 in the Philadelphia area by California Senator Edward D. Baker. It was thus nicknamed the "California Regiment." It rendezvoused in New York City before moving to Fort Monroe, where it remained until after the Federal defeat at First Manassas. On June 30, 1861, Lieutenant William A. Todd of Company C presented a silk national color to the regiment on behalf of Mrs. A. E. Yerger, whose husband was a member of the company.[1] This flag was carried until the disastrous defeat at Ball's Bluff, Virginia, on October 21, 1861. The 71st suffered more than three hundred casualties in this battle as it encountered a superior enemy force during a reconnaissance across the Potomac River into Virginia. Color-Sergeant Thomas Vansant stripped the flag from the staff and plunged into the river to escape capture. He became exhausted and was forced to jettison the flag to avoid drowning. It was never recovered.[2]

State Color

A state flag was sent to the State Agency in Washington sometime in November 1861 for presentation to the regiment.[3] As part of the Philadelphia Brigade of the Army of the Potomac's Second Corps, the 71st moved to the Yorktown Peninsula in March 1862. After taking part in the Siege of Yorktown, the regiment fought in the Battle of Fair Oaks on May 31-June 1. During the Seven Days' Battles, the regiment was engaged with the enemy at Savage's Station on June 29 and at Glendale on June 30. After the unsuccessful conclusion of the campaign, the army returned to northern Virginia. The Second Corps was not engaged in the Second Battle of Manassas and acted as rearguard when the beaten Federal troops retreated to Washington.

The army then moved into Maryland to counter General Lee's invasion of that state. The 71st fought in the Battle of Antietam on September 17, suffering 139 casualties in a very few minutes of fighting near the Dunker Church. At Fredericksburg on December 13, the regiment was detached from the brigade and

acted as pickets and skirmishers and did not suffer heavy casualties. After remaining in camp through the winter, the 71st next took part in the Chancellorsville Campaign of April-May 1863. The Second Division of the Second Corps aided the Sixth Corps to recapture Fredericksburg, the division then remaining behind to guard the city until the army retreated across the Rappahannock River. At Gettysburg, the regiment fought the enemy on July 2 and 3, losing heavily during Major-General George E. Pickett's attack on the Second Corps position on July 3. After taking part in the Bristoe Station and Mine Run campaigns, the regiment went into winter camp near Stevensburg, Virginia.

The regiment then fought in the Battles of the Wilderness (May 6-7, 1864), Spotsylvania (May 8-18), and Cold Harbor (June 1-3). Shortly after this latter battle, most of the soldiers in the 71st were sent home for mustering out. Those who had re-enlisted were transferred to the 69th Pennsylvania. The tattered state color was returned to the Commonwealth on July 4, 1866.[3]

State Color
Maker: HB
Size: 71³⁄₈" × 77¹⁄₂"
1985.111

Notes

[1] *Philadelphia Public Ledger*, July 1, 1861.

[2] Charles H. Banes, *History of the Philadelphia Brigade* (Philadelphia: J. B. Lippincott & Company, 1876), p. 29. A story in the *Philadelphia Inquirer*, October 26, 1861, identifies Vansant as the color-bearer. A letter in the *Bucks County Intelligencer*, November 12, 1861, has Vansant's name as well as that of Sergeant Randall C. Wood of Company I as the regiment's two color-bearers at Ball's Bluff. This article indicates that the colors were buried rather than thrown into the river.

[3] According to a letter from Richard P. Smith to Governor Curtin, April 29, 1864, RG 25, a second state color was requested and noted as ordered on May 17. Nothing else is extant to indicate if this flag was ever actually completed.

Bibliography

Baltz, John D. "Battle of Ball's Bluff. Death of Senator E. D. Baker." *United Service Magazine* 3rd series 4 (1903): 46-66.

———. *Hon. Edward D. Baker, U.S. Senator from Oregon, One of America's Heroes.* . . . Lancaster: Inquirer Printing Company, 1888.

Fifth Anniversary Banquet of the Survivors' Association, 71st P.V. (California Regiment), Monday Evening, April 13, 1891, at Colonnade Hotel, Philadelphia, and the Report of the Committee on the Monument at Gettysburg. Philadelphia, 1891.

Frazier, John W. "Colonel Baker's Regiment. How It was Raised in Philadelphia by Mr. Wistar." *Philadelphia Weekly Times*, September 20, 1879.

Harris, William C. *Prison-Life in the Tobacco Warehouse at Richmond.* Philadelphia: George W. Childs, 1862.

Hills, Alfred E. Papers. Chicago Historical Society.

Moore, John H. *Baker at Ball's Bluff, Address of J. Hampton Moore at Reunion of Survivors of the Seventy-first Pennsylvania (California) Regiment, G.A.R., and the Confederate Veterans, at Ball's Bluff, Potomac River, Virginia, on the Fiftieth Anniversary of the Battle, October 21, 1911.* N.p., n.d.

Ritman, George L. "Ball's Bluff." *Philadelphia Weekly Times*, April 20, 1878.

Slonaker, William H. "Ball's Bluff." *Philadelphia Weekly Times*, May 4, 1878.

Smith, Richard P. "The Battle. The Part Taken by the Philadelphia Brigade in the Battle." *Gettysburg Compiler*, June 7, 1887. (Gettysburg)

Vanderslice, Catherine H. (editor). *The Civil War Letters of George Washington Beidelman.* New York: Vantage Press, 1878.

Wistar, Isaac J. *Autobiography of Isaac Jones Wistar, 1827-1905, Half a Century in War and Peace.* Philadelphia: Wistar Institute, 1937.

———. "A Noted Charge at Antietam. The Part Borne by the Philadelphia Brigade in Sedgwick's Attack." *Philadelphia Weekly Times*, April 8, 1882.

72nd Infantry

State Color

Organized in August 1861, this fifteen-company regiment was popularly known as Baxter's Fire Zouaves, since many Philadelphia firefighters flocked to join the unit. The regiment went to Washington in September and was assigned to the Philadelphia Brigade, composed of the 69th, 71st, 72nd, and 106th Pennsylvania. The brigade spent the winter guarding the Maryland shore of the Potomac near Poolesville. While here, the 72nd received a state color sometime in November. The color was furnished to the State Agency in Washington by Horstmann Brothers & Company, and was presented to the regiment by agency director J. H. Puleston.

After taking part in some maneuvering in the northern Shenandoah Valley, the brigade rejoined the Army of the Potomac and moved to the Yorktown Peninsula in April 1862. As part of the Second Division, Second Corps, the 72nd participated in the Siege of Yorktown, then followed the retreating Confederate army toward Richmond. The regiment fought at Fair Oaks on June 1, suffering few casualties. During the Seven Days' Battles, the 72nd was engaged at Savage's Station on June 29. Including the sick and wounded captured by the Rebels during the campaign, the regiment lost 159 soldiers.

When the Army of the Potomac was withdrawn from the Peninsula and sent to northern Virginia, Second Corps men were among the last troops to board ships and were not engaged at Second Manassas. However, the corps was closely engaged with Lee's troops at the Battle of Antietam on September 17. The Second Division of the corps advanced to the Dunker Church area and was hit in the flank and driven from the field. In a very few minutes, the 72nd Pennsylvania suffered the third highest casualties of any Federal regiment that day, losing 38 killed, 163 wounded, and 36 missing, a total of 237, more than half of the men taken into action. The regiment next met the enemy at Frederickburg on December 13, losing seventy-one men in the fruitless attacks on Marye's Heights.

After wintering near Falmouth, the regiment played a minor role in the Chancellorsville Campaign of April-May 1863. The Second Division of the corps

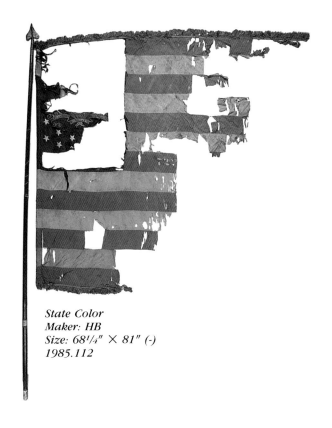

State Color
Maker: HB
Size: 68¹/₄″ × 81″ (-)
1985.112

cooperated with the Sixth Corps in recapturing Fredericksburg, then remained in the city as guards when the other troops moved on toward Chancellorsville. During the fighting at Gettysburg on July 3, the 72nd played a prominent role. The state color was kept out of this famous battle and was not used by the regiment.[1] When the two armies returned to Virginia after Gettysburg, the regiment took part in the Bristoe Station and Mine Run campaigns before entering winter quarters near Stevensburg, Virginia.

During the 1864 campaign in Virginia, the 72nd was heavily engaged in the Wilderness (May 5-7), Spotsylvania (May 8-18), and at Cold Harbor (June 4). The Army of the Potomac then crossed the James River and attacked Petersburg on June 16, the 72nd suffering a loss of fifty-five soldiers. Its last general fighting occurred on June 22 as the Second Corps attempted to cut the Weldon Railroad near Petersburg. In early August, the 72nd was relieved from duty and sent to Philadelphia, where it was mustered out of service on August 24. The battered state color was officially returned to the state on July 4, 1866.

Philadelphia Flags

Since a large number of Philadelphia firefighters joined the 72nd Pennsylvania, twenty-two companies gathered money to have a stand of colors prepared for the regiment. Both colors were presented to two companies of the 72nd on September 28, 1861. These flags were furnished by Evans & Hassall. One was a national color with the regiment's name painted on the center red stripe. The second was a regimental color with the state arms on one side and the national arms on the reverse. It was inscribed "The Philadelphia Fire Zouaves by the Fire Department of the City of Philadelphia, September 16, 1861." A silver plate attached to the staff contained the names of the donor companies.[2]

These flags seem to have been carried alongside the state color in the several engagements in which the 72nd fought. The national color was returned to Philadelphia in April 1863, and was given to the Union League for safekeeping.[3] A newspaper reporter who saw this flag described it as "battle-stained and bullet-riddled. The storms of Heaven have beaten upon them; the bolts of death have flown, winged with destruction, through the warm-breathing ranks that marched under them to victory. Upon their silken folds they wear the impress of the exposure and the service they have undergone." The staff had been shattered at Antietam and the blue field of stars "fearfully rent" in the same battle. The stripes were severely torn and mutilated. The present location of this flag is unknown.[4]

The regimental color was carried until the regiment disbanded in 1864. It was the lone flag taken by the regiment into the Battle of Gettysburg. On July 3, the 72nd stood in the path of Pickett's Charge and suffered heavy casualties. As the van of the Rebel assault reached the stonewall on Cemetery Ridge, the regiment fell back a few yards and both sides stood immobile, loading and firing at each other. Brigadier-General Alexander S. Webb, commanding the Philadelphia Brigade, saw that the enemy assault had spent itself and that a determined counterattack would win the day. Webb went to the front of the regiment, took

Left General Guide Marker
Size: 16" × 20¼"

hold of the flagstaff, and ordered the bearer, Sergeant William Finacy of Company H, to advance the colors. Even when threatened with a loaded pistol, the sergeant would not go forward. Webb gave up in disgust and made his way along the line to find other troops who would advance. Finacy soon moved forward with the flag but was quickly killed. Corporal Francis O'Donnell seized the flag and immediately fell wounded. Sergeant Thomas Murphy then took the flag and led the advance that captured or killed the grayclad survivors. As Murphy led the attack, a bullet hit the flagstaff and shattered the wood. When the regiment mustered out in 1864, this flag was left somewhere in Philadelphia and has since disappeared.[5]

Left General Guide Marker

In 1930, Mae L. Longaker donated this guidon to the State Museum. It was originally owned by Thomas F. Longaker, a lieutenant in Company E. There is no surviving evidence to indicate when this banner was carried by the 72nd.

Color-Bearer

Sergeant Frederick Mannes of Company B carried one of the regiment's flags for eighteen months prior to the Battle of Gettysburg. It is not known which color he bore.[6]

Notes

[1] *Paper Book of Appellants*, p. 95.

[2] "Flag Presentation to Baxter's Fire Zouaves," *Philadelphia Inquirer*, September 30, 1861; "Flags for Pennsylvania Regiments," *Philadelphia Inquirer*, September 17, 1861; "The Flags for Colonel Baxter's Regiment." *Philadelphia Public Ledger,* September 25, 1861; Scharf-Westcott 1: 779, 782.

[3] J. Warner Johnson to George H. Boker, April 27, 1863, archives of the Union League.

[4] "Consecrated Standard," *Philadelphia Inquirer*, April 15, 1863.

[5] *Paper Book of Appellants*, pp. 37, 57, 76-79, 86, 161, 171-172. The names of the bearers in the text is the author's reconstruction of the slightly conflicting court testimony of a number of the 72nd's veterans. As Sergeant Mannes stated to the court (p. 95), "We can't be particular—we don't look particular who picks up the colors in an engagement of that kind. Everything is confused the worst kind, and I couldn't see which man picked them up, and I couldn't see how often they went down." Indeed, Mannes claimed seven men were shot down on July 3.

[6] *Ibid.*, p. 85.

Bibliography

Fiftieth Anniversary of Baxter's Philadelphia Fire Zouaves, 72nd Regt. Penna. Vols., August 10th 1861, to August 10th, 1911, Association of the Survivors, of the 72nd Regt. Penna., Vols., Organized Sept. 30, 1882. Philadelphia: Bowers Printing Company, 1911.

Furness, William H. *A Word of Consolation for the Kindred of Those Who Have Fallen in Battle, A Discourse Delivered September 28, 1862 . . . with the Funeral Service at the Burial of Lieut. A. W. Peabody, September 26, 1862.* N.p., n.d.

Hall, William A. "The 72nd's Position [at Gettysburg]." *Philadelphia Weekly Press*, July 9, 1891.

Jones, A. Stokes. Letters, 1862-1864. USAMHI, HbCWRT Collection.

Longaker, Thomas F. Papers. Pennsylvania State Archives.

McClean, W. A. "The Third Day at Gettysburg. Fight at the Bloody Angle. The Master's Report." *Gettysburg Compiler*, February 3, 1891.

Maguire, Samuel K. Correspondence. Western Reserve Historical Society.

"A Monument Battle." *Gettysburg Compiler*, December 18, 1887.

Pennsylvania. Courts. Court of Common Pleas. Adams County. *Between Survivors of the 72d Regiment of Pennsylvania Volunteers, Plaintiffs and Gettysburg Battle-field Memorial Association and Commissioners Appointed by the Governor of the State of Pennsylvania, Defendants. Bill of Complaint by the Plaintiffs.* N.p., 1889.

Pennsylvania. Courts. Supreme Court, Middle District. *Appeal of the Gettysburg Battlefield Memorial Association and Commissioners Appointed by the Governor of the State of Pennsylvania, from the Decree of the Court of Common Pleas of Adams County. Paper Book of Appellants.* N.p., 1891.

Roberts, Samuel. "The 72nd Pennsylvania." *National Tribune*, September 1, 1887.

The Seventy-second Regiment, Pennsylvania Volunteers, at Bloody Angle, Gettysburg. Order of Exercises, and Addresses by John Reed and Capt. W. W. Ker, on the Occasion of the Temporary Erection of the Regiment's Monument on the Battlefield of Gettysburg, September 2, 1889. Philadelphia, 1889.

Webb, Alexander, and Banes, Charles H. *An Address Delivered at Gettysburg, August 27, 1883, by Gen. Alexander S. Webb, at the Dedication of the 72d Pa. Vols. Monument. Also, and Historical Sketch of the 72d Regiment, by Charles H. Banes.* Philadelphia: Porter & Coates, 1883.

73rd Infantry

First State Color

Known as the Pennsylvania Legion, the 73rd Infantry was recruited in Philadelphia and organized in August 1861. It left the city in late September and went into camp near Alexandria, Virginia, remaining in the general area until March 1862. On March 5, Representative Robert McKnight of Pittsburgh visited the division camp to present colors to the 27th, 73rd, 74th, and 75th Pennsylvania. The 73rd was absent on picket duty, but the officers and color-guard remained in camp to receive the new flag.[1]

The 73rd remained in northern Virginia until early April 1862, when the division to which it was attached was transferred to western Virginia, arriving in Petersburg on May 11. After moving about this area of Virginia, the division went into the Shenandoah Valley to reinforce Federal troops attempting to intercept Stonewall Jackson's Confederate army. Although present on the battlefield of Cross Keys (June 8), the 73rd was held in reserve. The regiment remained in the Valley on guard duty near Luray until late July, when it joined the new Army of Virginia. It fought in the Second Battle of Manassas on August 30, suffering 157 casualties. The colors of the regiment were badly torn during the fighting, in which five bearers were

First State Color
Maker: HB
Size: 64³/₈" (-) × 57" (-)
1985.115

shot down. At one point, a Confederate attack succeeded in capturing at least one of the flags carried by the regiment. Captain Henry J. Giltinan led a charge that reclaimed the flags. The captain would later be killed at Chancellorsville.[2]

After the beaten Federal army retired to Washington, the 73rd was attached to the new Eleventh Corps, which remained in the city and did not take part in the Maryland Campaign. The corps guarded the Army of the Potomac's supply lines and was also not engaged in the December repulse at Fredericksburg. Its next combat service occurred at Chancellorsville on the evening of May 2, 1863. Stonewall Jackson's late afternoon assault shattered the Eleventh Corps, the impetus of the massive charge driving the entire corps back. In this fighting, the 73rd lost more then one hundred men. In the succeeding Gettysburg Campaign, the regiment was engaged on Cemetery Hill on the evening of July 2, helping repulse an enemy assault on the hill.

In late September 1863, the Eleventh Corps was part of the reinforcements sent to Chattanooga. The 73rd took part in the Battle of Chattanooga on November 25, 1863, as part of General Sherman's attacks on the northern end of Missionary Ridge. Sherman's assaults were repulsed with heavy loss to the attacking regiments. The brigade to which the 73rd was attached gained a temporary foothold in the Rebel line, but supporting troops were driven off and the Southerners counterattacked, outflanking the brigade and taking large numbers of prisoners. As the enemy swept down on the 73rd, Color-Sergeant Charles Wendler tore the state color from its staff and gave it to Captain John Kennedy for safekeeping. Both men were included among the ninety-three prisoners taken by the enemy. Wendler died in Andersonville Prison but Captain Kennedy survived his internment. Kennedy kept the flag concealed beneath his uniform and the flag escaped notice while the captain was imprisoned in Richmond's Libby Prison. He was exchanged in March 1864 and brought the flag back with him. It was an object of special curiosity at the Philadelphia Sanitary Commission Fair later that year. The flag was returned to the state in 1866.[3]

Captain John Kennedy Saved the State Color at Chattanooga

Philadelphia Flags

During its term of service, the 73rd received at least two colors from Philadelphia friends. On October 24, 1861, ex-Governor James Pollock, on behalf of a Philadelphia committee, presented the 73rd with "a handsome suit of regimental flags."[4] These two flags

were carried by the regiment until it went home for a veterans' furlough in January 1864. At that time, a reporter described the national color as "so perforated with bullet holes as to render the Stars and Stripes utterly indistinguishable."[5] The regiment may have received a replacement stand of colors sometime in 1864 just prior to the Atlanta Campaign. In February 1863, the officers of the 73rd hesitated to accept new flags to replace their battle-worn colors.[6] A flag presented by Philadelphia ladies to the 73rd while the unit was encamped near Chattanooga was present at the regimental monument dedication at Gettysburg in 1889.[7] This color was carried by the 73rd during the Atlanta Campaign, where its heaviest losses occurred at Mill Creek (May 8, 1864) and near Kenesaw (June 15-16). The regiment accompanied General Sherman on his March to the Sea and the 1865 Carolinas Campaign. It was mustered out of service at Alexandria on July 14, 1865. None of these local presentation colors seem to have survived.

Second State Color

A replacement state color was supplied to the state in February 1865. This flag was probably not obtained by the 73rd until the regiment reached Virginia after the cessation of hostilities. Since the 28th and 46th Pennsylvania's replacement colors were not forwarded to Sherman's advancing army, the author assumes that the 73rd's also was not. It was carried in the 1866 parade.

Regimental Color

The remnant of this color precludes positive identification. A piece of the Lincoln mourning crepe is still

Second State Color   Size: 71³/4" × 76⁷/8"
Maker: EH   1985.114

Regimental Color   1985.113
Size: 70¹/4" × 73" (-)

attached to the flag, suggesting that it was carried sometime in 1865.

General Guide Marker

The 73rd carried general guide flags at Gettysburg and Missionary Ridge. During this latter battle, the left general guide, Sergeant Benjamin O'Donnell, was captured by the enemy. O'Donnell tore the small flag from its staff and stuck it under his jacket. A Confederate soldier saw him do this, ran up to him, and demanded the flag. The sergeant denied his action, whereupon the Rebel struck O'Donnell with his musket, crippling one of his hands for life. His assailant swept on by and O'Donnell retained his secret. He finally was interned in Andersonville Prison, where he became sick, and fearing he might die, gave the guide marker to Sergeant Zachariah Rost. This man was exchanged in May 1865 and brought the flag back safely. He eventually contacted O'Donnell, who also survived, and returned the flag to his care. O'Donnell gave the flag to the Regimental Association in 1889, which in turn gave it to the Commonwealth at some unspecified date. The flag no longer survives. In 1914, the now-blind O'Donnell carried one of the 73rd's flags in the parade, guided by the hand of Sergeant Rost.[8]

Color-Bearers

Names of two bearers who were both wounded at Second Manassas on August 30, 1862, have been located. One was Sergeant William Burkhardt, wounded in the left arm. The other was Sergeant Henry Hess, slightly wounded.[9]

Notes

[1]"Flag Presentation to Pennsylvania Regiments," *Philadelphia Inquirer*, March 8, 1862.

[2]*O.R.* 12.2, p. 308; "Captain Giltinan Killed," *Philadelphia Public Ledger*, May 9, 1863.

[3]Bates 2: 868; "An Hour Among the Battle-Flags," *Harrisburg Daily State Journal*, September 22, 1873.

[4]"Presentation of Flags," *Philadelphia Public Ledger*, October 25, 1861.

[5]"Arrival of the Seventy-third Pennsylvania Regiment," *Philadelphia Inquirer*, January 26, 1864.

[6]Officers to Lieutenant-Colonel William Moore, February 22, 1863, Regimental Letter Book, RG 94.

[7]*Pennsylvania at Gettysburg* 1: 400.

[8]*Ibid.*, p. 397; "Blind Veteran at Last Proves He Bore Colors," *Harrisburg Star-Independent*, June 16, 1914.

[9]"Official List of Killed and Wounded in the Seventy-third Pennsylvania, *Philadelphia Inquirer*, September 12, 1862.

Bibliography

Diembach, Andrew. "An Incident at Cemetery Hill." *Blue and Gray* 2 (July 1893): 21-22.

The Seventy-third Regiment Pennsylvania Volunteers at Gettysburg. Philadelphia, 1891.

74th Infantry

State Color

Composed primarily of German residents of Pittsburgh and vicinity, the 74th Pennsylvania was organized in September 1861, with a former Prussian officer, Alexander von Schimmelfennig, as colonel. The new regiment moved to Washington, where it remained in camp near the city until March 1862. While in a camp near Hunter's Chapel, Virginia, the 74th received its state color on March 5, 1862. Representative Robert McKnight of Pittsburgh presented the flag on behalf of the governor.[1]

Upon the opening of the 1862 campaign season, the regiment was assigned to western Virginia, and marched via Winchester to Franklin, where it remained a short time. It moved into the Shenandoah Valley as part of the troops sent there to counter Confederate General Stonewall Jackson's small army. After fighting in the Battle of Cross Keys on June 8, the regiment moved into northern Virginia as part of Major-General John Pope's Army of Virginia. When Pope was forced to withdraw his scattered forces to

Monument to the 74th Regiment at Gettysburg

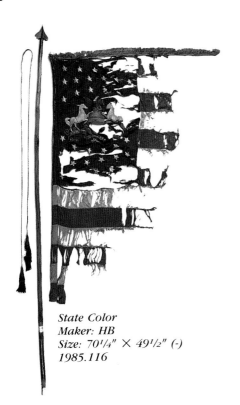

State Color
Maker: HB
Size: 70¼" × 49½" (-)
1985.116

oppose Jackson and Lee, the 74th was part of the rear-guard. It fought at Freeman's Ford (August 22), Sulphur Springs (August 24), and Waterloo Bridge (August 26) before taking part in the Second Battle of Manassas on August 29-30. Thereafter, the regiment was assigned to the Eleventh Corps, Army of the Potomac, but did not take part in the Maryland and Virginia campaigns of 1862. It joined the main army late in the year and went into winter camp near Stafford Court House.

The regiment next engaged the enemy during the Battle of Chancellorsville late on May 2, 1863. Stonewall Jackson's surprise attack struck the exposed right flank of the Eleventh Corps and drove the Yankee troops from the field. The 74th was caught up in the confusion of the retreat but managed to lose only fifty-two men. Color-Sergeant George Ekert was cited for his bravery in preserving the state color from capture.[2]

Part of the regiment arrived at Gettysburg on July 1 to engage the enemy north of the town before the corps was again flanked and driven back in confusion. During the three-day battle, the 74th suffered a loss of 110, its heaviest casualties in a single engagement during the war. Soon after the army returned to Virginia, the Third Division of the corps was detached from the army and sent to reinforce the Federal troops engaged in the siege of Charleston, South Carolina. The 74th remained near Charleston until August 1864, the men sometime acting as heavy artillery. The regiment fought numerous minor engagements with the enemy, most notably on Seabrook Island on November 15, 1863.

The regiment was ordered to Washington in August 1864, where it remained as part of the garrison for a month. It was then sent to West Virginia to guard a section of the Baltimore and Ohio Railroad. In the meantime, a considerable number of the men were mustered out of service, and the regiment was rebuilt with seven new companies in early 1865. The 74th remained in West Virginia until it was disbanded at Clarksburg on August 29, 1865. The state color carried by the regiment throughout its service was returned to the state on July 4, 1866.

Notes

[1]"Flag Presentation to Pennsylvania Regiments," *Philadelphia Inquirer*, March 8, 1862.

[2]*O.R.* 25.1, p. 666.

Bibliography

Schleiter, G. "The 11th Corps. Who was Responsible for the Disaster at Chancellorsville?" *National Tribune*, July 30, 1885.

75th Infantry

First State Color

Organized primarily of Philadelphia German-speaking men, the 75th Pennsylvania was formed in August 1861. After a month in camp outside the city, the new unit was sent to Washington, where it remained throughout the winter of 1861-62. On March 5, 1862, Representative Robert McKnight of Pittsburgh, acting on behalf of Governor Curtin, visited the camp and presented the regiment with a state color.[1]

After taking part in the March 1862 occupation of Manassas, the regiment was assigned to a division of troops sent to the Shenandoah Valley. The 75th at first remained in camp near Winchester, then marched south in pursuit of Stonewall Jackson's Confederates. Its first battle experience occurred at Cross Keys on June 8, when Federal troops caught up with Jackson's small force and fought an inconclusive engagement. Shortly after this battle, the Federal troops in northern Virginia were reorganized, the 75th being attached to Major-General Franz Sigel's First Corps, Army of Virginia. The regiment took part in the campaign that

culminated in the Second Battle of Manassas on August 29-30, 1862. It was engaged on the second day of the battle, suffering 150 casualties in the unsuccessful assaults on Jackson's entrenched Rebels.

Upon the army's withdrawal to Washington, the regiment was transferred to the new Eleventh Corps, Army of the Potomac. It remained near the capital and did not participate in the Maryland Campaign of September 1862. In early November, the corps finally moved south to rejoin the army, but did not take part in the defeat at Fredericksburg in December. The regiment went into winter quarters near Falmouth, remaining there until February 1863. It then moved back to Stafford Court House, where it remained until late April. At that time, General Hooker undertook the campaign that ended in the Federal defeat at Chancellorsville. When Jackson's Confederates surprised the Eleventh Corps on the evening of May 2, the 75th was one of the first units attacked and gave way in total confusion. Most of its casualties were captured in the rout. The regiment then moved north and fought at Gettysburg on July 1-3, suffering 111 casualties.

The regiment then accompanied the army on its pursuit of Lee's beaten troops. In late September, most of the Eleventh Corps was transferred by rail to Tennessee as reinforcements for the besieged Federal army in Chattanooga. Detraining at Bridgeport, Alabama, the 75th marched toward Chattanooga. It was under fire but suffered no losses at Wauhatchie on the evening of October 28-29. During the Battle of Chattanooga on November 25, the regiment was present on the field but lost no soldiers to enemy fire. After marching partway to Knoxville to relieve the Federal troops in that city, the regiment returned to Chattanooga and went into winter camp.

During the winter, the regiment re-enlisted and returned to Philadelphia for a furlough in January 1864. After returning to Chattanooga, the regiment was assigned to the Fourth Division of the new Twentieth Corps and was sent to Tennessee to guard railroads against guerrilla attacks. In May 1864, Lieutenant-Colonel Alvin V. Matzdorff requested a replacement state color. Upon receipt of this second flag, the first state color was sent to Nashville and from there Colo-

First State Color
Maker: HB
Size: 72" × 43¹⁄₂" (-)
1985.118

Second State Color
Maker: HB

Size: 71¾" × 76"
1985.117

After the Confederate defeat at Nashville in December, the 75th returned to Franklin and spent the winter in southern Tennessee, performing provost guard duties. It was finally mustered out of service on September 1, 1865. The second state color was officially returned to the state on July 4, 1866.

Philadelphia Flags

On September 27, 1861, Mrs. Sophia Bohlen, the colonel's wife, presented a national color to the regiment in front of the colonel's home at the corner of Walnut and Juniper Streets in Philadelphia. This flag was carried for an unspecified time by the regiment and was also used in the 1866 parade, after which it was deposited in Independence Hall. Its present whereabouts is unknown. Sometime in February 1862, George K. Ziegler presented the regiment with a set of guidons. Their subsequent history and disposition is unknown.[4]

nel James Chamberlin forwarded it to Harrisburg on August 22.[2] It was given to the state on July 4, 1866.

Second State Color

A new color was ordered in late May 1864 and sent to Nashville sometime in August.[3] By that time, the 75th was encamped near Nashville, with part of the unit spread out along the Nashville & Northwestern Railroad. Six companies were present at the Battle of Franklin on November 30, but suffered no casualties.

Color-Bearers

During the fighting at Second Manassas on August 30, 1862, Sergeant Robert Jordan of Company A was killed while carrying one of the flags. Sergeant John Emleben of Company D, though wounded, took the flag from Jordan's hands as he fell and bore it safely from the field. The regiment's second color-bearer, Sergeant Charles Haserodt, was cited for his bravery in this same battle.[5]

Notes

[1]"Flag Presentation to Pennsylvania regiments," *Philadelphia Inquirer*, March 8, 1862.

[2]Colonel James Chamberlin to Adjutant-General A. L. Russell, August 22, 1864, RG 25.

[3]Lieutenant-Colonel A. V. Matzdorff to Adjutant-General Russell, June 8, 1864, Regimental Letter Book, RG 94; Colonel Chamberlin to

Matthew S. Quay, August 9, 1864, RG 19, Quartermaster-General, Correspondence File.

[4]Scharf-Westcott p. 782; "Presentation of Colors," *Philadelphia Public Ledger*, September 28, 1861; "Colonel Bohlen's Regiment," *Philadelphia Inquirer*, September 28, 1861; *Pennsylvania at Chickamauga*, p. 169.

[5]*Pennsylvania at Chickamauga*, pp. 170-171.

Bibliography

Nachtigill, Hermann. *Geschichte des 75sten Regiments, Pa. Vols.* Philadelphia: C.B. Kretchman, 1886.

76th Infantry

First State Color

Known as the Keystone Zouaves, the 76th Pennsylvania was organized at Harrisburg's Camp Cameron during the fall of 1861. Late in the afternoon of November 18, the regiment marched into the city and halted behind the Capitol. The 55th Regiment marched in from Camp Curtin, and Governor Curtin then presented a state color to each regiment. The governor told the troops that both regiments had been assigned to the expedition about to move south to attack Charleston, South Carolina. Curtin hoped that the city would be laid waste in retribution for the state's part in starting the war. The Zouaves flung their caps in the air and cheered wildly for this rousing patriotic speech.[1]

The regiment then left Harrisburg for Fort Monroe, remaining there a week. It then sailed to Hilton Head Island, South Carolina, where it encamped until early April 1862, engaged in building fortifications and perfecting regimental drill. At this time, the 76th was detached to take part in the reduction of Fort Pulaski, situated at the mouth of the Savannah River. The Federal heavy artillery sufficed to force Pulaski's

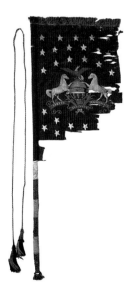

First State Color
Maker: HB
Size: 70½" × 27" (-)
1985.120

surrender, after which the 76th returned to Hilton Head. In early June, the regiment moved with an expedition to attack Charleston, which was repulsed at Secessionville on June 16. The regiment then returned to camp, where it remained until it took part in the attempted interdiction of the railroad between Charleston and Savannah. On October 23, the unit fought the enemy at Pocotaligo, suffering seventy-five casualties as the attack on the railroad's defenders was repulsed.

After this defeat, the 76th returned to Hilton Head and remained in the area until July 1863, when another expedition was formed to attack Charleston. On July 10, the 76th was among the first troops to land on Morris Island and drive the Confederates into their fortifications on the northern end of the island. The next day, the regiment formed part of the unsuccessful storming column against Fort Wagner, suffering almost fifty percent casualties. A second assault on July 18 was also repulsed. Shortly after this engagement, the 76th was sent back to Hilton Head as part of the garrison. It remained on the island performing guard duty until early May 1864.

At this time, the regiment, as part of the Tenth Corps, Army of the James, was transferred to Virginia to take part in Major-General Benjamin Butler's attack on Petersburg. The army rendezvoused at Yorktown, then landed at Bermuda Hundred. As the Federal troops moved to destroy the Petersburg and Weldon Railroad, Confederate troops marched to intercept them. The numerous skirmishes culminated in the Battle of Drewry's Bluff on May 16, which resulted in a Yankee defeat. Butler withdrew into his defensive line at Bermuda Hundred, then detached part of his army, including the 76th, to reinforce Grant's troops at Cold Harbor. The 76th was engaged from June 1-3, losing forty-nine soldiers. It then took a minor part in the June attacks on Petersburg.

Grant and Lee then settled into a static siege operation, and numerous engagements took place as the Federals attempted to cut supply lines and capture Petersburg. The 76th was engaged in the July 30 fighting near the Crater in one of the diversionary assaults, then took part in an unsuccessful attack at Deep Bot-

tom on August 14-17. During the fighting on August 14, Color-Sergeant Solomon C. Miller received a severe wound in his bowels.[2] Miller had been promoted color-bearer "for gallant and meritorious conduct in the field, and unexceptionable performance of his duties as a non-commissioned officer and soldier."[3] The regiment next fought at New Market Heights on September 29-30, and then took part in the engagement at the Darbytown Road on October 27-28. During this latter movement, Corporal Albert Sanders of Company C bore the state color, Sanders having been appointed bearer on September 27.[4] This was the last combat in which the original state color was carried. It was returned to Harrisburg and officially given to the state on July 4, 1866.

Second State Color

This flag was prepared for the regiment in mid-December 1864 and forwarded to the State Agency sometime thereafter. The new color saw its first and only combat on January 15, 1865. At that time, the 76th was part of the new Twenty-fourth Corps, part of which was detached to participate in the assault on Fort Fisher, the key to Wilmington, North Carolina. During the successful attack, the 76th suffered only twenty-one casualties, but the state color was pierced by eighty-nine bullets and shell fragments. The staff was broken but Corporal Sanders, still the bearer,

Second State Color
Maker: HB
Size: 72″ × 71⅝″
1985.121

Third State Color   *Size: 72¼″ × 76⅞″*
Maker: HB   *1985.122*

emerged unscathed.[5] The regiment then moved north to occupy Wilmington in February 1865. After performing provost guard duty in Raleigh, the regiment was mustered out of service on July 18. The second state color was returned to the Commonwealth in 1866.

Third State Color

This flag was delivered to the state on July 1, 1865, and forwarded to the State Agency in Washington.

Advance the Colors!

This late replacement flag was apparently never received by the 76th before it mustered out later in the month. It was returned to the state on July 4, 1866.

Regimental Color

This unmarked federal-issue infantry regimental color was carried by the 76th at some unspecified date, probably late in the war. Nothing has been found about its history.

Notes

[1]"Flag Presentation," *Harrisburg Patriot and Union*, November 19, 1861.

[2]"Casualties in the Seventy-sixth Pa. Regt.," *Philadelphia Inquirer*, August 25, 1864.

[3]Regimental Orders #238, July 22, 1864, Regimental Order Book, RG 94.

[4]Regimental Orders #259, September 27, 1864, *Ibid.*

[5]"Brevet Brigadier-General John S. Littell," *Pennsylvania Daily Telegraph*, July 25, 1865; Bates 2: 949.

Regimental Color
Maker: EH
Size: 71¹/₂″ × 76⁷/₈″
1985.119

Bibliography

Bennage, Simon. Diary, October 7, 1864-July 28, 1865. USAMHI.

Diller, William S. Papers. Historical Society of Pennsylvania.

Hildreth, Oscar. 1863 Letters. USAMHI, HbCWRT Collection.

Knox, W. H. "Morris Island Again." *National Tribune*, September 6, 1883.

McAbee, Daniel H. "Cold Harbor." *National Tribune*, July 29, 1886.

Miller, John J. Letters. In George Miller Collection, USAMHI.

Porter, John A. Personal Reminiscences. USAMHI, CWTI Collection.

Reinoehl, A. C. "The 76th Reg't. Penna. Vols. at the Capture of Ft. Wagner." *Philadelphia Weekly Press*, March 31, 1886.

Weigel, John. "The 76th Pennsylvania at Fort Wagner." *National Tribune*, January 14, 1886.

77th Infantry

First State Color

The 77th Pennsylvania was organized under the authority granted to Frederick S. Stumbaugh of Chambersburg in August 1861. The regiment formed at Camp Wilkins, located near Pittsburgh. Company I of the regiment was an artillery battery and was detached as an independent battery. Another company was understrength and soon broken up, so the 77th consisted of only eight companies throughout most of its existence. On October 17, 1861, Governor Curtin presented state colors to the 77th, 78th, and 79th Infantry, which composed a brigade of Pennsylvanians designated for service in Kentucky. The presentation took place in Allegheny City.[1]

The day after receiving the flags, the brigade went by boat to Louisville. After spending the winter in camp near the city, the 77th moved south to occupy Nashville in early March 1862. Soon thereafter, the Federal army led by Major-General Don Carlos Buell moved southwest, repairing the railroad as it went. Part of Buell's army reinforced Grant's troops during the Battle of Shiloh on April 6-7. Buell's troops

First State Color
Maker: EH
Size: 70" × 77⅝"
1985.124

arrived in time to fight on the second day of the engagement and helped turn the tide in favor of the North. The 77th was the only Pennsylvania command engaged in this battle.

The combined Federal army then marched south and forced the outnumbered Confederates to retreat from Corinth, Mississippi, in late May. Buell's troops then marched back into Tennessee as Braxton Bragg's Southern troops pushed north through Tennessee into Kentucky. As the main armies fought at Perryville on October 8, the 77th's division reached Frankfort and skirmished with the enemy near that location. As the enemy retreated, Buell's army returned to Tennessee and rested in the vicinity of Nashville before starting a new campaign.

Buell moved south and encountered Bragg's troops near Murfreesboro. On December 31, Bragg took the initiative and attacked his opponent. This battle, known as Stones' River, was initially a Southern success as Bragg's surprise assault drove many Yankees off the field. The 77th launched a counterattack to recover a captured Federal battery and take some nearby enemy guns. However, the assault was not supported and although the 77th retook the battery, it was forced to retreat, suffering heavy casualties. Color-Sergeant Scott R. Crawford was wounded in both legs during the attack. As Crawford fell, fifteen-year-old James A. Rodgers of Company E seized the flag but quickly fell wounded himself. Lieutenant John C. Shroad of Company K then grabbed the color and brought it from the field as the survivors withdrew. Sergeant Crawford had his left leg amputated but died on January 13, 1863.[2] The 77th was not engaged on the second day of the battle (January 2, 1863), which resulted in a Southern retreat.

The battle damage suffered by the state color at Shiloh (where it was "literally riddled" by a bursting shell) and Stones' River forced Captain Thomas E. Rose to request a replacement color. The captain wrote the following about his regiment's treasured banner:[3]

> The old flag was literally torn to pieces with grape shot when we charged the batteries and I think we must have a new one. I would send the old one home, but it would be

Advance the Colors!

like parting with an old friend. And I know the boys would shed tears. Two men were struck down while carrying it, but so quickly was it caught that the flag never fell, and by heaven, it never shall fall, while there is a man left in the old 77th strong enough to hold it up.

The remnant of the original state color was returned to Harrisburg sometime in 1863 and was officially returned during the 1866 ceremony.

Second State Color

A replacement color was finished in May 1863 and brought to the regiment on May 16 when Colonel Rose returned to the front after a visit to Pittsburgh.[4] In late June, the new commander of the Army of the Cumberland, Major-General William S. Rosecrans, finally left Murfreesboro and adroitly maneuvered Bragg's Confederates out of Tennessee in the Tullahoma Campaign. The 77th was engaged at Liberty Gap on June 24-25. Bragg was forced to abandon Chattanooga, and Rosecrans continued south into Georgia after the retreating enemy.

However, the Confederate army was reinforced and Bragg turned about and struck Rosecrans's army at Chickamauga Creek on September 19-20. This bitterly-contested struggle resulted in a Southern victory. On the evening of September 19, most of the 77th Pennsylvania was captured when the regiment was outflanked in the darkness. When it became apparent that the enemy was about to surround them, most of the soldiers in the 77th surrendered. As the men grounded arms, Colonel Alfred J. Vaughn, Jr., commanding a brigade of Confederate Tennessee troops, rode up and spied the state color. He inquired, "Who has those colors?" Corporal W. H. H. Woolslair glibly replied, "The color bearer." Vaughn then said, "Sir, to what command do you belong?" Once Woolslair stated his regiment, Vaughn took the flag and sent it to the rear for safekeeping. The flag was retaken in 1865 and returned to the state by the War Department in 1905. Corporal Woolslair did not survive the war; he died in Andersonville Prison on August 27, 1864.[5]

Third State Color

Once the beaten Federal army retired into the Chattanooga defenses, the remnant of the 77th was detached and acted as part of the garrison of Whiteside, Tennessee, where it remained until the men re-enlisted and went home for a furlough in early 1864. A new state color was furnished to the unit in April 1864. At this time, the 77th became part of the Fourth Corps, Army of the Cumberland. In May, General Sherman began the campaign for Atlanta, which lasted until September, when the city fell to the Union

Second State Color
Maker: HB
Size: 71" × 77⅛"
1985.125

army. The 77th was actively engaged in several of the battles and skirmishes of this campaign, including Resaca (May 14-15), Cassville (May 19), Dallas (May 27-June 3), Kenesaw Mountain (June 19-29), Smyrna (July 4), Atlanta (August 5), and Lovejoy Station (September 3).

The Fourth Corps remained behind when Sherman left Atlanta and headed toward Savannah because Confederate General John B. Hood took his troops and launched an invasion of Tennessee. Major-General George H. Thomas was placed in command to oppose Hood's advance. Hood's troops attacked at Franklin on November 29, where the 77th suffered

Third State Color
Maker: EH
Size: 70¾" × 78⅝"
1985.123

light casualties. The Federal troops retreated to Nashville, where Thomas reorganized his forces and finally struck at Hood's smaller army on December 15-16, completely shattering the Rebel troops. The 77th took part in the pursuit and went into winter camp at Huntsville, Alabama, where it remained until March 1865.

In March 1865, the 77th broke camp and moved by rail to Knoxville, remaining in that area for a month, when it moved to Nashville. In June, the 77th was ordered to Texas, where it was stationed near Victoria on garrison duty. In December 1865, the regiment began its return journey to Pennsylvania, being mustered out of service in Philadelphia on January 16, 1866. The third state color was returned to the Commonwealth on July 4, 1866.

Notes

[1]"Gen. Negley's Brigade—Presentation of Regimental Colors," *Pittsburgh Gazette*, October 18, 1861.

[2]"From the 77th Regiment," *Lancaster Daily Evening Express*, January 14, 1863; Obreiter (1908 edition), p. 140; "List of Casualties in the 77th Regiment Pennsylvania Volunteers in the Late Battle Before Murfreesboro, Tennessee," in Regimental Letter Book, RG 94.

[3]"The Flag, of the Seventy-seventh Pennsylvania," *Pittsburgh Gazette*, April 28, 1862; Captain Rose to Governor Curtin, January 26, 1863, Regimental Papers, RG 19.

[4]Kimber Moore Diary, May 16, 1863.

[5]*O.R.* 30.2, p. 108.

Bibliography

Cassel, J. E. "A Ludicrous Surrender." *Philadelphia Weekly Times*, March 5, 1881.

Duganne, P. S. "Battle of Resaca." *National Tribune*, April 18, 1889.

Erisman, Henry M. Letters, 1862-1864. USAMHI, HbCWRT Collection.

Franklin, Samuel B. Memoirs, 1861-1863. USAMHI, HbCWRT Collection.

Houck, M. W. "The 77th Pa. A Sketch of Its Part in the Battle of Stone River." *National Tribune*, December 30, 1886.

Moore, Kimber A. Papers. USAMHI, Save the Flags Collection.

Obreiter, John. *The Seventy-seventh Pennsylvania at Shiloh. History of the Regiment. The Battle of Shiloh.* Harrisburg: Harrisburg Publishing Company, 1905; revised edition, 1908.

———. Diary. Millersville University.

Robinson, William A. Diary. Western Reserve Historical Society.

Rose, Thomas E. *Col. Rose's Story of the Famous Tunnel Escape From Libby Prison.* N.p., n.d.

Truxall, Aida C. (editor). *"Respects to All;" Letters of Two Pennsylvania Boys in the War of the Rebellion.* Pittsburgh: University of Pittsburgh Press, 1962. Includes letters of Michael S. Bright.

78th Infantry

First State Color

The companies forming the 78th Infantry rendezvoused at Camp Orr near Kittanning in August and September 1861. In mid-October, the regiment moved to Pittsburgh, where it was assigned to a brigade of Pennsylvania troops designated for service in Kentucky. On October 17, the three regiments in camp marched to Allegheny City, where Governor Curtin presented state colors to the units.[1]

After being transported to Louisville, the brigade moved down the Green River & Nashville Railroad. In December, the 78th set up camp along the Green River near Munfordville, Kentucky, where it remained until mid-February 1862. The brigade then advanced south to Nashville, where the 78th was assigned to guard the railroad from Nashville to Columbia. From early May to mid-August, the 78th garrisoned Pulaski, then withdrew to Nashville when Braxton Bragg's Confederate army invaded Kentucky. At Nashville, the regiment was detached as part of the city's garrison until mid-December. It fought in several minor skirmishes outside the city, most notably at Lavergne (October 7) and Neely's Bend (October 19), as well as other encounters with enemy forces probing the city defenses.

In mid-December, the 78th rejoined the Army of the Cumberland, which pushed south to Murfreesboro and fought near that city at Stones' River on December 31, 1862-January 2, 1863. On the first day of the battle, the division to which the 78th was attached was forced back by superior numbers as Bragg's sunrise attack caught much of the Federal army by surprise. On January 2, the 78th reinforced the left flank and helped repulse a major enemy assault. During the two days of battle, the regiment suffered 188 casualties. Color-Sergeant George D. Hamm of Company D emerged unscathed, although the state color was "completely riddled."[2]

Soon after the battle, the Army of the Cumberland was reorganized and the 78th was assigned to the new Fourteenth Corps. Remaining at Murfreesboro until late April 1863, the 78th then took part in General William S. Rosecrans's Tullahoma Campaign of June-July, when Bragg's army was outmaneuvered and forced to withdraw to Chattanooga. After resting a month, Rosecrans marched further south and forced Bragg to retreat into northern Georgia. The 78th skirmished at Dug Gap on September 10-11 and although present at Chickamauga on September 19-20 was not actively engaged and suffered a mere five casualties.

After the defeat at Chickamauga, the Northern army retreated to Chattanooga, which was besieged until General Grant and numerous reinforcements defeated Bragg in late November. Again, the 78th was present on the battlefield but not engaged. It was then assigned to duty atop Lookout Mountain, remaining here until April 1864. The remnant of the first state color was sent to New Bethlehem sometime in early 1864. When the regiment mustered out of service, the flag was given to Sergeant Hamm to keep. The sergeant ignored the free railroad pass to go Philadelphia in 1866 to return the flag to the Commonwealth, and it remained in his possession until May 1907. At that time, a fire completely destroyed Hamm's dwelling, including the flag. The sergeant himself was badly burned trying to rescue the banner.[4]

Second State Color   Size: 71⅛″ × 77⅛″
Maker: EH   1985.126

National Color
Size: 57¹/₄" × 83¹/₄" (-)
1985.127

First Regimental Color   *1985.128*
Size: 69⁷/₈" × 65¹/₂" (-)

Second State Color

A replacement state color was authorized for the 78th as part of Joint Resolution #11 of April 11, 1863. However, on August 13, 1863, Lieutenant-Colonel Archibald Blakely informed Adjutant-General A. L. Russell that the promised replacement had not been received.[3] This second color was completed by Evans & Hassall in December 1863 and given to Colonel Sirwell on January 14, 1864, to deliver to the 78th.[5]

As part of the Fourteenth Corps, the 78th participated in the opening stages of General Sherman's Atlanta Campaign. It fought at Rocky Face Ridge on May 7, at Resaca on May 14, and at New Hope Church on May 27. During this last engagement, a young soldier from the 19th Ohio became detached from his unit and fell in with the 78th. This man was hit and decapitated by an artillery shell, which scattered the boy's head over the 78th's flag.[6] The regiment then fought in the series of engagements in the Kenesaw Mountain area until June 22. At that time, the regiment was relieved from duty and sent to Chattanooga in order to reinforce the troops guarding supply trains moving between that city and the army. The regiment performed this duty until late September, when it was transferred to Nashville. While in this area, the 78th participated in several minor skirmishes, including those at Pulaski (September 27) and Franklin (October 2). Most of the men in the regiment had not re-enlisted and were sent home in mid-October.

Those who had re-enlisted were consolidated into two companies, which remained at Nashville. Eight new companies were assigned to the 78th in 1865. The rebuilt regiment remained on duty in Tennessee until mustered out of service on September 11, 1865. The second state color was returned to the Commonwealth on July 4, 1866.

National Color

Judging from the attached streamers, this color was presented to the regiment by the ladies of Kittanning and was carried in the Battle of Stones' River. Nothing else has been located about its subsequent history.

Regimental Colors

One of these colors has a streamer marked "Stone River Flag." The author has not uncovered any further information about either of these unmarked colors.

Color-Bearers

On May 20, 1865, Sergeant J. Waream of Company C was relieved as bearer by Sergeant Thomas Evans of Company B.[7]

Second Regimental Color   *1985.002*
Size: 61" × 71¹/₂"

Advance the Colors!

Notes

[1]"Gen. Negley's Brigade—Presentation of Regimental Colors," *Pittsburgh Gazette*, October 18, 1861.

[2]"The Flag of the Seventy-eighth Pennsylvania Regiment," *Pittsburgh Gazette*, February 10, 1863; Gibson, p. 183.

[3]Blakely to Russell, August 13, 1863, RG 25.

[4]Flag of the 78th Pa., *National Tribune*, January 9, 1908.

[5]"Flag Memorandum," RG 25.

[6]Mary A. Livermore, *My Story of the War: A Woman's Narrative of Four Years Personal Experience as Nurse in the Union Army, . . .* (Hartford: A. D. Worthington and Company, 1890), p. 64.

[7]Special Orders #28, May 20, 1865, Regimental Order Book, RG 94.

Bibliography

Blakely, Archibald. *Address by Comrade Archibald Blakely, Delivered at Leechburg, Pa., September, 1880, at the Re-union of the 78th Regiment of Pennsylvania Volunteers.* Pittsburgh: W. V. Dermitt, Print, 1880.

_____. *Address of General Archibald Blakely at the Reunion of the Society of the Army of the Cumberland, Louisville, Ky., October, 1902.* Cincinnati: Robert Clarke Company, 1902.

Boney, W. W. "The Transport *Hastings*." *National Tribune*, March 15, 1888.

Doerr, Frederick. Letters, October 9, 1864-April 28, 1865. USAMHI.

Gibson, Joseph T. *History of the Seventy-eighth Pennsylvania Volunteer Infantry.* Pittsburgh: Pittsburgh Printing Company, 1905.

Wright, W. J. "New Hope Church." *National Tribune*, June 2, 1887.

79th Infantry

First State Color

With the exception of Company D (from Washington County), the 79th Pennsylvania was recruited solely in Lancaster County under authority granted to Henry A. Hambright, the unit's first and only colonel. The new regiment was organized at Camp Wilkins, Pittsburgh, for service with Brigadier-General James S. Negley's brigade, composed of the 77th, 78th, and 79th Infantry. On October 17, 1861, the three regiments left camp and marched into Allegheny City, where Governor Curtin addressed the 3,000 soldiers and presented each regiment with a state color.[1]

The very next day, the brigade left Pittsburgh by steamer for Louisville, Kentucky. After remaining here for a few weeks, the brigade moved south and went into winter camp along the Green River near Munfordville. In the Spring of 1862, the brigade was part of the force that marched south and occupied Nashville, where the 79th remained until late March. It was then detached and sent to garrison Columbia,

Tennessee. The regiment was in this area, guarding the Nashville and Decatur Railroad, until May 1862. At this time, the regiment took part in an expedition to Rodgersville and Florence, Alabama. After returning briefly to Columbia, the 79th was part of a two-week expedition that marched close to Chattanooga before retiring to Shelbyville, Tennessee.

In early August, the regiment was sent back to Nashville to help guard the capital. While here, the regiment spent part of its time guarding the railroad bridge at Gallatin. When Confederate General Braxton Bragg's army swept through Tennessee into Kentucky, the 79th joined Major-General Don Carlos Buell's army that moved to counter the enemy's northward advance. The two armies joined in battle at Perryville, Kentucky, on October 8. In this Federal victory the 79th suffered 216 casualties. During the return to Tennessee, the 79th's brigade was detached for a month to guard the railroad at Mitchellville, Tennessee.

In December, the regiment rejoined the Army of the Cumberland in time to take part in the second day of the Battle of Stones' River, on January 2, 1863. General Rosecrans's army went into camp near Murfreesboro after the battle. The regiment participated in expeditions to McMinnville and Liberty as Rosecrans prepared to move south after the spring rains. Beginning his campaign on June 24, Rosecrans maneuvered Bragg out of Tennessee and occupied Chattanooga. Bragg was reinforced and engaged Rosecrans in battle along Chickamauga Creek, located in northern Georgia, on September 19-20, 1863. The 79th, a part of the Fourteenth Corps, suffered 125 casualties in this Federal defeat. The army retreated to Chattanooga, where it remained until November, when reinforcements enabled the Yankees to defeat Bragg's army. During this battle, the 79th garrisoned part of the city fortifications and was not engaged.

A large number of soldiers re-enlisted and the regiment was granted a furlough in March 1864. The regiment returned to Lancaster for a month before returning to the army. During this time, the state color was apparently left in Harrisburg and was officially returned to the Commonwealth on July 4, 1866.[2]

First State Color
Maker: EH
Size: 72¼" × 77⅝"
1985.129

Lancaster Flags

Because of its gallantry at Perryville, several Lancastrians decided to procure a stand of colors for the 79th. A group of citizens spearheaded a drive to raise the money, and contracted with Evans & Hassall to supply the two flags. Philadelphia artist Isaac Williams painted both flags. One was a national color with "79th Regiment P.V." inscribed on the center red stripe. The second flag was a state regimental color. The national arms adorned the obverse, with the inscription "Presented by the Citizens of Lancaster, Pa., to the 79th Regiment P.V. for Gallant Conduct at Chaplain Hills, Ky., October 8, 1862" painted on a scroll beneath the eagle. The reverse depicted the state arms with the same presentation information. The gift included two general guide markers of blue silk with the regimental number in gold letters. These flags were obtained in December 1862. When word was received of the Stones' River fighting, this information was added to the regimental color. A deputation of citizens went to Tennessee and presented the flags on March 1, 1863.[3]

These flags seem to have been carried side by side with the state color throughout the 1863 campaigns. Judging from Confederate battle reports, one of the Lancaster flags was captured at Chickamauga on September 19, 1863. Major-General Patrick R. Cleburne reported the capture, as did Colonel F. C. Wilkes of the 24th Texas Cavalry (dismounted).[4] The captured flag was never recovered.

When the 79th returned from its furlough, it took part in General Sherman's Atlanta Campaign of May–September 1864. The regiment was principally engaged at Buzzard Roost, Kenesaw Mountain, and in the final struggle south of Atlanta just before the Confederates abandoned the city. In November 1864, Sherman began his famous March to the Sea, capturing Savannah, Georgia, on December 21. He then marched north through the Carolinas. The major engagement of the campaign occurred at Bentonville, North Carolina, on March 19, 1865. Here, the 79th lost fifty-four casualties in its final battle with the enemy. The regiment continued north with the army, took part in the Grand Review, and was mustered out of service on July 12, 1865. The final disposition of the surviving Lancaster flag is unknown.

Second State Color

A replacement state color was supplied to the state by Horstmann Brothers & Company in May 1864, but the regiment did not receive it until May 1865. It was apparently forwarded to the State Agency in Nashville and from there to Chattanooga, but never caught up

Second State Color
Maker: HB
Size: 71½" × 75¾"
1985.130

Monument to the 79th Regiment at Chickamauga, Showing Sergeant Dostman's Death

with the 79th. A letter written home in March 1865 by a veteran complained of the absence of the state color, and it seems that other regiments taunted the 79th over the missing flag, others thinking that they had been lost in battle. This flag was carried in the 1866 parade.[5]

Color-Bearer

During the fighting at Chickamauga on September 19, 1863, a shell exploded beside the colors and killed Corporal William F. Dostman, but the flag was caught before it fell. The incident does not show which flag Dostman was carrying.[6]

Notes

[1]"General Negley's Brigade—Presentation of Regimental Colors," *Pittsburgh Gazette*, October 18, 1861. Apparently, Governor Curtin became confused during the presentation and gave the wrong color to the 77th and 79th. See "The Colors of the 77th," *Lancaster Daily Evening Express*, January 1, 1862.

[2]"The Regimental Flag of the 79th Regiment P.V.," *Pennsylvania Daily Telegraph*, March 16, 1864.

[3]"Colors for the Gallant 79th," *Lancaster Daily Evening Express*, November 26, 1862; "The New Flags for the 79th," *Ibid.*, December 31, 1862; "The Flags for the 79th," *Ibid.*, February 12, 1863; Clark Diary, March 1, 1863.

[4]*O.R.* 30.2, pp. 154, 194.

[5]"From the Seventy-ninth," *Lancaster Daily Evening Express*, April 3, 1865.

[6]*Pennsylvania at Chickamauga*, p. 237.

Bibliography

Clark, William T. Diary. Lancaster County Historical Society.

Heisey, M. L. "The Gallant 79th Regiment." *Journal of the Lancaster County Historical Society* 66 (1962): 107-129.

Johnston, Adam S. *The Soldier Boy's Diary Book; or, Memorandums of the Alphabetical First Lessons of Military Tactics, Kept by Adam S. Johnston, from September 14, 1861, to October 2, 1864*. Pittsburgh, 1866.

Johnston, John M. "A Night with Bushwackers." *Blue and Gray* 2 (1893): 328-331.

Martin, Edwin K. "Oration, by E. K. Martin, Delivered in Fulton Hall, Lancaster, Pa., October 8th, 1877." Lancaster: New Era Print, 1877.

Nevin, Wilberforce. Letterbook, 1861-1864. Library of Congress.

"Sketch of the 79th Pa. Vols." *Grand Army Scout and Soldiers Mail*, April 5, 12, 19, 26, 1884.

7th Cavalry
(80th Regiment)

First State Standard

The 7th Pennsylvania Cavalry, one of the Commonwealth's best units, was organized at Camp Cameron in the fall of 1861, having been recruited under authority granted to William B. Sipes of Philadelphia. The troopers comprising the twelve companies came from more than fifteen counties spread across the state. On December 18, 1861, Colonel George E. Wynkoop marched the regiment into Harrisburg and halted it in massed formation in front of the Capitol. A member of Company E later recalled that after a few minutes, a group of gentlemen appeared on the piazza with a number of flags. The word soon spread that Governor Curtin himself was present to give a state standard and ten company guidons to the regiment. Most soldiers could not hear either the rousing presentation speech, which was occasionally interrupted with bursts of applause from those near the front, or Colonel Wynkoop's words of acceptance.[1]

On December 19, the 7th Cavalry left Harrisburg by train for Pittsburgh, then embarked on transports, which took the men to Louisville, Kentucky, where the unit remained until late January 1862. The regiment then marched south to Nashville, where the 7th was divided into its three battalions for duty in central Tennessee. It was the only cavalry regiment permanently assigned to duty in this part of the state, and the rigors of patrolling, chasing Confederate raiding parties, and garrisoning selected positions proved extremely taxing. Part of the regiment garrisoned Columbia for a short time, while the remainder of the unit was active in the area south of Nashville. The widely scattered regiment fought in numerous small engagements with enemy cavalry, the most important being Pulaski (May 1), Lebanon (May 5), Pikeville (June 19), Murfreesboro (July 13), McMinnville (August 10), and Gallatin (August 21).

The 1st Battalion of the regiment accompanied part of the main Federal army and took part in a diver-

sion toward Chattanooga, fighting at Sweden's Cove on June 6. The battalion was also engaged in the Battle of Perryville, Kentucky, on October 8, as Braxton Bragg's invasion of that state was turned back. When the Army of the Cumberland moved back to Nashville to rest and reorganize before advancing further south, the 7th Cavalry was finally reunited and assigned to this army's cavalry corps. During the Battle of Stones' River on December 31, 1862-January 2, 1863, the regiment was engaged in the army's rear, returning stragglers to the front and fighting a Confederate cavalry raid on part of the army's supply train.

During the winter and spring of 1863, the 7th was actively engaged in southern Tennessee. On January 31, the regiment attacked a rebel outpost at Rover, charging forward in advance of the other cavalry, utterly routing the enemy. The regiment again charged the enemy on March 4 at Unionville, again driving the opposing troops several miles toward Shelbyville. In April, the 7th fought at Franklin and McMinnville, both times driving the enemy cavalry from the field. Its use of sharpened sabers led the Confederate War Department to officially complain to the Lincoln government over this "barbaric" practice.

When the Army of the Cumberland advanced south in June, the cavalry again led the way. On June 25, Yankee troopers won a major victory at Shelbyville, where a large amount of military stores fell into Northern hands after the Rebel cavalry was again driven from the field. The 7th next engaged the en-

State Standard
Maker: HB
Size: 26³⁄₈" × 28⁷⁄₈"
1985.131

State Standard
Maker: HB
Size: 26" × 30⁷⁄₈"
1985.132

emy at Sparta on August 4 and 17. When the two major armies met at Chickamauga, Georgia, on September 19-20, the 7th Cavalry was engaged in the opening stages of the fighting while attempting to delay the enemy advance. After the army withdrew to Chattanooga, the regiment spent two weeks trying to intercept Confederate General Joseph Wheeler's cavalry raid into occupied Alabama and Tennessee in October. The regiment eventually moved to Huntsville, Alabama, where it remained throughout the winter of 1863-64.

In the spring of 1864, the regiment was briefly stationed at Columbia before rejoining the main army, now commanded by General Sherman. Atlanta was the objective of Sherman's army group, which captured the city in September. The 7th Cavalry was actively engaged throughout the campaign. It is not known when the first state standard was returned nor when the replacement flag was received by the regiment. This first standard was officially returned to the Commonwealth in 1866.

Second State Standard

A replacement standard was authorized for the 7th Cavalry as part of Joint Resolution #11, approved by the General Assembly and signed into law on April 11, 1863. This resolution authorized new colors for the 83rd and 111th, with amendments added to include the 78th Infantry and 7th Cavalry.[2] However, a second standard was not completed and sent to the State Agency in Nashville until mid-May 1864. It is not known when the regiment received this standard.

The regiment fought in several engagements during the Atlanta Campaign, most notably at Armuchy Creek (in Snake Creek Gap) on May 14, along the Villa Rica Road near Dallas on May 27, at McAfee's Cross Roads (June 11), Flat Rock (July 29), and Lovejoy Station (August 20), as well as many smaller skirmishes. At the conclusion of the Atlanta Campaign in October, the regiment was sent to Louisville for remounting, since most of the horses had been worn out from constant activity. The 7th moved to Nashville in January 1865, where it reorganized in preparation for the spring campaign.

In March 1865, Major-General James H. Wilson's Cavalry Corps swept through the lower southern states on a great raid. On April 2, the 7th Cavalry dismounted and took part in Wilson's successful attack on the Confederate defenses of Selma, Alabama, suffering fifty-three casualties. After fighting at Columbus, Georgia, on April 16, the regiment marched to Macon, where it remained on guard duty until mustered out of service on August 13. The second standard was returned to the state on July 4, 1866.

National Standard
Size: 26³/₄" × 30⁵/₈"
1985.133

National Standard

The remnants of this standard indicate that the flag is a federal-issue standard with battle honors evident. It was turned in to the state by February 1865, which indicates that the standard was carried sometime prior to that date. Nothing else has been found to verify its history.

1864 Pottsville
Standard
Size: 28³/₈" × 32"
S1984.012

1864 Pottsville Guidon,
Company I
Size: 26" × 37"
S1984.014

Pottsville Flags

On March 1, 1864, the ladies of Pottsville and St. Clair presented a standard and twelve company guidons to the 7th Cavalry. The presentation took place in Pottsville's Pennsylvania Hall, where the flags were received by Colonel Sipes.[3] These presented flags were apparently carried by the regiment during the remainder of its term of service. They were then kept by the Regimental Association until December 14, 1913, when they were given to the Historical Society of Schuylkill County for preservation. The flags were retained by the Historical Society until 1984, when the Society donated them to the Capitol Preservation Committee. The remnant of the standard and eight of the company guidons have been identified.

Advance the Colors!

Color-Bearers

On January 11, 1864, Sergeant John Ennis of Company A was appointed to carry the state standard.[4] He was carrying one of the two standards on April 2, 1865, during the charge of the regiment at Selma. Sergeant Ennis was mortally wounded, whereupon Sergeant Louis H. Bickel of Company I took the flag and planted it on the enemy entrenchments.[5]

Sergeant John Ennis

Notes

[1]*Clinton Democrat*, January 2, 1862; Sipes, p. 6.
[2]*Laws of Pennsylvania, 1863*, p. 610; "Presentation of Flags," *Pittsburgh Evening Chronicle*, March 27, 1863.

[3]"Presentation of Colors to the Seventh Pennsylvania Cavalry," *Pottsville Miners' Journal*, March 5, 1864.
[4]General Orders #5, January 11, 1864, Regimental Order Book, RG 94.
[5]Sipes, p. 159.

Bibliography

Dornblaser, Thomas F. *My Life-Story for Young and Old*. Chicago, 1930.
_____. *Sabre Strokes of the Pennsylvania Dragoons in the War of 1861-1865*. Philadelphia: Luthern Publication Society, 1884.
History and Roster of the Seventh Pa. Cavalry Veteran Volunteers, 1861-1865. Pottsville: Miners' Journal, 1904.
McCormick Family Papers. Pennsylvania State Archives.
Reed, Francis W. Papers. Pennsylvania State Archives; Historical Society of Schuylkill County ; USAMHI, CWTI Collection.
Sigmund, Jacob. Papers. Pennsylvania State Archives.
Sipes, William B. *The Seventh Pennsylvania Veteran Volunteer Cavalry,*

Its Record, Reminiscences and Roster. Pottsville: Miners' Journal, 1906.
Steahlin, George F. "Colonel Minty's Sabre Brigade at Guy's Gap." *National Tribune*, May 27, 1882.
Straub, Edward A. *Life and Civil War Services of Edward A. Straub of Co. B 7th Pennsylvania Cavalry, Written by Himself*. Milwaukee: Press of J. H. Yewdale & Sons Company, 1909.
Thompson, Heber S. *Diary of Capt. Heber S. Thompson, Seventh Pennsylvania Cavalry, Pottsville, May to December, 1864*. N. p., n.d.

81st Infantry

First State Color

Recruited primarily in Philadelphia and Carbon counties, the 81st Infantry presents an enigma because of the dearth of sources for this regiment. The companies rendezvoused at Easton before leaving for Washington in October 1861. It was assigned to the First Brigade, First Division, Second Corps, remaining in that brigade throughout its term of service. A state color was furnished to the state by Horstmann Brothers & Company in December 1861. It was sent to the State Agency in Washington and was given to the 81st at an unspecified date.

After taking part in the March 1862 occupation of Manassas, the corps, as part of the Army of the Potomac, was transferred to the Yorktown Peninsula. The 81st first engaged the enemy at Fair Oaks on May 31-June 1, suffering ninety-one casualties. During the Seven Days' Battles, the regiment fought at Glendale on June 30 and at Malvern Hill the following day. The Second Corps was among the last troops to leave the Peninsula in August and thus arrived too late to participate in the Second Battle of Manassas. During the fighting at Antietam on September 17, the 81st took part in the attacks on the Sunken Road. In its final battle of 1862, the regiment suffered 126 casualties out of 251 men taken into action at Fredericksburg on December 13. Color-Sergeant John B. Munyan of Company A was wounded three time before he relinquished the colors to James "Reddy" McHale of Company B. Young McHale, a twenty-year-old Philadelphia seaman, took the flag off the field, stopping to rescue the fallen banner of another regiment as he retreated.[1]

The regiment fought at Chancellorsville on May 1-3, 1863, then marched north and took part in the Battle of Gettysburg on July 2. The division moved to reinforce the Third Corps and fought in the Wheatfield. As the regiment charged across the field, color-bearer McHale surged forward in advance, urging the men on. He fell shot through the heart. McHale had carried the color ever since Fredericksburg, but because of his unkempt personal appearance, was deprived of carrying the flag at formal reviews. His nickname "Reddy" came from his "uncombed, uncut,

shaggy red hair." This "careless waif" was much loved by his comrades.[2]

After the conclusion of the Bristoe Station and Mine Run campaigns, the 81st went into winter camp near Brandy Station. The regiment was actively engaged in Grant's campaign against Lee's army in 1864. It was used as pickets on the army's left flank during the fighting in the Wilderness and suffered few casualties. It took part in the charge of the Second Corps at Spotsylvania on May 12, skirmished along the North Anna River, then participated in the unsuccessful charge at Cold Harbor on June 3. The army then crossed the James River and attacked Petersburg, the 81st being engaged primarily on June 16. At this time, the regiment seems to have obtained a new flag, but the disposition of the original color is shrouded in mystery. At some point prior to 1888, the War Department gave an 81st Pennsylvania flag to Captain James H. Mitchell. This banner had been marked as #247 on the list of recaptured Union flags, but it may have gotten into War Department control by mistake. When the regiment erected its monument at Gettysburg in 1889, Captain Harry Wilson remarked that the 81st never lost a color to the enemy. Once this flag was given to Mitchell, it disappeared from view.[3]

Second State Color

Although a bill for this flag does not exist in the State Archives, a pencilled note on the flags ordered from Horstmann Brothers & Company notes that a state color was ordered on January 20, 1864.[4] This flag seems to have been delivered to the 81st sometime later that year. It was first carried into combat at Deep Bottom on August 13-20, as the corps launched a diversion in this area. On August 25, the regiment fought at Reams' Station, suffering twenty-eight casualties. Color-Sergeant James B. Murray of Company H was killed. His successor, Sergeant John Hughs of Company E, was quickly wounded but refused to give up the flag until he fainted from loss of blood. A third sergeant, John Adams of Company D, then took the flag and carried it until after the reconnaissance to Hatcher's Run on December 9-10. At this time, Colonel William Wilson requested a new flag, noting that the second color was badly torn and could not be unfurled except in the calmest weather. It was returned to Harrisburg upon receipt of the replacement color.[5] It has not been identified and may perhaps be one of the flags marked "unknown."

Fourth State Color
Maker: HB
Size: 71⅝" × 76⅛"
1985.134

Third State Color
Maker: EH
Size: 71⅝" × 78¾"
1985.135

Third State Color

A replacement state color was sent to the State Agency in Washington and forwarded to the 81st on January 17, 1865.[6] This flag was carried by the regiment until the end of its combat service. On April 6, 1865, the regiment charged upon the enemy at Saylor's Creek, suffering few casualties; among the killed was Color-Sergeant William D. Parkhill of Company C. On April 7, the brigade unsuccessfully attacked a part of Lee's retreating army near Farmville. Sergeant Andrew J. Shiner was mortally wounded in the assault, which left a mere thirty-nine men with the flag.[7] After Lee's surrender at Appomattox, the remnant of the 81st returned to Washington and was mustered out of service on June 29. The third state color was retained by Colonel William Wilson, who returned it to the Commonwealth on July 4, 1866.[8]

Fourth State Color

Owing to the heavy battle damage sustained in the 1865 Campaign, Colonel Wilson asked for a new flag on June 14. This banner was received just prior to muster out while the 81st lay at Camp Cadwalader in Philadelphia. Colonel Wilson kept the flag until 1866, when he gave it back to the state.[9]

Regimental Color

This flag was obtained by the 81st on November 8, 1863, and carried until November 21, 1864. The color was badly damaged at Spotsylvania on May 12, 1864, and the finial was shot off during the charge at Cold Harbor on June 3. On June 17, the staff was broken by a bullet which grazed the forehead of the bearer, Sergeant Isaac McLean. Colonel Wilson sent the torn flag to the state on November 21, 1864.[10] It was an unmarked regimental and was included as an "unknown" flag by the time the collection was placed in the Rotunda.

Regimental Color (Probable)
Size: 70½" × 76½"
1985.178

Color-Bearer

One of the men who carried the colors in 1864 was Ephraim B. Davis of Company D. This man was mortally wounded and was buried in the Wilderness cemetery. Captain Harry Wilson recalled Davis's burial:[11]

> With and old shovel and some sharpened cracker-box lids we made the excavation, and wrapping him in his blanket all soaked with his blood, let him down, oh, so gently, in his grave. Then laying stones and lumps of earth along the sides, we placed pieces of rough boards across so that the falling earth might not strike his honored body. And we cried and could not help it as we filled the grave, and we cut his name deep in a piece of cracker-box lid with our pocket-knives, and filled the letters with ink to make them plain, and planted that poor tombstone at his head, the best and only tribute our loving hearts and willing hands could offer, ...

Notes

[1]Colonel H. B. McKeen to Governor Curtin, March 22, 1863, Regimental Papers, RG 19; *Pennsylvania at Gettysburg* 1: 417.

[2]*Pennsylvania at Gettysburg* 1: 417.

[3]*Ibid.*, p. 415; Captured Flags Document, p. 7.

[4]"Flags Purchased from Horstmann Bros & Co for Pennsylvania Regiments," RG 25.

[5]Wilson to Adjutant-General A. L. Russell, November 18, 1864, RG 19; Wilson to Colonel S. B. Thomas, October 31, 1864, Regimental Letter Book, RG 94; Wilson to Thomas, January 20, 1865, *Ibid.*

[6]Wilson to Colonel Frank Jordan, January 16, 1865; Wilson to Russell, June 14, 1865, both in Regimental Letter Book, RG 94.

[7]Wilson to Russell, June 14, 1865, *Ibid.*

[8]Wilson to Russell, May 23, 1866, RG 19.

[9]Wilson to Russell, June 14, 1865, RG 94; Wilson to Russell, RG 19.

[10]Wilson to Russell, November 21, 1864, Regimental Letter Book, RG 94.

[11]*Pennsylvania at Gettysburg* 1: 416.

Bibliography

Except for the sketches in Bates, Taylor, and *Pennsylvania at Gettysburg*, the author has not located any other information about the regiment.

82nd Infantry

State Color

Originally numbered as the 31st Pennsylvania, the regiment was renumbered 82nd shortly after the Battle of Fair Oaks, when several Pennsylvania units were redesignated to sort out the confusion over the double numbering system of the Reserve Corps. The 82nd was recruited primarily in Philadelphia and organized during the late summer of 1861, when it was rushed to Washington. Governor Curtin visited the regimental camp on February 15, 1862, and presented a state color.[1] The 82nd remained in camp near the city throughout the winter of 1861-62.

In March 1862, the unit took part in the occupation of Manassas, then moved with the Army of the Potomac to the Yorktown Peninsula. Its first combat action was at Fair Oaks on May 31-June 1, 1862, where, as part of the Fourth Corps, the 82nd contended with the Confederate attack on the corps. During the Seven Days' Battles, the 82nd was engaged only at Malvern Hill on July 1. After the army withdrew to Harrison's Landing, the 82nd participated in a reconnaissance to the Malvern Hill area on August 5. Upon the withdrawal of the army to northern Virginia, the Fourth Corps arrived too late to fight at Second Manassas. The corps remained in the Washington defenses, but the Second Division, to which the 82nd was attached, was detached to join the main army. The division arrived on the Antietam battlefield after the fighting there on September 17 had ended. As the army returned to Virginia, the division was added to the Sixth Corps as the Third Division. In its final action of 1862, the 82nd was present at Fredericksburg on December 13 but not actively engaged.

After spending the winter of 1862-63 in camp near Fredericksburg, the 82nd took part in the May 3 assault of the Sixth Corps on Marye's Heights. As one of the attacking columns started forward, the first two regiments suffered heavy casualties and the column faltered. Seeing this, Colonel Alexander Shaler of the 65th New York rode forward to the head of the 82nd, the third regiment in line. Colonel Shaler took the regiment's color and called upon the rest of the column

to follow him. The colonel's brave act inspired the attackers, who swept up the hill and captured the enemy's position. Shaler later was awarded a Medal of Honor for this action.[2]

The regiment then participated in the ensuing Battle of Salem Church on May 3-4 before the corps withdrew across the Rappahannock at Banks' Ford. During the Gettysburg Campaign, the Sixth Corps protected the army's right flank and did not arrive on the battlefield until late on July 2. The 82nd reinforced the Yankee troops on Culp's Hill but was not heavily engaged. It then aided in the pursuit of Lee's defeated army back to Virginia, taking part in the Bristoe Station and Mine Run campaigns before erecting winter quarters near Brandy Station. During the winter, several regiments of the corps including the 82nd, were detached and sent to the prison camp on Johnson's Island, Lake Erie, off Sandusky, Ohio. It was feared that an attempt would be made by Confederate agents in Canada to cross the frozen lake and attempt a rescue.

State Color
Maker: HB
Size: 72³/₈" × 77⁷/₈"
1985.137

The 82nd rejoined the Army of the Potomac in mid-May 1864, in time to take part in the skirmishing along the North Anna River. On June 1, the regiment was part of the unsuccessful attack at Cold Harbor, more than half of its effective strength being lost. During the initial assaults on Petersburg, the regiment suffered few casualties. In July, the corps was detached and sent to Washington to help drive away a Rebel attack on the city. It moved into the Shenandoah Valley and fought at Winchester on September 19. At this time, many of the 82nd's men were sent home when their enlistments expired. The remainder of the regiment was consolidated into a battalion of five companies.

After the successful conclusion of the Shenandoah Valley campaign, the corps returned to Petersburg and took part in the April 2, 1865, capture of the city. The 82nd's final engagement took place at Saylor's Creek on April 6, where it suffered about a hundred casualties. It returned to Washington and was mustered out of service on July 13, 1865. The state color was turned over to the Commonwealth on July 4, 1866, when General Meade used the flag to represent the entire collection.[3]

Philadelphia Flags

During its term of service, the 82nd received at least four colors from groups of Philadelphia friends. Two flags, one a national and the other a state regimental, were presented on October 23, 1861, at the regiment's Washington camp.[4] Two others were given on February 5, 1864, at an Independence Square ceremony. Colonel James Page presented all four flags in both ceremonies.[5] These latter two flags seem to have been carried in the 1864 and 1865 battles. As the regiment lay in battleline at Cold Harbor on June 2, 1864, an artillery shell severely damaged the staff of the na-

Left: *Repairs to the June 2, 1864, Damaged Staff of the National Color Carried by Sergeant Waterhouse*

Right: *One of the National Colors Carried by the 82nd Regiment*

tional color. Sergeant George Waterhouse, the bearer, spliced the staff together with pieces of a stair rod found in an abandoned house on the field.[6] The postwar history of these flags is difficult to discern with accuracy. The 1861 regimental color seems to have been given to the state sometime between 1887 and 1896. The Regimental Association gave four flags and

Obverse

Regimental Color
Size: 55½" × 72½"
1985.136

Reverse

Advance the Colors!

three guidons to G.A.R. Post One in April 1887, with the proviso that the Association could use them in local parades from time to time. On November 22, 1919, the G.A.R. Post gave its flag collection to the Union League. The list included four colors of the 82nd.[7] In 1977, the Union League donated its collection to the State Museum. Only the color that Waterhouse carried in 1864 could be identified. Two additional colors, a national and regimental (state arms on one side, national on the other) are owned by the Philadelphia Camp, Sons of Union Veterans.

Color-Bearer

At Fair Oaks, Sergeant William H. Gibson of Company C was wounded on May 31, 1862. The sergeant was struck in the pit of his stomach by a spent bullet and was bruised quite badly.[8]

Notes

[1]*Raftsman's Journal* (Clearfield), February 26, 1862.

[2]Beyer-Keydel, pp. 150-151.

[3]There was apparently a small controversy over the return of the state color. See Quartermaster-General James L. Reynolds's office to Captain F. H. Peters, April 13, 1866, and attached correspondence with Colonel Isaac Bassett, RG 19.

[4]Scharf-Westcott, p. 785; "Presentation of Standards," *Philadelphia Inquirer*, October 29, 1861.

[5]"Presentation of Flags," *Philadelphia Public Ledger*, February 6, 1864.

[6]*Union League of Philadelphia, Annual Report 1919*, p. 98.

[7]*Ibid.*; Document of Transferral, April 25, 1887, 82nd Pennsylvania to G.A.R. Post One, in "Flags Presentation" folder, Archives of the Union League.

[8]*O.R.* 11.1, p. 904.

Bibliography

Hug, Andrew. 1863 Diary. USAMHI.

Perry, W. W. "The Sixth Corps at the Wilderness." *National Tribune*, February 18, 1886.

Wetherill, John M. "The Eighty-second Regiment Pennsylvania Volunteers in the Gettysburg Campaign." *Philadelphia Weekly Press*, February 17, 1886.

83rd Infantry

First State Color

The 83rd Pennsylvania was recruited in the Commonwealth's northwest counties and was organized in September 1861 at a camp near Erie. The new regiment then moved directly to Washington, going into camp near Arlington. It remained here throughout the winter of 1861-62. On December 21, 1861, Senator Edgar Cowan arrived in camp to present a state color on behalf of Governor Curtin.[1] Over the winter, the 83rd was assigned to a brigade in Fitz John Porter's division, which later became part of the Fifth Corps when that unit was created in the spring of 1862.

In March 1862, the division accompanied the Army of the Potomac to the Yorktown Peninsula, taking part in the Siege of Yorktown. The regiment first encountered the enemy at Hanover Court House on May 27, as Porter's troops reconnoitered this area. On June 27, the 83rd took part in the Battle of Gaines' Mill. During the initial stages of this engagement, the enemy approached the 83rd's position with line after line of the soldiers, intent on driving the outnumbered Yankees off the field. In the words of Lieutenant-Colonel H. S. Campbell:[2]

> At this moment, Brigadier-General [Daniel] Butterfield, amidst a galling fire from his lines of support in the rear and that of the enemy in front, came coolly down to the knoll, and, sword in hand, seized our colors, waving them repeatedly aloft, and by all mortal means encouraged the valor of our regiment. His presence at once stimulated with new vigor our now thinned ranks, when the general loudly shouted out, "Your ammunition is never expended while you have bayonets, my boys, and use them to the socket."

The general later received a Medal of Honor for this act of personal bravery.

Sergeant Alexander Rogers with the First State Color

Advance the Colors!

Bearer after bearer fell that bloody day. The original color-sergeant, J. C. McKinley of Company C, apparently fell in this combat and died on July 1.[3] After the staff had been shattered and the silken folds "pierced by untold numbers of balls," Corporal Walter Ames of Company K took the flag as the regiment fell back. Ames was shot through the heart on July 1 during the Battle of Malvern Hill as he stood in front of the regiment, waving his color at the oncoming enemy.[4] The fallen banner was seized by Alexander Rogers of Company F, who was promoted to corporal on July 19, and who would carry the state colors of the 83rd until killed in 1864.[5] During the Seven Days' Battles, the 83rd suffered a loss of 362, the fourth highest total in the entire army.

In August, the Army of the Potomac was withdrawn from the Peninsula and sent to northern Virginia to reinforce Pope's Army of Virginia. The 83rd took part in the Second Battle of Manassas on August 30, losing 97 of the 224 men who entered the fighting. During the Battle of Antietam on September 17, most of the Fifth Corps remained in reserve and was not engaged. In its final combat of 1862, the 83rd fought at Fredericksburg on December 13, after which the unit went into winter quarters.

During the winter, Corporal Rogers was promoted to sergeant and continued to carry the flag. On April 11, 1863, the Legislature passed Joint Resolution #11, authorizing replacement colors for four regiments, including the 83rd. Colonel Strong Vincent approved of the new color, but felt his men's hesitation to accept a new flag, remarking that "a fresh, bright color assuming the place of the old one, makes them all look, the men say, like a new regiment. This sensitiveness is an honorable and a natural one, and I feel disposed, if possible, to gratify and respect it."[6]

A new state color was finished and sent to the 83rd sometime in May. It is not known if the 83rd carried their original color at Chancellorsville and Gettysburg. After this latter battle, Captain Amos Judson went home to Erie on leave and took the first state color with him. On July 30, Captain Judson presented the flag to the city of Erie. A large crowd witnessed the presentation, which took place at Brown's Hotel. A reporter noted that the flag was ". . . so pierced with bullet holes that it scarcely holds together."[7] This flag is presently housed in the Erie County Library System building in Erie.

Second State Color

The second flag given to the 83rd was originally intended for the 157th, and was altered for use by the 83rd. It is not known exactly when the regiment re-

Second State Color
Maker: HB
Size: 71" × 77¹⁄₈"
1985.140

ceived this banner, which was forwarded to the state on May 16, 1863. After participating in the fighting at Chancellorsville and Gettysburg, the 83rd returned to Virginia and took part in the Bristoe Station and Mine Run campaigns before settling into winter quarters.

During Grant's 1864 campaign against Lee's army, the 83rd fought in all the major engagements, beginning with the Battle of the Wilderness on May 5-7. On the first day of this battle, Sergeant Rogers was among the slain. As Rogers fell, Corporal M. Francis Vogus of Company G rescued the flag and carried it for three days. On May 8, the regiment charged the enemy breastworks at Laurel Hill at the opening of the series of engagements collectively known as Spotsylvania. During the assault, Vogus was severely wounded. Color-Corporal John Lillibridge then grabbed the flag and carried it forward a short distance until Vogus caught up with the regiment and reclaimed the flag. Vogus reached the enemy works and planted the flag. As he did, he was shot through the breast and fell, hurling the flag to the rear to prevent the enemy from capturing the banner. Corporal Daniel Jones rescued the colors but was quickly wounded. As he limped to the rear, Jones gave the battered flag to a member of the 44th New York, who took it to the rear as the attackers fell back. Eventually, Sergeant Isaac Keck reclaimed the flag for the 83rd.[8]

The regiment then took part in the fighting along the North Anna River (May 23-25), Cold Harbor (June 1-3), and the June assaults on Petersburg. During the operations around Petersburg, the 83rd fought in the engagement along the Weldon Railroad (August 18-21), Poplar Springs Church (September 30), and Hatcher's Run (October 27-28). Prior to the fighting at Poplar Springs Church, Corporal Vogus had recovered from his wounds and was appointed color-bearer.[9] In mid-September, many enlistments expired and the regiment was reduced to six companies. Four new companies were added to the 83rd in early 1865. The regiment's last engagements with the enemy were at Hatcher's Run (February 5-7, 1865) and Five Forks (March 31-April 1). After Lee's surrender at Appomattox the 83rd returned to Washington and was mustered out of service on June 28, 1865. The second state color was returned on July 4, 1866.

Third State Color

This banner was completed by Horstmann Brothers in late April 1865 and thus never saw combat. It was

Regimental Color
Size: 71¾" × 76⅝"
1985.139

Third State Color
Maker: HB
Size: 71" × 77¼"
1985.138

sent to the State Agency, forwarded to the 83rd, and taken home by Colonel Chauncey P. Rodgers. The colonel was contacted about returning the flag, but it was not received in Harrisburg until August 26, 1866.[10]

Regimental Color

According to the February 1865 quartermaster list, this national regimental color was returned in July 1865, suggesting that the 83rd carried it during its last months of service. Nothing else has been located to confirm its history.

Erie Flag

On January 8, 1862, Mrs. Colonel John W. McLane presented to the regiment a national flag of her own handiwork. Its subsequent history is unknown.[11] A flag marked as 83rd in the Erie County Library System building may be this very flag. According to the attached card, this banner was donated to the Library by G.A.R. Post 67 and the Ladies' Auxiliary on August 23, 1934.

Notes

[1]*Erie Weekly Gazette*, January 9, 1862.

[2]*O.R.* 11.2, p. 344.

[3]Judson, p. 29, mentions McKinley's name as bearer in March 1862. Bates 2: 1276, lists his death date.

[4]Judson, p. 48; *O.R.* 11.2, p. 345; Norton, p. 94.

[5]Judson, p. 48; Special Orders #89, July 19, 1862, Regimental Order Book, RG 94.

[6]Vincent to Matthew S. Quay, April 12, 1863, Regimental Letter Book, RG 94.

[7]"The 83rd's Battle Flag," *Erie Observer*, August 1, 1863.

[8]Judson, pp. 96-97.

[9]Special Orders #3, September 15, 1864, Regimental Order Book, RG 94.

[10]Rodgers to Adjutant-General A. L. Russell, May 28, 1866, RG 19.

[11]*Erie Weekly Gazette*, January 16, 1862.

Bibliography

Bedient, George H. "The 83rd Pennsylvania at Gaines' Mill." *National Tribune*, June 22, 1905.

Grimler, Joseph G. Letters, March 1862-August 1863. Erie County Historical Society.

Judson, Amos M. *History of the Eighty-third Regiment Pennsylvania Volunteers*. Erie: B. F. H. Lynn, 1865.

_____. Papers. Mercyhurst College.

Morrison, William J. Papers. Historical Society of Western Pennsylvania.

Norton, Oliver W. *Army Letters, 1861-1865*. Chicago: O. L. Deming, 1903.

_____. Scrapbooks. Central Michigan University.

Platt, Philander. "On Little Round Top." *National Tribune*, April 11, 1907.

Potter, J. B. "Rappahannock Station." *National Tribune*, May 24, 1888.

Stafford, David W. *In Defense of the Flag, a True War Story, a Pen Picture of Scenes and Incidents During the Great Rebellion, . . .* Erie: Warren Mirror Print, 1917.

Stoudt, David B. Letters, August-November 1864. USAMHI, CWTI Collection.

84th Infantry

State Color

Recruited in 1861 under the direction of Colonel William G. Murray, the 84th Regiment assembled at a camp near Huntingdon before moving to Camp Curtin in November. On December 21, Colonel Murray marched the regiment into the city and halted in front of the Capitol. Governor Curtin then appeared and presented a state color to the colonel, who in turn gave the banner to Sergeant Edward Stokes of Company B, who was admonished to protect it with his life. Stokes's reply was brief and to the point: "If I don't return this flag 'twill be because Ned Stokes will occupy five feet eight on the ground."[1]

Ten days later, the 84th was rushed to Hancock, Maryland, to reinforce the garrison at that point, which was threatened by a Confederate force under Stonewall Jackson's command. After the enemy moved out of the area, the regiment spent the winter helping guard the Baltimore and Ohio Railroad. In March, troops under Brigadier-General James Shields marched south and occupied Winchester. Jackson's

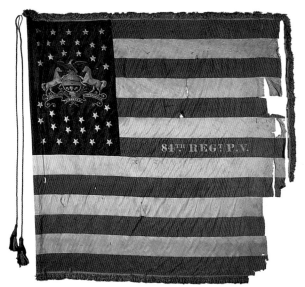

State Color
Maker: HB
Size: 72½" × 78¾"
1985.142

Rebels moved north and attacked Shields's division at Kernstown on March 23, 1862. The 84th lost heavily in this engagement as it charged a stonewall occupied by the enemy. Colonel Murray was killed and Color-Sergeant Hugh Smith of Company D was severely wounded as the regiment surged forward. Another bearer was shot down when Sergeant Thomas Gouldsberry of Company I seized the fallen color. The intrepid sergeant ran in front of the battleline, shouting defiance at the enemy before he was ordered back into line. After the battle ended in a Federal victory, Gouldsberry counted thirty-one bullet holes in the silken flag.[2]

During the succeeding operations in the Shenandoah Valley, the 84th was engaged at Port Republic on June 9. The regiment moved with its brigade to northern Virginia and became part of the Army of Virginia, taking a brief part in the concluding phase of the Battle of Cedar Mountain on August 9. It then fought at Second Manassas on August 30. Thereafter, the regiment remained in the Washington defenses and did not take part in the Maryland Campaign. The 84th was then assigned to the Third Corps, which rejoined the Army of the Potomac in October.

In early November, three captains of the 84th went to Harrisburg to return to the Commonwealth the battered state color, "nearly worn out by use." The flag was presented to the state and remained in Harrisburg until officially returned during the 1866 ceremony in Philadelphia.[3]

Williamsport Flag

On Saturday evening, September 20, 1862, Colonel Samuel M. Bowman received a "beautiful flag" from the ladies of Williamsport, the presentation taking place at the Lycoming County Courthouse. This banner was some type of national color containing the name of the regiment within the canton, and the battle honor "Winchester" on one of the stripes.[4]

This national color was apparently carried by the regiment during the remainder of its term of service, and was used in lieu of a replacement state color. The

Advance the Colors!

First Regimental Color
Maker: HB
Size: 68¹/₈″ × 79⁵/₈″
1985.143

Second Regimental Color
Size: 71⁷/₈″ × 80³/₄″
1985.141

84th rejoined the army in October and fought at Fredericksburg on December 13. After wintering near Falmouth, the regiment fought at Chancellorsville on May 3, 1863. During the close and bloody fighting that day, Color-Sergeant Charles White was "shot dead with the colors in his hands."[5] Of the 391 officers and men taken into the battle, 215 were casualties. Because of this heavy loss, the regiment was detached as wagon train guards and did not take part in the Battle of Gettysburg. It participated in the fall campaigns in northern Virginia, then went into winter quarters near Brandy Station.

In 1864, the regiment was transferred to the Second Corps when the Third Corps was discontinued as a separate organization. It then fought in the major battles of Grant's campaign, including the Wilderness (May 5-6), Spotsylvania (May 10 and 12 especially), North Anna River (May 23-24), Cold Harbor (June 2), and in the initial assaults on Petersburg. During the operations around Petersburg, the regiment fought twice at Deep Bottom (July 27-29 and August 15-16), Poplar Springs Church (October 2), and the Boydton Plank Road (October 27-28). By that time, the regiment had been consolidated into a four-company battalion, and in January 1865 was merged with the 57th Pennsylvania and served with that unit until mustered

out of service in June. The Williamsport flag seems not to have survived its postwar disposition.

Regimental Colors

There are two surviving regimental colors for the 84th. The first was presented to the regiment by Colonel Murray about the same time the state color was received. It was carried by the 84th at Kernstown, where at least one bearer was shot down and the staff broken by the enemy's bullets. The silk was pierced by thirty bullets. When three officers of the regiment went to Harrisburg in November 1862 to return the state color, they took this regimental color and presented it to the governor in person, noting that although the flag had suffered extensive battle damage, none of the stars had been injured. "As it is with those stars, may it be with the States they represent."[6]

The second regimental color seems to have been carried after the first was returned. It contains the remnant of the "Winchester" battle honor. The 84th was carrying two colors at Mine Run in November 1863, and the author assumes that the second flag was this regimental color. It was received by the state quartermaster-general on July 17, 1865, suggesting that it was carried until the regiment disbanded.[7]

Notes

[1]"Colonel Murray's Regiment—Flag Presentation," *Harrisburg Patriot and Union*, December 23, 1861; "Flag Presentation," *Muncy Luminary*, December 31, 1861.

[2]Thomas H. Craig, "Shields's Division," *National Tribune*, November 21, 1889; Thomas Gouldsberry to father, May 6, 1862, Gouldsberry Papers. Bates (2: 1331) as well as the pension letters in Gouldsberry's Papers, spell the sergeant's name "Goldsborough," but the sergeant spelled it "Gouldsberry" in his letters home.

[3]Colonel S. M. Bowman to Governor Curtin, October 23, 1862; Captain P. F. Walsh to Colonel Bowman, November 6, 1862, both in Regimental Papers, RG 19.

[4]"Flag Presentation," *Lycoming Gazette*, September 24, 1862.

[5]"The 84th Penn'a.," *Raftsman's Journal* (Clearfield), May 20, 1863. Bates 2: 1334, notes that Sergeant White was wounded and captured rather than killed.

[6]Walsh to Bowman, November 6, 1862; "Flag Presentation," *Harrisburg Patriot and Union*, November 7, 1862.

[7]*Pennsylvania at Gettysburg* 1: 461.

Bibliography

Aurandt, Alfred. Papers. The Pennsylvania State University.

Collins, Emerson. "Colonel Milton Opp." *Now and Then* 18 (October 1975): 229-231.

Craig, Thomas H. "Shields's Division. A Delayed Report of the 84th Pennsylvania at Kernstown." *National Tribune*, November 21, 1889.

Fowler, Thomas C. "Criticizing Capehart. The Troops that Captured the Stonewall at Kernstown." *National Tribune*, May 16, 1889.

Gouldsberry, Thomas. Papers. USAMHI, Save the Flags Collection.

Lamberton, Robert C. Diary. Cumberland County Historical Society.

Weidensall, J. "The 'Bull Pen.' A Few Incidents of the Fight at Hatcher's Run." *National Tribune*, January 14, 1886.

Wells, Harvey S. "The Eighty-fourth Pennsylvania Volunteer Infantry in the Late War." *Philadelphia Weekly Times*, April 10, 1886.

_____. "Second Bull Run." *Philadelphia Weekly Times*, July 18, 1885.

_____. "With Shields in 1862." *Philadelphia Weekly Times*, March 28, 1885.

85th Infantry

First State Color

Organized at Uniontown, Fayette County, under authority granted to Colonel Joshua B. Howell, the 85th Regiment was called to Washington in November 1861. The regiment's train arrived in Harrisburg for a brief stop late in the afternoon of November 21. The men formed line near the Round House and received a state color from Governor Curtin before continuing on to Washington.[1] During the winter of 1861-62, the regiment remained near Washington, drilling and preparing for the campaigns ahead.

In March 1862, the regiment, now attached to the Fourth Corps of the Army of the Potomac, moved by water to the Yorktown Peninsula, taking part in the April-May Siege of Yorktown. It was under artillery fire at Williamsburg on May 5, suffering few casualties. The regiment's first battle was at Fair Oaks on May 31, where the Second Division of the corps was driven from its position after delaying the enemy advance for several hours. During the Seven Days' Battles, the corps guarded the army's left flank and was not actively engaged with the enemy. When the army

withdrew from the Peninsula in August, the division remained behind as part of the garrison. The 85th was sent to Suffolk in September, remaining there until early December.

At that time, the brigade to which the 85th was attached was ordered to North Carolina, arriving at New Bern on December 9. Two days later, the bulk of the Federal troops concentrated there marched toward Goldsboro to interdict the railroad at that place. The 85th fought in several small engagements during this expedition, the most important being at Kinston on December 14. After returning to New Bern, the regiment remained in camp until late January 1863, when the brigade was transferred to South Carolina, arriving at Hilton Head Island on January 26.

The regiment remained on this island until April 1863, when it moved to Folly Island to take part in an expedition against Charleston. Federal troops toiled away in the heat until September 7, when the 85th was among the troops to occupy Battery Wagner as the Rebels withdrew from the island. The 85th remained as part of the garrison until December, when it returned to Hilton Head.

Second State Color

Information has not been found to indicate when the 85th returned its original state color. In addition to the first, there are two bills for 85th state colors. An Evans & Hassall bill is dated December 5, 1863, while a Horstmann bill is dated July 2, 1864. However, Lieutenant-Colonel Edward Campbell informed Adjutant-General Russell that the regiment received only two flags from the state.[2] The second flag's canton indicates that it is an Evans & Hassall manufacture, and was probably received by the regiment sometime late in December 1863, when Campbell returned from leave.[3]

The regiment moved to Virginia in April 1864 as part of the Army of the James. It fought in several skirmishes in the Bermuda Hundred area, most notably at Ware Bottom Church on May 20. After skirmishing with the enemy during the June 16-18 Petersburg assaults, the regiment charged the Confederate

First State Color
Maker: EH
Size: 71¾" × 40" (-)
1985.144

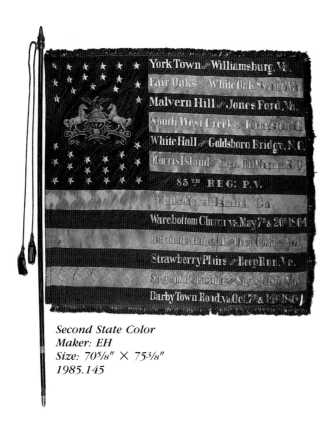

Second State Color
Maker: EH
Size: 70⁵⁄₈" × 75³⁄₈"
1985.145

Oaks. Corporal Richard Lincoln then grabbed the flag but was wounded and the staff was shattered by a bullet. Another bearer, Jacob Deffenbaugh of Company I, then carried the flag off the field as the regiment withdrew. Deffenbaugh was bearer until July 1863, when Private George Orbin of Company C carried the flag. On May 1, 1864, Corporal Alexander Ross was appointed bearer and carried the flag until November. During the fighting at Deep Bottom on August 16, a minie ball hit and embedded itself in the finial.

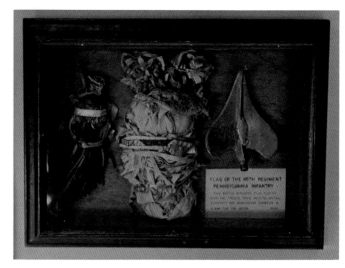

Surviving Relics of the Uniontown Flag

fortifications at Deep Bottom on August 16, losing more than one-third casualties. Sergeant John Moore, bearer of the state color, was mentioned by name in the battle report because of his gallantry in this engagement.[4] After this battle, the regiment fought at New Market Heights (September 29-30) and at the Darbytown Road (October 7 and 13). In November most of the regiment was sent home for muster out. Those who remained at the front were consolidated with the 188th Pennsylvania. The second state color was left in Harrisburg as the regiment passed through on its way to Pittsburgh; both were officially returned in 1866.

Uniontown Flag

On November 18, 1861, the 85th received a silk national flag from a committee of Uniontown ladies who had collected funds to buy the silk. The flag was sewn by Miss Elizabeth Hadden. Sergeant Joseph G. Reager was chosen to carry the flag, which he did until April 27, 1862. At this point, the booklet describing the history of this banner is confused. Apparently, the next bearer was wounded and captured at Fair

At the end of the war, the regiment gave the flag to Sergeant John G. Stevens. In 1873, the survivors began organizing annual reunions, and the flag was apparently shown at many of these until 1898, when the Regimental Association initiated court proceedings to obtain the banner from Sergeant Stevens. The flag had been given to different bearers at many of the reunions, and it appears that Stevens finally kept the flag, complaining that other members had all but destroyed the flag at the reunions by cutting off pieces as souvenirs. The case eventually went to the superior court in Pittsburgh, which ruled in favor of Sergeant Stevens, thus allowing him to keep the flag. It was eventually acquired by the Westmoreland-Fayette Historical Society, and recently by Ronn Palm. Pieces of the white stripes, a tassel, and the damaged finial are all that remain of this banner.[5]

Advance the Colors!

Notes

[1] "Presentation of a Flag to Col. Howell's Regiment," *Harrisburg Patriot and Union*, November 22, 1861.

[2] Campbell to Russell, May 31, 1866, RG 19.

[3] Campbell to Russell, December 15, 1863, Regimental Papers, RG 19.

[4] *O.R.* 42.1, p. 702.

[5] Information about this flag can be found in Hadden, *Old Flag*.

Bibliography

Dawson, Richard W. Papers. Duke University.

Dickey, Luther S. *History of the Eighty-fifth Regiment Pennsylvania Volunteer Infantry, 1861-1865, Comprising an Authentic Narrative of Casey's Division at the Battle of Seven Pines.* New York: J. C. & W. E. Powers, 1915.

Gordon, Marquis L. *M. L. Gordon's Experiences in the Civil War, From His Narrative, Letters and Diary.* Boston: Merrymount Press, 1922.

Hadden, James. *History of the Old Flag of the 85th Reg't.* Uniontown: The News Standard, 1901.

Howell, Joshua B. Papers. Duke University.

McHenry, S. L. "The Deeds and Sacrifices of the Eighty-fifth Pennsylvania." *Philadelphia Weekly Times*, July 3, 1886.

87th Infantry

State Color

The 87th Pennsylvania was organized at York in September 1861 and immediately dispatched to guard the Northern Central Railroad from the Pennsylvania border to Baltimore, a duty which lasted until late May 1862. On February 22, 1862, the seven companies of the regiment that were closest to Baltimore were assembled and marched into the city, halting at Monument Square. Here, one of Governor Curtin's staff presented a state color to the regiment.[1]

In late May, the entire regiment assembled for the first time and remained in Baltimore for a month, then was ordered to West Virginia for duty. The 87th was first stationed along the Baltimore and Ohio Railroad at New Creek, then took part in an August expedition that chased Confederate irregular forces south to Beverly. In September, the regiment retreated briefly to Clarksburg, then participated in much arduous marching through the mountains attempting to drive enemy guerrillas out of the area. The regiment was assigned to Major-General Robert Milroy's Eighth Corps division in October. Milroy's troops slogged through the winter mud and snow to reach Winchester, Virginia, in late December.

Battle Record Banner
Size: 31¼" × 54⅝"
1985.004b

The division remained near the town until June 1863. At that time, the Second Corps of General Lee's army, on its way north to Gettysburg, attacked the division and effectively scattered the outnumbered Yankees at Stephenson's Depot (or Carter's Woods) on June 15. The 87th suffered 112 casualties as Milroy's regiments were crushed by Lee's veterans. Part of the regiment managed to retreat to Harper's Ferry, while another column reached Bloody Run, Pennsylvania. After Lee's retreat, the division was reorganized and assigned to the Army of the Potomac's Third Corps, taking part in the Bristoe Station and Mine Run campaigns before erecting winter quarters near Brandy Station.

In 1864, the division was transferred to the Sixth Corps. The regiment fought in the Wilderness (May 5-7), at Spotsylvania (May 8-18), along the North Anna River (May 23-26), and at Cold Harbor (June 1-3). The army then crossed the James River and assaulted the Petersburg defenses. The 87th was engaged primarily on June 23 at the Weldon Railroad. The division then

State Color
Maker: HB
Size: 71⅝" × 41¼" (-)
1985.004a

was transferred to Washington as Jubal Early's Confederates' invaded Maryland. After fighting at Monocacy on July 9 to delay the advance, the Federals retired to the Washington defenses. During the succeeding Shenandoah Valley Campaign, the 87th fought at Winchester on September 19, Fisher's Hill on September 21-22, and at Cedar Creek on October 19.

By this time, the regiment had been reduced to five companies when those who had not re-enlisted went home. These men took the small remnant of the state color along home and gave it to George Hay, the regiment's first colonel. Hay kept the flag until early June 1866, when he was contacted about returning it for inclusion in the July 4 ceremony.[2] Since the flag had almost been completely shot to pieces, friends of the 87th presented the survivors with a small banner containing the names of the principal battles in which they had fought.[3] This banner was attached to the staff with the remaining portion of the state color and given to the Commonwealth in 1866.

National Color

Sometime in early 1864, Sergeant Jonathan J. Keesey of Company C procured a national color for the 87th. It was paid for by those soldiers who had re-enlisted for a second three-year term of service. Keesey apparently carried this flag until he was wounded at Winchester on September 19, 1864. Captain Murray S. Cross then retrieved the fallen banner and asked for a volunteer to carry it forward. Corporal Daniel P. Reigle of Company E stepped forward and took the flag. He was still carrying it at Cedar Creek when his captain was shot down. The corporal stuck the flag in the ground and helped carry his commander to the rear. As he did so, the Federal line began to fall back and the Rebels had approached to within ten yards before Reigle was able to reach the flag and save it

Above: *Sergeant Reigle (left) Poses with His Flag and a Fellow veteran*
Below: *Sergeant Reigle's Medal of Honor*

from capture. Later in the battle, Reigle led the regiment forward in a counterattack and captured an enemy battleflag. For his gallantry in this battle, Reigle received a Medal of Honor.[4]

After spending a thirty-five day furlough at home, Reigle came back and carried the flag until the end of the war. The 87th returned to Petersburg in Decem-

National Color After Conservation

ber 1864 and by early spring had been rebuilt with five new companies. It took part in the April 2, 1865, assault on Petersburg and fought at Saylor's Creek on April 6. After Lee surrendered, the 87th moved to Alexandria and was mustered out of service on June 29. On this date, the national color was given to Reigle to keep. He brought the banner to several postwar reunions as late as the 1897 reunion in York.[5] At some point both the flag and the Medal were acquired for the Rosensteel Collection in the Gettysburg National Museum, Incorporated, now owned by Gettysburg National Military Park. Reigle's items are on display in the Visitors' Center at the park.

Company F Flag

In early February 1862, Major C. H. Buehler presented a flag to Captain William J. Martin's Company F. No other information about this flag has been located.[6]

Notes

[1]"Flag Presentation," *York Gazette*, March 4, 1862.
[2]Colonel James Tearney to Adjutant-General A. L. Russell, May 24, 1866; Colonel John W. Schall to Russell, June 4, 1866, both in RG 19.
[3]Prowell, pp. 252-253.
[4]*Ibid*., pp. 207, 216, 303; General affadavit of Henry H. Smith, February 20, 1888, in Reigle File, Gettysburg National Military Park Library.
[5]Prowell, pp. 220, 261.
[6]"Flag Presentation," *Adams Sentinel*, February 5, 1862.

Bibliography

Crowl, Thomas O. Papers. The Pennsylvania State University.

Ebrehart, D. C. "In the Enemy's Lines After Winchester, What a Chaplain Saw." *Grand Army Scout and Soldiers Mail*, October 13, 20, 27, November 3, 1883.

Hartman, William. Letters, February 1862-January 1863. USAMHI, George Miller Collection.

Oren James. "The Sixth Corps at Cold Harbor." *National Tribune,* July 10, 1884.

Prowell, George R. *History of the Eighty-seventh Regiment, Pennsylvania Volunteers, Prepared from Official Records, Diaries, and Other Authentic Sources of Information.* York: Press of the York Daily, 1901.

Schaffner, Daniel. 1865 Diary, March 21-July 3. In Schaffner Family Papers, Pennsylvania State Archives.

Stahle, James A. Papers. USAMHI, HbCWRT Collection.

ATLAS

Theatres of Operations of
Pennsylvania Troops in the Civil War

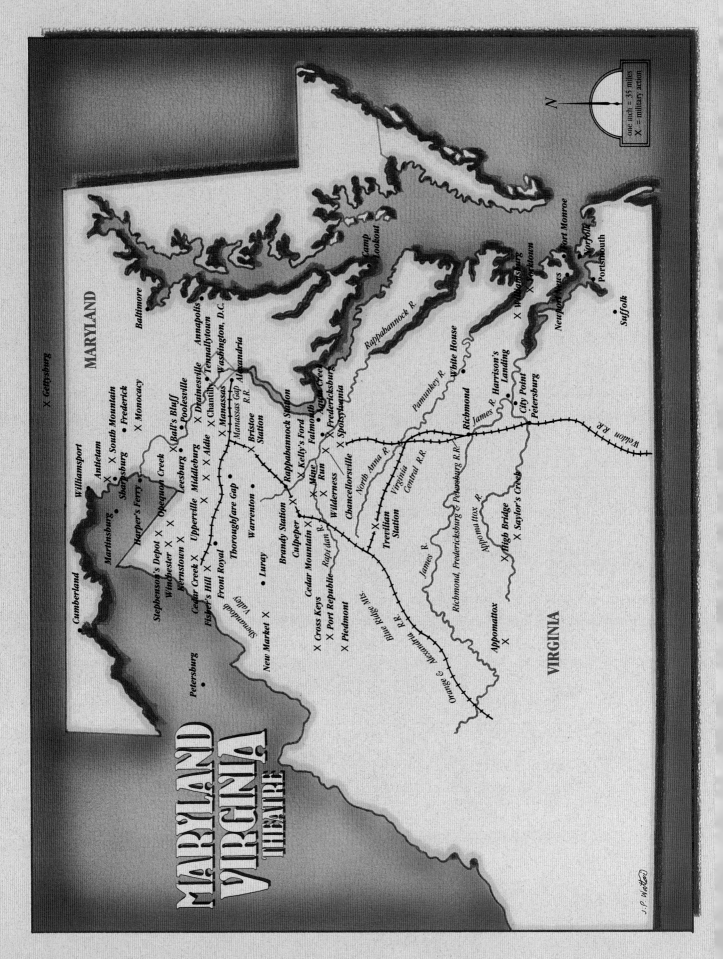

MARYLAND VIRGINIA THEATRE

one inch = 35 miles
X = military action

N

MARYLAND

Gettysburg X

Cumberland

Williamsport

Antietam
X South Mountain
X Frederick
Sharpsburg X
X Monocacy

Baltimore

Harper's Ferry

Opequon Creek

Ball's Bluff
X Poolesville
X Drainesville
Leesburg X Aldie
Middleburg
Upperville X

Annapolis
Tennallytown
Washington, D.C.
Alexandria

Martinsburg X
Stephenson's Depot X
Winchester X
Kernstown X
Fisher's Hill X
Cedar Creek X

Front Royal

Thoroughfare Gap

Manassas Gap R.R.

Manassas X
Bristoe Station X
Warrenton X

Rappahannock Station X

Camp Lookout

Rappahannock R.

New Market X

Luray

Cross Keys X
Port Republic X
Piedmont X

Shenandoah Valley

Brandy Station X
Culpeper X
Cedar Mountain X

Blue Ridge Mts.

Rapidan R.

Kelly's Ford X
Mine Run X
Wilderness X
Chancellorsville

Spotsylvania X
Fredericksburg X
Falmouth

Aquia Creek

North Anna R.

Trevilian Station X

Virginia Central R.R.

Pamunkey R.

White House

Richmond

James R.

Harrison's Landing
City Point
Petersburg

Williamsburg X
Yorktown X
Newport News
Fort Monroe
Norfolk
Portsmouth

Suffolk

Appomattox X

High Bridge X
Saylor's Creek X

Appomattox R.

Richmond, Fredericksburg & Petersburg R.R.

James R.

Orange & Alexandria R.R.

VIRGINIA

Weldon R.R.

Petersburg

J.P. Watters

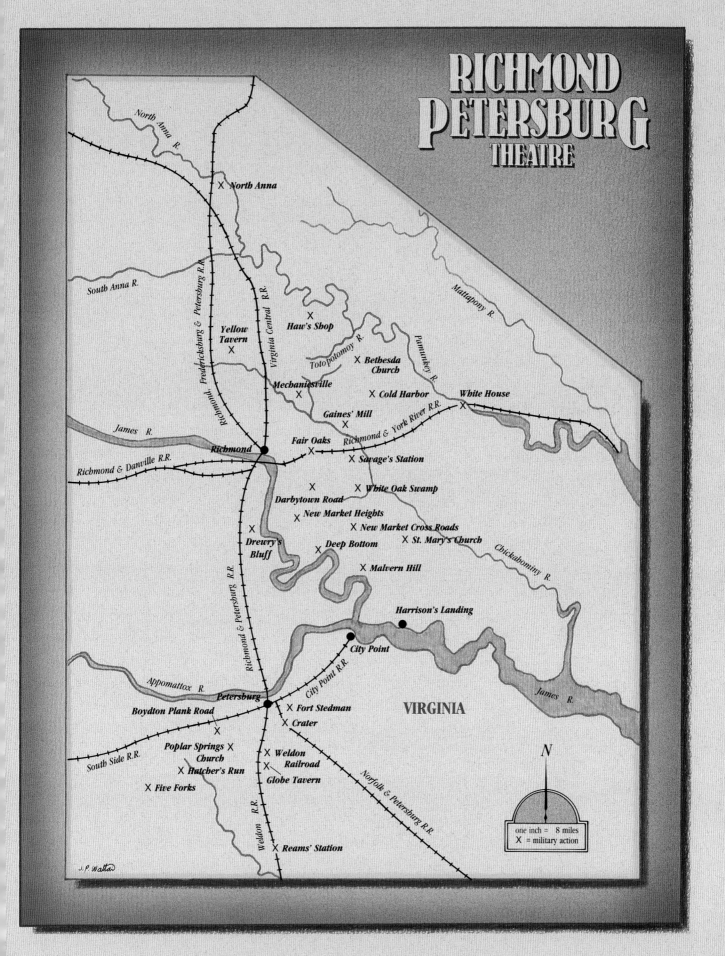

RICHMOND
PETERSBURG
THEATRE

North Anna R.

South Anna R.

X North Anna

Mattapony R.

Yellow
Tavern

Virginia Central R.R.

Richmond, Fredericksburg & Petersburg R.R.

X Haw's Shop

Totopotomoy R.

X Bethesda
Church

Pamunkey R.

Mechanicsville

X Cold Harbor

White House

James R.

Gaines' Mill

Richmond & York River R.R.

Richmond

Fair Oaks

X Savage's Station

Richmond & Danville R.R.

X White Oak Swamp

Darbytown Road

X New Market Heights

X New Market Cross Roads

Drewry's
Bluff

Deep Bottom

X St. Mary's Church

Chickahominy R.

Richmond & Petersburg R.R.

X Malvern Hill

Harrison's Landing

City Point

Appomattox R.

Petersburg

City Point R.R.

James R.

VIRGINIA

Boydton Plank Road

X Fort Stedman

X Crater

South Side R.R.

Poplar Springs X
Church

X Hatcher's Run

X Weldon
Railroad

X
Globe Tavern

Norfolk & Petersburg R.R.

X Five Forks

Weldon R.R.

N

X Reams' Station

one inch = 8 miles
X = military action

J.P. Walton

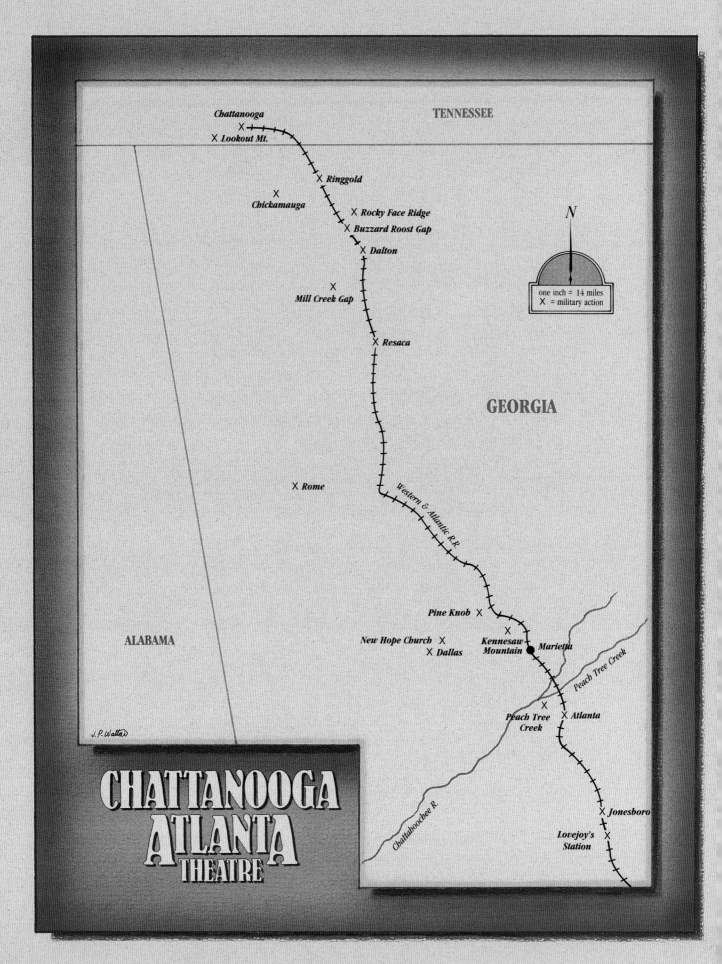

Chattanooga
X
X Lookout Mt.

TENNESSEE

X Ringgold

X Chickamauga

X Rocky Face Ridge
X Buzzard Roost Gap
X Dalton

X Mill Creek Gap

X Resaca

GEORGIA

N

one inch = 14 miles
X = military action

X Rome

Western & Atlantic R.R.

Pine Knob X

New Hope Church X
X Dallas

Kennesaw
Mountain ● Marietta

Peach Tree Creek

ALABAMA

Peach Tree
Creek
X
X Atlanta

Chattahoochee R.

X Jonesboro

Lovejoy's
Station
X

J. P. Wallai

**CHATTANOOGA
ATLANTA
THEATRE**

Advance the Colors!

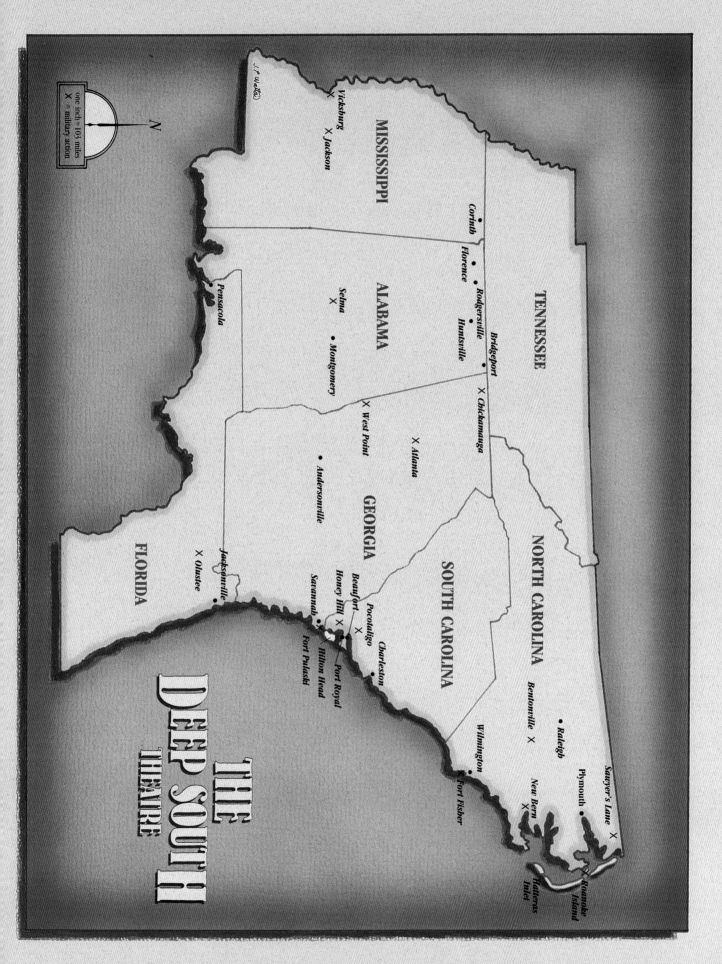

THE DEEP SOUTH THEATRE

one inch = 103 miles
X = military action

N

MISSISSIPPI

Vicksburg X

X Jackson

Corinth

Florence

Rodgersville

Huntsville

Pensacola

Selma X

Montgomery

ALABAMA

TENNESSEE

Bridgeport

X Chickamauga

X West Point

X Atlanta

Andersonville

GEORGIA

FLORIDA

Jacksonville

X Olustee

Savannah

Fort Pulaski

Hilton Head

Port Royal

Honey Hill X

Beaufort

Pocotaligo X

Charleston

SOUTH CAROLINA

NORTH CAROLINA

Bentonville X

Wilmington

Fort Fisher X

New Bern X

Raleigh

Plymouth

Sawyer's Lane X

Hatteras Inlet

Roanoke Island X

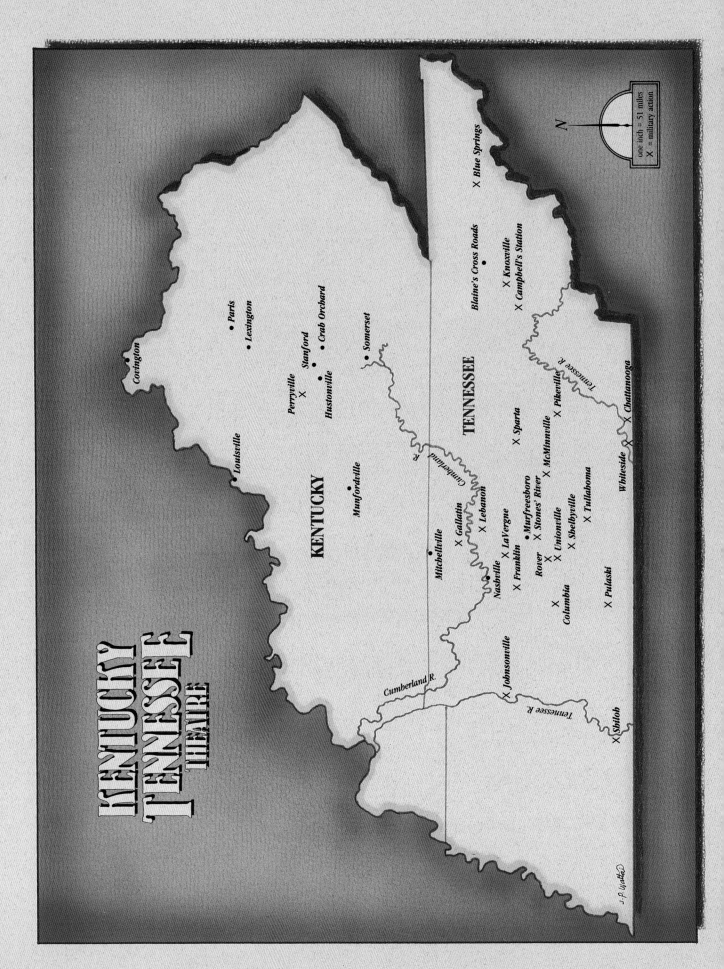

KENTUCKY/ TENNESSEE THEATRE

KENTUCKY

Covington

Paris
• Lexington

Stanford
Perryville • • Crab Orchard
X Hustonville   Somerset
•

Louisville

Munfordville
•

Mitchellville •

Blaine's Cross Roads
X
X Knoxville
X Campbell's Station

TENNESSEE

X Sparta
X McMinnville
X Pikeville

Tennessee R.

X Whiteside   X Chattanooga

X Blue Springs

R.
Cumberland

X Gallatin
X Lebanon
Nashville X LaVergne
X Franklin • Murfreesboro
Rover X Stones' River
X Unionville
X Shelbyville   X Tullahoma
Columbia
X Pulaski

Cumberland R.

X Johnsonville

Tennessee R.

X Shiloh

one inch = 51 miles
X = military action

N

J. P. Wyatt

Advance the Colors!

APPENDIXES

Appendix I
Pennsylvania Troops in the Civil War

Accoording to the 1866 State Adjutant-General's report, Pennsylvania furnished over 300,000 men during the war, from the President's first call for troops on April 15, 1861, to April 13,1865, when all recruiting for volunteer units ceased. The regiments and numbers furnished in response to the several calls were as follows:

Under the call of April 15, 1861, for 75,000 men for three months:

regiments #1-25, aggregating 20,979 men

Under the act of July 22, 1861, authorizing four independent regiments from Pennsylvania, for a term of three years:

regiments #26-29, 4,711 men

The Reserve Volunteer Corps of Pennsylvania, called into Federal service on July 22, 1861:

regiments #30-44, 15,856 men

On Presidential requisition, by act of Congress, July 22, 1861, together with units authorized by the War Department, to be raised by individuals, and placed under the control of Governor Curtin on September 25, 1861, the term of enlistment for three years.

regiments #11,23,45-115, strength of 89,048 men

Under the call of July 7, 1862, for 300,000 men, including eighteen nine-month regiments:

regiments #116-157, 159-164, 40,383 men

Organized under the draft of August 4, 1862, for a term of nine months:

regiments #158,165-179, 15,100 men

Organized in 1863 by authority of the War Department, for three years:

regiment #180, 1,066 men

Organized in 1864, for three years, on authority from the War Department:

regiments #181-191, 9,867 men

Under the call of July 6, 1864, for a term of one hundred days:

regiments #192-197, 1 infantry company, 5 cavalry companies, 1 independent battery, 1 artillery battalion, aggregating 7,675 men

By Presidential authority, July 27, 1864, for ten regiments under the call of July 18, for 500,000 men for a one year term of enlistment:

regiments #198-212, 16,094 men

Under the call of December 19, 1864, for 300,000 men for one year:

regiments #213-215, 75 infantry companies assigned to existing regiments, 9,645 men

Through 1862, eight independent artillery batteries, each for three years and one battery for one year, aggregating 1,358 men

Recruiting officers throughout the state forwarded the following number of volunteer recruits to existing regiments during the war:

1862	9,259
1863	4,458
1864	26,567
1865	9,133
	49,417

The following number of drafted men and substitutes was furnished during 1864 and 1865:

1864	10,651
1865	6,675
	17,326

United States recruiting officers forwarded to regular army units the following number of Pennsylvanians during the war. The 1861-62 total includes those men who enlisted in regiments from other states:

1861/2	5,000
1863	934
1864	2,974
1865	387
	9,295

In addition to the troops who entered Federal service, the following number of militia was enrolled during the emergency of 1863. This total includes those who enlisted in Federal service for six months:

Department of the Monongahela:	5,166
Department of the Susquehanna	31,422
	36,588

Finally, 17,876 men re-enlisted and were classed as "veteran volunteers" in late 1863. These soldiers are not included in any totals from the state, as they were counted in previous enlistments.

The total number of troops furnished by Pennsylvania, by year, was as follows:

1861	130,594
1862	71,100
1863	43,046
1864	73,828
1865	25,840
TOTAL	344,408

Appendix II
Composition of Pennsylvania Regiments

Having encountered numerous discrepancies between Bates, regimental histories, and county histories regarding the county origins of scores of companies, the author decided to resolve these differences by reading through the muster rolls in the State Archives. This appendix is the result of many months of work. Bates was correct in most instances, but he made several mistakes in attributing the wrong county to at least seventy companies of soldiers. He was also vague about county origins for thirty-three regiments and provided no county designations for eight regiments.

In general each regiment turned in three distinctly different forms of muster rolls:

1) muster-in roll, which was the unit's first nominal listing, and is useful in research because it shows the original members of a company before later recruits and conscripts joined.

2) alphabetical roll, which is what the author preferred to use because the alphabetical roll contains a column that specified place of residence for each soldier. The muster-in roll did not have this information, listing instead the place of enrollment, which was not always the same as place of residence.

3) muster-out roll, which was the final roll filled out just prior to disbanding, and accounted for every soldier who ever belonged to the company. This roll was of limited use because this roll lists place of enlistment, not county of residence.

The county listing in this appendix follows Bates in general. Where the muster rolls indicated a different county than Bates, the following symbols cite these changes:

* A single asterisk indicates that the county is completely different from that in Bates.

** A double asterisk signifies an addition to Bates. Generally, if the roll indicated at least twelve to fifteen men from another county in a company, then it was added to the list because this number of men is a significant portion of the company and

was included primarily to aid researchers. In regiments where Bates was vague (see below) this symbol indicates additions to Bates's county listing.

+ A cross indicates that the company was primarily composed of soldiers from the indicated county, with additions from several other counties as well. Taken alone, the dozen or less men from each of several other counties would not be enough strength to include in this listing, but when the small numbers of soldiers from neighboring counties are added together, they produce a sizeable portion of the company.

Bates was vague (listing counties in his regimental sketch but not specifying which companies came from which counties) in the following regiments:

108th, 111th, 112th, 113th, 121st, 141st, 147th, 149th, 152nd, 154th, 157th, 158th, 159th, 160th, 161st, 163rd, 168th, 171st, 172nd, 175th, 176th, 177th, 179th, 181st, 184th, 185th, 187th, 188th, 189th, 190th, 191st, 194th, 200th, 203rd, 204th, 206th, 210th, 212th, 213th, 214th, 215th

The muster rolls indicate county origins for all but four of the above regiments. The 190th and 191st were formed from the re-enlisted men of eleven infantry regiments of the Reserve Corps. The two veteran units were formed in Virginia, so the rolls do not indicate county origins. The 188th was formed from surplus recruits for the 152nd Regiment, and there are no separate muster-in rolls for the new regiment. Similarly, the 189th was formed from surplus men of the 112th Regiment. After suffering heavy losses in a few months, the 189th was broken up and the men returned to the 112th.

Where possible, the popular, local company nicknames are included. Unless noted, names have been taken from the muster rolls or election for officers forms in the regimental papers. All names found elsewhere are footnoted. Names for the Reserve Corps regiments are taken from Sypher's history, with additions as noted.

Sample Entry

Regimental number, including alternate designation, if necessary	Company letter	County of enlistment	Company nickname	Replacement Company, with dates of addition. Unless noted, all replacement companies were added during the winter of 1864/65
31st	A	Philadelphia	(Penn Rifles)	
(2nd	B	Philadelphia	(Governor's Rangers)	new B Philadelphia
Reserves)	C	Philadelphia	(Hibernian Target Company)	(?/62)
	D	Philadelphia	(Governor's Rangers)	
6/61-	E	Philadelphia	(Scotch Rifles)	
6/16/64	F	Philadelphia*	(Governor's Rangers)	new F Huntingdon (4/62) Blair
	G	Philadelphia	(Taggart Guards)	new G Lancaster
	H	Philadelphia	(Independent Rangers)	(7/62)
Dates of	I	Philadelphia*	(Constitution Rangers)	
Enlistment	K	Philadelphia	(Consolidation Guards)	

Advance the Colors!

1st	A	Northampton	(Washington Grays)
	B	Northampton	(Citizen's Artillery)[1,2]
4/20/61-	C	Northampton	(Easton Invincibles)[1]
7/24/61	D	Northampton	(Scott Guards)[1]
	E	Dauphin	(Cameron Guards)[1]
	F	Lancaster	(Lancaster Fencibles)[1]
	G	Berks	(Reading Artillery)[3]
	H	Northampton	(National Guards)[4]
	I	Lehigh	(Union Rifles)[1]
	K	Lancaster	(Jackson Rifles)[5]
2nd	A	Franklin	(Chambers Artillery)
	B	Franklin	(Chambers Artillery)
4/21/61-	C	Franklin	(Union Artillery)
7/26/61	D	Perry	(Independent Infantry)[4]
	E	Adams	(Independent Blues)
	F	Lancaster	(Shawnee Guards)
	G	Chester	(1st West Chester Rifles)
	H	Centre	(Bellefonte Fencibles)
	I	Dauphin	(State Capital Guards)
	K	York	(York Rifles)
3rd	A	Blair	(Hollidaysburg Fencibles)
	B	Blair	(Altoona Guards)
4/20/61-	C	Blair	(Wayne Guards)
7/29/61	D	Blair	(Tyrone Artillery)
	E	Blair	(Logan Rifle Rangers)
	F	Cambria	(Citizen Guards)
	G	Cambria	(Johnstown Infantry)
	H	Blair	(Juniata Riflemen)
	I	Allegheny	(Negley Zouaves)
	K	Cambria	(Johnstown Zouave Cadets)[6]
4th	A	Montgomery	(Wayne Artillerists)
	B	Montgomery	(Norris City Rifles)
4/20/61-	C	Montgomery	(Madison Guards)
7/27/61	D	Montgomery	(National Artillery)
	E	Montgomery	(Keystone Rifles)
	F	Delaware	(Union Rifles)
	G	Union	(Lewisburg Infantry)
	H	Centre	(Eagle Guards)
	I	Montgomery	(National Artillery)
	K	Montgomery	(2nd Norris City Rifles)
5th	A	Allegheny	(State Guards)[7]
	B	Allegheny	(Turner Rifles)
4/21/61-	C	Schuylkill	(Columbian Infantry)[8]
7/25/61	D	Huntingdon	(Standing Stone Guards)[9]
	E	Schuylkill	(Minersville Artillerists)[8]
	F	Schuylkill	(Scott Artillery)[10]
	G	Lebanon	(Lebanon Guards[11]
	H	Berks	(Union Light Infantry)[12]
	I	Schuylkill	(Ringgold Rifles)
	K	Allegheny	(United States Zouaves)[7]
6th	A	Carbon	(Anderson Greys)
	B	Schuylkill	(Port Clinton Artillery)
4/22/61-	C	Schuylkill	(Marion Rifles)
7/27/61	D	Schuylkill	(Nagle Guards)
	E	Schuylkill	(Ashland Rifles)
	F	Schuylkill	(Washington Jaegers)
	G	Schuylkill	(Llewellyn Rifles)
	H	Schuylkill	(Tower Guards)
	I	Carbon	(Anderson Greys)
	K	Carbon	(Anderson Greys)

7th	A	Allegheny	(Scott Legion)[13]
	B	Allegheny	(Allegheny Rifles)[13]
4/22/61-	C	Berks	(Washington Artillery)[12]
7/29/61	D	Berks	(Pennsylvania Artillery)[13]
	E	Allegheny	(Allegheny Light Guards)[13]
	F	Allegheny	(Pennsylvania Zouaves)[13]
	G	Berks	(Reading Rifles)[12]
	H	Centre	(Cameron Infantry)[14,15]
	I	Mifflin	(Burns Infantry)[16]
	K	Allegheny	(Pittsburgh Invincibles)[13]
8th	A	Northumberland	(Shamokin Guards)[17]
	B	Luzerne	(Covington Fencibles)
4/22/61-	C	Luzerne	(Wyoming Light Dragoons)
7/29/61	D	Luzerne	(Jackson Rifles)
	E	Luzerne	(Luzerne Guard)
	F	Luzerne	(Wyoming Artillerists)
	G	Luzerne	(Wyoming Jaeger Rifles)
	H	Luzerne	(Scranton Union Volunteers)
	I	Jefferson	(Brookville Rifles)
	K	Jefferson	(Brookville Rifles)
9th	A	Chester	(National Guards)[4]
	B	Armstrong	(Brady Alpines)
4/24/61-	C	Cumberland	(Sumner Rifles)[18]
7/29/61	D	Lehigh	(Catasaqua Rifles)[4]
	E	Chester	(National Guards)
	F	Chester	(National Guards)
	G	Northampton	(Easton Jaegers)[16]
	H	Schuylkill	(Wetherill Rifles)[19]
	I	Delaware	(Union Blues)[20]
	K	Schuylkill	(Keystone Rifles of Port Carbon)[19]
10th	A	Lancaster	(Maytown Infantry)
	B	Centre	(Curtin Guards)
4/26/61-	C	Shuylkilll	(Scott Rifles)
7/31/61	D	Schuylkill	(Washington Light Infantry)
	E	Lancaster	(Lancaster City Infantry)
	F	Dauphin	(Washington Rifles)
	G	Cambria	(Washington Rifles)
	H	Cambria	(Allegheny Guards)
	I	Huntingdon+	(Biddle Guards)
	K	Lancaster Allegheny**	(Steuben Guards)
11th	A	Lycoming	(Woodward Guards)[21]
	B	Clinton	(Lock Haven Artillery)[21]
4/26/61-	C	Clinton	(Keystone Infantry)[21]
8/1/61	D	Lycoming	(Williamsport Rifles)[21]
	E	Luzerne	(Pittston Volunteers)[21]
	F	Northumberland	(Sunbury Guards)[21]
	G	Lycoming	(Muncy Brady Artillery)[21]
	H	Montour	(Danville Rifles)[21]
	I	Westmoreland	(Westmoreland Guards)[21]
	K	Westmoreland	(Latrobe Light Infantry)[21]
11th	A	Cumberland Dauphin	(Sumner Rifles)[22]
12/11/61-	B	Clinton	
7/1/65	C	Westmoreland	
	D	Lycoming Northumberland**	
	E	Westmoreland Northumberland** Lancaster**	

11th	F	Westmoreland	(Salem Union Guards)[23]
(continued)	G	Allegheny	
	H	Carbon	
	I	Westmoreland	
	K	Westmoreland	
12th	A	Allegheny	(Jackson Independent Blues)[24]
	B	Allegheny	(Duquesne Greys)[24]
4/25/61-	C	Allegheny	(Fireman's Legion)[24]
8/5/61	D	Allegheny	(Union Guards)[24]
	E	Washington	(Washington's Invincibles)[24,25]
	F	Lawrence	(Lawrence Guards)[24]
	G	Washington	(Monogahela Artillery)[24]
	H	Lawrence	(Lawrence Guards)[24]
	I	Allegheny	(Zouave Cadets)[24]
	K	Allegheny	(City Guard)[24,26]
13th	A	Allegheny	(Washington Infantry)[7]
	B	Allegheny	(Union Cadets)[7]
4/25/61-	C	Allegheny	(Negley Cadets)[7]
8/6/61	D	Allegheny	(Washington Infantry)[7,27]
	E	Allegheny	(Fort Pitt Guards)[7]
	F	Allegheny	(Rowley Rifles)[7]
	G	Bedford	(Taylor Guards)[7]
	H	Butler	(Butler Blues)[7]
	I	Allegheny	(Shields Guards)[7]
	K	Allegheny	(Duquesne Greys)[7]
14th	A	Berks	(Union Guards)
	B	Schuylkill	(Lafayette Rifles)[28]
4/30/61-	C	Montour	(Columbia Guards)[29]
8/7/61	D	Clearfield	(Tyrone Cavalry)[4]
		Blair**	
	E	Berks	(Keystone Infantry)[12]
	F	Westmoreland	(North Huntingdon Guards)[30]
	G	Westmoreland	(Ridge Rangers)[31]
	H	Blair	(Scott Rifles)[4,32]
	I	Blair*	(Martinsburg Infantry)[32]
	K	Allegheny	(Alliquippa Guards)[13,33]
15th	A	Luzerne	(Keystone Guards)[30]
	B	Luzerne	(White Haven Jaegers)[30]
5/1/61-	C	Luzerne	(Lackwanna Rifles)[30]
8/7/61	D	Luzerne	(Pittston Artillery)[30]
	E	Dauphin	(Verbeke Rifles)[30]
	F	Lancaster	(Washington Rifles)[30,34]
	G	Luzerne	(Nagle Light Infantry)
	H	Huntingdon*	(Union Guards)[30]
	I	Centre	(Curtin Infantry)[30]
	K	Lancaster	(Marietta Cameron Guards)[30]
16th	A	York	(Worth Infantry)[35]
	B	Schuylkill	(German Light Infantry)
5/3/61-	C	Cumberland	(Slemmer Phalanx)[36]
7/30/61	D	Schuylkill	(Jackson Guards)
	E	Schuylkill	(Wynkoop Artillery)[28]
	F	York	(Marion Rifles)[37]
	G	York	(Hanover Infantry)[37]
	H	York	(York Voltigeurs)[35]
	I	Schuylkill	(Union Guards)
	K	Schuylkill	(Schuylkill Guards)[35]
17th	A	Philadelphia	(Washington Greys)[38]
	B	Philadelphia	(Philadelphia Greys)[38]
4/25/61-	C	Philadelphia	(West Philadelphia Greys)[38]
8/2/61	D	Philadelphia	(National Artillery)[38]

17th	E	Philadelphia	(State Guard)[38]
(continued)	F	Philadelphia	(2nd Co., Washington Greys)[38]
	G	Philadelphia	(2nd Co., Philadelphia Greys)[38]
Quaker	H	Philadelphia	(Cadwalader Greys)[38]
Regiment[39]	I	Philadelphia	(Independent Greys)[38]
	K	Philadelphia	(2nd Co., Cadwalader Greys)[38]
18th	A	Philadelphia	(2nd Co., Washington Blues)
	B	Philadelphia	(1st Co., National Greys)
4/24/61-	C	Philadelphia	(Garde Lafayette)
8/7/61	D	Philadelphia	(Philadelphia Zouaves)
	E	Philadelphia	(1st Co., State Fencibles)
	F	Philadelphia	(1st Co., Washington Blues)
	G	Philadelphia	(Minute Men of '76)
	H	Philadelphia	(2nd Co., National Greys)
	I	Philadelphia	(Voltigeurs)
	K	Philadelphia	(2nd Co., State Fencibles)
19th	A	Philadelphia	
	B	Philadelphia	
4/27/61-	C	Philadelphia	
8/29/61	D	Philadelphia	
	E	Philadelphia	
National	F	Philadelphia	
Guards[40]	G	Philadelphia	
	H	Philadelphia	
	I	Philadelphia	
	K	Philadelphia	
20th	A	Philadelphia	
	B	Philadelphia	
4/30/61-	C	Philadelphia	
8/6/61	D	Philadelphia	
	E	Philadelphia	
Scott Legion	F	Philadelphia	
Regiment[41]	G	Philadelphia	
	H	Philadelphia	
	I	Philadelphia	
	K	Philadelphia	
21st	A	Philadelphia	(Jackson Rifles)[42]
	B	Philadelphia	(Lafayette Rifles)[42]
4/29/61-	C	Philadelphia	(Pennsylvania Rifles)[42]
8/8/61	D	Philadelphia	(Washington Rifles)[42]
	E	Philadelphia	(Black Rifles)[42]
German	F	Philadelphia	(Steuben Rifles)[42]
Rifle	G	Philadelphia	(Philadelphia Rifles)[42]
Regiment[43]	H	Philadelphia	(DeKalb Rifles)[42]
	I	Philadelphia	(Scott Rifles)[42]
	K	Philadelphia	(Franklin Rifles)[42]
22nd	A	Philadelphia	
	B	Philadelphia	
4/23/61-	C	Philadelphia	
8/7/61	D	Philadelphia	
	E	Philadelphia	
Philadelphia	F	Philadelphia	
Light	G	Philadelphia	
Guards	H	Philadelphia	
Regiment	I	Philadelphia	
	K	Philadelphia	
23rd	A	Philadelphia	(Continental Guards)[44]
4/21/61-	B	Philadelphia	
7/31/61	C	Philadelphia	

23rd *(continued)*	D E F G H I K	Philadelphia Philadelphia Philadelphia Philadelphia Philadelphia Philadelphia Philadelphia	
23rd 8/31/61- 9/8/64 Birney's Zouaves[46]	A B C D E F G H I K L M O P R	Philadelphia Philadelphia Philadelphia Philadelphia Philadelphia Philadelphia Philadelphia Philadelphia Philadelphia Philadelphia Luzerne Philadelphia Philadelphia Philadelphia Philadelphia	 (Gymnast Zouaves)[45] (2nd Co., Gymnast Zouaves)[46a] (Independent Grays)[46b]
24th 5/7/61- 8/10/61 Irish Regiment[48]	A B C D E F G H I K	Philadelphia Philadelphia Philadelphia Philadelphia Philadelphia Philadelphia Philadelphia Delaware State Philadelphia Philadelphia	(Irish Volunteers)[47] (Hibernia Greens)[47] (Emmett Guards)[47] (Meagher Guards)[47] (Jackson Guards)[47] (1st Co., Shields Guards)[47] (Patterson Light Guards)[47] (2nd Co., Shields Guards)[47]
25th 4/18/61- 7/26/61	A B C D E F G H I K	Berks Schuylkill Berks** Berks Schuylkill** Schuylkill Mifflin Dauphin Lehigh Schuylkill Bucks Luzerne	(Ringgold Light Artillery) (Haskin Guards) (2nd Ringgold Artillery) (National Light Infantry) (Logan Guards) (Lochiel Grays)[49] (Allen Guards) (Washington Artillery) (Doylestown Guards)[50] (Carbondale City Guards)
26th 5/25/61- 6/18/64	A B C D E F G H I K	Philadelphia Philadelphia Philadelphia Philadelphia Philadelphia Philadelphia Philadelphia Philadelphia Philadelphia Philadelphia	(Washington Guards)[51] (Anderson Guards)[51] (1st Co., Monroe Guards)[51] (4th Co., Monroe Guards)[51] (Union Invincibles)[51] (Cameron Guards)[51] (2nd Co., Monroe Guards)[51] (3rd Co., Monroe Guards)[51] (2nd Co., Frankford Guards)[51] (1st Co., Frankford Guards)[51]
27th 5/31/61- 6/11/64	A B C D E F	Philadelphia Philadelphia Philadelphia Philadelphia Philadelphia Philadelphia	 (Harrison Guards)[38]

27th	G	Philadelphia	
(continued)	H	Philadelphia	
	I	Philadelphia	
	K	Philadelphia	

28th[52]	A	Luzerne	(Pardee Guards)[53]	
	B	Westmoreland		
6/28/61-	C	Philadelphia	(Geary Guards)[54]	
7/18/65	D	Philadelphia	(2nd Co., Independent Grays)[55]	
	E	Carbon	(Mauch Chunk Rangers)[56]	
	F	Allegheny	(Elizabeth Mountaineers)[57]	
	G	Allegheny	(Sewickley Rifles)[58]	
	H	Allegheny	(Zouave Cadets)[58]	
	I	Philadelphia		
	K	Philadelphia		
	L	Allegheny Philadelphia**	(McKnight Guards)[57]	
	M	Philadelphia	(Union Grays)[59,60]	
	N	Luzerne		
	O	Huntingdon	(Lawrence Rifles)[61,62]	
	P	Philadelphia	(Scott Legion)[63]	

29th[64]	A	Philadelphia	(Marion Guards)[65]
	B	Philadelphia	(2nd Co., West Philadelphia Grays)[65]
7/1/61-	C	Philadelphia	(United Rifles)[65]
7/17/65	D	Philadelphia	(Koska Guards)[65]
	E	Philadelphia	(Belmont Guards)[65]
Jackson	F	Philadelphia	(Warren Guards)[65]
Regiment	G	Philadelphia	(Federal Guard)[65]
	H	Philadelphia	(Henry Clay Fencibles)[65]
	I	Philadelphia	(Morgan Artillery)[65]
	K	Philadelphia	(Dougherty Guards)[65]

30th	A	Chester	(Brandywine Guards)
(1st	B	Lancaster	(Union Guards)
Reserves)	C	Delaware Chester	(Slifer Phalanx)
6/9/61-	D	Lancaster York	(Safe Harbor Artillery)
6/13/64	E	Lancaster	(Lancaster Guards)
	F	Delaware	(Archy Dick Rifles)[66]
	G	Chester	(Phoenix Artillery)
	H	Cumberland	(Carlisle Light Infantry)
	I	Cumberland	(Carlisle Guards)
	K	Adams	(Adams Infantry)[67]

31st	A	Philadelphia	(Penn Rifles)	
(2nd	B	Philadelphia	(Governor's Rangers)	new B Philadelphia
Reserves)[68]	C	Philadelphia	(Hibernian Target Company)	(?/62)
	D	Philadelphia	(Governor's Rangers)	
6/61-	E	Philadelphia	(Scotch Rifles)	
6/16/64	F	Philadelphia*	(Governor's Rangers)	new F Huntingdon (4/62)Blair
	G	Philadelphia	(Taggart Guards)	new G Lancaster
	H	Philadelphia	(Independent Rangers)	(7/62)
	I	Philadelphia*	(Constitution Rangers)	
	K	Philadelphia	(Consolidation Guards)	

32nd	A	Berks	(2nd Reading Artillery)[69]
(3rd	B	Wayne	(Salem Independents)
Reserves)	C	Bucks	(Union Rifles)
	D	Berks	(Mechanics' Infantry)
6/61-	E	Philadelphia	(DeSilver Greys)
6/17/64	F	Berks	(Washington Guards)

32nd	G	Philadelphia	(Germantown Guards)
(continued)	H	Bucks	(Applebachville Guards)
	I	Bucks	(Montgomery Guards)
	K	Philadelphia*	(Ontario Infantry)
33rd	A	Philadelphia	(Able Guards)
(4th	B	Philadelphia	(Quaker City Guards)
Reserves	C	Montgomery	(Montgomery Rifles)
		Philadelphia**	
6/61-		Bucks**	
6/17/64	D	Philadelphia	(Dickson Guards)
	E	Lycoming	(Williamsport Legion)
	F	Monroe	(National Guards of Monroe)
	G	Philadelphia	(Harmer Guards)
	H	Susquehanna	(Susquehanna Union Volunteers)
	I	Philadelphia	(Reed Guards)
	K	Chester	(Enton Guards)
34th	A	Lycoming	(Jersey Shore Rifles)
(5th	B	Northumberland	(Taggart Guards)
Reserves)	C	Clearfield	(Washington Cadets)
	D	Union	(Slifer Guards)
6/20/61-	E	Centre	(Centre Guards)
6/11/64	F	Bradford	(Bradford Union Guards)
	G	Huntingdon	(Huntington Infantry)
	H	Northumberland	(Pollock Guards)
		Lycoming	
	I	Huntingdon	(Scott Infantry)
	K	Lancaster	(Cookman Rangers)
35th	A	Columbia	(Iron Guards)
(6th	B	Snyder	(Union Guards)
Reserves)	C	Wayne	(Honesdale Guards)
	D	Franklin	(Washington Rifles)
6/61-	E	Montour	(Montour Rifles)
6/11/64	F	Bradford	(Northern Invincibles)
	G	Dauphin	(J. D. Cameron Infantry)
	H	Tioga	(Tioga Invincibles)
	I	Bradford	(Towanda Rifles)
	K	Susquehanna	(Susquehanna Volunteers)
36th	A	Cumberland	(Carlisle Fencibles)
(7th	B	Perry	(Biddle Rifles)
Reserves)	C	Lebanon	(Iron Artillery)[70]
	D	Clinton	(Lock Haven Rifle Guards)[71]
6/26/61-	E	Philadelphia	(Ridgway Guards)
6/16/64	F	Luzerne	(Wyoming Bank Infantry)
	G	Philadelphia	(2nd Philadelphia Guards)
	H	Cumberland	(Cumberland Guards)
	I	Lebanon	(Myerstown Rifles)
		Berks	
	K	Philadelphia	(Douglas Guards)
37th	A	Armstrong	(Armstrong Rifles)
(8th		Butler	
Reserves)	B	Allegheny	(Jefferson Riflemen)[72]
	C	Allegheny	(Anderson Cadets)
6/28/61-	D	Fayette	(Brownsville Greys)
5/24/64	E	Alletheny	(Duncan Guards)
		Philadelphia**	
	F	Bedford	(Hopewell Rifles)
	G	Fayette	(Fayette Guards)
	H	Clarion	(Clarion Union Guards)[73]
	I	Greene	(Greene County Rangers)[74]
	K	Washington	(Hopkins Infantry)

Composition of Pennsylvania Regiments

38th	A	Allegheny	(Pittsburgh Rifles)[75]	
(9th	B	Allegheny	(Garibaldi Guards)	
Reserves)	C	Allegheny	(Iron City Guards)	
	D	Allegheny	(Government Guards)	
6/28/61-	E	Allegheny	(Chartiers Valley Guards)	
5/13/64	F	Crawford	(Meadville Volunteers)	
	G	Allegheny	(City Guards)[76]	
	H	Beaver	(New Brighton Rifles)	
	I	Allegheny	(McKeesport Union Guards)	
	K	Allegheny	(Allegheny Rangers)	
39th	A	Somerset	(Somerset Infantry)	
(10th	B	Mercer	(Middlesex Rangers)	
Reserves)	C	Venango	(Venango Greys)	
	D	Washington	(Jefferson Light Guards)	
6/29/61-	E	Clarion	(Clarion River Guards)	
6/11/64	F	Beaver	(Curtin Rifles)	
	G	Mercer	(Mercer Rifles)	
	H	Warren	(Warren Guards)	
	I	Crawford	(Allegheny College Volunteers)[77]	
	K	Beaver	(Wilson Rifles)	
40th	A	Cambria	(Cambria Guards)	
(11th	B	Indiana	(Indiana National Guards)	
Reserves)	C	Butler	(Dixon Guards)	
	D	Butler	(Conongessing Rangers)	
7/1/61-	E	Indiana	(Washington Blues)	
6/14/64	F	Fayette	(Union Volunteers)[78]	
	G	Armstrong	(Apollo Independent Blues)[79]	
	H	Westmoreland	(Westmoreland Blues)	
	I	Westmoreland	(Washington Blues)	
		Indiana**		
	K	Jefferson	(Brady Guards)	
41st	A	Philadelphia	(Wayne Guards)	
(12th	B	Wyoming	(Factoryville Infantry)	
Reserves)	C	Bradford	(Troy Guards)	
	D	Dauphin	(Kepner Fencibles)	
7/25/61-		Philadelphia**		
6/11/64	E	Northampton	(Easton Guards)	
	F	Westmoreland	(West Newton Guards)	
	G	York	(Bailey's Invincibles)	
	H	Indiana	(Indiana County Infantry)	
	I	Huntingdon	(Huntingdon Guards)	
	K	Franklin	(McClure Rifles)	
42nd	A	Tioga	(Anderson Life Guards)	
(13th	B	Perry	(Morgan Rifles)	
Reserves)	C	Cameron+	(Cameron County Rifles)	
	D	Warren	(Ratfsman Guards)[80]	
6/61-	E	Tioga	(Tioga Rifles)	
6/11/64	F	Carbon	(Irish Infantry)	
	G	Elk	(Elk County Rifles)	
Bucktails	H	Chester	(Wayne Independent Rifles)	
	I	McKean	(McKean County Rifles)	
	K	Clearfield	(Raftsmen's Rangers)[81]	
43rd	A	Franklin		
(1st Light	B	Lawrence	(Mount Jackson Guards)	
Artillery)	C	Philadelphia	(Flying Artillery)	new C Philadelphia[82]
	D	Philadelphia	(Richmond Artillerists)[83]	
6/61-	E	York	(York Artillery)	
6—7/65	F	Schuylkill		
		Susquehanna**		
		Montour**		

43rd (continued)	G	Philadelphia Indiana**	
	H	Philadelphia Luzerne**	
	I	Pennsylvania	
44th (1st Cavalry) 7/61- 6/17/65	A	Juniata	(Juniata Cavalry)
	B	Montgomery	(Lower Merion Troop)
	C	Mifflin	(Mifflin County Cavalry)
	D	Clinton	(Smith's Cavalry)[84]
	E	Centre	(Centre County Cavalry)
	F	Greene	(Ringgold Cavalry)
	G	Blair* Cumberland**	(Blair County Cavalry)
	H	Fayette	(Dunlap Creek Cavalry)[85]
	I	Washington	(Winfield Hussars)[85]
	K	Allegheny Washington	(National Cavalry)[85]
	L	Berks	(Reading City Troop)
	M	Berks	(Reading Cavalry)[12]
45th 10/21/61- 7/17/65	A	Centre	(Bald Eagle Infantry)[86]
	B	Lancaster Centre**	
	C	Mifflin	(Belleville Fencibles)[87]
	D	Centre	
	E	Centre Huntingdon**	(Scott Guards)[88]
	F	Tioga Wayne	
	G	Tioga	(Charleston Rangers)
	H	Tioga	
	I	Tioga	(Fremont Rangers)[89]
	K	Lancaster	
46th 10/31/61- 7/16/65	A	Mifflin	(Logan Guards)
	B	Allegheny	(Frisbee Infantry)[90]
	C	Lehigh Northampton	(Lehigh Valley Guards)[91,92]
	D	Dauphin	(Verbeke Rifles)[93]
	E	Berks	(Reading Rifles)[93]
	F	Allegheny Beaver**	(Pittsburgh Rifles)[90]
	G	Potter	(Oswayo Rifles)[94]
	H	Potter	(Curtin Rifle Guards)[94]
	I	Luzerne	
	K	Northumberland	(National Guard)[95]
47th 8—9/61- 1/9/66	A	Northampton	
	B	Lehigh	
	C	Northumberland Juniata**	(Sunbury Guards)[96]
	D	Perry	
	E	Northampton	
	F	Lehigh	
	G	Lehigh	
	H	Perry Dauphin**	
	I	Lehigh	
	K	Lehigh Luzerne** Berks**	
48th 10/1/61- 7/17/65	A	Schuylkill	(Port Clinton Artillery)[97]
	B	Schuylkill	(Haskin Guards)[97]
	C	Schuylkill	(Tower Guards)[97]

48th *(continued)*	D	Schuylkill	(Nagle Guards)[97]	
	E	Schuylkill	(Wynkoop Artillerists)[97]	
	F	Schuylkill	(Ringgold Rifles)[97]	
	G	Schuylkill		
	H	Schuylkill		
	I	Schuylkill	(Anthracite Guards)[97]	
	K	Schuylkill	(Wilder Guards)[98]	
49th[99]	A	Centre Clinton**	(Milesburg Infantry)[100]	
9/14/61- 7/15/65	B	Chester	(O. S. Frazer Rifles)[101]	
	C	Huntingdon	(Craig Biddle Guards)	
	D	Huntingdon		
	E	Mifflin	(Burns Infantry)[102]	new E drafted men
	F	Chester		new F drafted men
	G	Centre	(Penn's Valley Infantry)[86]	new G drafted men
	H	Mifflin Snyder**		new H drafted men
	I	Juniata Perry**		new I Snyder
	K	Mifflin*	(Governor Guards)[102a]	new K Allegheny
50th	A	Schuylkill		
	B	Berks	(Ellsworth's Zouaves)[12,103]	
9/25/61- 7/31/65	C	Schuylkill		
	D	Susquehanna	(Susquehanna County Rifle Company)[104]	
	E	Berks Lebanon**	(Reading Light Infantry)[12]	
	F	Lancaster+		
	G	Bradford	(Goodrich Guards)[105]	
	H	Berks Chester**	(Union Light Infantry)[12]	
	I	Luzerne Schuylkill**		
	K	Bradford		
51st	A	Montgomery		
	B	Northampton		
11/16/61- 7/27/65	C	Montgomery		
	D	Montgomery		
	E	Union	(Shriner Guards)[106]	
	F	Montgomery		
	G	Centre	(McAllister Rifles)[86]	
	H	Union Lycoming Snyder	(Linn Rifles)[106]	
	I	Montgomery		
	K	Union Northampton	(Walls Guards)[106,107]	
52nd	A	Luzerne		
	B	Wyoming		
10/7/61- 7/12/65	C	Clinton		
	D	Union Snyder**	(Cameron Rifles)[108,109]	
	E	Bradford		
Luzerne Regiment	F	Bradford		
	G	Columbia Luzerne**		
	H	Luzerne Wyoming**		
	I	Luzerne		
	K	Luzerne Schuylkill		

53rd	A	Montgomery	
	B	Montgomery	
11/7/61-	C	Blair	
6/30/65		Huntingdon	
	D	Centre	
		Clearfield	
	E	Carbon	
		Union	
	F	Luzerne	(Wyoming Guards)[110]
	G	Potter	(Jones Rifles)[111]
	H	Northumberland	(Rooke Guards)[112,112a]
		Montour**	
	I	Juniata	
	K	Westmoreland	(Latrobe Light Guards)[113]
54th	A	Cambria	(Johnstown Zouave Cadets)[114]
		Indiana	
2/27/62-	B	Somerset	
7/15/65	C	Somerset	
	D	Somerset	
		Cambria**	
	E	Cambria	
	F	Dauphin+	
		Lehigh**	
	G	Somerset	
	H	Cambria	
		Northampton	
		Somerset	
	I	Cambria	(McClellan Guards)[114]
		Jefferson**	
	K	Lehigh	
55th	A	Cambria	
	B	Berks	(Washington Legion)[12]
12/4/61-	C	Cambria	(Sarsfield Guards)[114]
8/30/65	D	Bedford	(Bedford Riflemen)[115]
	E	Schuylkill	(Schuylkill Guards)[116]
	F	Indiana	
	G	Dauphin	(Roberts Guards)[117]
	H	Bedford	(Schellsburg Riflemen)[118]
	I	Bedford	
		Blair	
	K	Bedford	(Taylor Guards)[119]
56th	A	Susquehanna*	
		Wayne	
3/7/62-	B	Indiana	(Blairsville Guards)[120]
7/1/65	C	Luzerne*	
	D	Luzerne+	
		Northumberland**	
		Philadelphia	
	E	Lycoming*[121]	
	F	Centre*	
		Snyder*	
		Union*	
	G	Luzerne	
		Wayne**	
	H	Centre	
	I	Centre	
		Luzerne	
		Philadelphia**	
	K	Schuylkill	
		Susquehanna	

57th[122]	A	Susquehanna Wyoming	(Susquehanna Rifles)[123,124]
12/14/61- 6/29/65	B	Mercer	
	C	Mercer	
	D	Tioga	
	E	Allegheny Mercer Centre**	(Verner Greys)[90,125]
	F	Mercer	
	G	Bradford	
	H	Bradford	
	I	Mercer Venango	
	K	Crawford	
58th	A	Philadelphia Delaware**	
9/61—3/62- 1/24/66	B	Philadelphia	
	C	Philadelphia	
	D	Philadelphia	
	E	Erie McKean Tioga	
	F	Elk McKean Warren	
	G	Clinton Warren**	
	H	McKean	
	I	Luzerne Northumberland	(Augusta Rangers)[125]
	K	Philadelphia	
59th (2nd Cavalry)	A	Philadelphia	
	B	Philadelphia	
	C	Philadelphia	
	D	Lancaster	(Pequea Dragons)[126]
9/61—4/62- 6/17/65	E	Philadelphia	
	F	Centre	
	G	Philadelphia	
	H	Northampton*	
	I	Crawford	
	K	Berks Philadelphia	
	L	Tioga	
	M	Armstrong	(James E. Brown Dragoons)[127]
60th (3rd Cavalry)	A	Philadelphia	(Philadelphia Merchant Troop)[128]
	B	Philadelphia	
	C	Philadelphia	
	D	District of Columbia	(President's Mounted Guards)[128]
	E	Philadelphia	
	F	Philadelphia	
7—8/61- 5/9/65	G	Allegheny	
	H	Cumberland Franklin**	(Big Spring Adamantine Guard)[129]
	I	Philadelphia	
	K	Philadelphia	
	L	Schuylkill	
	M	Philadelphia	
61st[130]	A	Indiana	(Mahoning Rifles)[131,132]
	B	Allegheny	(Ellsworth Legion)[90]
9/7/61- 6/28/65	C	Allegheny	(Baxter Guards)[90,133]
	D	Luzerne	

61st	E	Allegheny	(Simpson Infantry)[90,134]	
(continued)	F	Allegheny	(Allegheny Guards)[90]	
	G	Philadelphia	(Lyon Guards[90]	
	H	Philadelphia	(Marshall Guards)[135]	new H Allegheny
	I	Philadelphia		new I Allegheny
	K	Allegheny	(Pennsylvania Zouaves)[90]	new K Allegheny
62nd	A	Allegheny	(Federal Guards)[136]	
	B	Allegheny	(McKee Rifle Cadets)[136]	
7/4/61-	C	Clarion	(Lyon Guards)[136]	
7/13/64	D	Armstrong	(Finlay Cadets)[136]	
	E	Clarion	(Reimersburg Guards)[136]	
	F	Allegheny	(Eighth Ward Guards)[136]	
	G	Allegheny	(Kramer Guards)[136]	
	H	Allegheny	(St. Clair Guards)[136]	
	I	Jefferson	(Jefferson Guards)[136]	
	K	Allegheny	(Eighth Ward Guards)[136]	
	L	Allegheny	(Chambers Zouaves)[136]	
	M	Blair	(Blair County Sharpshooters)[137]	
63rd	A	Allegheny	(Kelly Guards)[90]	
	B	Allegheny	(Sharpsburg Guards)[90,138]	
8—10/61-	C	Beaver*	(Hanna's Light Guards)[90]	
9/9/64	D	Allegheny	(Pittsburgh Fire Zouaves)[90]	
	E	Allegheny	(Etna Guards)[90,139]	
	F	Clarion		
	G	Armstrong	(Morgan Guards)	
		Venango**		
	H	Allegheny	(McCullough Guards)[90]	
	I	Allegheny	(McKeesport Greys)[90,140]	
	K	Allegheny	(Hays Guards)	
64th	A	Northampton	(Bethlehem Cavalry)[141]	
(4th	B	Allegheny		
Cavalry)	C	Westmoreland		
	D	Westmoreland	(Covode Cavalry)[142]	
8—10/61-	E	Allegheny		
7/1/65	F	Lebanon		
	G	Allegheny		
	H	Venango		
	I	Venango		
	K	Venango		
	L	Venango	(Oil Creek Cavalry)[142a]	
	M	Luzerne		
65th	A	Philadelphia		
(5th	B	Philadelphia		
Cavalry)	C	Philadelphia		
		New Jersey**		
7—9/61-	D	Philadelphia		
8/7/65		Delaware**		
	E	Philadelphia		
	F	Philadelphia		
Cameron	G	Philadelphia		
Dragoons	H	Philadelphia		
	I	Philadelphia		
	K	Lycoming	(First Lycoming Troop)[143]	
		Philadelphia		
	L	Allegheny		
	M	Allegheny		
		Venango		
67th	A	Carbon	(Carbon Guards)[143a]	
	B	Philadelphia	(Schuylkill Rangers)[144]	new B Indiana
8/61—3/62-	C	Pike		
7/14/65		Wayne		

67th *(continued)*	D	Monroe Wayne		
	E	Indiana Westmoreland Philadelphia		
	F	Clarion Jefferson	(United Eagles)[145]	
	G	Monroe		
	H	Carbon Northampton		
	I	Philadelphia		new I Allegheny
	K	Schuylkill		
68th 8—9/62 6/9/65 Scott Legion	A	Philadelphia		
	B	Philadelphia		
	C	Philadelphia		
	D	Philadelphia		
	E	Philadelphia		
	F	Philadelphia		
	G	Philadelphia		
	H	Philadelphia[146]		
	I	Philadelphia[146a]		
	K	Philadelphia		
69th 8/9/61- 7/1/65	A	Philadelphia		
	B	Philadelphia		
	C	Philadelphia		
	D	Philadelphia		
	E	Philadelphia		
	F	Philadelphia		
	G	Philadelphia		
	H	Philadelphia		
	I	Philadelphia	(Tiger Zouaves)[147]	
	K	Philadelphia		
70th (6th Cavalry) 8—10/61- 6/17/65 Rush's Lancers	A	Philadelphia		
	B	Philadelphia		
	C	Philadelphia		
	D	Philadelphia		
	E	Philadelphia Luzerne**		
	F	Philadelphia		
	G	Berks	(Reading Dragoons)[12]	
	H	Philadelphia		
	I	Philadelphia		
	K	Philadelphia		
	L	Philadelphia		
	M	Philadelphia		
71st[148] 8/61- 7/2/64 California Regiment	A	Philadelphia		
	B	Philadelphia		
	C	Philadelphia		
	D	Philadelphia		
	E	Philadelphia		
	F	Philadelphia		
	G	Philadelphia		
	H	Chester Philadelphia		
	I	Bucks* Philadelphia	(Middletown Guards)[149]	
	K	Chester Philadelphia	(Wayne Guards)[150]	
	L	Philadelphia		
	M	Philadelphia		
	N	Philadelphia		

71st (continued)	P	Philadelphia		
	R	Philadelphia		
72nd[148]	A	Philadelphia		
	B	Philadelphia		
8/10/61-	C	Philadelphia		
8/24/64	D	Philadelphia		
	E	Philadelphia		
Baxter's	F	Philadelphia		
Fire	G	Philadelphia		
Zouaves	H	Philadelphia		
	I	Philadelphia		
	K	Philadelphia		
	L	Philadelphia	(Keystone Guards)[151]	
	M	Philadelphia		
	N	Philadelphia		
	P	Philadelphia		
	R	Philadelphia		
73rd	A	Philadelphia		
	B	Philadelphia	(Read Guards)[152]	
9/19/61-	C	Philadelphia		
7/14/65	D	Philadelphia		
	E	Philadelphia		
Pennsyl-	F	Philadelphia		
vania	G	Philadelphia		
Legion		Lancaster**		
	H	Philadelphia		
	I	Philadelphia		
	K	Philadelphia		
		Lancaster**		
74th	A	Philadelphia		new A Columbia
	B	Allegheny	(Turner Rifles)[153]	new B Allegheny
9/30/61-	C	Allegheny		new C Northumberland
		Snyder**		(Rohback Guards)[154]
8/29/65	D	Allegheny	(Kossuth Guards)[153]	new D Union
				Snyder
	E	Allegheny	(Alliquippa Rifles)[153]	new E Northumberland
				Union**
				Berks**
	F	Allegheny	(Sigel Guards)[153]	new F Indiana
	G	Allegheny	(Lyon Guards)[153]	new G Adams
				Berks
	H	Allegheny	(Pittsburgh Infantry)[153,155]	
	I	Allegheny	(Hooveler Zouaves)[153]	
	K	Allegheny		
		Philadelphia		
75th	A	Philadelphia		
	B	Philadelphia		
8/9/61-	C	Philadelphia		
9/1/65	D	Philadelphia		
	E	Philadelphia		
	F	Philadelphia		
	G	Philadelphia		
	H	Philadelphia		
	I	Philadelphia		
	K	Philadelphia		
76th	A	Lawrence		
	B	Mercer		
9—11/61-	C	Blair		
7/18/65	D	York	(Union Guard)[155b]	
		Snyder**		

76th *(continued)* Keystone Zouaves	E	Bedford York**		
	F	Blair		
	G	Lawrence Westmoreland Indiana**		
	H	Luzerne Dauphin**		
	I	York		
	K	Allegheny Beaver Schuylkill	(Hampton Guards)[156]	
77th 9—10/61- 1/16/66	A	Franklin		
	B	Allegheny	(Union Rifles)[156]	
	C	Huntingdon		
	D	York* Lancaster* Cumberland*		new D Allegheny
	E	Mercer Allegheny*	(Bell Guards)[157]	new E Allegheny
	F	Fulton*	(Fulton Rifles)[158]	new F Blair
	G	Luzerne*		
	H	Franklin Luzerne Allegheny**		new H Beaver Lawrence
	I	None		new I Dauphin
	K	Lancaster Allegheny*		
78th 10/18/61- 9/11/65	A	Indiana		
	B	Armstrong		
	C	Clarion		new C Mifflin+ (Bower Guards)[158a]
	D	Cambria Indiana		new D Cumberland Dauphin** (Russel Guards)[159]
	E	Clarion	(Perry Rifles)[160]	new E Butler
	F	Armstrong		new F Allegheny
	G	Armstrong	(Buffington Blues)[161]	new G Beaver Lawrence**
	H	Butler		new H Allegheny+
	I	Armstrong		new I Allegheny+
	K	Armstrong		new K Huntingdon+
79th 9—10/61- 7/12/65	A	Lancaster	(Jackson Rifles)[162]	
	B	Lancaster		
	C	Lancaster		
	D	Washington	(Mallinger Guards)[163]	
	E	Lancaster	(Normal Rifles)[164]	
	F	Lancaster	(German Sharpshooters)[162]	
	G	Lancaster		
	H	Lancaster		
	I	Lancaster		
	K	Lancaster		
80th (7th Cavalry) 9—2/61- 8/23/65	A	Schuylkill		
	B	Lycoming Tioga		
	C	Bradford Tioga		
	D	Montour	(Washingtonville Cavalry)[165]	
	E	Centre Clinton	(Nittany Valley Dragoons)[166]	
	F	Philadelphia Schuylkill		

80th (continued)	G	Chester Lycoming Tioga		
	H	Allegheny Chester Montour		
	I	Dauphin Lycoming	(First City Cavalry)[167,168]	
	K	Cumberland Fayette		
	L	Berks Northumberland		
	M	Allegheny	(S. Bradley Independent Cavalry Scouts)[169]	

81st	A	Philadelphia		
	B	Philadelphia		
8—10/61-6/29/65	C	Philadelphia		
	D	Philadelphia Carbon		
Chippewa Regiment[170]	E	Philadelphia		
	F	Philadelphia	(2nd Co., Cadwalader Greys)[171]	
	G	Carbon		
	H	Carbon		
	I	Carbon		
	K	Luzerne Carbon**		

82nd	A	Philadelphia		
	B	Allegheny	(Siegel Guards)[172]	
7—9/61-7/13/65	C	Philadelphia		
	D	Philadelphia	(2nd Co., Garde Lafayette)[173]	
	E	Philadelphia		
	F	Philadelphia		
	G	Philadelphia		
	H	Philadelphia	(Greble Guards)[173]	
	I	Philadelphia		
	K	Philadelphia		

83rd	A	Crawford	(Watson Guards)[174]	
	B	Crawford	(McLane Guards)[175]	
9/13/61-6/28/65	C	Erie		
	D	Erie		
	E	Erie	(LeBoeuff Guards)[174]	
	F	Crawford		
	G	Forest		new G Allegheny
	H	Crawford		new H Allegheny
	I	Erie		new I Berks Dauphin
	K	Erie		new K Dauphin

84th	A	Blair Bedford**		
11/22/61-1/13/65	B	Lycoming Sullivan** Bradford**		
	C	Blair		new C Westmoreland (9/62) (Foster Guards)[176]
	D	Columbia	(Hurley Light Guard)[177]	
	E	Blair		
	F	Lycoming	(Muncy Rifles)[178]	
	G	Cameron		
	H	Dauphin		new H Clearfield (10/62)Philadelphia** Columbia**

84th (continued)	I	Blair Indiana** Wayne** Clearfield	(Mechanics' Rifle Co.)[179]	new I Wayne (9/62)
	K	Clearfield		
85th 11/12/61- 11/22/64	A	Washington	(Union Guards)[180]	
	B	Washington	(Ellsworth Cadets)[180]	
	C	Fayette Somerset** Washington**	(Red Stone Blues)[180]	
	D	Washington	(Lafayette Infantry)[180]	
	E	Washington Fayette	(Washington Guards)[180]	
	F	Greene	(Ten Mile Greys)[180]	
	G	Fayette Greene	(Monongahela Guards)[180]	
	H	Somerset	(Independent Blues)[180]	
	I	Fayette	(Howell Invincibles)[180]	
	K	Fayette	(Mountain Rifles)[180]	
87th 9/61- 6/29/65	A	York	(Ellsworth Zouaves)[181]	
	B	Dauphin York	(Washington Guards)[181,182]	
	C	York		
	D	York		
	E	York Cumberland**	(Worth Infantry)[182a]	
	F	Adams	(Independent Blues)[183]	new F Allegheny
	G	York		new G Allegheny
	H	York		new H Lawrence Washington
	I	Adams	(National Guards)[184,184a]	new I Dauphin
	K	York	(York Rifles)[185]	new K Franklin
88th 9/61—4/62- 6/30/65 Cameron Light Guards	A	Berks	(Junior Fire Zouaves)[12]	
	B	Berks	(Neversink Zouaves)[12]	
	C	Philadelphia		
	D	Philadelphia		
	E	Philadelphia		
	F	Philadelphia		
	G	Philadelphia		
	H	Berks	(Union Guards)[12]	
	I	Philadelphia		
	K	Philadelphia		
89th (8th Cavalry) 8—10/61- 7/24/65	A	Chester		
	B	Lycoming		
	C	Philadelphia		
	D	Philadelphia		
	E	Philadelphia		
	F	Philadelphia		
	G	Philadelphia		
	H	Philadelphia		
	I	Philadelphia		
	K	Philadelphia		
	L	Philadelphia		
	M	Philadelphia		
90th 10/61—3/62- 11/26/64 National Guards[186]	A	Philadelphia		
	B	Philadelphia		
	C	Philadelphia		
	D	Philadelphia		
	E	Philadelphia		
	F	Philadelphia		

90th (continued)	G	Philadelphia		
	H	Philadelphia		
	I	Philadelphia		
	K	Philadelphia		
91st	A	Philadelphia		
	B	Philadelphia		
9—12/61-	C	Philadelphia		
7/10/65	D	Philadelphia		
	E	Philadelphia		
	F	Philadelphia		
	G	Philadelphia		
	H	Philadelphia		
	I	Philadelphia	(Union Guards)[186a]	
	K	Philadelphia		
92nd (9th Cavalry)	A	Perry Lehigh**		
	B	Dauphin		
	C	Dauphin Perry**		
10—11/61 7/18/65	D	Luzerne		
	E	Dauphin Susquehanna		
Lochiel Cavalry	F	Lancaster	(Old Guard Mounted Volunteers)[187]	
	G	Lancaster	(Greider's Mounted Rangers)[188]	
	H	Cumberland Dauphin** Luzerne**		
	I	Cumberland		
	K	Dauphin Luzerne		
	L	Luzerne Mifflin		
	M	Huntingdon Blair**		
93rd	A	Lebanon	(Perseverance Co. 1)[189]	
	B	Berks	(Union Zouaves)[189]	
10/28/61-	C	Lebanon	(Quittapahilla Guards)[189]	
6/27/65	D	Lebanon	(Union Guards)[189]	
	E	Clinton Centre	(Washington Guards)[189]	
	F	Lebanon	(Perseverance Co. 2)[189]	
	G	Berks Montgomery**	(Coleman Rifles)[189]	
	H	Montour	(Baldy Guards)[189]	
	I	Dauphin Lebanon	(McCarter Guards)[189]	
	K	Lebanon	(Annville Guards)[189]	
95th	A	Philadelphia		
	B	Philadelphia		
8/23/61-	C	Philadelphia		
7/17/65	D	Philadelphia		
	E	Philadelphia		
Gosline's Zouaves	F	Philadelphia		new F Philadelphia
	G	Philadelphia		
	H	Philadelphia		
	I	Philadelphia		new I Philadelphia
	K	Philadelphia		
96th	A	Schuylkill	(National Light Infantry)[141]	
9/23/61-	B	Schuylkill	(Pine Grove Sharpshooters)[190]	
10/21/64	C	Schuylkill	(Good Intent Light Artillery)[190]	

96th	D	Schuylkill	
(continued)	E	Schuylkill	
		Luzerne	
	F	Schuylkill	(Union Guards)[191]
	G	Schuylkill	
		Berks	
		Dauphin	
	H	Schuylkill	
	I	Schuylkill	
	K	Schuylkill	
97th	A	Chester	(Guss Fencibles)[192]
	B	Chester	(Chester County Grays)[192]
8—10/61-	C	Chester	(Paoli Guards)[192]
8/28/65	D	Delaware	(Concordville Rifles)[192]
		Chester**	
	E	Chester	(Mulligan Guards)[192]
	F	Chester	(National Guards)[192]
	G	Delaware	(Broomall Guards)[192]
	H	Chester	(Greble Guards)[192]
	I	Delaware	(Brooke Guards)[192]
	K	Chester	(Wayne Guards)[192]
98th	A	Philadelphia	
	B	Philadelphia	
8/17/61-	C	Philadelphia	
6/29/65	D	Philadelphia	
	E	Philadelphia	
	F	Philadelphia	
	G	Philadelphia	
	H	Philadelphia	
	I	Philadelphia	
	K	Philadelphia	
99th	A	Philadelphia	
	B	Philadelphia	
7/61—2/62-		Lancaster**	
7/1/65	C	Philadelphia	
	D	Philadelphia	
Lincoln		Lancaster**	
Legion[193]		Schuylkill**	
	E	Philadelphia	
	F	Philadelphia	
	G	Philadelphia	(Union Zouaves)[194]
	H	Philadelphia	
	I	Philadelphia	
	K	Philadelphia	
100th[195]	A	Washington	(Washington Greys)[196]
	B	Lawrence	
8/31/61-		Mercer**	
7/24/65	C	Butler	
		Lawrence**	
Roundhead	D	Beaver	(Darlington Blues)[197]
Regiment	E	Lawrence	
		Butler**	
	F	Lawrence	(Slippery Rock Guards)[198]
	G	Mercer	(Worth Guards)[199]
	H	Lawrence	
	I	Lawrence	
	K	Lawrence	
	L	Beaver**	
		Susquehanna**	
		Cumberland**	
	M	Westmoreland	
		Allegheny	

101st	A	Allegheny Perry**	(Duquesne Guards)[200]	new A Dauphin
11/61—2/62-6/25/65	B	Tioga	(Tioga Mountaineers)[201]	new B Westmoreland Indiana
	C	Beaver Lawrence	(Agnew Guards)[202]	new C Union
	D	Bedford	(All Hazard Boys)[203]	new D Dauphin
	E	Allegheny	(Wilson Guards)[156]	new E Juniata Dauphin
	F	Beaver	(Roberts Infantry)[202]	new F Cumberland Allegheny
	G	Allegheny Bedford		new G Adams Allegheny Dauphin
	H	Beaver Butler**		new H Allegheny
	I	Allegheny Dauphin**	(McFarland Rangers)[200]	
	K	Adams	(Unger Guards)[204]	
102nd	A	Allegheny	(Washington Infantry)[205]	
	B	Allegheny	(Union Cadets)[205]	
8/61-6/28/65	C	Allegheny	(Birmingham Zouaves)[205]	
	D	Allegheny	(Pennock Guards)[205]	
	E	Allegheny	(Union Cadets)[205]	
	F	Allegheny		
	G	Allegheny	(Johnston Cadets)[205]	
	H	Butler		
	I	Allegheny	(Iron City Zouaves)[205]	
	K	Allegheny	(Vierheller Infantry)[205]	
	L	Allegheny	(Rowley Rifles)[205]	
	M	Allegheny	(Pittsburgh Zouaves)[205]	
103rd	A	Clarion	(Constitution Rangers)[206]	new A Adams Franklin
9/61—2/62-6/25/65	B	Armstrong Butler Venango	(Curry Rifles)[206]	new B Columbia
	C	Allegheny	(McClellan Guards)[206]	new C Northumberland
	D	Armstrong	(Finlay Rifles)[206]	new D York Perry
	E	Butler		new E Crawford Beaver
	F	Clarion Armstrong**		new F Westmoreland
	G	Indiana Clarion** Allegheny**		new G Dauphin York
	H	Clarion		new H Blair
	I	Allegheny Butler Venango**		
	K	Allegheny Armstrong Butler**		
104th	A	Bucks	(Young Guard)[207]	
	B	Bucks	(Old Guard)[207]	
9—10/61-8/25/65	C	Bucks	(McClellan Rangers)[207]	
	D	Bucks		
	E	Bucks		new E Blair
Ringgold	F	Bucks		new F Perry
Regiment[208]	G	Bucks		new G Schuylkill
	H	Berks*	(Lauer Infantry)[209]	
	I	Bucks		new I Luzerne

104th *(continued)*	K	Philadelphia Bucks		Montour** new K Armstrong Allegheny
105th 9/9/61- 7/11/65	A	Jefferson Indiana**	(Mahoning Rifles)[210]	
	B	Jefferson	(Brookville Rifles)[210]	
	C	Clarion Clearfield	(Limestown Guards)[210]	
	D	Clearfield Jefferson**	(Jackson Blues)[210]	
	E	Westmoreland	(Sewickley Infantry)[211]	
	F	Clearfield Indiana Venango	(Union Guards)[210]	
	G	Jefferson	(Ringgold Artillery)[210]	
	H	Jefferson	(Washington Guards)[210]	
	I	Jefferson		
	K	Indiana		
106th 8/28/61- 6/30/65	A	Philadelphia		
	B	Philadelphia		
	C	Philadelphia Bradford**		
	D	Philadelphia Bradford**		
	E	Philadelphia		
	F	Lycoming* Bradford** Philadelphia**	(Hughesville Guards)[212]	
	G	Philadelphia Montgomery**		
	H	Philadelphia		
	I	Philadelphia		
	K	Philadelphia Bradford**		
107th 2—3/62- 7/13/65	A	York Cumberland** Luzerne**	(Union Infantry)[213]	
	B	Franklin Cumberland** Berks**	(R. P. McClure Light Guards)[214]	
	C	Sullivan* Lycoming*	(Jackson Guards)[215]	
	D	Schuylkill* Mifflin*		
	E	Lancaster*+ Dauphin*	(Union Fencibles)[216]	
	F	Mifflin* Dauphin* Wyoming*	(Slemmer Guards)[216a]	
	G	Schuylkill*+ Bradford*		
	H	Franklin Fulton* Bedford**		
	I	Dauphin* Lebanon*		
	K	Franklin		
108th (11th Cavalry)	A	Iowa		
	B	Chester*		
	C	Philadelphia*		
	D	Franklin*		

108th		Dauphin*		
(continued)	E	New York	(Cameron Light Horse)[217]	
		Philadelphia**		
	F	Bradford*	(Troy Cavalry)[218]	
		Tioga*		
8—10/61-	G	Cambria*		
8/13/65	H	Northampton*	(2nd Co. Bethlehem Cavalry)[219]	
	I	New Jersey		
Harlan's		Lancaster**		
Light		York**		
Cavalry		Warren**		
	K	Luzerne*		
	L	Clarion*		
		Allegheny*		
		Jefferson*		
	M	Ohio		
109th	A	Philadelphia		
	B	Philadelphia		
3—5/62	C	Philadelphia		
3/31/65	D	Philadelphia		
	E	Philadelphia		
Curtin	F	Philadelphia		
Light	G	Philadelphia		
Guard	H	Philadelphia		
	I	Philadelphia		
	K	Philadelphia		
110th	A	Blair	(Tyrone Infantry)[220]	
	B	Huntingdon	(Union Guards)[220]	
10/24/61-	C	Bedford	(Woodbury Guards)[220,221]	
6/28/65	D	Huntingdon	(Hart's Loq. Infantry)[220]	
	E	Philadelphia	(Dare Guards)[220]	
Juniata	F	Philadelphia	(Scott Fusiliers)[220]	
Regiment[222]	G	Philadelphia	(Lewis Guards)[220]	new G Philadelphia
	H	Philadelphia	(Fitz Greys)[220]	
	I	Philadelphia	(Henry Guards)[220]	
	K	Centre	(Slifer Guards)[220]	
		Clearfield		
		Blair**		
111th	A	Erie		
	B	Warren		
1/24/62-	C	Erie		
7/19/65	D	Warren		
	E	Crawford		
	F	Erie		
	G	Crawford		
		Erie		
	H	Erie		
		Warren		
	I	Crawford		
		Erie		
	K	Erie		
		Mercer**		
		Elk**		
112th	A	Philadelphia		
(2nd Heavy	B	Philadelphia		
Artillery)	C	Philadelphia		
		Wayne**		
2/8/62-	D	Philadelphia		
1/29/66	E	Philadelphia		
		Wayne**		
	F	Philadelphia		

112th		Montour**		
(continued)		Lycoming**		
		Columbia**		
	G	Philadelphia		
	H	Philadelphia		
		Carbon**		
	I	Philadelphia		
		Allegheny		
	K	Fayette*		
	L	Luzerne*		
	M	Luzerne*		
113th	A	Philadelphia		
(12th	B	Crawford*		
Cavalry)	C	Philadelphia		
	D	Northampton		
12/61—4/62-		Philadelphia		
7/20/65	E	Lancaster		
	F	Mifflin		
Curtin		Union*		
Hussars		Juniata**		
	G	Blair		
		Dauphin		
	H	Blair		
		Dauphin		
		Lebanon*		
	I	Lancaster		
		Philadelphia		
	K	Warren		
	L	Erie		
		Dauphin		
	M	Cambria		
114th	A	Philadelphia	(Zouaves d'Afrique)	
	B	Philadelphia		
8—9/62	C	Philadelphia	(Cooper's Guard)[223]	
5/29/65	D	Philadelphia		
	E	Philadelphia		
	F	Philadelphia		
	G	Philadelphia		
	H	Philadelphia		
	I	Philadelphia		
	K	Philadelphia		
115th	A	Philadelphia		
	B	Philadelphia		
1/28/62-	C	Philadelphia		
6/22/64[224]	D	Cambria		
		Blair**		
	E	Philadelphia		
	F	Philadelphia		
	G	Lebanon		
		Lancaster		
		Northampton**		
	H	Philadelphia		
	I	Philadelphia		
	K	Philadelphia		
116th[225]	A	Philadelphia		
	B	Philadelphia		
8/30/62-	C	Philadelphia		
7/14/65	D	Philadelphia		
	E	Philadelphia		new E Philadelphia
	F	Philadelphia		new F Schuylkill
	G	Philadelphia		new G Schuylkill

116th	H	Philadelphia		new H Allegheny
(continued)	I	Philadelphia		new I Allegheny
	K	Philadelphia		new K Fayette
117th	A	Philadelphia		
(13th	B	Philadelphia		new B Huntingdon
Cavalry)				(8/63)
	C	Philadelphia		new C Dauphin(8/63)
				York
12/61—3/63-	D	Philadelphia		new D Blair(8-9/63)
7/14/65	E	Allegheny		
	F	Cumberland		
Irish	G	Lycoming		
Dragoons	H	Philadelphia		
	I	Philadelphia		
	K	Philadelphia		
	L	Philadelphia*		
	M	Philadelphia		
118th	A	Philadelphia		
	B	Philadelphia		
8/30/62-	C	Philadelphia		
6/1/65	D	Philadelphia		
	E	Philadelphia		
Corn	F	Philadelphia		
Exchange	G	Philadelphia		
Regiment	H	Philadelphia		
	I	Philadelphia		
	K	Philadelphia		
119th	A	Philadelphia		
	B	Philadelphia		
9/1/62-	C	Philadelphia		
6/19/65	D	Philadelphia		
	E	Delaware*	(Delaware County Guards)[226]	
	F	Philadelphia		
	G	Philadelphia		
	H	Philadelphia		
	I	Philadelphia		
	K	Philadelphia		
121st	A	Venango	(Venango Blues)[226a]	
	B	Philadelphia		
9/1/62-	C	Philadelphia		
6/2/65	D	Philadelphia		
	E	Philadelphia		
	F	Venango		
	G	Philadelphia		
	H	Philadelphia		
	I	Philadelphia		
	K	Philadelphia		
122nd	A	Lancaster		
	B	Lancaster		
8—9/62-	C	Lancaster		
5/16/63	D	Lancaster		
	E	Lancaster		
	F	Lancaster		
	G	Lancaster	(Jefferson Guards)[227]	
	H	Lancaster		
	I	Lancaster		
	K	Lancaster	(Schaeffer Zouaves)	
123rd	A	Allegheny	(Cass Infantry)[228]	
8/62-	B	Allegheny	(Butchers Infantry)[228]	
5/13/63	C	Allegheny	(Clark Infantry)[228]	

123rd	D	Allegheny	(Walker Infantry)[228]
(continued)	E	Allegheny	(Clark Infantry)[228]
	F	Allegheny	(Tarentum Infantry)[228]
	G	Allegheny	(Powers Infantry)[228,229]
	H	Allegheny	(Clark Infantry)[228]
	I	Allegheny	(Howe Engineers)[228]
	K	Allegheny	(Watt & Butchers Infantry)[228]
124th	A	Chester	
	B	Delaware	(Delaware County Fusiliers)[230]
8/62-	C	Chester	(Oxford Guards)[231]
5/17/63	D	Delaware	(Gideon's Band)[230]
	E	Chester	
	F	Chester	
	G	Chester	
	H	Delaware	(Delaware County Volunteers)[230]
	I	Chester	
	K	Chester	
125th	A	Blair	
	B	Blair	
8—9/62	C	Huntingdon	(Huntingdon Bible Company)[232]
5/19/63	D	Blair	
		Huntingdon**	
	E	Blair	
		Bedford**	
	F	Huntingdon	(S. M. Kier Rifles)[233]
	G	Blair	
	H	Huntingdon	
	I	Huntingdon	
	K	Blair	
		Cambria**	
126th	A	Franklin	(Chambers Infantry)[234]
	B	Franklin	
8/62-		Fulton	
5/20/63	C	Franklin	(Mercersburg Guards)[235]
	D	Franklin	(Franklin Rifles)[234]
	E	Franklin	(Waynesboro Sharpshooters)[234]
	F	Juniata	
	G	Franklin	(Easton Avengers)[234]
	H	Franklin	(Washington Blues)[236]
	I	Juniata	
	K	Franklin	
127th	A	Dauphin	(First City Zouaves)[237]
	B	Dauphin	(Harrisburg Fire Zouaves)[238]
8/62-	C	Dauphin	(Derry Fencibles)[237]
5/9/63	D	Dauphin	(Boas Guards)[237]
	E	Lebanon	(Lebanon Guards)[239,240]
	F	Dauphin	(Russell Guards)[237]
	G	Dauphin	(City Guards)[237,241]
		Crawford**	
	H	Dauphin	(Susquehanna Rangers)[242]
	I	Adams	(Londonderry Volunteers)[242a]
		Lebanon	
	K	Lebanon	(Lebanon Valley Rifles)[243]
		Schuylkill	
128th	A	Berks	(Washington Infantry)[12]
	B	Berks	(Muhlenberg Infantry)[12]
8/62-	C	Bucks	
5/20/63	D	Lehign	
	E	Berks	(Reading Artillerists)[12]
	F	Bucks	

128th	G	Lehigh	
(continued)	H	Berks	(Felix Light Guard)[12]
	I	Berks	(Reading Iron Works Guard)[12]
	K	Berks	(Reading City Guards)[244]
129th	A	Schuylkill	
	B	Schuylkill	
8/62-	C	Northampton	
5/18/63	D	Northampton	
	E	Schuylkill	
	F	Northampton	
	G	Schuylkill	(Cleaver Guards)[245]
	H	Schuylkill	
	I	Montgomery	
	K	Northampton	
130th	A	Cumberland	
	B	York	
8/62-	C	Montgomery	
5/21/63		York	
	D	Cumberland	(Shippensburg Guards)[246]
	E	Cumberland	(Newville Infantry)[246]
	F	Cumberland	(Pope Fencibles)[246a]
		Dauphin**	
	G	Cumberland	(Carlisle Infantry)[246]
	H	Cumberland	(James Guards)[246]
		Chester	
		Dauphin	
	I	York	
	K	York	
131st	A	Union	(Union County Fencibles)[247]
	B	Northumberland*	
8/62-	C	Northumberland	(Northumberland County Tigers)[248]
5/23/63	D	Mifflin*	
	E	Northumberland*	(Davis Sharpshooters)[249]
	F	Snyder*	
	G	Lycoming*	
	H	Lycoming	
	I	Lycoming	
	K	Mifflin*	
132nd	A	Montour	(Danville Fencibles)[250]
	B	Wyoming	(Wyoming Tigers)[251]
8/62-	C	Bradford	
5/24/63	D	Bradford	
		New York*	
	E	Columbia	(Bloomsburg Guards)[251]
	F	Carbon	(Lehigh Valley Guards)[251]
	G	Carbon	
	H	Columbia	(Catawissa Guards)[251]
	I	Luzerne	(Railroad Guards)[252]
		New York*	
	K	Luzerne	(Scranton Guards)[251]
133rd	A	Cambria	
	B	Cambria	
8/62-	C	Bedford	
5/26/63	D	Somerset	
	F	Somerset	
	F	Cambria	(2nd Co., Cambria Guards)[253]
	G	Perry	
	H	Perry	
	I	Perry	
	K	Bedford	

134th	A	Lawrence	
	B	Lawrence	
8/62-	C	Butler	
5/26/63	D	Lawrence	
	E	Beaver	(Beaver County Greys)[254]
	F	Butler	
	G	Butler	
	H	Lawrence	
	I	Beaver	
		Lawrence**	
	K	Butler	
135th	A	Indiana	
	B	Jefferson	
8/62-	C	Lancaster	
5/24/63	D	Indiana	
	E	Lancaster	
	F	Westmoreland	
	G	Westmoreland	
	H	Lancaster	(Marietta Braves)[255]
	I	Indiana	
	K	Lancaster	
136th	A	Tioga	
	B	Luzerne	(Lackawanna Tigers)[256]
8/62-		Tioga	
5/29/63	C	Dauphin	
		Northumberland**	
	D	Tioga	
	E	Allegheny	(Union Infantry)[257]
	F	Allegheny	(Sumner Infantry)[257]
	G	Allegheny	(McClintock Guards)[257]
	H	Allegheny	(Keystone Infantry)[257]
		Westmoreland**	
	I	Centre	
		Columbia	
		Crawford	
	K	Cambria	(Morrell Guards)[258]
137th	A	Wayne	
	B	Crawford	
8—9/62-	C	Clinton	
6/2/63	D	Butler	
	E	Clinton	
	F	Butler	
	G	Butler	
	H	Clinton	
	I	Blair*	(Hammond Guards)[259]
	K	Schuylkill	
		Wayne**	
138th	A	Montgomery	
	B	Adams	
8—9/62-	C	Montgomery	
6/23/65	D	Bedford	
	E	Bedford	
	F	Bedford	
	G	Adams	
	H	Bucks	
	I	Montgomery	
	K	Montgomery	
139th	A	Mercer	(Mercer Guards)[257]
	B	Armstrong	(Armstrong Guards)[257]
9/1/62-	C	Armstrong	(Dudley Infantry)[257]
6/21/65		Westmoreland**	

139th (continued)	D	Allegheny	(Semple Infantry, Co. B)[257]
	E	Allegheny Armstrong	(Graham Rifles)[257]
	F	Allegheny	(Logan Guards)[257]
	G	Allegheny	(Semple Infantry, Co. C)[257]
	H	Allegheny Beaver	(Rudd Infantry)[257]
	I	Allegheny	(Semple Infantry, Co. A)[257]
	K	Allegheny	(Semple Infantry, Co. D)[257]
140th	A	Greene	(Greene County Rifles)[260]
	B	Mercer	(Stewart's Infantry)[261]
8—9/62-	C	Washington	(Brady Infantry)[260,262]
5/31/65	D	Washington	(Ten Mile Infantry)[260]
	E	Washington Fayette**	(Lawrence Guards)[260]
	F	Beaver	(R. L. Baker Guards)[260]
	G	Washington	(Brown Infantry)[263,264]
	H	Beaver	(Ormond Rangers)[260]
	I	Beaver	(Darragh Infantry)[260]
	K	Washington	(Reed Infantry)[260]
141st	A	Bradford	
	B	Bradford	
8—9/62	C	Bradford	
5/28/65	D	Bradford	
	E	Bradford	
	F	Susquehanna	
	G	Wayne	(Union Guards)[265]
	H	Susquehanna	
	I	Bradford	
	K	Bradford Sullivan**	
142nd	A	Mercer	
	B	Westmoreland	
8/62-	C	Somerset	
5/29/65	D	Somerset	
	E	Union	
	F	Somerset	
	G	Monroe Pike**	
	H	Fayette	
	I	Venango	(Petroleum Guards)[266]
	K	Luzerne Lebanon**	
143rd	A	Luzerne	(Ross Rifles)[267]
	B	Luzerne	
8—10/62-	C	Luzerne	(Wyoming Artillerists)[267]
6/12/65	D	Luzerne	(Wyoming Light Dragoons)[267]
	E	Luzerne	
	F	Luzerne	
	G	Luzerne	
	H	Susquehanna	
	I	Luzerne	
	K	Lycoming Wyoming	
145th	A	Erie	
	B	Erie	
8—9/62-	C	Erie	
5/31/65	D	Erie	
	E	Warren Erie**	
	F	Warren	

145th	G	Mercer	
(continued)	H	Crawford	
	I	Erie	
	K	Erie	
147th	A	Allegheny	(Old Company L, 28th Regiment)
		Philadelphia**	
10/28/62-	B	Huntingdon	(Old Company O, 28th
7/15/65		Philadelphia	Regiment)
	C	Luzerne	(Old Company N, 28th
			Regiment)
		Carbon**	
	D	Philadelphia	(Old Company M, 28th
			Regiment)
	E	Philadelphia+	(Old Company P, 28th Regiment)
	F	Luzerne	
	G	Snyder*	(Keystone Guards)[268]
	H	Lehigh*+	
		Berks*	
	I	Philadelphia	(Schuylkill Arsenal Guard)[269]
		Berks**	
	K	Carbon*[270]	
148th	A	Centre	
	B	Centre	
9/1/62-	C	Centre	
6/1/65	D	Centre	
	E	Indiana*	
		Jefferson*	
	F	Centre	
		Cameron**	
	G	Centre	
	H	Centre	
	I	Jefferson*	
	K	Clarion*	
149th	A	Tioga	
	B	Clearfield	
8/30/62-	C	Lebanon	(Jackson Guards)[271]
6/24/65	D	Allegheny	
	E	Clearfield	
		Luzerne	
	F	Luzerne	(Huntingdon Valley Rifles)[272]
	G	Potter	
		Tioga	
		Perry**	
	H	Mifflin	
	I	Huntingdon	
	K	Potter	
150th	A	Philadelphia	
	B	Philadelphia	
8—9/62-	C	Crawford	
6/23/65	D	Union	
	E	Philadelphia	
	F	Philadelphia	
	G	McKean	
	H	Crawford	
	I	Crawford	
	K	Crawford	
151st	A	Susquehanna	
	B	Pike	
10—11/62-	C	Susquehanna	
7/27/63	D	Juniata	

151st		Snyder**	
(continued)	E	Berks	
	F	Warren	
	G	Berks	
	H	Berks	
	I	Berks	
		Schuylkill	
	K	Berks	
152nd	A	Philadelphia	
(3rd Heavy		New Jersey**	
Artillery)	B	Philadelphia	
		New Jersey**	
10/62—2/63-	C	Philadelphia	
7—11/65		Dauphin	
		Adams	
	D	Dauphin	
		Northumberland	
		Montour	
		Erie	
		York	
	E	Philadelphia	
		York	
	F	Philadelphia	
	G	Philadelphia	
	H	Philadelphia	
		Lebanon**[273]	
	I	Philadelphia	
	K	Philadelphia	
		Berks	
	L	Philadelphia	
	M	Philadelphia	
153rd	A	Northampton	
	B	Northampton	
9/62-	C	Northampton	
7/24/63	D	Northampton	
	E	Northampton	
	F	Northampton	
	G	Northampton	
	H	Northampton	
	I	Northampton	
	K	Northampton	
154th	A	Philadelphia	(Arsenal Guard)[274]
	B	Philadelphia	
12/62—1/63-	C	Philadelphia	
9—10/63			
155th	A	Allegheny	(Hiland Guards)[275]
		Westmoreland**	
9/62-	B	Allegheny	(Howard Rifles)[275]
6/2/65	C	Allegheny	(Park Engineers)[275]
	D	Allegheny	(McAuley Guards)[275]
	E	Allegheny	(Kier Rifles)[275]
	F	Allegheny	(Kier Rifles)[275]
		Westmoreland**	
	G	Clarion	(Clarion Guards)[275]
	H	Clarion	(Clarion Rifles)[275]
	I	Allegheny	(Park Zouaves)[275]
	K	Armstrong*	
157th	A	Philadelphia	
	B	Philadelphia	
10/62—2/63-	C	Philadelphia	
3/21/65	D	Philadelphia	

Composition of Pennsylvania Regiments

158th	A	Cumberland	(Silver Spring Guards)
	B	Franklin	(Lederkenny Guards)
11/62-	C	Cumberland	(Cumberland Guards)
8/12/63	D	Franklin	(Wiestling Guards)
	E	Franklin	(Border Guards)
	F	Cumberland	(Oakville Guards)
		Franklin	
	G	Franklin	(Franklin Guards)
	H	Fulton	(Fulton County Guards)
	I	Franklin	(Mountain Rangers)
		Fulton	
	K	Cumberland	(Mifflin Guards)
		Fulton	
159th	A	Philadelphia	(Washington Cavalry)[276]
(14th	B	Fayette	
Cavalry)	C	Allegheny	
	D	Allegheny	
10—11/62-	E	Fayette	
11/2/65	F	Fayette	
	G	Allegheny	
Stanton	H	Allegheny	
Cavalry[277]	I	Erie	
	K	Armstrong	
	L	Armstrong	
	M	Armstrong	
160th	A	Allegheny+	
(15th		Philadelphia	
Cavalry)	B	Philadelphia	
	C	Philadelphia	
8—10/62-		Cumberland**	
6/21/65	D	Philadelphia	
		Dauphin**	
Anderson	E	Philadelphia	
Cavalry		Adams**	
	F	Allegheny	
	G	Allegheny+	
		Philadelphia	
	H	Philadelphia	
		Westmoreland**	
	I	Philadelphia	
		Westmoreland**	
		Dauphin**	
	K	Greene*	
		Cumberland*	
	L	Philadelphia	
	M	Philadelphia	
		Allegheny	
161st	A	Fayette	
(16th	B	Fayette	
Cavalry)	C	Erie	
	D	Bradford	
9—11/62-		Dauphin	
8/11/65		Tioga	
	E	Dauphin	
		Franklin	
		Mifflin	
	F	Juniata	
		Montour**	
	G	Fayette	
	H	Franklin	
	I	Philadelphia	
	K	Washington	(Prosperity Cavalry)[278]

161st		Greene**	
(continued)	L	Erie	
		Crawford**	
		Warren**	
	M	Mifflin	(Kishacoquillas Cavalry)[278a]
		Perry	
		Huntingdon**	
162nd	A	Beaver	(Irwin Cavalry)[279]
(17th	B	Susquehanna	
Cavalry)	C	Lancaster	(Ephrata Mountain Cavalry)[280]
	D	Bradford	
9/1/62-	E	Lebanon	(Jackson Cavalry)[281]
6/16/65	F	Cumberland	
	G	Franklin	
	H	Schuylkill	
	I	Perry	
		Philadelphia	
	K	Luzerne	
		Susquehanna**	
	L	Chester	
		Montgomery	
	M	Wayne	
163rd	A	Greene	
(18th	B	Crawford	
Cavalry)	C	Greene	
	D	Crawford	
10/62—2/63-	E	Dauphin	
6/24/65	F	Washington	
	G	Greene	
	H	Allegheny	
	I	Lycoming	
	K	Somerset	
		Cambria**	
		Bedford**	
	L	Philadelphia	
		Bucks	
		Delaware**	
		Montgomery**	
	M	Philadelphia	
165th	A	Franklin	(Green Township Rangers)
	B	Cumberland	(Union Guards)
11—12/62-	C	Adams	
7/28/63	D	Adams	
	E	Adams	
	F	Adams	
	G	Adams	
	H	Adams	
	I	Adams	
	K	Adams	
166th	A	York	
	B	York	
10—12/62	C	York	
7/28/63	D	York	
	E	York	
	F	York	
	G	York	
	H	York	
	I	York	
	K	York	

167th	A	Berks	
	B	Berks	(Mount Penn Guard)[282]
11—12/62-	C	Berks	
8/12/63	D	Berks	
	E	Berks	
	F	Berks	
	G	Berks	
	H	Berks	
	I	Berks	
	K	Berks	
168th	A	Greene	
	B	Fayette	
10—12/62-	C	Westmoreland	
7/25/63	D	Fayette	
	E	Fayette	
	F	Erie	
		Westmoreland	
	G	Beaver	
	H	Westmoreland	
	I	Westmoreland	
	K	Westmoreland	
169th	A	Mercer	
	B	Clarion	
10—11/62-		Armstrong**	
7/27/63	C	Crawford	
	D	Mercer	
	E	Butler	
	F	Erie	
	G	Erie	
	H	Crawford	
	I	Crawford	
	K	Crawford	
171st	A	Tioga	
	B	Bradford	
10—11/62-		Potter**	
8/8/63		Wyoming**	
	C	Bradford	
		Tioga	
	D	Bradford	
	E	Somerset	
		Cambria**	
	F	Juniata	(Pennsylvania Railroad Guards)
	G	Bradford	
		Cambria**	
	H	Somerset	
	I	Bedford*	(Bedford County Guards)
	K	Somerset	
		Cambria**	
172nd	A	Snyder	(Chapman Guards)
		Dauphin**	
10—11/62-	B	Northumberland	(Woods Brown Fencibles)
8/1/63	C	Snyder	(Franklin Guards)
	D	Northumberland	(Mountain Tigers)
	E	Clearfield	
		Elk	
	F	Snyder	(McClellan Guards)
	G	Snyder	(Beaver Guards)
		Union	
	H	Northumberland	(Northumberland County Rangers)
		McKean	

172nd		Montour**	
(continued)	I	Snyder	(Washington Guards)
	K	Northumberland	
		Schuylkill**	
173rd	A	Schuylkill	
		Lancaster**	
10—11/62-	B	Lebanon	(Coleman Legion)
8/18/63	C	Lebanon	
	D	Schuylkill	(Bierer Guards)
	E	Perry	
		Luzerne**	
	F	Schuylkill	
		Luzerne**	
	G	Schuylkill	
	H	Schuylkill	
	I	Lebanon	(Heidelberg Guards)
		Schuylkill	
	K	Dauphin	
174th	A	Bucks	
	B	Bucks	
10—11/62-	C	Bucks	
8/7/63	D	Bucks	
	E	Bucks	
	F	Bucks	
	G	Bucks	
	H	Northampton	
	I	Northampton	
		Philadelphia**	
	K	Bucks	
175th	A	Montgomery	
	B	Chester	
11/6/62-	C	Chester	
8/7/63	D	Chester	
	E	Chester	
	F	Chester	
	G	Chester	
	H	Montgomery	
	I	Chester	
	K	Chester	
176th	A	Lehigh	
	B	Lehigh	
11/62-	C	Monroe	
8/19/63	D	Lehigh	
	E	Lehigh	
	F	Monroe	
	G	Lehigh	
	H	Monroe	
	I	Lehigh	
	K	Lehigh	
177th	A	Lycoming	
	B	Luzerne	
11/62-		Susquehanna	
8/7/63	C	Dauphin	
	D	Lycoming	
	E	Indiana	
		Susquehanna	
	F	Lancaster*	
		Perry	
	G	Luzerne	(Pittston Rangers)
	H	Luzerne	

177th *(continued)*		Susquehanna	
	I	Dauphin	(Lykens Valley Guards)
	K	Indiana	(Indiana Guard)
178th	A	Columbia	
	B	Lancaster	
10—11/62- 7/27/63	C	Luzerne	
		Lancaster**	
	D	Lancaster	
	E	Lancaster	
	F	Montour	(Keystone Guards)
		Columbia**	
	G	Montour	(Montour Guards)
		Columbia**	
	H	Columbia	(Union Guards)
	I	Columbia	(McClellan Guards)
	K	Lancaster	(Lancaster County Guards)
179th	A	Montgomery	
		Philadelphia	
10—12/62- 7/27/63	B	Pike	
		Carbon**	
	C	Montgomery	
		Philadelphia	
	D	Wayne	(Chestnut Hill Hospital Guard)[283]
	E	Wayne	
	F	Lancaster	
	G	Montgomery	
		Philadelphia	
	H	Lancaster	
	I	Berks	
	K	Berks	
180th (19th Cavalry)	A	Philadelphia	
	B	Philadelphia	
	C	Philadelphia	
	D	Philadelphia	
6—8/63- 5/14/66	E	Philadelphia	
	F	Philadelphia	
	G	Philadelphia	
	H	Philadelphia	
	I	Philadelphia	
	K	Philadelphia	
	L	Huntingdon	
		Blair	
	M	Huntingdon	
		Blair	
181st (20th Cavalry)	A	Perry	
		Dauphin	
	B	Philadelphia	
	C	Philadelphia	
7/63- 1/7/64	D	Cumberland	
	E	Huntingdon	
	F	Dauphin	
	G	Philadelphia	
	H	Lancaster	
	I	Lancaster	
	K	Philadelphia	
	L	Philadelphia	
	M	Huntingdon	
		Philadelphia	
181st (20th Cavalry)	A	Cumberland	
		Dauphin	
	B	Cumberland	

181st		Dauphin	
(continued)		Lancaster**	
		York**	
2/64-	C	Philadelphia	
6/17/65	D	Dauphin	
		Lancaster**	
		Philadelphia	
	E	Dauphin	
		Mifflin**	
		Huntingdon**	
	F	Philadelphia	
	G	Philadelphia	
	H	Philadelphia	
	I	Philadelphia	
		Lancaster**	
	K	Lancaster*	
		Lebanon*	
	L	Bucks*	
	M	Chester	
		Philadelphia	
182nd	A	Lancaster	
(21st		Dauphin	
Cavalry)		York	
	B	Adams	(Adams County Cavalry)[274]
7/63-	C	Lancaster	(Lancaster City Troop)[284]
12/63	D	Franklin	
	E	Bedford	
		Cambria	
		Mifflin	
	F	Cambria	
	G	Lancaster	
		Dauphin	
	H	Franklin	
	I	Franklin	
	K	Franklin	
	L	Franklin	(McClure Dragoons)[285]
	M	Somerset	
		Franklin	
		Warren	
182nd	A	York	
(21st		Franklin**	
Cavalry)		Dauphin**	
	B	Franklin*	
2/64-	C	Lancaster	
7/8/65		Dauphin**	
	D	Franklin	
	E	Bedford	
		Franklin**	
	F	Blair*	
		Franklin*	
		Dauphin*	
	G	Lancaster	
		Franklin*	
	H	Berks*	
	I	Luzerne*	
		Dauphin*	
	K	Franklin	
		Schuylkill**	
	L	Franklin	
		Luzerne**	
	M	Franklin	
		Philadelphia**	

183rd	A	Philadelphia	
	B	Philadelphia	
12/63—3/64-	C	Philadelphia	
7/13/65	D	Philadelphia	
	E	Philadelphia	
4th Union	F	Philadelphia	
League	G	Philadelphia	
	H	Philadelphia	
	I	Philadelphia	
	K	Philadelphia	
184th	A	Bedford	
	B	Centre	
5/13/64-		Montour	
7/14/65	C	Lancaster	
	D	Blair	
		Mifflin	
		Dauphin	
	E	Blair	
		Mifflin	
		Centre	
	F	Snyder	
		Schuylkill	
		Franklin	
	G	York	
		Centre	
		Mifflin	
	H	Mifflin	
		Snyder	
	I	Snyder	
	K	Adams	
185th	A	Huntingdon	
(22nd	B	Bedford	
Cavalry)		Cumberland	
	C	Bedford	
6/63-		Blair	
2/5/64	D	Bedford	
		Blair	
185th	A	Washington	(Ringgold Cavalry)[286]
(22nd	B	Washington	(Washington Cavalry)[286]
Cavalry)	C	Washington	(Keystone Cavalry)[286]
	D	Washington	(Beallsville Cavalry)[286]
2/64-	E	Washington	(Independent Cavalry)[286]
7/19/65	F	Washington	(Patton Cavalry)[286]
	G	Washington	(Lafayette Cavalry)[286]
		Greene**	
	H	Blair	
		Bedford	
	I	Blair	
		Bedford	
		Huntingdon	
	K	Huntingdon	
		Fulton	
		Cumberland	
	L	Bedford	
		Cumberland	
		Franklin	
	M	Cumberland	
		Blair	
		Bedford	
		Fulton	

186th	A	Philadelphia	
	B	Philadelphia	
1—5/64- 8/15/65	C	Philadelphia	
	D	Philadelphia	
	E	Philadelphia	
	F	Philadelphia	
	G	Philadelphia	
	H	Philadelphia	
	I	Philadelphia	
	K	Philadelphia	
187th	A	Tioga	
	B	York	
3—5/65 8/3/65	C	Montour+	
	D	Cumberland	
		Perry	
	E	Philadelphia	
	F	Philadelphia	
		Cumberland	
	G	Luzerne+	
		Susquehanna	
	H	Luzerne	
		York	
		Susquehanna	
		Somerset	
	I	Bradford	
		Tioga	
		New York	
	K	Bradford	
		Blair	
		Lycoming	
		Philadelphia	
		New York	
188th	Regiment formed 4/1/64 from surplus recruits of the 152nd Pennsylvania; mustered out 12/14/65.		
189th	Regiment formed 4/64 from surplus men of the 112th Regiment; regiment known as the 4th Pennsylvania Heavy Artillery and as the 2nd Provisional Heavy Artillery; merged back into 112th on 8/26/64.		
190th	Regiment formed 6/64 from re-enlisted men of the 30th, 36th, 37th, 38th, 39th, 40, 41st, and 42nd Regiments, mustered out 6/28/65.		
191st	Regiment formed 6/64 from re-enlisted men of the 31st, 34th, 35th, and 39th Regiments, mustered out 6/28/65.		
192nd	A	Philadelphia	
	B	Philadelphia	
7/15/64- 11/11/64	C	Philadelphia	
	D	Philadelphia	
	E	Philadelphia	
	F	Philadelphia	
	H	Philadelphia	
	I	Philadelphia	
	K	Philadelphia	
	L	Philadelphia	
	M	Philadelphia	
	N	Philadelphia	
	P	Philadelphia	
192nd	A	Ohio	
	B	Huntingdon	(Taylor Guards)[287]
3/65- 8/24/65		Blair	
	C	Dauphin	
		Cumberland	
	D	Blair	
	E	Philadelphia	
	F	Berks	

192nd *(continued)*	G	Cambria	
		Lycoming	
	H	Dauphin	
	I	Northumberland	
		Union	
	K	Cumberland	
		Dauphin	
		York	
193rd	A	Allegheny	
	B	Allegheny	
7/24/64-	C	Allegheny	
11/9/64	D	Allegheny	(Heath Guards)[288]
	E	Lawrence*	
	F	Allegheny	
	G	Allegheny	
	H	Allegheny	
	I	Allegheny*	
	K	Allegheny	
194th	A	Lycoming	
	B	Montour	
7/24/64-	C	Schuylkill	
11/6/64	D	Dauphin	
	E	Dauphin	(Curtin Fencibles)[289]
		Schuylkill	
	F	Cambria	
		Mifflin	
		Dauphin	
	G	Dauphin	
	H	Dauphin	
		Schuylkill	
	I	Bedford	
		Berks	
	K	Dauphin	
		Luzerne	
		Schuylkill	
195th	A	Berks**	
	B	Berks[290]	
7/25/64-	C	Lancaster	
11/4/64	D	Lancaster	
	E	Lancaster	
	F	Union*[291]	
	G	Lancaster	
	H	Mifflin*	
	I	Cumberland*	
	K	Lancaster	
195th	A	Berks	
	B	Lancaster	
2/65-	C	Lancaster	
1/31/66	D	Lancaster	
	E	Lancaster	
	F	Lancaster	
	G	Lancaster	
	H	Lancaster	
	I	Lancaster	
	K	Lancaster	
196th	A	Philadelphia	
	B	Philadelphia	
7/20/64-	C	Philadelphia	
11/17/64	D	Philadelphia	
	E	Bucks*	
		Philadelphia	

196th	F	Philadelphia	
(continued)	G	Philadelphia	
	H	Philadelphia	
5th Union	I	Philadelphia	
League	K	Philadelphia	
197th	A	Delaware*	
	B	Philadelphia	
7/22/64-	C	Lancaster*	
11/11/64	D	Philadelphia	
	E	Philadelphia	
3rd Coal	F	Montgomery*	
Exchange	G	Montgomery*	
	H	Philadelphia	
	I	Delaware*	
	K	Philadelphia	(Courtland Saunders Minute Men)[292]
198th	A	Philadelphia	
	B	Philadelphia	
8/64-	C	Philadelphia	(Saunders Guards)[293]
6/4/65	D	Berks*	
	E	Philadelphia	
6th Union	F	Philadelphia	
League	G	Berks*	
	H	Luzerne*	
		Bradford*	
	I	Philadelphia	
	K	Philadelphia	
		Delaware**[294]	
	L	Philadelphia	
	M	Philadelphia	
		Chester**[294]	
	N	Northampton*[294]	
	O	Philadelphia	
199th	A	Philadelphia	
		Montgomery**	
9—11/64-	B	Philadelphia	
6/28/65	C	Philadelphia	
		Luzerne**	
Commercial	D	Philadelphia	
Regiment	E	Philadelphia	
	F	Crawford*	
	G	Philadelphia	
		Luzerne**	
		Lancaster**	
	H	Philadelphia	
		Erie**	
		Fayette**	
		Allegheny**	
	I	Luzerne*	(Alleman Fencibles)[295]
		Lycoming*	
	K	Lancaster*	
		Erie*	
200th	A	York	
	B	York	
9/3/64-	C	Dauphin+	
5/30/65		York	
		Lancaster**	
	D	York	
	E	Cumberland	
		York	
	F	Lebanon	

200th *(continued)*		Lancaster** Centre**	
	G	York Dauphin Franklin** Lancaster**	
	H	York	
	I	Cumberland York	
	K	York	
201st 8/29/64- 6/21/65	A	Dauphin+ Cumberland** Berks** Perry**	
	B	Dauphin+ Cumberland**	
	C	Dauphin+ Perry** Berks**	(Verbeke Guards)[296]
	D	Dauphin York** Cumberland**	
	E	Dauphin+ Lancaster**	
	F	Dauphin York** Lancaster**	
	G	Dauphin York** Perry**	
	H	Dauphin+ Lancaster**	
	I	Dauphin Lebanon** Franklin**	
	K	Cumberland Franklin Lebanon**	
202nd 8—9/64- 8/3/65	A	Carbon Schuylkill**	
	B	Juniata+ Perry**	
	C	Adams York	
	D	York*+	
	E	Lehigh Berks	
	F	Northampton+ Lehigh	
	G	Cumberland+ Franklin	
	H	Cumberland+ Perry	
	I	Union+ Lycoming	
	K	Huntingdon+	
203rd 8—9/64- 6/22/65	A	Lancaster	(Lancaster Sharpshooters)[297]
	B	Chester Delaware	
	C	Luzerne** Susquehanna**	

203rd *(continued)*	D	Wyoming**
		Chester
		Philadelphia
		Luzerne**
Birney's Sharp-shooters	E	Lancaster
		Luzerne**
	F	Lancaster
		Luzerne**
	G	Lycoming
		Clinton**
		Centre**
	H	Lancaster
	I	Lycoming
	K	Lancaster
		Luzerne**
204th (5th Heavy Artillery)	A	Allegheny
	B	Beaver
		Lawrence
	C	Allegheny
8—9/64- 6/30/65	D	Cambria
		Somerset**
	E	Allegheny+
		Westmoreland
	F	Allegheny+
		Westmoreland
		Clearfield**
	G	Allegheny
	H	Allegheny
		Beaver
	I	Allegheny
		Westmoreland
		Armstrong
	K	Greene
		Somerset**
	L	Allegheny
	M	Armstrong
205th	A	Blair+
	B	Berks
8—9/64- 6/2/65	C	Blair
		Bedford**
	D	Huntingdon
	E	Berks
	F	Mifflin+
	G	Huntingdon
		Franklin**
	H	Berks
	I	Blair+
		Huntingdon
		Adams**
	K	Mifflin+
206th	A	Indiana
	B	Jefferson[298]
9/12/64- 6/26/65	C	Indiana
	D	Indiana
	E	Westmoreland
	F	Indiana
	G	Indiana
		Westmoreland
	H	Indiana
	I	Indiana+

206th (continued)	K	Westmoreland
		Cambria**
		Somerset**
207th	A	Tioga
		Bradford
9/12/64-	B	Bradford+
5/31/65		Lycoming**
	C	Clinton+
		Lycoming**
	D	Tioga
		Potter**
	E	York
		Tioga
	F	Cumberland
		Franklin
	G	Lancaster+
	H	Tioga
		Lycoming**
		New York**
	I	Lycoming
		Clinton**
	K	Tioga
		Clinton**
		New York**
208th	A	Snyder+
		Dauphin**
8—9/64-		Northumberland**
6/1/65	B	Blair
		Huntingdon**
		Franklin**
	C	Lebanon+
		Juniata**
		Dauphin**
	D	Snyder
		Union**
		Northumberland**
	E	Perry+
	F	Perry+
	G	Perry+
	H	Bedford
	I	Perry
		Dauphin**
	K	Bedford
209th	A	Cumberland+
		Adams**
9/64-	B	York
5/31/65	C	Cambria
		Huntingdon**
	D	Franklin+
	E	Columbia
	F	Cumberland
		Lehigh**
	G	Adams
		Franklin**
	H	Lehigh+
	I	York
		Adams**
	K	Lebanon
210th	A	Dauphin
8—9/64	B	Lebanon
5/30/65		York**

210th *(continued)*	C	Montour York**	
	D	Columbia Franklin	
	E	Columbia Schuylkill	
	F	Potter+ Northumberland** New York**	
	G	Centre Clinton** Wyoming** Luzerne**	
	H	Dauphin+	
	I	Franklin Adams**	
	K	Perry+ Columbia Snyder**	
211th 9/17/64- 6/2/65	A	Crawford+	
	B	Jefferson Clarion**	
	C	McKean Elk**	
	D	Mercer Crawford**	
	E	Westmoreland	
	F	Erie+	
	G	Warren	
	H	Westmoreland Somerset**	
	I	Westmoreland	
	K	Westmoreland	
212th (6th Heavy Artillery) 9/13/64- 6/13/65	A	Allegheny Butler	
	B	Allegheny Butler Armstrong**	
	C	Allegheny Butler	
	D	Allegheny Butler Westmoreland	
	E	Allegheny Fayette Washington	
	F	Allegheny	
	G	Allegheny	
	H	Allegheny Westmoreland Armstrong**	
	I	Lawrence Butler Beaver** Mercer**	
	K	Fayette Allegheny Somerset**	
	L	Allegheny Westmoreland Indiana**	

212th *(continued)*	M	Lawrence Washington Mercer**	
213th 3/2/65- 11/18/65 7th Union League	A B C D E F G H I K	Philadelphia Philadelphia Philadelphia Berks Philadelphia Chester Philadelphia Philadelphia Delaware** Philadelphia Philadelphia Bucks** Philadelphia Bucks**	
214th 3/65- 3/21/66 8th Union League	A B C D E F G H I K	Philadelphia Lancaster Philadelphia Schuylkill** Lebanon** Philadelphia Philadelphia Philadelphia Philadelphia Northampton Monroe** Philadelphia Philadelphia	
215th 4/21/65- 7/31/65 9th Union League	A B C D E F G H I K	Northampton Philadelphia Lancaster Philadelphia Bucks** Philadelphia Montgomery** Philadelphia Montgomery** Philadelphia Montgomery** Northampton Philadelphia Carbon** Lancaster Philadelphia Philadelphia Montgomery** Philadelphia	
Independent Batteries:			
9/16/61- 6/30/65	A	Philadelphia	
8/61- 10/12/65	B	Erie Allegheny Franklin	(William L. Scott Artillery Co.)[299]
9/24/61- 6/30/65	C	Allegheny	
9/24/61- 6/14/65	D	Berks Bucks	(Ringgold Battery)[300]

Independent Batteries (continued)

9/61-6/14/65	E	Allegheny Philadelphia
12/7/61-6/26/65	F	Allegheny
8/22/62-6/18/65	G	Allegheny
10/21/62-6/18/65	H	Allegheny
6/63-6/23/65	I	Lancaster

Notes

Abbreviations
I: Books & Documents

AG1866	*Annual Report of the Adjutant General of Pennsylvania, Transmitted to the Governor in Pursuance of Law, for the Year 1866.* Harrisburg: Singerly & Myers, State Printers, 1867.
Amann	Amann, William F. (editor). *Personnel of the Civil War.* 2 volumes. New York: Thomas Yoseloff, 1961. All references are to volume 2.
Africa	Africa, J. Simpson. *History of Huntingdon and Blair Counties, Pennsylvania.* Philadelphia: Louis H. Everts, 1883.
Ashmead	Ashmead, H. G. *History of Delaware County, Pennsylvania.* Philadelphia: Louis H. Everts & Company, 1884.
Boucher	Boucher, J. M. *History of Westmoreland County, Pennsylvania.* 3 volumes. New York: Lewis Publishing Company, 1906. All references are to volume 1.
Crumrine	Crumrine, Boyd. *History of Washington County, Pennsylvania.* Philadelphia: Louis H. Everts & Company, 1882.
Egle	Egle, William H. *History of the Counties of Dauphin and Lebanon in the Commonwealth of Pennsylvania.* Philadelphia: Everts & Peck, 1883.
FERA	Federal Emergency Relief Administration. A series of cards compiled by this agency, and now a part of RG 19.
Juniata/ Susquehanna Valleys	*History of that Part of the Susquehanna and Juniata Valleys Embraced in the Counties of Mifflin, Juniata, Perry, Union and Snyder . . . of Pennsylvania.* Philadelphia: Everts, Peck & Richards, 1886.
Linn	Linn, James B. *History of Centre and Clinton Counties, Pennsylvania.* Philadelphia 1883.
McKnight	McKnight, William J. *Jefferson County of Pennsylvania.* 2 volumes. Chicago: J. H. Beers & Company, 1917. All references are in volume 1.
McFarland	McFarland, Joseph F. *Twentieth Century History of Washington and Washington County.* Chicago: Richmond-Arnold Publishing Company, 1910.
Montgomery	Montgomery, M. L. *History of Berks County in Pennsylvania.* Philadelphia: Everts, Peck & Richards, 1886.
OSANJ	*Our State Army and Navy Journal.*
Prowell	Prowell, G. R. *History of York County, Pennsylvania,* 2 volumes. Chicago: J. H. Beers & Company, 1907. All references are to volume 1.
RG 19	State Archives, Record Group 19. All references are to Civil War Service, Miscellaneous Box 2.
RRAC	*The Rebellion Record of Allegheny County, from April, 1861, to October, 1862.* Pittsburgh: W. A. Lare and W. M. Hargzell, 1862.

Schalck	Schalck, Adolf W., and Henning, D. C. *History of Schuylkill County, Pennsylvania.* 2 volumes. Madison: State Historical Association, 1907.
Smith	Smith, Robert W. *History of Armstrong County, Pennsylvania.* 2 volumes. Chicago: Waterman, Watkins & Company, 1883. References are to volume 1.
Stewart	Stewart, J. T. *Indiana County, Pennsylvania.* 2 volumes. Chicago: J. H. Beers & Company, 1913. All references are to volume 1.
Taylor	Taylor, Frank H. *Philadelphia in the Civil War 1861-1865.* Philadelphia: Dunlap Printing Company, 1913.
Wing	Wing, C. P. *History of Cumberland County, Pennsylvania.* Philadelphia: 1879.

II: Newspapers

AS	*Adams Sentinel* (Gettysburg)
BCI	*Bucks County Intelligencer* (Doylestown)
BCP	*Bellefonte Central Press*
BI	*Bedford Inquirer*
BWA	*Beaver Weekly Argus*
CR	*Clearfield Republican*
CVJ	*Cumberland Valley Journal* (Mechanicsburg)
CVST	*Chambersburg Valley Spirit and Times*
DI	*Danville Intelligencer*
EWG	*Erie Weekly Gazette*
HG	*Huntingdon Globe*
HPU	*Harrisburg Patriot and Union*
JT	*Johnstown Tribune*
LC	*Lebanon Courier*
LDEE	*Lancaster Daily Evening Express*
LI	*Lancaster Intelligencer*
LTD	*Lewistown True Democrat*
MD	*Montrose Democrat*
ML	*Muncy Luminary*
MVR	*Monongahela Valley Republican*
NCJ	*Northampton County Journal* (Easton)
PDT	*Pennsylvania Daily Telegraph* (Harrisburg)
PEC	*Pittsburgh Evening Chronicle*
PG	*Pittsburgh Gazette*
PhP	*Philadelphia Press*
PI	*Philadelphia Inquirer*
PMJ	*Pottsville Miners' Journal*
PNA	*Philadelphia North American and United States Gazette*
PP	*Pittsburgh Post*
PPL	*Philadelphia Public Ledger*
RDT	*Reading Daily Times*

RJ	*Raftsman's Journal* (Clearfield)	WBRT	*Wilkes-Barre Record of the Times*
SA	*Sunbury American*	WCVR	*West Chester Village Record*
SG	*Sunbury Gazette*	WRT	*Washington Reporter and Tribune*
UCSLC	*Union County Star & Lewisburg Chronicle*	YG	*York Gazette*
WA	*Wellsboro Agitator*		

[1]*PDT*, May 2, 1861.

[2]As Citizen Artillery in *Easton Argus*, April 25, 1861.

[3]As Reading Artillerists in Montgomery, p. 195.

[4]RG 19.

[5]*LDEE*, May 3, 1861.

[6]*JT*, April 19, 1861.

[7]*RRAC*, p. 5.

[8]Schalck, p. 143.

[9]Africa, p. 113.

[10]*PMJ*, April 27, 1861.

[11]Egle, p. 71.

[12]Montgomery, p. 195.

[13]*RRAC*, p. 6.

[14]Linn, pp. 106-107.

[15]As Cameron Guards in *BCP*, April 25, 1861.

[16]*LDEE*, April 24, 1861.

[17]As National Guards in *Shamokin Register*, April 25, 1861, and *SA*, May 18, 1861.

[18]*Carlisle Herald*, May 3, 1861.

[19]*OSANJ*, April 1924, p. 12.

[20]Ashmead, p. 116.

[21]*SA*, May 11, 1861.

[22]*Carlisle American*, November 27, 1861.

[23]*PG*, February 21, 1862.

[24]*RRAC*, p. 4.

[25]Name changed to Washington Greys, *WRT*, May 2, 1861.

[26]As City Guards in *PG*, May 16, 1861.

[27]Muster Roll as Rowley Infantry.

[28]Schalck, p. 144.

[29]*PDT*, May 6, 1861.

[30]*PDT*, May 9, 1861.

[31]As Blair County Rifles in *DI*, May 10, 1861.

[32]*HPU*, May 10, 1861.

[33]As Alliquippa Rifles in RG 19.

[34]As Mount Joy Rifles in *LI*, July 9, 1861.

[35]*YG*, May 21, 1861.

[36]*Carlisle Herald*, June 14, 1861.

[37]*YG*, May 14, 1861.

[38]*PI*, May 6, 1861.

[39]Bates 1: 159.

[40]Bates 1: 176.

[41]*PPL*, April 29, 1861.

[42]*PPL*, April 25, 1861.

[43]Taylor, p. 36.

[44]*PPL*, May 9, 1861.

[45]*PNA*, July 22, 1861.

[46]Companies L,O,P, and R transferred to 61st Regiment, Company M disbanded, February 1862.

[47]*PI*, May 1, 1861.

[48]Amann, p. 215.

[49]*PDT*, June 24, 1861.

[50]*BCI*, April 23, 1861.

[51]*PNA*, May 3, 1861.

[52]Companies L-P transferred to 147th Regiment, October 28, 1862.

[53]*WBRT*, June 26, 1861.

[54]*PPL*, June 27, 1861.

[55]*PPL*, July 1, 1861.

[56]*PPL*, July 8, 1861.

[57]*PP*, September 16, 1862.

[58]*PI*, July 12, 1861.

[59]*PPL*, June 26, 1861.

[60]As Korponay Rifles in *PPL*, November 21, 1861.

[61]*HG*, October 31, 1861.

[62]As McCabe Rifles in *PPL*, November 21, 1861.

[63]*PPL*, November 21, 1861.

[64]Taylor, p. 61, has several different company names.

[65]David Monat, "Three Years With Company G in the 29th Pennsylvania Volunteers," in 29th Regiment Collection, Historical Society of Pennsylvania.

[66]As Archy Dick Volunteers in Ashmead, p. 120.

[67]*AS*, July 3, 1861.

[68]Companies B,F,G, and I disbanded August 27, 1861.

[69]As Reading Artillerists in Montgomery, p. 195.

[70]As Iron Artillerists in *LC*, June 6, 1861.

[71]*Clinton Democrat*, September 12, 1861.

[72]As Jefferson Rifles in *RRAC*, p. 19.

[73]*RRAC*, p. 19.

[74]Muster Roll as Waynesburg Infantry.

[75]As Pittsburgh City Rifles in *RRAC*, p. 19.

[76]As City Guards, 2nd Company, *PG*, July 3, 1861.

[77]Muster Roll As Meadville Volunteers.

[78]Muster Roll as Fayette Volunteers.

[79]Muster Roll.

[00]As Raftsmen's Guard in *Warren Mail*, May 25, 1861.

[81]As Raftsmen Rangers in *CR*, May 15, 1861, and *RJ*, May 15, 1861.

[82]Original Company C consolidated with Company D, October 23, 1863.

[83]*PPL*, June 17, 1861.

[84]As Clinton County Cavalry in *Clinton Democrat*, August 29, 1861.

[85]Lloyd, *First Cavalry*, pp. 189, 194, 199.

[86]Linn, p. 108.

[87]*Juniata/Susquehanna Valleys*, p. 203.

[88]*Bellefonte Democratic Watchman*, 1894. (FERA).

[89]*WA*, November 27, 1861.

[90]*RRAC*, P. 29.

[91]*PDT*, September 17, 1861.

[92]As Washington Greys in Levering, p. 74.

[93]*PDT*, October 28, 1861.

[94]*Potter Journal*, September 25, 1861.

[95]*RDT*, September 20, 1861.

[96]*SA*, September 14, 1861.

[97]*PMJ*, August 24, 1861.

[98]*PMJ*, November 16, 1861.

[99]Consolidated to four companies, January 1863; new Companies E, F, and G added December 1863; Company H, February 1864; Company I, March 1864; Company K, April 1865.

[100]*BCP*, August 23, 1861.

[101]*WCVR*, October 1, 1861.

[102]*Lewistown Gazette*, October 2, 1861.

[102a]*LTD*, November 13, 1861.

[103]As Ellsworth Guards in *RDT*, September 20, 1861.

[104]*MD*, October 17, 1861.

[105]*Bradford Reporter*, August 22, 1861.

[106]*UCSLC*, February 12, 1864.

[107]As Scott Guards in *NCJ*, November 6, 1861.

[108]*UCSLC*, November 29, 1861.

[109]As Cameron Guards in *UCSLC*, May 23, 1862.

[110]*WBRT*, January 1, 1862.

[111]*Potter Journal*, October 30, 1861.

[112]*UCSLC*, February 7, 1862.

[112a]As Lawson Guards in *Miltonian*, November 1, 1861.

[113]*PP*, December 20, 1861.

[114]*JT*, August 30, 1861.

[115]*BI*, September 20, 1861.

[116]*PMJ*, August 17, 1861.

[117]*HPU*, December 12, 1861.

[118]*BI*, October 11, 1861.

[119]*BI*, September 6, 1861.

[120]Stewart, p. 117.

[121]Muster rolls are deficient for this regiment, which began the war with only nine companies. Company E from *AG1866*, p. 276. A letter from Colonel Hofmann to Adjutant-General Russell, July 23, 1863, Folder 18, Muster Rolls, lists officers from Luzerne, Wayne, and Centre counties.

[122]Companies D and G disbanded, September 25, 1862. Regiment consolidated to six companies on January 11, 1865, then transferred to 84th Regiment until mustered out on June 29, 1865.

[123]*MD*, October 31, 1861.

[124]As Wyoming and Susquehanna Rifle Company in *MD*, November 14, 1863.

[125]As Verner Guards in *PP*, September 16, 1862.

[125a]*SA*, October 19, 1861.

[126]*LDEE*, October 24, 1861.

[127]*PEC*, December 19, 1861.

[128]Taylor, p. 157.

[129]Wing, p. 136.

[130]Companies D, G, H, and I were respectively, Companies L, O, P, and R of the 23rd Regiment.

[131]*PEC*, August 22, 1861.

[132]As Mahoning Rifle Guards in *PG*, August 23, 1861.

[133]As Richard Guards in *PEC*, January 29, 1862.

[134]As Simpson Light Infantry in *PG*, September 12, 1861.

[135]*PEC*, October 3, 1861.

[136]*RRAC*, pp. 27-28.

[137]*Altoona Mirror*, August 29, 1861.

[138]As Collier Guards in Hays, *Red Patch*, p. 299, and as Werner Guards in *PG*, August 2, 1861.

[139]As Etna Infantry in Hays, *Red Patch*, p. 408.

[140]As McKeesport Rifle Greys in Hays, *Red Patch*, p. 409.

Advance the Colors!

141OSANJ, May 1924, p. 3.

142Amann, p. 210.

142aVenango Spectator, September 18, 1861.

143ML, July 30, 1861.

143aFrom recruiting poster in private collection.

144PNA, August 1, 1861.

145McKnight, p. 180.

146Company origin indicated as Chester County in Taylor, p. 83.

147PI, September 20, 1861.

148Companies L-R disbanded during the fall of 1862.

149BCI, June 11, 1861.

150PPL, June 7, 1861.

151PPL, September 7, 1861.

152PPL, July 3, 1861.

153RRAC, p. 30.

154SA, May 6, 1865.

155As National Guard in PEC, October 22, 1861.

155bHanover Citizen, August 29, 1861.

156PEC, October 22, 1861.

157PG, October 8, 1861.

158Company Memorial in Moore Papers, USAMHI.

158aLTD, March 29, 1865.

159PDT, March 11, 1865.

160PEC, August 23, 1861.

161Smith, p. 70.

162LDEE, August 26, 1861.

163MVR, December 5, 1861.

164WCVR, September 28, 1861.

165DI, November 22, 1861.

166Williamsport Grit, May 2, 1909.

167HPU, January 24, 1863.

168As Harrisburg City Cavalry in PDT, January 13, 1862.

169PG, October 17, 1861.

170NCJ, October 16, 1861.

171PbP, September 12, 1861.

172PP, August 23, 1861.

173PPL, June 24, 1861.

174EWG, August 15, 1861.

175EWG, September 19, 1861.

176Boucher, p. 435.

177DI, October 11, 1861.

178ML, October 29, 1861.

179Altoona Tribune, September 19, 1861.

180Regimental History, pp. 6-8.

181Prowell, p. 364.

182As Colder Fencibles in PDT, October 4, 1861.

182aCVJ, September 5, 1861.

183AS, August 28, 1861.

184AS, October 9, 1861.

184aAs New Oxford National Guard in Hanover Citizen, September 5, 1861.

185YG, August 27, 1861.

186PbP, November 20, 1861.

186aRecruiting broadside, MOLLUS.

187LDEE, November 18, 1861.

188PDT, September 27, 1861.

189Regimental History, pp. 50-62.

190Letter of David A. Ward, December 11, 1984.

191PMJ, August 24, 1861.

192Regimental History, p. vi.

193PPL, July 29, 1861.

194PI, October 22, 1861.

195Company L transferred to 105th Regiment; Company I transferred to Companies G, H, and K, January 16, 1863.

196WRT, August 22, 1861.

197BWA, December 18, 1861.

198Lawrence Journal, April 27, 1861.

199PP, September 2, 1861.

200RRAC, p. 30.

202WA, December 11, 1861.

201BWA, January 29, 1862.

203BI, October 25, 1861.

204AS, February 5, 1862.

205RRAC, p. 28.

206Regimental History, pp. 2-3.

207BCI, September 24, 1861.

208BCI, October 22, 1861.

209RDT, October 4, 1861.

210PP, September 10, 1861.

211PEC, November 26, 1861.

212MI., August 20, 1861.

213PDT, October 26, 1861.

214Shippensburg News, March 15, 1862.

215ML, January 14, 1862.

216PDT, April 2, 1862.

216aLTD, March 12, 1862.

217PPL, July 27, 1861.

218WA, January 15, 1862.

219NCJ, September 4, 1861.

220PI, January 2, 1862.

221As Woodbury Riflemen in BI, January 3, 1862; as Union Riflemen in BI, October 4, 1861; as Woodbury Guards in BI, January 10, 1862.

222PNA, November 1, 1861.

223PI, August 5, 1862.

224Consolidated to three companies on June 22, 1864, and merged with the 110th Regiment.

225Consolidated to four companies, January 15, 1863; new companies added in May 1864.

226Ashmead, p. 133.

226aVenango Spectator, August 13, 1862.

227LDEE, May 14, 1863.

228RRAC, p. 34.

229PP and PG of September 9, 1862, both have McCandless Infantry; PEC, September 21, 1864, has J. M. Powers Infantry.

230Ashmead, p. 135.

231WCVR, September 9, 1862.

232HG, August 19, 1862.

233Pittsburgh Leader, December 31, 1898 (FERA).

234CVST, August 13, 1862.

235CVST, October 1, 1862.

236CVST, September 3, 1862.

237PDT, September 6, 1862.

238Regimental History, p. 34.

239PP, August 15, 1862.

240As Greenawalt Guards in PDT, May 19, 1863, and LC, August 28, 1862.

241As Harrisburg Guards in LC, August 14, 1862.

242PDT, May 19, 1863.

242aLebanon Advertiser, September 3, 1862.

243LC, August 14, 1862.

244RDT, August 26, 1862.

245PMJ, October 4, 1862.

246PP, August 15, 1862.

246aCVJ, August 21, 1862.

247Mifflinburg Telegraph, August 19, 1862.

248SA, August 23, 1862.

249Miltonian, August 15, 1862.

250SG, June 6, 1863.

251Bradford Reporter, September 4, 1862.

252Hitchcock, War From the Inside, p. 247.

253JT, August 29, 1862.

254BWA, August 13, 1862.

255LI, September 2, 1862.

256WBRT, August 27, 1862.

257RRAC, p. 37.

258JT, August 29, 1862.

259Altoona Tribune, September 11, 1862.

260WRT, August 28, 1862.

261PG, September 2, 1862.

262As Brady's Artillery in McFarland, p. 135.

263WRT, August 21, 1862.

264As Canonsburg Guards in WRT, September 11, 1862.

265Wayne County Herald, August 21, 1861.

266Venango Specator, August 13, 1862.

267Zierdt, 109th Field Artillery, p. 70.

268Lumbard History, Chapter One.

269PI, January 14, 1863.

270Company organized February 1864, broken up in March 1864.

271LC, August 21, 1862.

272WBRT, August 20, 1862.

273LC, September 25, 1862.

274Amann, p. 207.

275RRAC, pp. 37-38.

276Taylor, p. 174.

277PG, December 18, 1862.

278WRT, November 13, 1862.

278aLTD, November 5, 1862.

279BWA, September 3, 1862.

280LI, November 4, 1862.

281LC, September 25, 1862.

282RDT, November 7, 1862.

282aAs Coleman Rifles in Lebanon Advertiser, November 19, 1862.

283RG 19, Folder 3, Muster Rolls.

284LDEE, July 22, 1863.

285Franklin Repository, October 14, 1863.

286Crumrine, p. 353.

287HG, March 15, 1865.

288PEC, August 22, 1864.

289PDT, July 20, 1864.

290Muster roll indicates Dauphin, but Montgomery, p. 196, and AG1866, p. 937, both indicate Berks.

291Muster roll indicates Union, but HG, September 14, 1864, contains the muster roll.

292PPL, July 23, 1864.

293PI, April 15, 1865.

294Indicated changes based on Regimental History, pp. 108,117,120.

295PDT, October 19, 1864.

296PDT, August 24, 1864.

297LDEE, September 20, 1864.

298Change based on McKnight, pp. 185-186, and AG1866, p. 975.

299EWG, October 10, 1861.

300BCI, November 19, 1861.

Company/County Index

If there were two regiments with the same number, an asterisk(*) after the number indicates the short-term regiment. An asterisk after a company denotes a later replacement company.

Advance the Colors!

Butler	13	H
	37	A
	40	C,D
	78	E*,H
	100	C,E
	101	H
	102	H
	103	B,E,I,K
	134	C,F,G,K
	137	D,F,G
	169	E
	212	A,B,C,D,I
Cambria	3	F,G,K
	10	G,H
	40	A
	54	A,D,E,H,I
	55	A,C
	78	D
	108	G
	113	M
	115	D
	125	K
	133	A,B,F
	136	K
	163	K
	171	E,G
	182*	E,F
	192	G
	194	F
	204	D
	206	K
	209	C
Cameron	42	C
	84	G
	148	F
Carbon	6	A,I,K
	11	H
	28	E
	42	F
	53	E
	67	A,H
	81	D,G,H,I,K
	112	H
	132	F,G
	147	C,K
	179	B
	202	A
	215	G
Centre	2	H
	4	H
	7	H
	10	B
	15	I
	34	E
	44	E
	45	A,B,D,E
	49	A,G
	51	G
	53	D
	56	F,H,I
	57	E
	59	F
	80	E
	93	E
	110	K
	136	I
	148	A,B,C,D,F,G,H
	184	B,E,G
	200	F
	203	G
	210	G
Chester	2	G
	9	A,E,F
	30	A,C,G
	33	K
	42	H
	49	B,F
	50	H
	71	H,K

Chester (continued)	80	G,H
	89	A
	97	A,B,C,D,E,F,H,K
	108	B
	124	A,C,E,F,G,I,K
	130	H
	162	L
	175	B,C,D,E,F,G,I,K
	181	M
	198	M
	203	B,D
	213	F
Clairon	37	H
	39	E
	62	C,E
	63	F
	67	F
	78	C,E
	103	A,B,F,G,H
	105	C
	108	L
	148	K
	155	G,H
	169	B
	211	B
Clearfield	14	D
	34	C
	42	K
	53	D
	84	H*,I,K
	105	C,D,F
	110	K
	149	B,E
	172	E
	204	F
Clinton	11*	B,C
	11	B
	36	D
	44	D
	49	A
	58	G
	80	E
	93	E
	137	C,E,H
	203	G
	207	C,I
	210	G
Columbia	35	A
	52	G
	74	A*
	84	D,H*
	103	B*
	112	F
	132	E,H
	136	I
	171	K
	178	A,F,G,H,I
	209	E
	210	D,E,K
Crawford	38	F
	39	I
	57	K
	59	I
	83	A,B,F,H
	103	E*
	111	E,G,I
	113	B
	127	G
	136	I
	137	B
	145	H
	150	C,H,I,K
	161	L
	163	B,D
	169	C,H,I,K
	199	F
	211	A,D
Cumberland	9	C
	11	A

Cumberland (continued)	16	C
	30	H,I
	36	A,H
	44	G
	60	H
	77	D
	78	D*
	80	K
	87	E
	92	H,I
	100	L
	101	F*
	107	A,B
	117	F
	130	A,D,E,F,G,H
	158	A,C,F,K
	160	C,K
	162	F
	165	B
	181*	D
	181	A,B
	185*	B
	185	K,L,M
	187	D,F
	192	C,K
	195*	I
	200	E,I
	201	A,B,D,K
	202	G,H
	207	F
	209	A,F
Dauphin	1	E
	2	I
	10	F
	11	A
	15	E
	25	F
	35	G
	41	D
	46	D
	47	H
	54	F
	55	G
	76	H
	77	I*
	78	D*
	80	I
	83	I*,K*
	84	H
	87	B,I*
	92	B,C,E,H,K
	93	I
	96	G
	101	A*,D*,E*,G*,I
	103	G*
	107	E,F,I
	108	D
	113	G,H,L
	117	C*
	127	A,B,C,D,F,G,H
	130	F,H
	136	C
	152	C,D
	160	D,I
	161	D,E
	163	E
	172	A
	173	K
	177	C,I
	181*	A,F
	181	A,B,D,E
	182*	A,G
	182	A,C,F,I
	184	D
	192	C,H,K
	194	D,E,F,G,H,K
	200	C,G
	201	A,B,C,D,E,F,G,H,I
	208	A,C,I
	210	A,H

Delaware		
	4	F
	9	I
	30	C,F
	58	A
	65	D
	97	D,G,I
	119	E
	124	B,D,H
	163	L
	197	A,I
	198	K
	203	B
	213	G
Elk	42	G
	58	F
	111	K
	172	E
	211	C
Erie	58	E
	83	C,D,E,I,K
	111	A,C,F,G,H,I,K
	113	L
	145	A,B,C,D,E,I,K
	152	D
	159	I
	161	C,L
	168	F
	169	F,G
	199	H,K
	211	F
	Battery	B
Fayette	37	D,G
	40	F
	44	H
	80	K
	85	C,E,G,I,K
	112	K
	116	K*
	140	E
	142	H
	159	B,E,F
	161	A,B,G
	168	B,D,E
	199	H
	212	E,K
Forest	83	G
Franklin	2	A,B,C
	35	D
	41	K
	43	A
	60	H
	77	A,H
	87	K*
	103	A*
	107	B,H,K
	108	D
	126	A,B,C,D,E,G,H,K
	158	B,D,E,F,G,I
	161	E,H
	162	G
	165	A
	182*	D,H,I,K,L,M
	182	A,B,D,E,F,G,K,L,M
	184	F
	185	L
	200	G
	201	I,K
	202	G
	205	G
	207	F
	208	B
	209	D,G
	210	D,I
	Battery	B
Fulton	77	F
	107	H
	126	B
	158	H,I,K
	185	K,M

Greene		
	37	I
	44	F
	85	F,G
	140	A
	160	K
	161	K
	163	A,C,G
	168	A
	185	G
	204	K
Huntingdon	5	D
	10	I
	15	H
	28	O
	31	F*
	34	G,I
	41	I
	45	E
	49	C,D
	53	C
	77	C
	78	K*
	92	M
	110	B,D
	117	B*
	125	C,D,F,H,I
	147	B
	149	I
	161	M
	180	L,M
	181*	E,M
	181	E
	185*	A
	185	I,K
	192	B
	195*	F
	202	K
	205	D,G,I
	208	B
	209	C
Indiana	40	B,E,I
	41	H
	43	G
	54	A
	55	F
	56	B
	61	A
	67	B*,E
	74	F*
	76	G
	78	A,D
	84	I
	101	B*
	103	G
	105	A,F,K
	135	A,D,I
	148	E
	177	E,K
	206	A,C,D,F,G,H,I
	212	L
Jefferson	8	I,K
	40	K
	54	I
	62	I
	67	F
	105	A,B,D,G,H,I
	108	L
	135	B
	148	E,I
	206	B
	211	B
Juniata	44	A
	47	C
	49	I
	53	I
	101	E*
	113	F
	126	F,I
	151	D

Juniata _(continued)_		
	161	F
	171	F
	202	B
	208	C
Lancaster	1	F,K
	2	F
	10	A,E,K
	11	E
	15	F,K
	30	B,D,E
	31	G*
	34	K
	45	B,K
	50	F
	59	D
	73	G,K
	77	D,K
	79	A,B,C,E,F,G,H,I,K
	92	F,G
	99	B,D
	107	E
	108	I
	113	E,I
	115	G
	122	A,B,C,D,E,F,G,H,I,K
	135	C,E,H,K
	162	C
	173	A
	177	F
	178	B,C,D,E,K
	179	F,H
	181*	H,I
	181	B,D,I,K
	182*	A,C,G
	182	C,G
	184	C
	195*	C,D,E,G,K
	195	B,C,D,E,F,G,H,I,K
	197	C
	199	G,K
	200	C,F,G
	201	E,F,H
	203	A,E,F,H,K
	207	G
	214	B
	215	B,H
	Battery	I
Lawrence	12	F,H
	43	B
	76	A,G
	77	H*
	78	G*
	87	H*
	100	B,C,E,F,H,I,K
	101	C
	134	A,B,D,H,I
	204	B
	212	I,M
Lebanon	5	G
	36	C,I
	50	E
	64	F
	93	A,C,D,F,I,K
	107	I
	113	H
	115	G
	127	E,I,K
	142	K
	149	C
	152	H
	162	E
	173	B,C,I
	181	K
	200	F
	201	I,K
	208	C
	209	K
	210	B
	214	C

Advance the Colors!

Lehigh	1	I
	9	D
	25	G
	46	C
	47	B,F,G,I,K
	54	F,K
	92	A
	128	D,G
	147	H
	176	A,B,D,E,G,I,K
	202	E,F
	209	F,H
Luzerne	8	B,C,D,E,F,G,H
	11*	E
	15	A,B,C,D,G
	23	L
	25	K
	28	A,N
	36	F
	43	H
	46	I
	47	K
	50	I
	52	A,F,G,H,I,K
	53	F
	56	C,D,G,I
	58	I
	61	D
	64	M
	70	E
	76	H
	77	G,H
	81	K
	92	D,H,K,L
	96	E
	104	I*
	107	A
	108	K
	112	L,M
	132	I,K
	136	B
	142	K
	143	A,B,C,D,E,F,G,I
	147	C,F
	149	E,F
	162	K
	173	E,F
	177	B,G,H
	178	C
	182	I,L
	187	G,H
	194	K
	198	H
	199	C,G,I
	203	C,D,E,F,K
	210	G
Lycoming	11*	A,D,G
	11	D
	33	E
	34	A,H
	51	H
	56	E
	65	K
	80	B,G,I
	84	B,F
	89	B
	106	F
	107	C
	112	F
	117	G
	131	G,H,I
	143	K
	163	I
	177	A,D
	187	K
	192	G
	194	A
	199	I
	202	I

Lycoming (continued)	203	G,I
	207	B,C,H,I
McKean	42	I
	58	E,F,H
	150	G
	172	H
	211	C
Mercer	39	B,G
	57	B,C,E,F,I
	76	B
	77	E
	100	B,G
	111	K
	139	A
	140	B
	142	A
	145	G
	169	A,D
	211	D
	212	I,M
Mifflin	7	I
	25	E
	44	C
	45	C
	46	A
	49	E,H,K
	78	C*
	92	L
	107	D,F
	113	F
	131	D,K
	149	H
	161	E,M
	181	E
	182*	E
	184	D,E,G,H
	194	F
	195*	H
	205	F,K
Monroe	33	F
	67	D,G
	142	G
	176	C,F,H
	214	H
Montgomery	4	A,B,C,D,E,I,K
	33	C
	44	B
	51	A,C,D,F,I
	53	A,B
	68	H
	93	G
	106	G
	129	I
	130	C
	138	A,C,I,K
	162	L
	163	L
	175	A,H
	179	A,C,G
	197	F,G
	199	A
	215	D,E,F,I
Montour	11*	H
	14	C
	35	E
	43	F
	53	H
	69	D
	80	D,H
	93	H
	104	I*
	112	F
	132	A
	152	D
	161	F
	172	H
	178	F,G
	184	B

Montour (continued)	187	C
	194	B
	210	C
Northampton	1	A,B,C,D,H
	9	G
	41	E
	46	C
	47	A,E
	51	B,K
	54	H
	59	H
	64	A
	67	H
	108	H
	113	D
	115	G
	129	C,D,F,K
	153	A,B,C,D,E,F,G,H,I,K
	174	H,I
	198	N
	202	F
	214	H
	215	A,G
Northumberland	8	A
	11*	F
	11	D,E
	34	B,H
	46	K
	47	C
	53	H
	56	D
	58	I
	74	C*,E*
	80	L
	103	C*
	131	B,C,E
	136	C
	152	D
	161	L
	172	B,D, H,K
	192	I
	208	A,D
	210	F
Perry	2	D
	36	B
	42	B
	47	D,H
	49	I
	92	A,C
	101	A
	103	D*
	104	F*
	133	G,H,I
	149	G
	161	M
	162	I
	173	E
	177	F
	181*	A
	187	D
	201	A,C,G
	202	B,H
	208	E,F,G,I
	210	K
Philadelphia	17	A,B,C,D,E,F,G,H,I,K
	18	A,B,C,D,E,F,G,H,I,K
	19	A,B,C,D,E,F,G,H,I,K
	20	A,B,C,D,E,F,G,H,I,K
	21	A,B,C,D,E,F,G,H,I,K
	22	A,B,C,D,E,F,G,H,I,K
	23*	A,B,C,D,E,F,G,H,I,K
	23	A,B,C,D,E,F,G,H,I,K,M,O,P,R
	24	A,B,C,D,E,F,G,H,K
	26	A,B,C,D,E,F,G,H,I,K
	27	A,B,C,D,E,F,G,H,I,K
	28	C,D,I,K,L,M,P
	29	A,B,C,D,E,F,G,H,I,K
	31	A,B,B*,C,D,E,F,G,H,I,K
	32	E,G,K

Philadelphia (continued)	33	A,B,C,D,G,I
	36	E,G,K
	37	E
	41	A,D
	43	C,C*,D,G,H
	56	D,I
	58	A,B,C,D,K
	59	A,B,C,E,G,K
	60	A,B,C,E,F,I,K,M
	61	G,H,I
	65	A,B,C,D,E,F,G,H,I,K
	67	B,E,I
	68	A,B,C,D,E,F,G,H,I,K
	69	A,B,C,D,E,F,G,H,I,K
	70	A,B,C,D,E,F,H,I,K,L,M
	71	A,B,C,D,E,F,G,H,I,K,L,M,N,P,R
	72	A,B,C,D,E,F,G,H,I,K,L,M,N,P,R
	73	A,B,C,D,E,F,G,H,I,K
	74	A,K
	75	A,B,C,D,E,F,G,H,I,K
	80	F
	81	A,B,C,D,E,F
	82	A,C,D,E,F,G,H,I,K
	84	H*
	88	C,D,E,F,G,I,K
	89	C,D,E,F,G,H,I,K,L,M
	90	A,B,C,D,E,F,G,H,I,K
	91	A,B,C,D,E,F,G,H,I,K
	95	A,B,C,D,E,F,F*,G,H,I,I*,K
	98	A,B,C,D,E,F,G,H,I,K
	99	A,B,C,D,E,F,G,H,I,K
	104	I
	106	A,B,C,D,E,F,G,H,I,K
	108	C,E
	109	A,B,C,D,E,F,G,H,I,K
	110	E,F,G,I
	112	A,B,C,D,E,F,G,H,I
	113	A,C,D,I
	114	A,B,C,D,E,F,G,H,I,K
	115	A,B,C,E,F,H,I,K
	116	A,B,C,D,E,E*,F,G,H,I,K
	117	A,B,C,D,H,I,K,L,M
	118	A,B,C,D,E,F,G,H,I,K
	119	A,B,C,D,E,F,G,H,I,K
	121	B,C,D,E,G,H,I,K
	147	A,B,D,E,I
	150	A,B,E,F
	152	A,B,C,E,F,G,H,I,K,L,M
	154	A,B,C
	157	A,B,C,D
	159	A
	160	A,B,C,D,E,F,G,H,I,L,M
	161	I
	162	I
	163	L,M
	174	I
	179	A,C,G
	180	A,B,C,D,E,F,G,H,I,K
	181*	B,C,G,K,L,M
	181	C,D,F,G,H,I,M
	182	M
	183	A,B,C,D,E,F,G,H,I,K
	186	A,B,C,D,E,F,G,H,I,K
	187	E,F,K
	192*	A,B,C,D,E,F,G,H,I,K,L,M,N,P
	192	E
	196	A,B,C,D,E,F,G,H,I,K
	197	B,D,E,H,K
	198	A,B,C,E,F,I,K,L,M,O
	199	A,B,C,D,E,G,H
	203	D,F
	213	A,B,C,E,F,G,H,I,K
	214	A,C,D,E,F,G,I,K
	215	A,C,D,E,F,G,H,I,K
	Batteries	A,E
	Engineer Company	
Pike	67	C
	142	G
	151	B
	179	B

Potter	46	G,H
	53	G
	149	G,K
	171	B
	207	D
	210	F
Schuylkill	5	C,E,F,I
	6	B,C,D,E,F,G,H
	9	H,K
	10	C,D
	14	B
	16	B,D,E,I,K
	25	B,C,D,H
	43	F
	48	A,B,C,D,E,F,G,H,I,K
	50	A,C,I
	52	K
	55	E
	56	K
	60	L
	67	K
	76	K
	80	A,F
	96	A,B,C,D,E,F,G,H,I,K
	99	D
	104	G*
	107	D,G
	116	F*,G*
	127	K
	129	A,B,E,G,H
	137	K
	151	I
	162	H
	172	K
	173	A,D,F,G,H,I
	182	K
	184	F
	194	C,E,H,K
	202	A
	210	E
	214	C
Snyder	35	B
	49	H,I*
	51	H
	52	D
	56	F
	74	C*,D*
	76	D
	131	F
	147	G
	151	D
	172	A,C,F,G,I
	184	F,H,I
	208	A,D
	210	K
Somerset	39	A
	54	B,C,D,G,H
	85	C,H
	133	D,E
	142	C,D,F
	163	K
	171	E,H,K
	182*	M
	187	H
	204	D,K
	206	K
	211	H
	212	K
Sullivan	84	B
	107	C
	141	K
Susquehanna	33	H
	35	K
	43	F
	50	D
	56	A,K
	57	A
	92	E

Susquehanna (continued)	100	L
	141	F,H
	143	H
	151	A,C
	162	B,K
	177	B,E,H
	187	G,H
	203	C
Tioga	35	H
	42	A,E
	45	F,G,H,I
	57	D
	58	E
	59	L
	80	B,C,G
	101	B
	108	F
	136	A,B,D
	149	A,G
	161	D
	171	A,C
	187	A,I
	207	A,D,E,H,K
Union	4	G
	34	D
	51	E,H,K
	52	D
	53	E
	56	F
	74	D*,E*
	101	C*
	113	F
	131	A
	142	E
	150	D
	172	G
	192	I
	202	I
	208	D
Venango	39	C
	57	I
	63	G
	64	H,I,K,L
	65	M
	103	B,I
	105	F
	121	A,F
	142	I
Warren	39	H
	42	G
	58	F,G
	108	I
	111	B,D,H
	113	K
	145	E,F
	151	F
	161	L
	182*	M
	211	G
	Independent Company C	
Washington	12	E,G
	37	K
	39	D
	44	I,K
	79	D
	85	A,B,C,D,E
	87	H*
	100	A
	140	C,D,E,G,K
	161	K
	163	F
	185	A,B,C,D,E,F,G
	212	E,M
Wayne	32	B
	35	C
	45	F
	56	A,G
	67	C,D

Wayne	84	I,I*
(continued)	112	C,E
	137	A,K
	141	G
	162	M
	179	D,E

Westmoreland	11*	I,K
	11	C,E,F,I,K
	14	F,G
	28	B
	40	H,I
	41	F
	53	K
	64	C,D
	67	E
	76	G
	84	C*
	100	M
	101	B*
	103	F*
	105	E
	135	F,G
	136	H

Westmoreland	139	C
(continued)	142	B
	155	A,F
	160	H,I
	168	C,F,H,I,K
	204	E,F,I
	206	E,G,K
	211	E,H,I,K
	212	D,H,L

Wyoming	41	B
	52	B,H
	57	A
	107	F
	132	B
	143	K
	171	B
	203	C
	210	G

York	2	K
	16	A,F,G,H
	30	D
	41	G

York	43	E
(continued)	76	D,E,I
	77	D
	87	A,B,C,D,E,G,H,K
	103	D*,G*
	107	A
	108	I
	117	C*
	130	B,C,I,K
	152	D,E
	166	A,B,C,D,E,F,G,H,I,K
	181	B
	182*	A
	182	A
	184	G
	187	B,H
	192	K
	200	A,B,C,D,E,G,H,I,K
	201	D,F,G
	202	C,D
	207	E
	209	B,I
	210	B,C

Photograph Credits

Unless otherwise noted, all color photographs of the flags and the close-ups of the damaged staffs are courtesy of the Capitol Preservation Committee and are not to be reproduced without the express written consent of the Committee.

3: First Troop, Philadelphia City Cavalry
4: (both) State Museum of Pennsylvania, PHMC
5: (left) Soldiers & Sailors, courtesy Al Richardson, (right) State Museum of Pennsylvania, PHMC
6: (left) The Historical Society of Pennsylvania, (above right) State Museum of Pennsylvania, PHMC
7: (both) State Museum of Pennsylvania, PHMC
8: State Museum of Pennsylvania, PHMC
9: (above right) State Museum of Pennsylvania, PHMC
13: Governor's Private Office, State Capitol Building, Commonwealth Media Services
14: RG 19, Division of Archives and Manuscripts, PHMC
15: *McElroy's Philadelphia City Directory for 1864*
18: (upper left) USAMHI, MASS-MOLLUS
21: Courtesy of the Cooper-Hewitt Museum, The Smithsonian Institution's National Museum of Design, 1912-12-136
22: (upper left) Soldiers & Sailors, courtesy Al Richardson, (bottom left) Chester County Historical Society, (right) War Library and Museum, MOLLUS
23: J. Craig Nannos
24: Peter Kersten
31: (left) *Harper's Weekly*, July 5, 1879, (right) *Smull's Legislative Hand Book, 1888*
32: (top right) postcard in possession of Capitol Preservation Committee, (bottom) Daniel Hastings Papers, MG 145, Division of Archives and Manuscripts, PHMC
33: (all) RG 25, Division of Archives and Manuscripts, PHMC
35: Capitol Preservation Committee
36: Capitol Preservation Committee
41: Bustill-Bowser-Asbury Collection, Moorland-Spingarn Research Center, Howard University
44-57: all flag photographs courtesy of the Edward L. Bafford Photography Collection, Albin O. Kuhn Library and Gallery, University of Maryland, Baltimore County
45: Beyer-Keydel
66: Wray, *History of the Twenty-third*
69: Beyer-Keydel

75: USAMHI, Ron Beifuss Collection
77: (top right) GAR Memorial Hall, Philadelphia Camp, Sons of Union Veterans, (bottom right) Ronn Palm
78: Ronn Palm
94: Ronn Palm
95: State Museum of Pennsylvania, PHMC
99: Ronn Palm
100: Robert S. Ulrich
102: National Archives photograph 111-B-446
104: Soldiers & Sailors, courtesy Al Richardson
116: Wyoming Historical & Geological Society, Courtesy Mike Winey, USAMHI
118: War Library and Museum, MOLLUS
128: Gould, *Story of the Forty-eighth*
130: Gould, *Story of the Forty-eighth*
131: Bosbyshell, *48th in the War*
134: (both) Ronn Palm
140: Ronn Palm
145: Ronn Palm
146: Ronn Palm
151: GAR Memorial Hall, Philadelphia Camp, Sons of Union Veterans
167: *History of the Third Pennsylvania Cavalry*
170: GAR Memorial Hall, Philadelphia Camp, Sons of Union Veterans
171: Beyer-Keydel
178: (left) Ronn Palm, (right) Hays, *Under the Red Patch*
189: Library of Congress photograph B817-7267
190: John Stanchak
191: War Library and Museum, MOLLUS
192: (left, guidon) First Troop, Philadelphia City Cavalry, (right) Howard M. Madaus
196: State Museum of Pennsylvania, PHMC
199: USAMHI, MASS-MOLLUS
201: *Pennsylvania at Gettysburg*
206: USAMHI, PHMC Collection
215: *Pennsylvania at Chickamauga*
219: Sipes, *Seventh Cavalry*
224: (staff) State Museum of Pennsylvania, PHMC, (flag) Ronn Palm
226: Ronn Palm
234: (right) Ronn Palm
237: (left) Mike Wiltshire, National Park Service, (both right) Gettysburg National Military Park, Lane Studios